Peresvet.   Steam-barge.   Variag.   Osliaba.

OW IN THE HARBOR OF NEW YORK.

CZARS and PRESIDENTS

To America and old Russia who gave me so much and to whom I gave

so little, I dedicate this book.

czars and presidents

BY ALEXANDRE TARSAÏDZÉ

McDOWELL / OBOLENSKY / NEW YORK

preface

Russia, up to the Revolution of 1917, was the only major power in the world with which the United States had neither a war nor a serious diplomatic dispute. Yet at no time in the history of the United States was there full, unreserved American approval of the Russian form of government, save perhaps for those few months between the abdication of Czar Nicholas II and the Bolshevik revolution—that brief period when Russia had what David Francis, the last American Ambassador to the Court at St. Petersburg, called "government by consent of the governed."

In form and in social implications the American Government and that of Czarist Russia had many antagonistic differences. But during all the years of the Czars Russian-American relations were remarkably friendly and cooperative. Jefferson did not believe in monarchy, but that did not prevent him from feeling respect for the efforts made by Czar Alexander I to improve the lot of mankind. Alexander did not believe in the principles of representative democracy, but that did not prevent him from watching with interest and enthusiasm the progress toward human freedom which was being made by the infant western Republic. Lincoln, emancipator of the American Negro, and Alexander II, who freed the Russian serfs, were as far apart in political method as two men could possibly be, yet each respected and applauded the other for the similar blows which they had struck for human freedom.

Not until the Russian Monarch was supplemented by the Soviets, whose "people's government" more closely resembled that of the United States, at least on the surface, did the two nations fall into enmity. This enmity, after the brief respite of a somewhat nervous alliance during the Second World War, has risen to such extravagant proportions that the fate of the world presently hangs in the balance. Besides the abandonment of the principle of *laissez faire* in both trade and politics, which was the basis of all earlier Russian-American relations, one of the most important causes has been the increasing determination, which first began in Soviet Russia and now has infected the United States, of each country to indoctrinate the other with its own particular national beliefs.

In Soviet Russia, this has been characterized by open contempt for "capitalistic democracy" and by shrewdly organized schemes to supplant American political, social, and economic beliefs with the current communist ideology. Americans split into two camps: the partisan pros, who found their support in the dissatisfied and pseudo-liberal elements of American society; and the anti-communists, whose sense of fair play was shocked by the extremist methods of revolution and terrorism, and by the death of political freedom in Russia.

It is not the intention of this book to enter into a prolonged debate relative to the virtues and sins of Soviet Russia, but to remind both sides of their extremely amicable pasts. The United States and the U.S.S.R. will have to make an effort to understand the political, social, and economic histories of each other's people, if only to rid the world of the darkness they have created, a darkness which today is as impenetrable as that of the Middle Ages. It is highly unlikely that this can come about while both nations minutely scrutinize the wash hanging in the other's back yard and attempt to dictate methods to cleanse the other's stains.

This book deals with an earlier period, prior to the revolution of 1917, when freedom-loving Americans and freedom-loving Russians, both born in lands of vast, open spaces, were more understandable to each other. It is the story of the friendly development of diplomatic relations between two countries far apart in space and in their principles of government. It is also the story of individual men, ranging from John Paul Jones to a very young American who carried acorns from Washington's tomb to plant them in Russian soil and of many others who attempted to bridge the gulf of distance.

And in a more final sense it is a story of sorrow, sorrow that the efforts of men failed to dispel the clouds of ignorance. For if understanding is not a magic key to the peace and harmony of nations, it remains the sole assurance that men will continue to remember, in the ultimate hour of crisis, the brotherhood of man.

ACKNOWLEDGMENTS

The author expresses his appreciation to Mr. Roger Dow of Washington, D. C., for his help with the early stages of this book and for the use of the material from his articles: "Prostor," *The Russian Review,* November, 1941, Vol. 1, No. 1; "Seichas," *The Russian Review,* Autumn, 1947, Vol. VII, No. 1.

The author wishes to thank Warren Eyster, whose work in editing made possible the publication of this book. His appreciation goes also to the staff of McDowell, Obolensky Inc. for their cooperation, particularly to Irene Glynn and Dr. Richard Carlton; to Stefan Salter for his help with the selection of the photographic material and to Christine Leusch for the arrangement of the Bibliography.

The author gratefully remembers the late Prince Georges Matchabelli, who was the first one to lend sympathetic and generous help.

Belatedly the author thanks the officers and crew of the *USS Whipple,* who, during the Civil War in Russia, brought him to safety in the free world.

contents

iLLustRatioNs

THE IMPERIAL FAMILY OF ROMANOV,

showing only members mentioned in this book. The dates shown are reigning years.

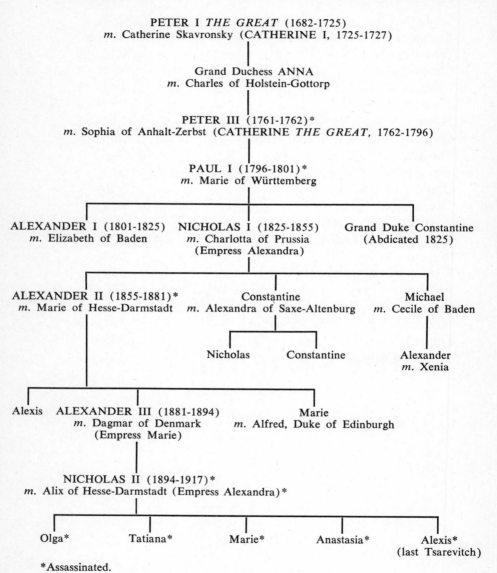

PETER I *THE GREAT* (1682-1725)
m. Catherine Skavronsky (CATHERINE I, 1725-1727)

Grand Duchess ANNA
m. Charles of Holstein-Gottorp

PETER III (1761-1762)*
m. Sophia of Anhalt-Zerbst (CATHERINE *THE GREAT,* 1762-1796)

PAUL I (1796-1801)*
m. Marie of Württemberg

ALEXANDER I (1801-1825)   NICHOLAS I (1825-1855)   Grand Duke Constantine
m. Elizabeth of Baden   *m.* Charlotta of Prussia   (Abdicated 1825)
                              (Empress Alexandra)

ALEXANDER II (1855-1881)*   Constantine   Michael
m. Marie of Hesse-Darmstadt   *m.* Alexandra of Saxe-Altenburg   *m.* Cecile of Baden

                        Nicholas   Constantine   Alexander
                                                            m. Xenia

Alexis   ALEXANDER III (1881-1894)   Marie
         m. Dagmar of Denmark   *m.* Alfred, Duke of Edinburgh
            (Empress Marie)

NICHOLAS II (1894-1917)*
m. Alix of Hesse-Darmstadt (Empress Alexandra)*

Olga*   Tatiana*   Marie*   Anastasia*   Alexis*
                                                               (last Tsarevitch)

*Assassinated.

NOTE:

Emperor Paul I established the rule of succession in 1800. By it, the eldest son of the reigning monarch succeeds to the throne, or, in the absence of a male heir, the next eldest brother.

CZARS and PRESIDENTS

Peter the Great
and Catherine I

empress's doorstep

By the mid-Eighteenth Century, England's Colonies in America were in turmoil over the arbitrary policies of Whitehall. Lexington, Concord, Bunker Hill, Ticonderoga, and Crown Point—these were the subsequent blows in a family quarrel. They punctuated the divergence of opinion between Englishmen at home and Englishmen abroad. The American Revolution was not a war of liberation, but rather a violent expression of disapproval for the policies of an absent and distant Government.

In England the official attitude was to view it as an insurrection by rebellious subjects of the crown which the red-coated soldiers of General Gage would disperse. In America, no one, neither the embattled farmers and tradesmen, the colonial militia, the Minutemen—those oddly assorted, lawless sons of Liberty—nor even George Washington, foresaw the result of the armed conflict.

3

Only in the minds of a few extremists, Samuel Adams, Thomas Paine, and Richard Price, was the eventual objective full independence.

Yet in June, 1775, hearing that British soldiers and American colonists had clashed, Empress Catherine II of Russia, better known as Catherine the Great, predicted that the Revolution would succeed. She said, "England has lost her American colonies forever." Perhaps her words never reached George III, perhaps he disregarded them as having come from "the half-barbarian sovereign of a half-barbarian nation." In any case, he sent Catherine a request for the loan of a few Cossack regiments to help stamp out the American insurrection. The British assumed as a matter of course that the request would be granted, and Gibbon, the British historian, wrote to a friend in America, "When the Russians arrive, go see their camp."

Catherine replied to the British King: "I am just beginning to enjoy peace. Your Majesty knows that my empire needs repose. He must also know what is the condition of an army, though victorious, when it emerges from a long war in a murderous climate [Her first Turkish War]. There is impropriety in employing so considerable a military force in another hemisphere, under a power almost unknown to it, and deprived of correspondence with its sovereign. Peace, which has cost me such great efforts, demands absolutely that I do not deprive myself of so large a part of my forces. Affairs in Sweden are but put to sleep and those of Poland not yet terminated. Moreover, I cannot prevent myself from reflecting on the consequence that would result to our own dignity, that of the monarchies and the two nations, from a conjunction of our forces simply to calm a rebellion which is not supported by any foreign power."

George III commented that her letter contained expressions that "may be civil to a Russian ear, but certainly not to more civilized ones."

The dawn of 1776 brought evidence that Catherine had prophesied accurately. On January 10th, Thomas Paine's *Common Sense* was published in Philadelphia, and in a short time 100,000 copies were sold. By June 7th Richard Henry Lee of Virginia had moved that "these colonies are, and ought to be, free and independ-

Empress Catherine the Great when still a Grand-Duchess

ent states." The July 4th Declaration of Independence—that monument to Eighteenth Century thought, with its still debated theory that all men are created equal—charged the Revolution with the fervor of a religious war. The colonies settled into a determined liberty-or-death effort.

The ministers of George III, finally realizing the seriousness of the rebellion, once more turned their thoughts toward Russia. The mercenaries, bought from the Landgrave of Hesse at $900 a man, were not dependable soldiers. What was needed, they said, was "barbarians" to fight barbarians, hard-riding, hard-fighting Cossacks, accustomed to great tracts of wilderness. When Sir James Harris arrived in St. Petersburg as British Ambassador, his first task was to urge Catherine to reconsider her decision of 1775. He pointed out to her that the proposed loan of Cossacks was no longer merely a favor to England; the whole future status of monarchical rule was involved, and it was to Russia's advantage to maintain the status quo. He stated bluntly that a second refusal would incur the displeasure of England.

Catherine replied, "I do not choose to mar the last years of my reign with war."

"Suppose," said Sir James, "the colonies were yours. Would you give them independence?"

"I would rather lose my head!" said Catherine. "But the American colonies are not mine, fortunately."

"The interests of Europe are the interests of Russia," said Sir James. "Russia is too powerful to remain aloof."

But Catherine was not persuaded. English blood would have to pay for England's mistakes.

In 1779, Sir James Harris made a final attempt to obtain Russian naval and military assistance. Armed with a letter from King George, offering the island of Minorca, Harris suggested that if the Empress did not want Minorca, she might choose a "sugar island," perhaps Jamaica. "The war has dragged on too long," he said. "England wants to end it."

"If England desires peace," replied Catherine, "she must renounce her struggle with the colonies."

That same year, after rejecting a proposed alliance with England, Catherine offered to mediate between the Colonies and England, drafting an armistice proposal which both sides rejected. Catherine blamed the failure of her attempt on British obstinacy.

In 1780, as a result of losses to the Russian shipping trade which had occurred during the wars between England and France, the Empress issued her famous armed-neutrality declaration, urging neutral nations to form a Maritime Confederation to protect their merchant ships from seizure. Defining contraband as arms and munitions, she declared that all other goods carried in the bottoms of neutral nations were free from seizure.

John Adams, in Paris, trying to negotiate a peace treaty with England, sent word of the Confederation to his countrymen, reminding them that the United States would always be a shipping nation. From Amsterdam, where he was placing his son, John Quincy, in school, he sent further particulars, ending with the regret that there was no American envoy in Russia.

The American Continental Congress, without investigating

the nature of the Maritime Confederation, acted promptly. Had they sought further information, they would have learned that the States could not join this league, for they were certainly not neutral. Besides, they had their backs to the wall. The fall of Charleston had given the British control of the South, and in the battle of Camden the Colonial Army had suffered a severe defeat. Furthermore, the Colonial States were not even considered to be a nation, except by France. Nevertheless Congress decided to "adhere" to the Confederation, and on December 19, 1780, Francis Dana, a distinguished Boston lawyer, was appointed Minister to Russia.

It was March before the appointment reached Paris where Dana was serving as secretary to John Adams. Benjamin Franklin and Adams both advised Dana to go immediately to Russia without inquiring whether he would be accepted or not. Dana, who knew no French and no Russian, took with him fourteen-year-old John Quincy Adams, who spoke French with reckless fluency. This oddly matched pair, with a goodly supply of wool comforters and specifics for the intense cold, sped across Europe by post chaise, through

John Quincy Adams at the age of 28
from a picture by J. S. Copley

Prussia, skirted the bleak Pomeranian coast, and arrived in Riga on a blustery Sunday. They demanded fresh horses of an innkeeper for the last lap of the journey, but he staunchly believed it was sinful to travel on the Sabbath. Young Adams argued and protested, but the innkeeper, with true Russian disdain for those who attach importance to the minutes and hours of time, replied, "Petersburg won't run off. It's been there since Peter the Great—may he rest in peace!"

When Dana arrived in St. Petersburg he learned the real truth of the innkeeper's words. He might as well have remained weeks or months in Riga. Empress Catherine was not in St. Petersburg, and during her absence none of the Russian officials were willing to see him. One of the ageless beliefs of Russian government officials was that if they did nothing, they could do nothing wrong.

In despair Dana turned to the Marquis de Verac, the French Ambassador. The Frenchman received him coolly. Verac had known an American was coming, but had expected Silas Deane, Franklin's collaborator in the Franco-American alliance. Finding himself confronted by an unknown man who could not even speak French, with a suite consisting of a young boy who told him that they had come to join the Maritime Confederation, Verac uttered the single word, "Impossible!" He urged Dana not to make his presence known to the Imperial Foreign Office. "If you do," Verac said, "you risk a humiliating rebuff."

After a second consultation with the French Ambassador failed, Dana, whose name St. Petersburg changed to the more fashionable sounding term, *d'Aena,* was convinced that Verac not only would not support American recognition, but would oppose it. The Bostonian was certain his mail was being opened and his activities closely watched. He wrote home, complaining of this, to Philip Livingston, Secretary of State. Livingston replied that Dana should not be so suspicious, the Empress could not receive an American envoy openly if she hoped to mediate between the Franco-American allies and Great Britain; Verac had been right in advising caution.

So Dana waited. Finally he sent a message to the Russian Foreign Office suggesting the value of a commercial treaty. For nearly a century Russians had been using Virginia and Maryland snuff and tobacco. He mentioned other American products, and indicated that the United States would be interested in Russian hemp, cordage, sailcloth and linen, articles which hitherto had been imported from England. He received no reply.

After Dana had been in Russia more than a year, young John Quincy packed his bags and left, Dana stayed on. Cornwallis had long since surrendered at Yorktown. The American Republic was a fact. On November 30, 1782, Great Britain and the United States signed the articles preliminary to a peace treaty. In Russia, still nothing happened. Dana, armed against another Russian winter with his fur *shuba,* watched the Winter Palace wistfully, and wandered up and down Nevsky Prospect. He must have envied the success of another American then in St. Petersburg, Mr. Blank, a puppeteer, who was drawing tremendous crowds to his Punch-and-Judy shows, his "Tyrolean maiden who guessed thoughts and performed wizardry," his drum which "beat by itself," and his stunt of having a pistol fired at him from point blank range.

Dana began to feel that by the time Russia granted recognition the United States would no longer need it. Russian recognition, if given promptly, would have enhanced American diplomatic status and prestige in Europe, thereby bringing additional pressure on England at the peace conference. To John Adams he wrote, "Do they not see that America is independent? That they must soon admit it?"

The Russian Foreign Office went placidly about its business. Then, one day, it was called to Dana's attention that the sum of £4500 might awaken interest in the hearts of the four principal Russian Ministers. This was a shock to the puritanical Dana, the first of many rude awakenings which American representatives were to have. "The diplomatic technique of the Eighteenth Century," said historian W. P. Cresson, "reserved certain peculiar rewards. Accepted custom provided that costly gifts should be bestowed on foreign diplomats and the ministers of the European courts. These gratuities generally took the form of snuff boxes or *objets d'art* studded in such a manner as to make the removal of the diamonds possible without difficulty."

With anger and shame Dana sent this information to Paris, where Franklin, more urbane in such matters, calmly replied that it could be arranged.

Meanwhile, Dana learned that England, France and Spain had agreed on the preliminaries for peace. On March 5th he was informed that Russian Vice-Chancellor Count Ostermann could be approached. Without consulting the Marquis de Verac, Dana wrote a brief courteous request for Russian recognition of the United States and asked for an audience with the Empress. The Russian officials counseled patience. Russia was sympathetic, but an immediate reply should not be expected; the delay must not be regarded by Mr. Dana as a reflection on either himself or the country he represented.

For a month the Russian Foreign Office was silent. Dana, whose patience was wearing thin, demanded an immediate conference with the Vice-Chancellor. The Foreign Office explained that Mr. Dana's credentials bore a date prior to the formal recognition of American independence by England—it was a legal matter which must be cleared. The Foreign Office did not mention that Sir James Harris, on behalf of Britain, had voiced a strong protest when he learned that Russian recognition of the United States was imminent.

After pondering a fortnight, Dana replied that, in regard to his credentials, the position of the Russian Foreign Office was not supported by international law. The United States could not agree to remove seven years from their actual independence, particularly when that meant acknowledgment of their independence as an act of the King of England. Dana cited the Declaration of Independence as the hour of actual freedom. In an angry mood he wrote to Livingston that he did not think Russian recognition was important. "Furthermore, I do not think the advantage of being a minister of this court will compensate for the expense of it."

Count Ostermann, however, explained that there had been a misunderstanding about the credentials. Russia was not trying to invalidate the sovereign acts of the United States during the years before England had recognized their independence. Dana would be received by the Empress as soon as the final articles of peace were signed. So encouraging were these assurances that Dana wrote, "The ports of the Empress are open to the United States and our independence is completely acknowledged."

But the American Congress, partly as a result of the discour-

Russian Coins

aging reports which Dana had sent, decided that Russian recognition was no longer important, and that a commercial treaty obtained by bribery would not be worthwhile. Dana was instructed to come home. Perhaps it was just as well. "To have received Dana officially," wrote historian Frank Golder, "would have compromised Russia and wounded the pride of England without in the least advancing the interests of the United States."

Diplomatic relations between the two countries remained at a standstill. In 1784 Congress resolved that a treaty of "amity and commerce" should be made. No pact was signed.

Count Vergennes, French Minister for Foreign Affairs, asked the United States to join the Armed Neutrality League, but England opposed admission of her former colonies.

Empress Catherine and George Washington corresponded about her plan to include American Indian words in a universal dictionary. Washington, who was sometimes absurd with his courteous generalities, hoped it "might in some measure lay the foundation for that assimilation of manners and interests which should one day remove many of the causes of hostility from amongst mankind."

Another important American of the time was honored by the Russia of his day. In 1752 Benjamin Franklin was hailed by the Russian press for the discovery of atmospheric electricity. He entered soon after into personal contact with Russian scientists and scholars. Catherine's interest in George Washington is too coincidental at this time for her not to have had something to do with Franklin's becoming the first American to be elected a member of the Russian Academy of Science in 1789. It was Franklin who in return apprised Americans of the period of Russia's cultural power.

Empress Catherine died of apoplexy in November, 1796. She was succeeded by her son, Paul I, who, it was said, hovered on the edge of insanity.

George Washington from a lithograph by N. Currier

A new American attempt to gain Russian recognition began in 1798, when, as a result of the halting of American ships on the high seas and the rude treatment of American Commissioners (the X-Y-Z affair), diplomatic relations with France were broken. War seemed so likely that President Adams wrote George Washington that the Nation would look to him to command the Army. England and the United States drew together, and Russia, as a British ally, tried to bring the United States into an alliance against France. Count Worontzov, the Russian Minister to London, communicated with Rufus King, the American Minister to Great Britain, suggesting that since the United States was trading in the Baltic, the two countries should have diplomatic relations. He indicated that Emperor Paul was willing to conclude a commercial treaty and would aid the Americans in obtaining a similar trade agreement with Turkey.

Rufus King, remembering the unhappy expedition of Dana, was non-committal. He did notify his Government. President Adams, eager to increase trade with his native city, Boston, instructed King to negotiate with the Russian Government. But nothing came of the King-Worontzov negotiations, because shifting international relations made London an unsuitable place for them. Czar Paul, in one of his fits of madness, refused to take part in military operations against France and recalled his Ambassadors from London and Vienna. The Russian Fleet, stationed in English waters, sailed for the Baltic. Anglo-Russian affairs became muddled, formal negotiations between Russia and the United States were again postponed, while the violent Eighteenth Century passed into history.

This first phase of Russian-American relations was indicative of the problems which the two nations would encounter. England was the lifeline of Russian commerce, and to have recognized American independence before it had been permanently established would have been a belligerent act. Empress Catherine had established a policy of non-intervention that was to become the keystone of Russian-American relations. Indeed, the entire pattern of these relations was already visible. Russia and the United States, separated by two vast oceans, were by geographical necessity doomed to have England, mistress of the seas, as the pivotal point in their relations. Only when Russia and the United States were both friendly or both hostile toward England could their own friendship thrive. That was the genesis of Russian-American history.

During this early stage of diplomatic relations, there were few Russians in the United States, almost no Americans in Russia, and no trade and no contact between the two nations. There were, therefore, few reasons to establish permanent relations. The American Colonies had sought Russian recognition only because it would have placed pressure on England to accept their independence. Once that independence was established, the Americans no longer cared too much whether Russia opened diplomatic relations or not.

This hints at a basic problem, for with the exception of a few men, such as Jefferson and Franklin, Americans were blind to the real need for the establishment of diplomatic relations, the essential function of which is to enable each nation to be aware of the ideas, opinions and shifting political forces of all other nations. Sir Henry Wotton, a British diplomat of an earlier time, defined an ambassador as "an honest man sent to lie abroad for the good of his country." Diplomatic relations, at their best, are a means of promoting a healthy international climate and of arriving at peaceful solutions to international problems before they reach such magnitude as to become insoluble. At their worst, they are an instrument for espionage.

The United States, however, was innocent of both of these functions of diplomatic relations. When diplomatic relations finally were established between the two nations, the pressure that induced it came from the Boston sea trade. And because it was the Boston merchants who felt the need for representation in St. Peterbsurg, instead of the American government, the character of relations between the two countries, albeit friendly for more than a century, never properly assumed the true functions of diplomacy. The result was that the two nations suffered from a mutual ignorance of each other. The effects of this, in our own times, have become obvious.

Catherine II, in 1762, vowed to make her rule an enlightened one. A prolific letter writer, she corresponded with the most advanced thinkers in Europe, including Voltaire, Diderot, D'Alembert, Grimm, and Joseph II of Austria. She compiled an "instruction" from Montesquieu and Beccaria, by which a new code of laws was to be composed, giving her subjects a measure of freedom hitherto undreamed of in Russia. However, opposition from the gentry was so great that the Statute of Provinces, 1775, bore little relation to the original instructions. It made the lot of the serfs no better. It did create local administrative and judiciary units.

Catherine, by turns reactionary and liberal, was not sentimental in international matters. Her attitude toward the American Colonies bore little sympathy for their cause or suffering. She had used the British request for Cossacks as an opportunity to show her opposition to England, which she felt needed shaking up. She had felt contempt for England's admitted inability to control its empire. Her longing for peace, at moments genuine, at other times a political maneuver, never prevented her from seizing an opportunity for Russian expansion. Like Peter the Great, her eyes were fixed on Constantinople. She wanted her grandson, Constantine, named with antiquity in mind, to set on his brow the crown of a restored Byzantium.

The Treaty of Kuchuk-Kainardji, 1774, was the most profitable treaty any Russian sovereign ever concluded with the Turk. By it large pieces of Turkish territory were added to Russia, and it was only a matter of time before the Crimea became Russian. Empress Catherine's method was simple. She organized a minor civil war, so that the Tartar population in the Crimea could ask her to take the territory under her protection and restore order.

In April, 1783, the Crimea became part of the Russian Empire.

England, France and Prussia began to goad the Sultan of Turkey with dark prophecies that the Black Sea would soon become a "Russian lake." In August, 1787, he declared war. Catherine would have preferred to wait. There had been an uprising of Volga peasants led by the Cossack, Pugachev. Throughout Europe she had enemies. There were hostile indications along the Baltic shores. But, having no choice, she went about the task of setting her military and naval forces in order. The Black Sea Fleet was still being built. It was stationed at Sevastopol, "Beautiful City." With the Swedes making it necessary to keep the Baltic Fleet fully manned, there was a shortage of Russian naval officers.

English, French, Greek, German and Italian officers were often in charge of Russian crews, and there were the usual animosities, jealousies and conflicting ambitions that arise from such a situation.

Prince Potemkin was Commander-in-Chief of both land and sea forces. From 1771 to 1776 he had been Catherine's lover. He was a weak, proud, fearful, irritable man, constantly complaining about military affairs and Russian unpreparedness. He believed the war would be hopeless, futile, and though Catherine placed her ablest men at his disposal, and all the resources of her empire, it nevertheless took all her ability, not only as a ruler, but as a woman, to keep him from despair. By turns a gentle mother, tactful friend, appealing woman, and stern ruler, she kept his trembling hand at the helm.

In September, 1787, Potemkin ordered the Black Sea Fleet to destroy or blockade the Turkish Fleet at Ochakov. A storm flung the Russian ships far and wide, driving some of them into the Bosporus. Potemkin wrote the Empress that he would evacuate the Crimea and relinquish his command.

"You are tired and ill," replied Catherine, "or you would never have thought of such a thing. There is neither honor nor glory in beginning something and not finishing it. Your bad mood would pass if you would take the offensive and seize Ochakov. You are as impatient as a child, when war requires unshakable patience. Adieu, my friend. Neither time, distance, nor anyone in this world can change my personal feelings toward you."

But when the burden of a war with Sweden was added to the one currently being waged against the Turks, Catherine decided that new strength must be injected into the Russian Navy. She knew there was no one available in Russia. Her eye was on Admiral Jonkheer Jan Hendrik van Kinsbergen of Holland. When approached, he consented, and started toward Russia; but in Berlin, after consultations with diplomats of other nations who wanted Russian expansion stopped, he rejected her offer. Catherine then invited Lafayette to enter her Army, and John Paul Jones to enter her Navy. Lafayette refused and after a series of conferences in Paris between Paul Jones, Thomas Jefferson, and Simolin, the Russian Ambassador, at which Jefferson recommended Jones highly and made it clear that he would work best

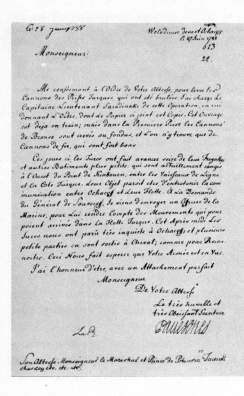

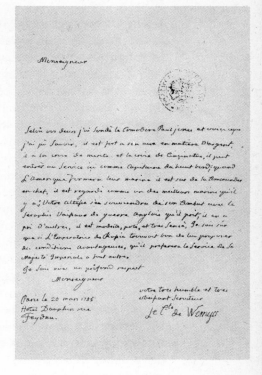

Facsimile of Jones' letter to Potemkin,
June 27, 1788

Facsimile of Count Wemyss' letter
recommending Commodore Paul Jones

only if given complete authority, John Paul Jones entered the
Empress' service on February 26, 1788.

To her friend, Baron von Grimm, Catherine wrote, "Paul
Jones will be well received . . . but have the kindness not to make
a great noise about it, so that no one may prevent my getting him."

Having crossed the icy waters from Denmark in an open
boat, Jones arrived in St. Petersburg. Catherine wrote to Grimm,
"I saw him today. I think he will suit our purposes admirably."

From a contemporary diary: "Paul Jones has made a good
impression, has entree to the Hermitage [Catherine II's private
palace], is welcomed everywhere except among the English, who
cannot bear him."

The English did everything possible to discredit the "traitor."

When a rumor spread that Jones was to be put in charge of the Baltic Fleet, British naval officers in Russian service threatened to resign and English businessmen in Russia closed their shops. Jones, accustomed to English enmity, in London he was carica- tured as a whiskered, sabered pirate, paid no attention to these threats, though numerous references in Catherine's correspond- ence show that she was worried. She could ill afford to lose her English officers. This may have caused her decision to send him to the Black Sea. She wrote to Potemkin, "The notorious English subject, Paul Jones, who, while in the service of the American colonies became a scourge to the English, despite his small force, is desirous of entering my service. I have commanded him to waste no time but to proceed directly to you. This man is capable of inspiring much fear and dread in the enemy . . ."

Perhaps Potemkin was prejudiced by the English officers serving under him. Perhaps he resented Jefferson's insistence that Jones be given full authority. Perhaps he was irked by the praise Jones had received at the Russian court and the interest which Catherine had shown, for, though she was sixty, her preference for young men was never more marked. Certainly it was less than diplomatic, as attractive as Paul Jones was to women, royal or otherwise, for him to have written to Potemkin: "All my life I shall remember with joy the gracious and noble welcome with which I was honored by Our August Catherine. If her Majesty were not the Empress of all Russia, she would always be, in my estimation, the most delightful of women. I will gladly give my blood . . ."

Potemkin immediately made sure the American would not be in a position to steal the whole naval show. He gave Prince Nassau-Siegen, a German-French adventurer who disliked Jones, the rank of Rear Admiral, the same rank the Empress had given Jones. He put Nassau-Siegen in charge of all ships especially designed for Black Sea navigation, while assigning the American to the more clumsy sailing vessels.

The moment that Jones raised his flag on the *Vladimir,* trouble began. English officers announced they would take no orders from him, and Russians and Greeks joined them. Jones asserted his authority sternly, declaring that he intended to prosecute the war vigorously, and that he would use severe punishment on those who did not obey. Once he had brought the rebellious crews under control, he sent word to General Suvorov to fortify Kinburn to prevent the Turkish Fleet from being able to sail near that part of the coast. Of all the brass hats present, Suvorov, Potemkin, Mordvinov, Nassau-Siegen, Suvorov was the only one willing to listen to Jones and the only one whose name has come down through history as a great leader. Suvorov, by his extraordinary campaign in Italy against Napoleon and his conquest of the Alps, later carved his name as one of the great military men of the century.

After heated arguments with Nassau-Siegen, Jones persuaded him to withhold his attack until the batteries at Kinburn were ready. He then ordered the Fleet drawn up to prevent the Turks from entering or leaving the Dniester River estuary in which they had sought refuge. The Turks, commanded by Hassan, came out on June 7th, but contrary winds made the use of Jones' unwieldy ships impossible. On the 16th Hassan came out again but ran his flagship aground, and it was dark before the Turks got it afloat. In the confusion the Turkish flagship went aground a second time, and Nassau raced to attack it with his fast ships, leaving Jones, with his wallowing boats, at the mercy of the Turkish guns. Jones, however, managed to lead the Turkish ships close to the shores of Kinburn, and when the fortifications opened fire, nine Turkish vessels were soon piled up on the shoals. Nassau-Siegen, having destroyed the flagship, gleefully set fire to another seven of them.

Part of the Turkish Fleet had been destroyed. The coveted St. George Cross was awarded to Potemkin and Nassau-Siegen. Jones received the extremely modest Cross of St. Anne. On July 1st the Russians met the Turks again and, following the American's tactical plan, Nassau-Siegen covered himself with glory, and was sent as a "naval expert" to examine the squadron at Sevastopol.

Jones was left in sole command. He had no expectations of glory. The political machinations which had all his life prevented him from using efficiently his genius in tactics were still to plague him. Potemkin sent him unintelligible, contradictory orders to block the Liman River and unblock it, to flee and then to attack.

Finally, Potemkin demanded that Jones withdraw his fleet from the area, and Jones, after pointing out that the Russian position was the best possible one, bowed to authority and withdrew. The Turks immediately attacked the evacuated harbor. Potemkin was enraged and condemned Paul Jones for inefficiency.

The American sent an angry reply. Potemkin's next order rather bluntly suggested that Jones receive the enemy "courageously" and not retreat. That was more than Paul Jones could bear. He wrote, "As I am here neither as an adventurer nor a mountebank, nor to repair a ruined fortune, I hope in the future to suffer no humiliation, but soon to be in the position which was promised me when I was invited to enter her Imperial Majesty's Navy."

At this very moment, Nassau-Siegen, who earlier had written to his wife, "I shall make enough noise to get the attention of the world. I have enough determination to act against this Jones," sent her the brief message, "I cannot help telling you that I am pleased with myself."

Having resigned his command, October 20th, Paul Jones visited Suvorov. "He is the soul of truth and honor," wrote Jones.

General, Prince Suvorov

"While under the evil command of Potemkin he never made reports of his operations because Potemkin would not let him write
the truth. . . . When I departed, he took from one of his camp
chests a fur cloak made of Siberian sea otter skins, lined with
yellow China silk, and long enough to reach my heels. This was
not all. He next produced a hussar jacket of solid ermine, white
as driven snow. 'Take these, Jones,' he said. [He knew that Jones
was going to St. Petersburg to try to get an independent commission.] 'For me, the coarse gray greatcoat of my soldiers and a
pair of muddy boots . . .' "

In St. Petersburg, Jones was pleasantly received by the
Empress and became as great a favorite among the ladies at Peterhof as he had been at Versailles. Catherine hinted that he would
get a new appointment in the spring.

Then, unexpectedly, a woman accused him of raping her
daughter. At first Jones did not take the charge seriously. He did
not believe the unsupported word of a woman living in a bawdy
house would be accepted against his own. He found he was in
error. He was placed under house arrest and his friends and even
his lawyer were forbidden to see him. Catherine refused him an
audience. In desperation he turned to Potemkin. By letter he
explained the case in detail. The girl had, for several months,
been the mistress of one of his servants, and therefore was able
to describe his house. The girl's mother had deserted her husband.
The mother was forcing the girl to work with her in a St. Petersburg bawdy-house. The mother herself privately admitted that she
was taking orders from a man "with gold lace." Her affidavit
accused Jones of a long conversation with the girl, importuning
her in Russian to become his mistress. Jones could not speak
Russian.

With utter frankness he wrote, "I love women, I confess,
and the pleasures one can enjoy only with that sex, but enjoy-
ments by force fill me with horror. I could not think of gratifying
my passions at the expense of their freedom and their modesty.
I give you my word, as a soldier and an honest man, that if the
Girl in question had never passed through other hands than mine,
she would still be a Virgin."

Potemkin never replied. Jones finally returned to Paris, his honor stained and his heart sore. One is forced to wonder whether Catherine had ever received him as "graciously" as the official reports stated. Her rage was terrible when she heard a rumor that he might enter the Swedish service. When Paul Jones made a last appeal to be cleared of the charges and reinstated, she replied that she had given him his release "so that he might leave here, without disgrace." "I have nothing more to say to Paul Jones," she wrote to Grimm. She even accused Jones of having turned Turco-Swede during the Ochakov campaign.

On July 9, 1790, Nassau-Siegen was decisively defeated by the Swedes, losing fifty-two ships and 7600 men. The career he had obtained at the expense of the American was at an end.

In July, 1792, Paul Jones was buried in an obscure Paris cemetery. His funeral was attended only by a few ruffians who used the occasion to get drunk. Catherine wrote to Grimm, "It is quite fitting that he should be celebrated by a rabble of detestable creatures."

This was the fate of the first important American who had turned his eyes toward Russia. But it must be remembered that John Paul Jones had had almost as much difficulty during his years in the American Navy, winning his reputation in spite of handicaps and restrictions which were imposed upon him. For his bravery and tactical genius, America gave him a few copper pennies, and for his pains on her behalf Russia cast a slur upon his honor.

CHAPTER TWO

RUSSIAN AMERICA

The northwest coast of North America, meanwhile, drew the destinies of Russia and the United States toward each other.

In the Sixteenth Century Ivan IV's warriors had assaulted Kazan, and Cossack Yermak had pushed relentlessly across the trackless wastes of Siberia. Sixty years later, another Cossack explorer, Dezhnev, sailed the waters separating Siberia from America and unknowingly was the first European to sight the northwest coast of America.

In 1698, William Penn had tried to convert Peter the Great to Quakerism. Penn failed, but young Czar Peter listened carefully when Penn informed him that although Spain, Portugal, Holland, England, Denmark and Sweden had established colonies in the new world, they had overlooked the northwest coast. Peter, who like all Russians of his time had considered America as being

23

Peter the Great

inaccessibly distant, suddenly realized that it might be quite close to Siberia. Encouraged by Leibnitz, German scientist and philosopher, he began to make plans for the exploration of that area. In the wars with the Swedes, many men skilled in shipbuilding had been captured. Peter ordered them sent to the northeastern Siberian coast, thereby making it possible for ships to be constructed in Siberia, and avoiding the long, long voyage from the Baltic Sea. These men were responsible for building ships suited to the Sea of Okhotsk, saving a month of travel overland, and bringing the Russians closer to Alaska.

After several unsuccessful expeditions, in 1724 Peter ordered Commodore Vitus Bering to build ships at Okhotsk and find out whether Siberia and the North American continent were joined by land. Six months later the Emperor died, but his widow, Catherine I, ordered the project to be continued. In 1728 the first Northern Expedition set sail.

Four years later Bering returned with a chart of Kamchatka and insisted that Asia and America were not joined by a land corridor, but he had almost no geographical evidence to support his claim. He based his belief primarily on a group of tales which he had heard from the Chuckchi, savages who lived along the Siberian coast. Actually, an accident of weather had made it impossible for Bering to be certain. Twice he had passed islands which he had named Diomede, but on both occasions heavy Arctic fog had obscured his view. If the mists had dissolved either of these days he would have seen the coast of America to the east and that of Siberia to the west.

St. Petersburg scientists felt his investigations had been inconclusive, although the maps which Bering's expedition made of the Polar regions of Siberia were the most accurate in existence for more than a century. The only error of consequence in the Bering Report was his statement that a northeastern passage from the White Sea to Siberia was infeasible. His pronouncement discouraged further interest in opening up such a waterway for a hundred and fifty years. Since all the major rivers in Siberia flow from south to north, with their outlets in Arctic waters, the rivers were largely useless as means of transportation and supply which had to travel east and west. The importance of this can be realized only if one tries to imagine the development of the United States without the Ohio and Missouri tributaries.

Presently, an illiterate Cossack officer, Shestakov, proposed a plan to subjugate the Chuckchi. The Russian Senate gave him permission and assigned Gvozdev, a geodesist, and Pavlutsky, a captain of Dragoons, to the expedition. Shestakov and Pavlutsky quarreled and split, Shestakov sailing from Okhotsk to conquer the Chuckchi, and in his first battle with the savages every man in his party was killed. The other ship, with Gvozdev in command, because scurvy had incapacitated Pavlutsky and the officers, skirted the Diomede islands and continued eastward until a strip of coast was sighted. Shoals and headwinds prevented a landing, and Gvozdev stood out to sea on a southwest course, without realizing that he had done accidentally what Bering, after immense

The Diomede Islands in Bering Straits: Russian (l.) and American (r.)

preparation, had failed to do. The "Large Country" which Gvozdev thought to be an island was the coast of America. Five years later a Cossack sent to St. Petersburg on a criminal charge mentioned it and the Admiralty College immediately demanded more information. Ten years after the voyage, Gvozdev, who informed them that he had sent his report shortly after the completion of the voyage, re-wrote it, as best he could, from memory. No other information could be obtained, since Pavlutsky in the meantime had led another expedition against the Chuckchi, who had removed and dried his head.

Bering's second expedition, The Great Northern, was ordered to survey Siberia from the Lena to the Anadyr and Kamchatka Rivers, to investigate Japan and the possibilities of Japanese trade, and to find out what connection existed between Asia and America. In September, 1740, the *St. Peter* and *St. Paul* rounded the point at Kamchatka and hove-to in Avacha Bay, where Bering built a settlement, Petropavlovsk. His plan was to set out in May, winter in America, and return the following spring. His plan went awry. A cargo of ship's biscuit was lost in the Okhotsk River, freight boats were unable to make the hazardous trip around the southern point of the Kamchatka, and the natives staged a rebellion. June was upon him and the short northern summer well advanced before the expedition put to sea, with Bering on the

St. Peter and Chirikov on the *St. Paul*. Two weeks later they became separated.

Chirikov searched three days, then continued on his course. On July 22nd wild ducks and landfowl warned him that land was near, and on the 26th came the cry, "Land ho!" Two days later the ship manoeuvered into a wide, placid harbor, Sitka or Latuiya Bay, and a landing party was sent ashore to hunt for fresh water. It never returned. An armed search party was sent inland, and it, too, vanished. Desperate for water, with his crew almost mutinous, Chirikov ordered full sail and turned back towards Asia, abandoning forever the first Russians to set foot on the western coast of North America. On one of the Aleutian Islands the sailors searched the entire island, but found no water. On October 19th, with rotted sails and the crew bordering on madness, Petropavlovsk came into view. Chirikov lay sick in his cabin with tuberculosis.

Meanwhile, Bering had sailed northeast for nearly a month with fair winds. He was almost convinced he had missed the American coast when shallow-water seaweed and kelp were encountered. The next day a chain of rugged mountains behind a heavily indented coast was sighted, fifty-nine hours after Chirikov had made his discovery. Bering, gloomy, disconsolate, sick with scurvy, allowed Dr. Steller only one day in which to go ashore. Steller remarked bitterly that ten years of unremitting toil and hardship had been endured so that he might make ten hours of scientific investigation. Yet he made remarkable observations in those few hours, most of which were substantiated by later research. From the remains of a fire, a dwelling containing some utensils, a heap of shells and bones, some dried fish, he decided that America and Asia were closer than the long voyage had suggested, and that it was inhabited by natives closely akin to the Siberians and possessing a high state of material culture.

The return voyage was a repetition of the hardships that had harassed previous Russian expeditions into sub-Arctic waters. Bering was so anxious to get away that he hoisted anchor while twenty casks were yet to be filled. Rain, storm and fog pursued the *St. Peter*. Scurvy was a curse. So many of the crew were laid up that the ship was often out of control. Once it drifted ashore on a tiny island. A storm blew it miles off the course.

Men died. Brackish water taken on at the tiny island intensified the sickness. Only ten men were above deck when the ship ran aground on a large island.

Bering decided to spend the winter there. He was carried ashore in a dying condition. The crew were greeted by thousands of blue foxes. As Bering lay in a sand-pit, the men surrounded him to ward off the foxes that tugged at him inquisitively, as if they had never seen human beings. In the last hours of his life a blizzard piled snow, sleet and sand upon his body. Shortly after he died, the storm dashed the *St. Peter* to pieces on the rocks.

A few days later, foxes could be seen dragging frozen human bodies around, playing with them and fighting over them. As the foxes became more vicious, desperate men fought them off with pikes and clubs. Crude huts were built, and scores of foxes that had been beaten to death were used whole to form walls and stuff cracks. It was so cold that neither dead animals nor dead men could decay.

After a ghastly winter, the survivors built a small boat and managed to get back to Kamchatka. History is replete with accidents and ironies. To men of the sea, to merchants and traders, Bering's discovery meant nothing, but when the remnants of his expedition straggled ashore, clad in crude garments of sea otter, seal and Arctic blue fox, the news spread of the fortunes that could be had to the north and east. In 1745, a group of fur prospectors returned from a trip in small boats laden with furs. The following year Mikhail Nevodchikov discovered the island of Attu in the Aleutians. Each summer saw the departure of ships which brought back furs to the value of hundreds of thousands of rubles. Fur prospectors pushed farther and farther north. Ever more money was needed to finance their expeditions, and, as it became increasingly difficult for individuals to provide adequate funds, fur companies sprang up.

England, France and Spain began to cast longing eyes toward the fur lands. Spain hurried her California colonization and fortified San Francisco. England offered 20,000 pounds sterling to anyone who discovered a Northwest Passage. Captain Cook, searching for it, discovered the Hawaiian Islands and made scattered visits along the Russian-American coast. France sent an expedition under La Perouse. In the wake of exploration came the "Boston men" and the "King George men" who bought, stole, raped and murdered, but worst of all, from the Russian point of view, depleted the supply of furs. The merchants of Irkutsk urged Catherine II to proclaim the northwest coast Russian territory.

"It is for traders to traffic where they please," she wrote in 1769. "I will furnish neither men, ships nor money. I renounce forever all possessions in America." She said later, "England's experience with the American colonies should be a warning to other nations to abstain from such efforts."

But Russian traders and fur merchants would not give in so easily. Shelikhov, a merchant of Rylsk who dealt in Alaskan furs, knew that permanent settlements in America would decrease the rising costs of trade and make Russian control over the land more certain. He sensed that an appeal to the Empress to help him prevent "the extermination of fur-bearing animals" might arouse her sympathy. In 1784, he sent a small group of fur prospectors to Kodiak Island, where a few buildings were erected. This done, he went to St. Petersburg to explain his plan to the Empress. He took with him his partner, Golikov, who was astute

Gregory Shelikhov

enough to send in advance a map of the new land and a present of costly furs. Catherine was so pleased with the gifts and the "noble idea" that all taxes on the new company were discontinued and exclusive trading rights in Russian America were granted.

Delarov, a Russo-Greek merchant, was appointed manager, and a huge crate filled with shields, emblems, and plates, all bearing the Imperial arms of Russia, were shipped to Russian America (later Alaska), where they were to "be placed at the point where a British ship anchored in 1784, so that the continent of Western America, called Alaska, would henceforth be recognized by all as one of the domains of the Empress of Russia." Delarov was told to bury near each shield an iron plate engraved with a cross and the words, "Territory of the Russian Empire," so that, if some impudent Englishman or Spaniard removed the shields, ownership could still be proved by digging up the plates.

While Shelikhov-Golikov tightened their hold on Russian America, in 1785 there appeared in Paris an adventuresome American, John Ledyard. Educated at Eleazar Wheelock's Indian Charity School (Dartmouth College), he became so interested in the Indians that he threw aside his books and went to live among them. Later, he made a canoe, paddled to Hartford, Connecticut and boarded a ship bound for the Mediterranean. At Gibraltar he jumped ship and enlisted in the British Army. Reaching London by an unrecorded course, he pestered men of influence until he was given a place on Cook's last expedition. Several years later, in Paris, he called on Jefferson, John Paul Jones, and Lafayette and related to them glowing tales of what he had seen in the Northwest. He believed there was a close connection between Asia and Alaska, either land or a chain of islands. Leaning over a map, Jefferson traced with his finger a route to Philadelphia by way of St. Petersburg, Siberia, Russian America. That was the feat Ledyard believed he could accomplish if he were given a little assistance.

Jefferson agreed to arrange for his credentials. Sir Thomas Banks, who had been on the Cook expedition, would provide money. Jefferson wrote Catherine and waited five months for her reply. Ledyard waited for neither his credentials nor money, but set out on foot during the winter of 1786, going to Stockholm and crossing the frozen Gulf of Bothnia. He reached St. Petersburg without shoes, stockings or money. In seven weeks he had walked 1400 miles. Ragged, impoverished, undaunted, he decided to get assistance from the Empress, but was informed that she was not in St. Petersburg.

He met a Scotsman, one Dr. Browne, who befriended him by accompanying him to the border of Siberia. From there Ledyard traveled alone the trail across the frozen wastes that had turned back many a well-equipped expedition. When he was within six hundred miles of the Pacific Ocean, he was arrested by soldiers on horseback whom Catherine had dispatched after him. The Empress, learning that Ledyard had been on the Cook expedition, had decided it would be unwise to allow him to continue his explorations. He was brought back to St. Petersburg, deported to Poland, and warned never again to enter Russia.

While England was losing part of its Empire in America, Russia was attempting to expand its holdings on the North American continent. In 1790, Delarov, manager of the Shelikhov-Golikov Company in Alaska, was replaced by Alexander Baranov, who was eager to move southward, but was hampered by the Nootka Sound Convention, signed by Russia, Spanish California, and Great Britain, which restricted Russian settlements to lands north of the 60th degree of latitude. Baranov had no intention of observing the convention, but the moment was not propitious for pressing forward. Russia did not want to quarrel with England.

To understand the real difficulties of the Alaskan settlements, one must remember the words of Nansen, famous Arctic explorer, "An unending stream of straggling, struggling, frostbitten men bundled in heavy clothing, some erect and powerful, some so skinny and bent that they could hardly drag themselves or their sleds; wasted, starved, plagued with scurvy, but all gazing forward into the unknown, beyond the edge of the northern sun toward the dream which they sought."

Food was difficult to obtain in Alaska. Supplies had to be brought by caravan across Siberia, then across the Pacific, and were always late arriving and frequently insufficient in quantity. The wooden supply ships were not suited to the rough northern

Alexander Baranov

waters and many were lost or wrecked. The Russians at Sitka went on protracted fasts in order to conserve their tiny, dwindling food supplies.

There were other troubles. The warlike Kolosh tribe, which had invaded Sitka a few years earlier, was again threatening. Spanish California, by refusing to trade with Russian ships, had made the food shortages alarming. The Shelikhov-Golikov Company, though still powerful financially, was not centralized, and its widely spread enterprises had so little contact with each other that the whole organization was in danger of collapse.

After Captain Robert Gray, on the *Columbia,* in 1792 discovered the mighty river which he named in honor of his ship, the Northwest swarmed with Boston ships. Baranov, unable to prevent the Americans from coming, refused to allow his Aleuts to aid them, and since the Aleuts were the best trappers, the Russians were able to keep the bulk of the fur-trade for themselves. But the cycle was vicious. The race for fur was causing the annihilation of the seals and otters and left little time for agricultural pursuits; importing food increased company expenses, and the higher the expenses, the more furs the home office demanded from the colonists.

Nicholas Rezanov

Shelikhov died in 1795. The company passed into the hands of Nicholas Rezanov. Rezanov wanted a national fur monopoly. Empress Catherine was about to grant it when her death in 1796 forced him to negotiate with her son, Paul I. Rezanov managed to win the confidence of Paul and was granted a twenty-year charter giving the company all trading rights in Russian America north of 55°, as well as in all islands and lands adjacent thereto which might be discovered. The new company, the Russian-American Company, under its favorable charter, became the Slavic replica of such great empire-builders as the British and Dutch East India Companies. Its power in Siberia was supreme and it carried on international intercourse almost as a sovereign power.

On March 11, 1801, Paul I was murdered in his bedroom in St. Michael Palace. Alexander I ascended to the throne.

Rezanov, who had long speculated on the advantages of a Russian economic agreement with Japan, broached to Alexander I a plan for a voyage around the world to increase Russian naval prestige. The voyage would include visits to Japan, Alaska, and the Spanish possessions in Central and South America. Rezanov's plan preceded Commodore Perry's by half a century and Roosevelt's World Cruise by more than twice that. His idea was basically that of empire salesmanship.

Czar Alexander I, like Rezanov, thought in large terms. He appointed Rezanov Imperial Envoy to Japan and placed the ships *Neva* and *Nadezhda* at his disposal. The first part of the trip went smoothly, the ships stopping at Brazil, Argentina, and most of the ports of western South America. Rezanov did not make serious attempts to obtain trade pacts with these countries because the shipping distances were too large. But when he stopped at Honolulu, he suggested to King Kamehameha the possibility of trading food to the Russian-American colony in exchange for sea-otter pelts.

After leaving Hawaii, the *Neva* was sent to Russian America where it arrived in time to aid Baranov in the recapture of Sitka, under attack by the natives. Rezanov went on to Japan. Though his interest in and knowledge of Japan probably surpassed that of any Russian of his time, having written a grammar and compiled a dictionary with the help of Japanese immigrants in Siberia, he had never been to that country before. Rezanov was one of those rare men in whom personal curiosity, esthetic appreciation, and practical knowledge caused no conflict.

In Japan, he was forbidden to visit the Imperial Court, and for five months he was kept in a house in Nagasaki which the Japanese had built for him. The guard stationed outside the entrance of his door was not to protect him from the natives, who showed no signs of hostility, nor to make him feel imprisoned, which the Japanese would have felt was discourteous, but simply to protect the natives from being corrupted by him. There was no personal feeling against him. Japan simply did not want foreigners or foreign customs to taint their own culture.

Rezanov remained as cool and unperturbed as his hosts, occupying his leisure by collecting some five thousand words to add to his dictionary and gathering pertinent information on their observable mores and modes of living. He was determined, if he succeeded in nothing else, to leave a good impression of himself. Finally, however, having sent the *Nadezhda* to chart the islands and make maps, having failed to get permission from Japan for Russian trade (even his gifts, including porcelain vases, mirrors, rugs and furs, English cloths, rifles, and a bronze elephant clock, were returned without comment), he chartered a vessel and sailed for Sitka.

Affairs were going none too happily there. Yankee traders and fur-hunters had increased. By 1803 they were a veritable curse. Baranov had finally come to accept a Yankee political maxim, "When you can't beat 'em, j'ine 'em." The food situation was critical. Rezanov wrote, "The founder of this settlement lives in a miserable hut so damp that the floor is always covered with water. During heavy rains the place has to be abandoned." During the autumn and early winter Rezanov investigated the entire colony from Sitka to Three Saints. He established a school, writing the text books himself, and organized housekeeping classes for the young girls. He tried to raise the morale of the colony. But he knew that as long as starvation loomed always in the immediate future, the settlers could not be expected to have much spirit.

The winter was terrible that year. Another such winter, Rezanov decided, would see Russian territories in America a thing of the past. When a schooner from Bristol, Rhode Island arrived, he negotiated the purchase of her cargo of foodstuff. Then, changing his mind, he bought from Captain DeWolfe not merely the cargo, but the *Juno* herself, for a price of some 68,000 dollars. He decided, as soon as weather permitted, to sail the cargo ship to San Francisco.

Rezanov, one of the most far-sighted men in the annals of Russian diplomacy, saw clearly that Russia could not survive as a trans-Pacific power unless she colonized the northern California coast. "If this is not done in our own lifetime," he wrote, "we need never expect to reap the tremendous potential benefits of America." His travels in the Pacific had not been aimless, and his eye had been attentive to the geographical importance of Hawaii, to the important trade which Japan would have to offer once it had shaken off the chains of centuries of sleep. But the present Russian position required immediate alleviation and he was making the trip to California, partly to scout the shoreline for the site of a settlement, but also to try to obtain a trade agreement with the Spanish.

The voyage to San Francisco was hazardous in the early

March weather. He was unable to put the ship into harbor anywhere along the coast. Anxious to explore the Columbia River,
for two days he fought high seas, contrary winds and shallow
reefs, before giving up the attempt. When he arrived in San Francisco, it took all his perseverance and persuasion to be allowed to
put into port. But once this was done, he soon found favor among
the Spaniards and installed himself in the home of Don Jose Daiso
Arguello, Commandante of San Francisco.

He wrote to the Emperor, "The Spanish are weak in this
region. If, in 1798, when war was declared by Spain, Russian
America had had a force equal to its present one, it would have
been easy to seize from 34° to Santa Barbara and keep this territory forever, since the geographical position of Mexico is such
as to prevent her from sending much assistance overland. Even
now, if we can obtain the means for the beginning of this penetration of California, in the course of ten years we would be strong
enough to make use of any favorable turn in European politics
to include the coast of California among Russian possessions."

In June, 1806, he wrote, "If Russia had followed the foresight of Peter the Great, one can definitely state that California
would never have been a Spanish possession." In the same letter
he admitted that a difficult political situation in California had
forced him to alter his policy. "I decided to change from a polite
man to a stern one, and I begin every day to court the Spanish
Beauty . . ."

The "Spanish Beauty" was Maria Concepçion, fifteen-year-
old daughter of the Commandante, who had become fascinated
by this mature man from a land far across the seas. Rezanov had
used her, much to her delight, to advance his political interests.
Shortly after having written the above letter, after overcoming
considerable parental opposition, Rezanov and Maria Concepçion
were betrothed. All that remained was to obtain the sanction of
the Czar and the consent of the Pope.

His sojourn in California was drawing to a close. He had
every reason to be pleased. Relations between Russian America
and Nueva California were vastly improved; trade seemed imminent. He had assured the Governor of California that as soon as
he returned to Russia, he would go at once as Envoy Extraordi-

nary to Madrid, to bind Spain in friendly accord with Russia. Then he would return to California to claim Doña Concepçion as his bride.

His happiness was marred, however, by dispatches from Mexico. Napoleon had defeated the Austrians, the French had occupied Vienna, and the Russian Army was in retreat. One newspaper, under a Hamburg date-line, announced that a revolution had broken out in St. Petersburg. "My God!" Rezanov cried in consternation. "What is happening to my unhappy country!"

The commercial agreement finally settled, Rezanov bade goodbye to his friends in San Francisco, boarded the *Juno,* which was loaded with Spanish grain, and sailed to Sitka, where he spent the summer. It was October before he reached Okhotsk on the last lap of his journey. He complained of feeling physically exhausted. By the time he reached Yakutsk in February, 1807, he was desperately ill. He pushed on towards Krasnoyarsk, almost in the dead center of freezing Siberia.

Ten years later Captain Otto von Kotzebue, aboard the Russian warship, *Rurik,* entered San Francisco. He had with him a small book, *Voyages and Travels,* by Heinrich von Langsdorff. In this book Doña Concepçion, who had clung to her scattered memories—the cannon by which they had exchanged vows, the cotton-wood trees beneath which they had strolled in the evenings—read the words which caused her to take the veil and dedicate her life to works of charity and love: "They consigned him to God in the churchyard at Krasnoyarsk. His tomb is marked by a large stone in the fashion of an altar, but without any inscription."

The Seal of the Russian-American Company

father dimitri
of loretto, pa.

Frequently the ties that bind nations together are forged, not over council tables, but in the hearts of individuals whose activities are far removed from diplomacy and statesmanship. One memorial to such a tie stands on a wooded height of Pennsylvania, between Johnstown and Altoona, in the village of Loretto. In front of St. Michael's Church a small monument bears this Latin inscription:

SACRUM MEMORIAE
DEM. A.E. PRINCIPIBUS GALLITZIN
NAT. XXII DECEMB. A.D. MDCCLXX
QUI SCHISMATE EJURATO
SACRO. MINISTERIO PER
TOT HANC REG. PERFUNCTUS
FIDE ZELO CHARITATE PERFUNCTUS
HEIC. OBIT DEI VI MAII MDCCCXL

It is the tomb of a Russian prince, a Roman Catholic priest, and one of the best loved men America has ever known.

The Golitzin estate just outside Moscow contained the finest private residence in the province. Alexander I expressed envy of its owner. In more modern times it became the country residence of Joseph Stalin. Any door in Europe opened to the name Golitzin. That the Golitzin family was one of the most distinguished in Russia is demonstrated by the story of a child, who, when told by his grandmother the story of Jesus, asked, "Was he a Golitzin too?"

The late Eighteenth Century buzzed with new ideas, and the acknowledged center of this intellectual ferment was Paris. Prince Golitzin, a wise, witty, worldly nobleman, was a star of the first magnitude in this atmosphere during the fourteen years in which he was the Russian Ambassador. The Russian Embassy was frequented by the foremost men of the Age of Reason, including Voltaire, D'Alembert, and Diderot, and many of the controversial articles of the famous encyclopedia were written there. When Prince Golitzin was transferred to The Hague, his residence again became the center of the most brilliant company of the day, including French, Dutch and German philosophers. It was in this mansion that Empress Catherine, charmed by three-year-old Dimitri, the Prince's son, held him on her lap and commissioned him an Ensign in a Guard regiment.

The elderly Prince Golitzin had married Amalie Schmettau, barely twenty, daughter of a famous Prussian field-marshal. Though baptized a Roman Catholic, she, like many young women who felt "enlightened," did not take religious matters seriously. She threw herself into the atmosphere of the intellectual life about her and enjoyed every minute of it. She talked endlessly, read novels, and even started to write one, *Simon: or, The Faculties of the Soul.* She was also interested in music and dabbled in the study of Greek. But one afternoon she told Diderot that she was bored with social life. He suggested that she devote more time to the care and education of her children. Amalie promptly employed a tutor, "for the children," who spent most of his time in conversation with her, and whom she soon preferred to address as "Our dear Socrates."

When Diderot passed through the Hague again, he listened to her enthusiastic report on the education of her children, politely praised their and her progress, and suggested that she leave society altogether and go to some blessed spot where she (and of course the children) could commune with nature. Having read Rousseau's *Noble Savage,* the idea appealed to her. Prince Golitzin, amused, good-naturedly offered her a house he owned between the Hague and Scheveiningen. There Amalie took her children and "Our dear Socrates." She cut off her long hair, wore plain clothes, and spent her days in plain living, with merely a cook and two maids to handle the routine housework. She named the house Niethuis (nobody home!) and spent the evenings reading Plato and the Stoics. The children were compelled to take cold water baths each morning and to sleep in the dark to harden them for the rigors of Hellenic thought. When they cried, which they seemed to do from time to time in spite of her efforts to make them more rational, she comforted them with Socratic dialogues.

When the children were older, and the tutor had become rather boring, she heard of a marvelous new school at Munster, and decided to visit it. She planned to go on to Geneva but was so entranced by the learned atmosphere that she remained at Munster. In 1783 she fell ill of a fever and nearly died. During her illness, Baron von Fürstenberg, founder of the school, sent his own confessor, Father Overberg, to talk with her on spiritual matters. Amalie was too sick. She did promise, however, that if God spared her life she would seriously investigate religion. Two years later she was received into full communion with the Roman Church, and shortly afterward her son, Dimitri, was baptized and confirmed.

Prince Golitzin accepted his son's conversion as calmly as he had accepted everything else engineered by his extraordinary wife. He knew that her enthusiasm for religion would follow the same course as her enthusiasm for philosophy. It might not even last as long. He sensed too that his son was merely riding in the wake of her impulsiveness, and in a letter he wrote to his wife he merely reminded her that Dimitri would soon have to choose a career, and that it would be wise for the boy, now seventeen, to get some military experience. Amalie, who did not want to return to Russia, consulted with her brother, General von Schmettau, who felt the best place for a Roman Catholic was in the Austrian army. An appointment was secured for Dimitri as aide-de-camp to General von Lillien, but lasted only a few months, because the mysterious death of Leopold and the assassination of the King of Sweden led to an order that discharged all foreigners holding commissions.

General Schmettau, a great admirer of George Washington, suggested that the boy be sent to America. When Prince Golitzin was informed, he heartily endorsed the idea as the most sane his wife had ever proposed. The Prince, also an admirer of Washington, and like all good Eighteenth Century gentlemen deeply interested in the American Constitution as the apotheosis of rationalist thought, had followed the course of the American Revolution, and felt America was a fine place to harden a young man for later obligations.

When travel arrangements were made, it was found that a Father Brosius could accompany Dimitri to America, where he would be placed under the protection of John Carroll of Baltimore, the first Roman Catholic Bishop in the United States. On the advice of his father, to avoid being fleeced by unscrupulous fellow-travelers, Dimitri traveled incognito as "Augustine Schmett." Shortly after his arrival in America he found himself being called Schmidt and Smith. In October, 1792, Dimitri took up residence at the new seminary in Baltimore. Two months later he announced his intention of becoming a priest. Bishop Carroll advised him to think it over. But when Dimitri showed no sign of changing his mind, the bishop agreed that he should inform his family of his intentions.

Amalie was dismayed. She refused to believe it. She had failed to notice that her own enthusiasm for religion, which had long since waned, had made a deep impression on her son. Having never had a high regard for his willpower, she was convinced that he had gotten into the hands of bad priests who intended to use him. She wrote letter after letter, imploring him to come home. She stated that she could not believe he was cut out for the priesthood. She wrote that she was afraid to tell her husband, that she felt it was all her fault, and that she did not know what to do.

A strange thing happened. The military appointment which Empress Catherine had given to the child, and which had been forgotten, came due, and an official message, ordering Dimitri to join his regiment within six months, was sent to Prince Golitzin. The Prince informed his wife and asked her to write Dimitri that he must start for home. Amalie was forced to confess everything.

Prince Golitzin was stunned. In a pathetic letter he wrote his wife that he had no intention of censuring her. "Above all, I beg you to unite with me to discuss that which is properly our common trouble and to seek some means of solving it. I do not know what to write to my son."

Dimitri remained unmoved throughout the whole affair. He had found his true vocation. He was happy for the first time in his life. Kneeling before Bishop Carroll on March 18, 1795, he was the first Catholic priest within the United States to receive all the orders from tonsure to ordination. He was sent to the mission in Conowago, Pennsylvania.

When he had been at the mission nearly a year, he received a call to the Maguire Settlement, where a dying woman wished to become a Catholic. The settlement was beyond the crest of the Allegheny Mountains, a hundred and fifty miles westward and a week's journey. When Dimitri reached the small group of houses along Clearfield creek, he found he had come too late. The woman had died. He remained there for a time, celebrated mass, baptised a number of children and heard confessions. He learned that Captain Maguire, a Revolutionary War officer, had purchased 1200 acres of land and started the settlement. He had wanted a church and a priest, and, at his death, had bequeathed a third of his land to Bishop Carroll. When Dimitri returned to Conowago, he consulted with the Bishop and told him that he wanted to build a parish at the Maguire Settlement. With considerable misgivings, since there was a need for priests in more populous areas, Bishop Carroll, after more than three years of delay, finally agreed to establish the mission.

In August, 1799, Dimitri left civilization and plunged into the forests and mountains that were to be his home for forty years. It was harvest time when he reached the Maguire Settlement, and after the harvest was in the men cut white pine logs for the church and the women molded candles and sewed altar cloths. The winter snows had begun before the last logs were in place, the roof shingled, and the little church ready for occupancy. People came from twenty and thirty miles around to attend the first service held at midnight on Christmas Eve.

In the years that followed Dimitri knew heartache and trouble, but he never faltered. For twenty years he worked his vast vineyard alone. The settlement grew and his flock increased. Nine years after St. Michael's was built it had to be doubled in size. At his own expense, using money he received from his mother, he bought land, improved its soil, and resold it for less than it had cost. Land for which he had paid four dollars an acre he sold to poor settlers at a dollar an acre. Altogether he purchased 20,000 acres and in the village of Loretto, which he named in honor of the Italian shrine, he built a tannery, a grist-mill and a sawmill.

His mother sent him money until her death in 1806. Then, as the heir to a large fortune, he borrowed on his expectations, determined to do everything he could for the land and people he loved. It was a kind of generosity that is rare even among men of God. The interminable litigation over the estate began to worry him, though he did not fear that he would eventually receive his share of the estate. In 1803 the Russian Senate handed down a decision excluding him from the estate on grounds of religious faith and profession. Emperor Alexander signed it.

Dimitri's sister wrote that he need not worry, she was sending him 5000 rubles. Once he received a $2000 draft from King William of the Netherlands, labeled as payment for some trifling articles which he had left behind in the royal summerhouse when he and the King had been boyhood playmates. Despite these bright moments he was in difficult circumstances, for he had borrowed heavily on what had been vast expectations. He went to Washington to see the Russian Minister, to whom he owed $5000, and laid his case before him and promised what restitution he could. The Minister, however, suggested that the discussion of financial matters be postponed until after dinner. Present at dinner were Henry Clay and the Dutch Envoy. After the plates had been removed, a servant brought in a candle to be used by the gentlemen in lighting their cigars. The Russian Minister rolled a spill, thrust it into the flame of the candle, lighted his cigar leisurely, and smiled. A black ash was all that remained of the $5000 bond.

Not all Dimitri's debtors were able, or inclined, to duplicate such a gesture. In the end the priest was forced to appeal for contributions. Money came from as far away as Rome, where Cardinal Cappellari (Pope Gregory XVI) sent a draft for $200. Dimitri did not live to see all his debts paid and the lands he loved fully settled. Bishop Carroll tried to transfer him to the prosperous town of Lancaster. When a diocese was established in Cincinnati, Bishop Flaget urged Golitzin to be the new bishop. Archbishop Maréchal wanted to appoint him bishop of a new diocese at Detroit. Dimitri protested that it would be easy to find men more deserving and fitted to bear the honors and burdens of an episcopate, but it would be impossible to fill his place in Loretto.

By 1840 there were many priests under his charge, but he continued to visit the outlying settlements, to ride the mountain trails, to tramp through woods and along streams. He died in May, too soon to see the mountain laurel. From the length and breadth of his parish people came for his funeral. The only instructions he left was the wish that his grave might be midway between the church and his little house. But his devoted parishioners formed a procession and bore his body all through the village, and the pallbearers were changed every few yards so that as many as possible could share in this last homage.

I will lift up mine eyes unto the hills from whence cometh my strength.

Three years later another member of the Golitzin family died in America. Princess Elizabeth Golitzin, influenced by her relative, Dimitri, abandoned the Russian for the Roman Church. She joined the Society of the Sacred Heart, came to America, was an indefatigable worker in the yellow fever epidemic in Louisiana, was stricken and died.

Today the former parish of Dimitri Golitzin makes up the dioceses of Pittsburgh, Erie and part of Harrisburg. Within a few miles of Loretto there are now twenty parishes. It is staggering to realize that one man once administered the whole of this and brought the word of God to ten thousand souls.

diplomatic mélange

Although Great Britain steadfastly refused to negotiate a commercial treaty with her ex-colonies and forbade American trade with the British West Indies, American shipping grew. New Englanders, a bit heady with their new independence, were extending their operations in all directions. Boston, yielding first place in size to New York and Philadelphia, was still the center of foreign trade. Massachusetts merchants began to open the Baltic ports to American commerce. In exchange for West Indian goods which Russia needed, American ships were being loaded with iron, duck, canvas, hemp, linen, candles and soap. By the time Napoleon closed the ports of western Europe nearly two hundred American vessels were trading with Russia. The fortunes of the Derbys of Salem, the Cabots and Peabodies of Boston were being made.

In 1790, a citizen of Amesbury constructed a nail machine and the Old Bay State became the center of nail manufacture.

Though Pennsylvania ironmasters had made progress in developing
their ore resources, overland shipments were financially prohibitive,
and it was cheaper to bring Russian iron across the sea. There
resulted a complicated international trade, for Russia imported
Welsh coal to smelt the iron, and Massachusetts paid for it with
West Indian rum. Between 1806 and 1811 American exports to
Russia increased from $12,407 to $6,137,657, chiefly at the expense of England. The twin arms of British trade were the Baltic
and the West Indies, and Massachusetts seamen were cutting into
both. The English retaliated with new laws and a new rigid interpretation of old laws. The American government, determined to
end the difficulties of their merchants, passed the Non-Importa-
tion Act.

Russian relations remained cordial with both nations. American seamen wintering in Riga brought back tales of skating parties,
balls, open sleighs, and all-night drinking bouts. Not only American
goods but American ideas were finding their way into Russia.
Alexander Radishchev, the distinguished Russian philosopher of
the time, in his "Voyage from Petersburg to Moscow," wrote:
"According to Pennsylvania law, people have the right to speak,
write and express any opinion. Unrestricted printing is practiced
there. Freedom of printing is one of the greatest freedoms in the
democratic experiment."

But while unofficial relations and trade were increasing,
Russia still dared not risk incurring British animosity. Moreover,
Russia was undergoing serious financial difficulties. The task of
maintaining a large army throughout long wars had caused inflation
and skyrocketing food prices.

In 1806, the Fourth Coalition was organized and Europe
plunged once more into war. Napoleon at Jena gave Prussia her
most humiliating defeat since Tannenberg. Early the following year
he met the Russians at Eylau in one of the bloodiest battles ever
fought. At Friedland, Napoleon won a clear-cut victory over the
Russian General, Bennigsen, and Alexander decided to make
peace. The Treaty of Tilsit in June, 1807, changed the outlook of
European affairs. Russia, forced by the treaty to become an ally
of France, declared war on England, and seizures and confiscations
were made. London placed an embargo on all ports that refused to

welcome the British flag. Napoleon retaliated with his Milan Decree, announcing confiscation of any ship, neutral or otherwise,
which had stopped or intended to stop at a British port anywhere
in the world.

The United States was hit from both sides. If she traded with
France, the British seized her ships. If she traded with England, the
French seized her ships. Yet both belligerents were using American
harbors freely. It took this remarkable, even weird situation to open
the gates between Russia and America. The declaration of war on
England freed Russia from her chains of diplomatic bondage, per-
mitting her at last to express her friendship to the United States.

President Jefferson and Czar Alexander I had been corresponding for some time. In 1805, the Emperor had written to Jefferson congratulating him on his re-election and making several
inquiries concerning the Constitution. Jefferson had sent him
several books, including *The Federalist,* and wrote, "I am happy
that the principles in which the American people believe are placed

Thomas Jefferson

Emperor Alexander I of Russia

under the protection of an umpire who, looking beyond the narrow bounds of an individual nation, will take under the cover of his equity the rights of the absent and unrepresented." To a friend Jefferson wrote, "Russia is the most cordially friendly to us of any power on earth."

Jefferson, quick to take advantage of the situation created by the Treaty of Tilsit, determined to send a special representative to St. Petersburg, one with more powers than Harris, the American Consul. He chose William Short of Pennsylvania. Knowing how unpopular he was in the Senate, fearing the rejection of his appointment, he kept it secret, and sent Short without the necessary Senate confirmation. He waited until the following February, on the eve of his return to private life, to report his act, believing the Senate would not carry its opposition to the point of persecuting a retiring President. But the Senate refused its consent. Short, already in Paris and in communication with Russian officials, suddenly discovered he had no diplomatic standing. Due to slow communications, however, one important event had already taken place. When Rumiant-zev, the Russian Chancellor, learned that Short was enroute to Russia to negotiate a commercial treaty, he inquired what rank Short had. Short replied that he held the rank of Minister. Rumiant-zev said, "Good! Russia will immediately appoint an Envoy of equal rank." In May, 1809, Count Theodore Pahlen was dispatched to America with full diplomatic powers.

President Madison, immediately after his inauguration, asked the Senate to confirm John Quincy Adams as American Minister to Russia. The Senate first rejected, then finally approved his nomi-nation. Adams had been in the diplomatic service since he was fourteen and was probably one of the very few Americans who knew anything about Russia. He had so few illusions about the probable duration of his appointment that he left his family in Quincy, Massachusetts, and set out on a private ship. The passage was uneventful until at Christiansand the ship was halted by a Danish privateer and ordered to enter the harbor for investigation.

Adams was furious. His indignation increased when he found that thirty-eight other American ships were being held. Sensing that Britain was responsible, he called on British Admiral Bertie and demanded an explanation. Bertie did not like Americans, cer-tainly not arrogant ones. He did not even offer Adams a chair. He informed the American that neither he nor his ship could pro-ceed toward Russia. Adams insisted on his diplomatic status and hinted that he had access to higher authorities who might not approve of the Admiral's conduct. After blustering a while, Bertie gave in, and the ship was allowed to sail on to Kronstadt.

Emperor Alexander received him cordially, and said, "The American desire to keep apart from the unhappy disturbances that agitate Europe is a wise and just policy. I assure you I will do noth-ing to withdraw you from it." Later that same afternoon, after the formalities of his arrival had been completed, Adams went to the Russian Foreign Office and asked Chancellor Rumiantzev to secure the release of the American ships being held in Denmark. The Chancellor commented on the hazards traders must expect in time of war and advised dropping the matter. But Adams persisted. He went to see Alexander. Finally Rumiantzev reported, "Our Danish Minister will make urgent representations to his court regarding the

matter. I am sure the King of Denmark will see fit to comply."
Shortly afterward the American ships were released.

Adams was not merely an excellent envoy, but probably
enjoyed his years in St. Petersburg, though it was never his custom
to admit that he was happy. He spoke always in terms of "duty"
rather than pleasure. But when Madison offered him a release, and,
a year later, he was offered a place on the Supreme Court, he
refused. Even his rather crotchety remarks about St. Petersburg
indicate that he was not dissatisfied. "I engaged an apartment of
five indifferent chambers, said to be the best in the city." He spoke
of the "queer double-windows," precursors of storm-windows.
"There is a princess, Golitzin," he wrote, "venerable by the length
and thickness of her beard, resembling a Grecian philosopher."

Chancellor Rumiantzev wanted to establish diplomatic relations in order to obtain trading advantages and to protect Russian
America. His deep interest in the Rezanov fur monoply, the
Russian-American Company, caused him to complain almost daily
to Adams about the Boston ships in Alaskan waters, and to object
to the sale of firearms to the natives. One day he made a grandiose
proposal, in which he stated that Russia would be content to extend
her lands only as far south as the Columbia River, and that
Russians in Alaska would trade only with Boston ships, if the
Americans would let the Russians into the China trade.

Adams almost fell out of his chair. This was a direct violation
of the Nootka Sound Convention. It would give Russia a huge
chunk of land and the Columbia River. As for Alaska, the starving
Russians were only too glad to see Yankee ships, loaded with food,
enter their harbors. To give Russia part of the lucrative China
trade would be ridiculous. Adams flatly refused to even consider
such a proposal and was so indignant that Rumiantzev said, "Forget it, I was speaking of a matter of no real importance." Adams,
who believed in plain-talking, never really understood European
diplomats and their methods of sounding out each other. He did not
understand that the Russian Chancellor had taken an extreme position as the starting point at which bargaining would have been
begun, so that both sides would have had more space in which to
maneuver.

It was this same blindness to European diplomatic methods

that caused Adams to make bewildered protests whenever Russia prevented American ships from entering her ports, at the very same time that Russia was declaring her warmest friendship for the United States. The situation was simple. Russia had lost a war to France and was still under the thumb of Napoleon, who did not want Russia to trade with America. Chancellor Rumiantzev was constantly assuring the French that "steps were being taken" to prohibit the Yankees. From time to time, as a hoax to fool the French, he refused permission for American ships to unload. A few days later the American ships would be permitted to quietly land their goods and take on Russian cargoes. But the strategy went wide of its mark, for the French were not fooled, while Adams was so completely fooled that he sent protest after protest to the Chancellor.

Russia, however, had gained her purpose, which was to get enough time to rebuild her military. When Napoleon made an outright demand that Russia confiscate all American ships and cargoes, Alexander defiantly issued a *Ukase* in December, 1810, opening his ports to all vessels not English. Adams reported that Alexander did want American trade, but that he feared French pressure might force the Emperor to rescind his order.

In both Russia and the United States the confused international situation had developed pro-French and pro-British parties. The Federalists favored England, while the Jeffersonians, despite Citizen Genêt, preferred France. In Russia, Rumiantzev headed the Francophile party and in 1811 his party was losing ground. If Rumiantzev fell, Great Britain would once more send her ships to Russia and American trade would be seriously damaged. Moreover, both countries were drifting toward war, Russia with France, the United States with England. The Congressional election of 1810 brought the "warhawks," ardent young men led by Henry Clay and John C. Calhoun, into the House of Representatives. James Monroe, a career diplomat who had little faith in British or French pledges, became Secretary of State. In February, Minister William Pinkney was withdrawn from London.

On June 18, 1812, after a battle between *H.M.S. Little Belt* and the *U.S.S. President,* the United States declared war on Great Britain. On August 9th Adams learned of this. In June also,

Napoleon invaded Russia, and shortly thereafter Russia allied herself with England. John Quincy Adams was bewildered. While at war with England, the United States sought to keep the friendship of Russia, who was now allied with England. Adams sat on the powder keg and waited. Communications between Washington and St. Petersburg were slow and uncertain — the early news that trickled through was not cheering. The French Grand Army was driving deep into Russia, and, in the middle of September, Napoleon quartered his troops in the Holy City of Moscow. Adams wished for the downfall of Napoleon yet knew that that would mean the release of Wellington's troops for use against the United States.

Cartoon depicting Russia's mediation in the War of 1812

Czar Alexander had the Russian Chancellor inform Adams on the very day before Napoleon entered Moscow, that he was grieved to hear of the new British-American war (War of 1812), and that he would be pleased to offer his mediation. The United States accepted this offer and sent a delegation consisting of Secretary of the Treasury, Albert Gallatin, and Senator James A. Bayard. They arrived at St. Petersburg to learn that Great Britain had refused the mediation. Alexander, to show his friendship to the United States, requested the honor of paying the expenses of the Commission, and bestowed on each Commissioner a small gift. But when it was suggested that the Emperor present Mrs. Madison with a portrait of the Empress, Alexander smiled and said, "Entertain our guests by all means. But owing to our relations with England it is perhaps better not to present the Empress' portrait."

A year later, on September 1, 1813, a second offer of mediation by the Czar caused Anglo-American negotiations to take place, resulting in the Treaty of Ghent in 1814. By 1815 the world had come a long way. Russia had survived a baptism of fire which had left her at the pinnacle of European power. When Alexander entered Paris, Europe regarded him as its savior. His personal power was greater than that of any other ruler in the world. His insistence on a just peace, his generous attitude toward his vanquished enemies, spared the world many bitter recriminations that might have ensued.

Across the Atlantic, the Americans had undergone a test proportionately even more severe. The year 1815 saw them surveying a burned Capital, but the threat of Napoleon to England had extricated them from a war of attrition that could have negated the psychological impact of their belated victory in New Orleans under Andrew Jackson. In any case, England had to gird her loins, while the United States, unencumbered once again, set forth on a path that was to make her the counterpart in the West of Russian power in the East.

In June, 1808, Andrei Dashkov had been appointed Consul-General and "Chargé d'Affaires near the Congress of the United States." The indefinite nature of his title was due to the constant shifts of locale of the American Capital. Dashkov was crossing the Atlantic when Alexander I, as a return courtesy for Jefferson's appointment of William Short as American Minister to Russia, designated Count Pahlen as the Russian Minister to the United States. Therefore, for some time, Dashkov remained the only Russian representative in America.

President Madison, who had succeeded Jefferson, received Dashkov in Washington. Dashkov was astonished to learn that William Short, whom he had met in Paris, was not, despite his credentials, the Minister-Designate to Russia. Madison explained,

"The rejection of the Senate is entirely a partisan matter. The Senate is, indeed, as anxious as we all are to exchange envoys with Russia."

When Dashkov learned that President Madison had sent a new name to the Senate for confirmation, John Quincy Adams, and that it also had been rejected, he could be pardoned if his introduction to American politics left him doubtful of the vaunted excellence of democratic methods. The subsequent approval of Adams by the Senate bewildered him. Dashkov believed that if a system of checks and balances meant anything, it should mean the checking of a bad appointment, not the withholding, for no reason, of an appointment to which no one had any objection. He never got over the feeling that democratic government was wasteful and blundering.

Following the instructions of Chancellor Rumiantzev, he lodged frequent complaints against the Boston ships sailing in the Northwest and the sale of firearms to the Kolosh natives. He urged the American government to prohibit trade with anyone except Russian merchants in the Northwest. Secretary of State Robert Smith felt that such a law could never be enforced and that since Dashkov had no power to settle on a demarcation line, there was no reason for further discussion.

The arrival of Count Pahlen relieved Dashkov of almost all of his duties. Pahlen went straight to Washington and found it a desolate place. The streets were unpaved. The venerable oaks made the razed capital seem more permanently ruined. In bad weather Pennsylvania Avenue was impassable. The comment by the Minister from Portugal, "The city of magnificent distances," which Americans considered a compliment, was a European way of expressing distaste. A French diplomat stated it more directly, "My God! What have I done to deserve having to reside in such a city!"

In the confusion concerning the Short and Adams appointments, the Russian government, feeling it had been tricked into sending a Minister, informed Count Pahlen that he could remain in Washington or go to Rio de Janeiro. Pahlen immediately presented a letter of recall and hurried on to Brazil, leaving Dashkov as "Minister-ad-Interim." Dashkov, by this time, had so little regard for his appointment that he remained in Philadelphia, which, if not European, was at least civilized. Having never been in sympathy with republican forms of government, and feeling affronted by the confused political processes of the United States, he failed completely in his mission.

Two of his aides, however, were making important contributions to cultural exchange. Paul Svinin, a Russian painter who had been elected to the Academy of Fine Arts in St. Petersburg, traveled the United States from Maine to Virginia. "He acquainted himself," says the historian Avrahm Yarmolinsky, "with manners, customs and institutions. He enquired into the new mechanical devices, into the state of the fine arts. He attended revival meetings, mixed with street crowds, visited churches, prisons, mills and factories. He made acquaintances with engineers, captains-of-industry and government officials." Svinin contributed sketches and articles to the *Philadelphia Portfolio* "to enable Americans to see my own Russia." He sent his impressions of America to a monthly magazine in St. Petersburg. He wrote, "The United States present an example unprecedented in history. The Americans have shown themselves worthy of enjoying the rights of true liberty. The spirit of their government, to my mind, excels in this respect all the ancient and modern republics. Hence the incredible headway made by this country, an advance which seems more like a dream than a reality."

Hearing of J. J. Astor's plan to colonize the Columbia River, Svinin wrote, "What an enterprise for a private citizen! May it be crowned with success!" Fascinated by Fulton's steamboat, he wrote, "Conceive a vessel unafraid of storms, independent of wind, careless of foul weather, moving with amazing speed and security . . . such is the picture of an American steamboat!" He wrote to Rumiantzev suggesting a plan to build steamboats for Russia. When he found out Fulton was already doing this, he wrote Fulton, offering his services and his knowledge of the Neva River and its channel.

Svinin's enthusiasm for America was a forerunner of the early Whitman. But he loved too his native Russia. He wrote, "What pleasure for a Russian, what food for his complacency, what glory for his government, when, traveling through the vast lands of America and seeing inhabitants hailing from all the well-ordered countries of Europe, priding themselves on their liberty and wealth, he does not come upon a single Russian who has fled here, as did all the others, from the injustice of his country's laws, from religious persecution, or to find freedom for his industry!" On his return to Europe, he was asked by a British publisher to write his American experiences. "The thought that I would have to write contrary to my inclination and ideas, not as I felt, but as the policy of England demanded, or to gratify my publishers, who would use me as a tool to gratify their hatred of the United States, forced me to reject these advantageous offers."

The other aide, Alexis Evstafiev, a Cossack by birth, was the first Russian businessman of importance to visit Boston. He wrote a number of plays, several of which were produced in Boston, and became so Americanized that he wrote his official despatches to St. Petersburg in English. Boston newspapers printed his dramatic and literary criticisms. Before Napoleon invaded Russia, he published a booklet, *The Resources of Russia in Event of War with France.* In 1813, he translated Colonel Tchuykevitch's *Reflections on the War of 1812.* In 1814, he published a biography of Peter the Great.

But while Svinin and Evstafiev were engaged in cultural activities, another Russian diplomat, Kozlov, Consul-General, accidentally caused a great amount of harm to Russian-American relations. Kozlov, if not a brilliant man, was the pleasant, gay sort who should have filled his function nicely, without denting the pages of history. But among the servants in Kozlov's Philadelphia residence was a maid with large eyes and pink cheeks, whose silhouette looked far more mature than her twelve years. Kozlov found his gaze constantly settling on her. Finally, one cold November evening he decided, with his sense of European privilege, to visit her room. Unaccustomed to being refused by a woman of the lower classes, or mistaking her refusal for coquettery, or perhaps in that state of emotion where vanity made him willing to satisfy his desires by force, he got into bed with her. As soon as he left her room, the girl ran to the nearest police-station and swore out a warrant for his arrest. The police acted promptly and Kozlov spent the remainder of the night in jail.

Andrei Dashkov, the Russian Minister, entered the police-station in a towering rage. He would not tolerate the imprisonment of a Russian diplomatic representative. The police sergeant, who was not keen on foreigners, was in no mood to be told his duties. When Dashkov offered to pay to obtain the Consul-General's release, the police sergeant told him rape was not a bailable offence; it did not matter how much money Kozlov was willing to offer, the prisoner would remain in jail until he had appeared before a judge.

"Then in heaven's name bring him before a judge at once!" said Dashkov.

The police sergeant knew of no judge who could be awakened during the middle of the night, at least not without immediately pronouncing the prisoner guilty.

"But you can't arrest a Consul-General," shouted Dashkov. "He has diplomatic immunity."

"Never heard of it," replied the sergeant. "He's raped a girl and he stays in jail until a judge lets him out. And if you keep pestering me, you'll find yourself sitting in there beside him."

When morning came Dashkov went straight to the United States Attorney. He demanded that Kozlov be freed and interference with the affairs of the Russian Legation be stopped. The District Attorney, once he managed to get the facts straight, informed Dashkov that the State of Pennsylvania had made the arrest and the affair was in the hands of the State courts. He explained in detail States Rights and limited jurisdictions. He would do what he could, but only in an unofficial capacity. Dashkov, on his advice, obtained a writ of habeas corpus, Kozlov was brought immediately before a judge, and the case was remanded to the next Court session. Kozlov was sent home to brood over this strange country and its strange laws in which he had entangled himself.

Dashkov, however, hurried to Washington and called on President Monroe. Monroe was courteous, anxious to be helpful, but when he understood the trouble he looked worried, and informed Dashkov that it was outside Federal jurisdiction. The State Court could not be overruled except on a question of constitutional guarantees. Dashkov was astounded. Here was the President telling him that a representative of the Czar had been locked up in a filthy jail and that he could do nothing about it. A provincial court was taking precedence over a national government! Monroe's promise that Kozlov would be guaranteed "all the rights belonging to his character as a Consul-General" did not appease him. He wrote an urgent message to the Czar. His somewhat hysterical report was a long time in reaching St. Petersburg, and the official explanation from Washington took even longer. The Russian Foreign Office never did arrive at a full understanding of the situation.

President Monroe, who knew that politics could take the place of the law, that the case could be dismissed on a technicality, did not worry much over the affair. When trial was held the following spring, 1816, the defense asked that the charge be dismissed, first, because international law granted Consuls immunity from criminal prosecution, second, because any case involving a Consul must appear before Federal courts. The Court admitted the second count and dismissed the case. There the matter rested. The State court could not continue the case for want of competence and Federal courts could not take it up for the same reason. President Monroe felt everything had been happily concluded.

Dashkov, however, felt that the whole matter had been badly mismanaged. Kozlov was still guilty in the eyes of the law, and the American government owed an apology to Russia for a serious breach of international law. He demanded that a Federal court try the case and give Kozlov a chance to clear himself. He was informed that the only way the defendant could clear himself would be to sue the girl for defamation of character, and, if successful, he would be automatically exonerated.

"That's not the point," said Dashkov. "The point is that you would not arrest a Senator on such a charge."

"No. Provided Congress was in session."

"And you can't arrest me on such a charge," said Dashkov.

"No. A Minister cannot be arrested unless his own Foreign Office permits it."

"Then how the devil can you arrest a Consul, who also has diplomatic immunity?"

That, Dashkov was informed, was the trouble. According to the American concept of international law, Consuls did not have immunity; they were neither the personification of their Sovereign, as was an Ambassador, nor of their Foreign Minister, as was the head of a Legation.

The Russian government began to take steps which could have made a *casus belli* of the case. Adams having left St. Petersburg to negotiate peace with the British, Levett Harris had been left behind, and Count Nesselrode icily informed Harris that the affair was strangely reminiscent of the *lettres de cachet* of Bourbon France, and that until an apology was made by Washington he must ask Mr. Harris to refrain from appearing at Court. Meanwhile, Dashkov wrote an offensive letter to the Secretary of State, accusing the President of backing an impertinent official. The State Department at Washington and the Chancellery in St. Petersburg were in a furor, charges and countercharges, notes and explanations shuttling back and forth across the Atlantic. William Pinkney, who was to succeed Adams as Minister, was on the point of entering Russia when he found the two countries on the verge of a rupture in diplomatic relations. He decided to remain where he was until it was settled.

Matters were also complicated by the fact that there was a joint Foreign Ministership; Nesselrode was one, Capo d'Istria, the other. Levett Harris, abandoning hope of settling matters with Nesselrode, appealed to Capo d'Istria, a Greek and an old enemy of Napoleon. Capo d'Istria admitted that Dashkov had handled the affair stupidly, but that, for all that, the dignity of the Nation was involved. He said that an explanation by the President of the United States was the only solution. Monroe wrote this letter, but Dashkov refused to send it to Nesselrode, broke off diplomatic relations, and started packing his bags. A year had passed since Kozlov had visited the bedroom of a maidservant and no one remembered what all the shouting was about or how things had become so snarled. One diplomat was banned, another insulted the President and demanded his passports, and the Foreign Offices of both nations were in turmoil. Monroe decided it was time for the nonsense to end. He sent a letter of explanation to St. Petersburg aboard a Sloop-of-War, and after a few more negotiations Nesselrode accepted the explanation on behalf of the Emperor and Harris was restored to his place in Court. Only Dashkov was dissatisfied and would not resume his official position for nearly a year.

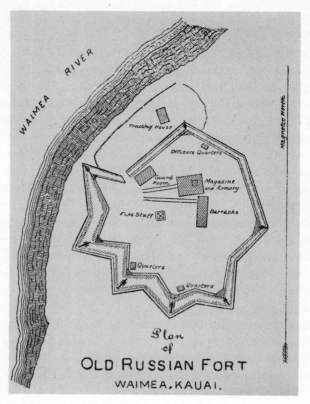

Plan
of
OLD RUSSIAN FORT
WAIMEA, KAUAI.

CHAPTER FIVE

Russian hawaii

"Father told me of Mr. John Jacob Astor's generous offer to take him into partnership in a business whose profits were $100,000 a year," wrote James Gallatin. "His reasons for refusing were, although he respected Mr. Astor, he could never place himself on the same level with him. I am not surprised, as Astor was a butcher's son, and came to this country with a pack on his back. He peddled furs, was very clever, and is, I believe, one of the kings of the fur trade. He dined here and ate his peas and ice-cream with a knife." In another entry: "Mr. Astor is dreadful. He came to *déjeuner* today; we were simply *en famille,* he sitting next to Frances. He actually wiped his fingers on her white spencer. Mama, in discreet tones, said, 'Oh, Mr. Astor, I must apologize, they have forgotten to give you a serviette!'"

If John Jacob Astor was uncouth, he was also shrewd. He learned the efficacy of lobbying and managed to achieve powerful connections in Washington. The great Astor fortune, like the Stroganov in Russia, was founded on the fur trade, and only later did real estate play an important part in it. Astor entered the China trade about 1800 as an adjunct to his fur business. By 1805 he had begun to build his own ships. He planned to hold not only a monopoly on furs but also on the Northwest-China-New York triangular commerce. With the organization of Astor's fur company there were four in the field, the Russian-American, the Canadian Northwest, and the Michilimackinac. With the Canadian company Astor made an agreement to divide the whole northwest coast, so that he would have everything south of the Columbia River. It was a clever arrangement. Astor had no rivals in his section except the Northwest Company, while the Canadians had the other two to contend with. Astor planned to build a two million dollar factory on the Columbia, into which he, aware of the hazards, did not intend to invest more than fifty thousand.

In December, 1807, Jefferson, because of unsettled international affairs, sent a message to Congress urging that all foreign-bound ships be detained in ports of the United States. This resulted in the Embargo of 1808. All American commerce abroad was halted. One ship, owned by Astor, managed to slip out of port and cross the Pacific to Canton. The embargo, however, threatened to delay Astor's plans, and he searched desperately for ways to circumvent it. Finding a Chinaman in New York, Astor invented a tale of his being a powerful mandarin unable to return to his homeland, obtained an audience with the President, presented this story and hinted that to refuse the Chinese dignitary might cause retaliation by the Chinese government. By pure coincidence Astor had a ship that could set sail in a few days, and he would be glad to place the ship at the disposal of the government. Jefferson, whose greatness was in extracting the maximum from generalities, was not as keen in understanding a man like Astor. Despite warnings from Gallatin that he should investigate the Chinaman, Jefferson allowed the ship to sail. It left so hurriedly that there was no time to remove its cargo, which, of course, were the American goods that would bring the highest profit in Canton. And since this cargo was the only one to reach China that year, Astor could command his own price. As Astor jokingly said, "Selflessness and patriotism bring their own rewards."

In March, 1809, the embargo was removed, except against Britain and France. Astor plunged into his many projects. He decided to make an agreement with Russian America, went to Dashkov and offered a promise not to trade with the natives in the vicinity of Sitka, if the Russians would make a similar pledge for the Columbia Valley. Astor also offered to supply sufficient food and goods to Sitka if the Russians agreed to trade only with his ships. Dashkov, not empowered to conclude such an agreement, urged Astor to send someone to Sitka to negotiate direct with Baranov, the new manager.

On the 16th of November, 1809, Captain John Ebbets, on the *Enterprise,* cleared New York for the northwest coast. He had written orders authorizing an agreement with Baranov. He arrived at the mouth of the Columbia in June and, after a week of exploration, pushed on toward Sitka. Sitka had become the liveliest and gayest city north of New Orleans and Charleston, booming with wealth and increased population, and with an air of permanence which it had never achieved in the earlier period. On the velvet and silk gowns of the women, diamonds were liberally sprinkled, and there were balls and parties with true Slavic frequency. Massive wooden towers had been built on the fortress and a high stockade protected the colony. Cannon were posted at holes cut at regular intervals in the walls.

Captain Ebbets found that Baranov's house was well furnished, with thick carpets covering the puncheon floor, fine pictures hanging along the walls, and a library of books in all the principal languages. Ebbets immediately encountered difficulties, Baranov having had no communication with his superiors for three years and therefore hesitant to sign any agreement. Baranov was not able to read the contract, since he knew no English and almost no French. Matters were at a standstill until the *Diana* arrived, and Ebbets turned over his papers to her captain, Golovin, who read the proposed agreement and the contract. Then Golovin came to some other papers that were mixed among them which contained confidential instructions to Ebbets, telling him to sell his cargo in California and to inform the Russians that he had supposed them well-supplied; but in case the cargo could not be sold in California, he was to explain the diligence and care with which the Astor company had selected the cargo for the Russians alone. Furthermore, Ebbets was to spy on the defences of Sitka and to find out how vulnerable to attack it would be.

The Russian officer, after translating this to Baranov, indignantly urged that Ebbets be forced to leave Sitka immediately. Baranov, however, merely laughed. He had understood Yankee business methods for a long time and this seemed merely an honest statement of them. "After all," Baranov said, "we should treat him well. He came here to get information and has given it to us instead." Baranov of course refused to sign the contract, but he did buy the cargo of the *Enterprise* and sent $65,000 worth of furs to China, paying Ebbets a five percent commission and $1800 carriage.

"You see," Baranov explained to the Russian officer, "we have his cargo, we have sold furs to a market unavailable to us, he has made his pocket money, and, for the time being, his ship might as well be flying the Russian flag. If you can't beat 'em, j'ine 'em."

Meanwhile, Astor had begun his expedition to the Columbia River. His settlers were moving overland by the Oregon Trail, while ships loaded with supplies were being sent around the Horn. On June 4th, 1809, the Winships of Massachusetts attempted to make a settlement near the site Astor had chosen, but were driven away by Indians. The supply ship *Tonquin* of the Astor expedition was boarded by Indians at the mouth of the Columbia and most of her crew massacred. Despite these difficulties, Astoria was founded in 1811. But when the War of 1812 broke out, Astor could not maintain communication with the outpost, though he resorted to the device of sailing his ships under false colors. Astoria was seized by the British and it was not until 1817 that an American warship reoccupied the settlement.

The Russians met with more success. In 1808, Baranov sent two ships to explore Bodega Bay, the site Rezanov had selected. The *St. Nicholas* was wrecked, but the *Kadiak* reached Bodega Bay, renamed it Port Rumiantzev, and returned to Sitka with 1400 pelts. It was not, however, until 1812 that the St. Petersburg directors gave permission to make the new settlement. A second exploration trip convinced Baranov that Port Rumiantzev was not the best site because of a lack of forests, and he chose another point a few miles to the northwest. Kuskov, with 95 Russians, landed there in March, 1812, and by September enough buildings had been constructed to house them for the winter. The settlement was named Ross—a shortened, poetic word for Russia. A priest of the Holy Orthodox Church presided over the christening. In 1814, a fort was built, a high stockade of redwood planted deep into the earth to prevent the Indians from tunneling an entrance, and protected by bastions that commanded a view of the entire valley. This same year the Russians complained of swarms of grasshoppers. Since the chief function of Ross was to supply food for Sitka, gardens were planted and land cleared for cultivation. The Spaniards, though displeased with this descent from the north, soon began a little clandestine trading.

With Fort Ross established, Baranov turned his eyes toward Hawaii. Rezanov had made him aware of the political, strategic, and economic possibilities of these islands. He bought two Yankee ships, the *Atahualpa* and the *Lady,* and hired all those of their crews who would sail under the Russian flag. Some historians believe he intended to annex the entire archipelago. But, whatever his ultimate plans, immediate annexation, or even close commercial relations were not among the orders he gave to Captain Bennet.

The *Lady* never did reach her destination; she ventured too near the Spaniards along the California coast and lost most of her crew. Bennett, aboard the *Atahualpa,* carried out his mission, bought a cargo of provisions from Kamehameha, and turned his ship northward toward the rugged coast of Kauai. While crossing Kaieie Waho channel the ship sprang a leak and lay to for repairs. A January storm caught the ship before it could get underway and dashed it against the rocks. The island was inhabited by natives under the rule of King Tomaree, the only native sovereign who had been able to hold out against Kamehameha. The natives gleefully confiscated the remains of the cargo and the useful portions of the ship. They did not however harm Bennett or his crew, and the captain eventually found his way back to Alaska.

Baranov was seriously annoyed by the loss of this ship. The

Kamehameha giving audience to the Russian Officers

Fort Ross venture was not turning out as well as he had anticipated. He decided to protest the ransacking of the *Atahualpa* and use the situation to obtain a favorable commercial treaty with the Hawaiian king.

Georg Anton Scheffer, a devious and talented man, a German adventurer who had been a physician for the Moscow police and who had constructed balloons for the Russian army, had decided, after an unsuccessful balloon flight of the *Areostat,* to escape Napoleon's army which was marching into Moscow. He had fled to the sea and to Russian America as a doctor aboard the *Suvorov*. Baranov decided to send Scheffer to Hawaii. Scheffer sailed in October, 1815, on the *Isabella* and had an uneventful voyage.

He received a warm welcome from King Kamehameha, who placed a staff of servants and a large plantation at his disposal. Scheffer, something of a botanist, spent the early portion of his visit raising a garden and studying various kinds of vegetation. Leisurely he gathered impressions of the political organization of the islands and of the relationship between Kamehameha and Tomaree, who was supposed to be a vassal king, but who seemed to have more independence than the Hawaiian ruler wanted known.

One afternoon, when Scheffer decided it was time to bring up his real purpose, he asked Kamehameha whether he intended to make restitution for the ship that had been pillaged. The king was seated at the opposite side of the room, a naked soldier, who followed the monarch wherever he went, standing beside him, holding a small black box that might have been a snuff-box. It was, however, a spitting box, in which the royal saliva was preserved. Kamehameha protested that he knew nothing about the Russian ship, but promised to replace the lost cargo. But the king, despite questioning, refused to reveal information about Tomaree.

Scheffer remained on the island long enough to change his occupation from botanist to militarist. He erected a fort and raised the Russian flag above Oahu. As a result, the friendship between Scheffer and the king waned. Scheffer next went to the island of Kauai, which could have been dangerous, since the natives on some of the northern islands were cannibalistic. But his medical training worked to his advantage, for he found Tomaree suffering from dropsy and his wife deathly ill of fever. Tomaree would not let Scheffer touch him, but did agree to let the white man try his magic on the Queen. He could always get a new queen. When she made a swift recovery, Tomaree decided he would risk being a patient, and though he was not completely cured, he was so delighted to feel better that he insisted on making Scheffer Physician-to-the-Crown.

From Tomaree, Scheffer learned the truth of the political situation in the Hawaiian Islands. Tomaree's father had once ruled over five islands. Kamehameha had originally ruled only a small part of northern Oahu. All of southern Oahu, including Honolulu, had been divided among local rulers, whom Kamehameha, with the aid of foreigners, had overthrown. Kamehameha had killed Tomaree's father and Tomaree was sworn to revenge. He explained that he had looted the Russian ship in the hope that Kamehameha would be blamed and perhaps punished by the Russians. Tomaree insisted that Kauai did not belong to the English, that Captain Cook had never been on the island. (It was at Waimea, on Kauai, that Cook first set foot on Hawaiian soil, January 20,

1778.) Scheffer sensed that he had at his fingertips an opportunity to become the Viceroy of an island empire. He offered Tomaree military assistance in retaking the islands of his patrimony in return for becoming a part of the Russian Empire. He drew up a formal agreement of allegiance to the Russian Emperor, on which Tomaree made his mark. This document was dispatched to St. Petersburg on the *Discovery,* a Russian ship then in Hawaii. In his report Scheffer wrote, "The king promptly asked for the Russian flag, which he hoisted over his house. He also asked for the uniform of a Naval officer, which he put on . . ."

Scheffer obtained permission to build a fort overlooking Waimea Bay. The fort consisted of twenty-four walls, each thirty feet thick at their widest point. Nearly three acres were enclosed, with a large magazine, and barracks for soldiers. It was nearly impregnable, so strong indeed that Tomaree's son held it successfully with a handful of men against the entire military force on the island. Three smaller forts were constructed. Tomaree expressed his doubts about building forts on Kauai when the battles were to be fought on Oahu, but Scheffer assured him that it was the invariable practice of European rulers before commencing a military expedition. However, to prove to Tomaree that his alliance with Russia would soon make him a powerful ruler, one of the Russian ships, with a number of Kauai warriors aboard, made a harmless bombardment of Kailua.

Meanwhile, two Russian ships, the *Myrtle* and *Ilmen,* anchored off Honolulu, and their armed crews, bearing the Russian flag, went ashore and erected a block house, and brought cannon to the beach in small boats. Shortly before, one of these two ships had delivered new orders from Sitka urging Scheffer to obtain further concessions from Tomaree and land on which to build a factory. At this time Scheffer sent to Baranov a complete report of everything he had accomplished. He stated bluntly that with a little military assistance he could put the Hawaiian Islands into the Russian Empire.

But since Baranov had sent the *Myrtle* and *Ilmen,* pressure had been brought on him by the Yankee brothers, Winship, who had no intention of abdicating their trading posts at Honolulu. From the Russian Foreign Office came warnings. When Baranov received a request from King Tomaree for 200,000 rubles, as a token of gratitude for his submission, he ordered Scheffer to stall the king until the treaty had been ratified by the St. Petersburg directors. He hinted that it probably would not be ratified, since Hawaii was technically under British protection. The annexation must wait until a favorable international situation developed.

Scheffer ignored these instructions, knowing that if he waited the whole project might as well be abandoned. The *Ilmen* had a cargo of lumber and furs, and he ordered the lumber to be put ashore to build homes for the colonists whom he hoped Russia would send. Farm sites had already been laid out in the Hanalei Valley.

Oahu had been alarmed by the bombardment of Kailua and the presence of Russian cannon and the fort. The Americans, annoyed by the Russian penetration, warned Kamehameha that a Russian fleet might soon try to take possession of his domain. There was a wholesale desertion of the Americans who had been serving aboard Russian ships, which paralyzed Russian activity and communications. Another group of Americans, at the suggestion of John Young, a renegade Englishman, destroyed the small Russian factory on Oahu. Natives then seized all Russian property on the island. The dissatisfaction spread to Kauai. Tomaree began to doubt whether the Russians would help him regain his island empire. The natives had begun to dislike Scheffer, and a plot to dispose of him by boring holes in the small boat he used to sail the Kauai coast almost succeeded.

Scheffer decided to go to St. Petersburg and urge immediate action. Though aware that the long journey might give the Americans time to consolidate their position in the islands, he could think of no other remedy. Baranov had left him in the lurch at the crucial moment. With the arrival at Waimea of a Russian ship, he sold its cargo of furs and grain, pocketed the money, and went off on an American ship commanded by an old friend, Captain Luns. During the voyage he became acquainted with a Swede, Ljungstedt, and while drinking rum punch told the Swede of the island empire that had almost been his. Eventually Scheffer arrived in Canton, and from there made his way across Siberia, arriving in St. Petersburg early in 1819.

The directors of the Russian-American Company were impressed by the glowing account of his activities. But they were inclined to discredit his forecast of the ease with which the islands could be seized. Seizure, aside from diplomatic problems with England, would be dangerous because of the extreme distance between Hawaii and Russian bases. Scheffer insisted that the safety of Alaska and Fort Ross depended on these islands. The directors, sympathetic as they were to the idea of making money, hesitated to urge the Emperor to pursue a course of which they were themselves in doubt.

Scheffer wrote to the Emperor. "The Sandwich Islands are the keys to China, Japan, the Philippines, India and the Northwest Coast of North America. By holding Honolulu, Russia can, with the posts she already holds at Petropavlovsk, Sitka and Fort Ross, control the entire Pacific."

The Czar replied that the lands ceded to the Russian-American Company by Tomaree might be retained, but all other lands, treaties and documents must be returned and the request for Russian protection refused. He sent presents to King Tomaree, among them a handsome cutlass set with jewels, and a fur mantle. He also bestowed on Tomaree the Medal of St. Anne, a decoration usually reserved for servants, porters and lowly government clerks. Sent aboard the gunboat *Kamchatka,* they never reached their destination, for they turned up, in 1844, in the archives of the Ministry of Commerce and Industry.

Scheffer disappeared. Years later he became an agent of Don Pedro I, Emperor of Brazil. Bearing the title of Count von Frankenthal, which he had purchased from the Emperor for $10,000, he recruited soldiers for His Majesty's Imperial Life Guards. The Emperor of Brazil, who sold titles to everyone he could, used this source of income to build a lunatic asylum in Rio de Janeiro. Its façade bears the slogan—"From the vain to the foolish."

After the departure of Scheffer, King Tomaree and his court moved into the massive fort which the Russians had built. Tomaree, feeling the necessity of some sort of emblem and having none, kept the Russian flag flying over his island. It was all that remained of the man who had nearly founded an empire.

Enroute to Sitka and exploration of the Arctic circle, Captain Otto von Kotzebue stopped at Oahu to replenish his water casks and take on food. King Kamehameha, who made foreigners welcome despite his unpleasant experiences with some of them, invited the captain to a roast pig dinner. The captain's escort was mahogany-skinned John Adams, who, by the Hawaiian custom, had exchanged names with an American visitor. The palace was a one-room bamboo and palmleaf house—the most modest royal dwelling the Captain had ever seen. Kamehameha, a striking figure in a white shirt, black neckband, scarlet waistcoat and sky-colored pantaloons, explained that his policy as a ruler was to let his subjects be happy rather than make them feel the importance of government.

Nobles to whom the captain was introduced wore whatever they had of elegant clothes and when they lacked an essential article of dress simply ignored it. Frock coats made the nakedness of the remainder of their bodies a bit startling, but their dignity, the way the coats were properly buttoned, preserved them from indecency. The guards were naked, except around their waists where a narrow belt was used to hold two pistols; they carried muskets without powder horns.

During dinner the King related the villainy of Georg Anton Scheffer, and the Captain made the apologies which he felt obliged to make for a fellow-countryman. He made assurances that the Russian Emperor was a peace-loving man who would never consider taking land that was not his. Kamehameha urged the Captain to partake of more roast pig, apologizing for eating taro-paste. It was a Hawaiian fast day.

In the afternoon the Captain was taken on a tour of the island. He noticed that everywhere people were smoking. Noblemen wore pipes strung about their waists—the higher their political status the larger and more numerous their pipes. Women kept their pipes going full blast. Babies too young to walk were old enough to puff on pipes as big as their heads. Borrowing one, he noticed that its bowl was lined with copper, and he nearly choked on it. He was not surprised to learn that people sometimes fell unconscious from its effects.

Aside from smoking, the chief occupations of the women

seemed to be eating, combing their hair and swatting flies. Yet they were healthy-looking, with beautiful skin. When one of the King's wives sliced a watermelon, he noticed that her hands and wrists were strong and agile. The men seemed to occupy themselves as little as the women and in the same manner except that they did not bother to comb their hair. The men were more degenerate in appearance. They had acquired one other habit, a taste for liquor in varying degrees of excess; but, in contrast with Europeans, alcohol seemed to make them even more peaceful and contented, a bit vague, and dreamy.

Passing an artificial coral lagoon where an enormous shark swam idly, it was explained to the Captain that men were sometimes tossed in, but children were regarded as finer sacrifices and more of the islanders would come to watch the ceremony that made the bigger magic. The shark was their great God. Thus, the pond was never used to punish thieves or murderers, since there was too much honor in sacrificial death for it to be granted to the undeserving. The King did not bother to punish crimes, unless they became annoyingly frequent. The Captain was not able to find out how the shark had been captured and transported from the sea, for some told him that nets had been used to drive it into the shallow beach water, and others insisted that it had been there for centuries.

The Captain was led into a dark hut, where, surrounded by naked guards, Prince Liholiho, *dog-of-all-dogs,* so fat and unwieldy that he spent most of his life lying on the ground in a kind of religious retirement, roused himself long enough to glance at his visitor. Liholiho was sulking. He had purchased a yacht from two Americans for sandalwood worth somewhere between twenty and eighty thousand dollars and had renamed it *Cleopatra's Barge,* only to discover that the timbers along one side were rotten. For this reason Liholiho had decided not to converse with foreigners.

The last evening in Honolulu, the King and several local chieftains were invited aboard the *Rurik* for dinner. One chieftain sent his regrets at being unable to attend, explaining that his favorite wife was too drunk to be left alone. Another came wearing a tall silk hat, which he was unwilling to remove. During dinner the Captain became aware of a commotion on the opposite side of the ship, and was about to investigate when the King leaped to his feet and ran to the railing. Two women were swimming naked in the water alongside the ship, attempting to converse with a group of sailors. The sailors could not understand them, but were shouting in Russian and trying to coax them to come aboard. The King leaned over the rail and chatted with the Queen of Hawaii and one of her *Dames d'Honneur* for a few minutes and then waved to them as they, with the grace of women who seemed to have been born without fear of water, swam slowly away. The King turned to the Captain, shrugged, and said, "The curiosity of women!"

The following morning Captain Kotzebue presented the King with two mortars and a barrel of wine. During the presentation the King espied an apple and asked if he might taste it. He liked its flavor so much that, on departure, a bag of them was given to him, with instructions to preserve the cores for planting.

The next Russian to visit Hawaii was an Irishman by birth, Peter Dobell, a professional soldier who had served in Ireland, England, France, China and the American Revolution. While in China, he had performed some trifling service for the Russians. The Emperor had given him a ring. Dobell apparently felt that this ring made him a personal favorite of the Czar. In 1812, he sold two profitable shiploads of food in Kamchatka and, seeing the incredible richness of the land, formed a plan to exploit its minerals and furs. With his Gaelic imagination, he dreamed up a scheme worthy of the greatest empire builders. The Pacific Ocean, he was convinced, could be made into a Russian lake. Russia could extend its empire from Mexico to the Arctic.

In the summer of 1813, he set out, accompanied by two Chinese servants, for St. Petersburg. He arrived at Christmas time, and Russia was still in turmoil. Napoleon had been defeated at Leipzig, but the war was raging and Alexander I was away with his armies. Dobell trailed after him across Europe for several months. Then, failing to catch up with him, Dobell returned to St. Petersburg and applied for Russian citizenship and a commission in the army, citing the Whiskey Rebellion as proof of his military ability. He presented the Russian Foreign Office with a long memorandum, urging them to transport Roman Catholic refugees from Ireland to the Kamchatka, because they were a hard working people who would settle permanently in any land of opportunity. Once Russia was firmly entrenched in the Kamchatka, commerce with China must be cultivated and Japan must be forced to open her doors. The next logical step was to establish strong naval bases in the Philippines and Hawaii, which would close the gates of Asia to England and the United States, and make California vulnerable to Russian expansion. Dobell believed that, since the Hawaiians were incomparable sailors, with Russian technical aid Honolulu could become a Russian Gibraltar. Because the Philippines would be the most difficult area to penetrate, Dobell suggested that he be named Consul-General at Manila.

Though the Russian Foreign Office objected to sections of the plan, they were impressed, and in March, 1817, they appointed Dobell Consul-General and ordered him to proceed to Manila on receipt of instructions. Dobell did not wait. He struck out across Siberia with all possible speed and was halfway across when a courier caught up with him and gave him the news that his appointment had been cancelled because Spain did not look with favor upon his presence in Manila. Dobell decided to go ahead anyway. Exhausted by the time he reached Kamchatka, he was delayed more than a year by ill health. Then, apparently unable to get passage to the Philippines, he boarded a ship enroute to Hawaii.

By one of those accidents which occur in all human lives, but which seem to bear fruit only in men with a sense of destiny, he met Ljungstedt, the Swede to whom Scheffer had revealed his plans for the conquest of the Hawaiian Islands. After hearing Scheffer's story, Dobell decided to go to Kauai Island. He spent two months there, finding King Tomaree still anxious to regain his northern island empire.

Kamehameha was dead; and Liholiho, his fat, unworthy son, ruled over Oahu. Dobell, realizing that the Hawaiian Islands could easily be captured, followed in Scheffer's footsteps by striking a bargain with Tomaree. He promised King Tomaree that if he were allowed to plant the Russian flag on Kauai, and if Tomaree's warriors were able to capture the island of Oahu, Russian troops and ships would come to aid him and make him ruler of the entire archipelago.

Tomaree, victim for a second time of Russian ventures and of his own vanity, gathered his small army and attacked Oahu. King Liholiho, frightened, took the advice of a French beachcomber, Jean Rivas, and composed a letter to Czar Alexander I. His pathetic request in French for mercy, in which he offered the Russian Emperor a fine canoe in return for his personal liberty, contained at least forty-four grammatical errors, some sort of record for royal communications.

Dobell, knowing he must act quickly, went on to Macao, enroute to the Philippines. From Macao he sent Chancellor Nesselrode the details of his plan. The four largest islands, Oahu, Kauai, Maui and Hawaii were to be taken immediately, before foreign powers could interfere. To accomplish this he needed five thousand men and eight warships. With a firm hold on these islands, the rest of the archipelago would gradually fall under Russian domination. "Nature," he concluded, "has lavished her bounties on these islands for no other reason than to invite us to make our home on them."

Nesselrode, who had never had much interest in Asia or the Pacific, never bothered to reply. Dobell wrote again and again. Finally he returned to St. Petersburg, his health destroyed, his fortune dissipated, and his enthusiasm for trans-Pacific expansion gone. The next communication from the Hawaiian Islands was in the 1840's, a letter from a Robert C. Wyllie to Czar Nicholas I, advertising some choice Honolulu real estate. Hawaii never did get a Russian Consul. One was appointed in 1853, but he never went, feeling that the islands were too distant and unimportant.

One might be tempted to imagine that the Americans understood the value and importance of Hawaii, and that the present domination of the Pacific by the United States was planned and foreseen. Actually, the Russians had more foresight into the strategic value of Hawaii, the Philippines, Alaska and California than the Americans had almost a century later.

The American Government had little interest in the Hawaiian Islands. Not until 1893, when a revolution overthrew Queen Liliuokalani and forced the American marines to establish a Provisional Government, did President Harrison send a treaty of annexation to Congress. The incoming President, Grover Cleveland, withdrew the treaty, ordered the marines out of Hawaii and the American flag lowered from the Government building in Honolulu.

Five years later, in 1898, the Hawaiian Islands were annexed. But not because of American interest in them, for, with the exception of a few sugar-cane speculators who saw commercial possibilities, no one saw any value in them. President Cleveland, by being so high-handed in his withdrawal of the marines, caused Congress and the American people to react against him. History, like a game of dice, seems to make certain nations fortunate in their blindest hours. It is indeed worthy of some thought that three of the world's greatest empires, Russia, China, and the United States, rose to power not primarily by aggression, but by resisting other nations' attempts to dominate their respective domains.

In 1896, the Grand Duke Alexis proposed a "fantastic scheme" to acquire Hawaii as a naval base. He wanted to send warships and colonists. Baron Rosen, the Russian diplomat to whom the scheme was proposed, treated it with the ridicule which he thought it deserved. This was the last Russian dream about the Pacific Ocean, which had been the graveyard of so many Russian dreams.

Fort Ross was situated on the California coast, about seventy miles north of San Francisco. Twelve cannon, said to have been among those fired on Napoleon, were mounted in the log bastions. The house of Ivan Kuskov had a piano, carpets, and windows of real glass. At the opposite side of the stockade was a chapel with the Slavonic cross above its doors. In 1820 an orchard of pears, cherries and Bellflower and Gravenstein apples was planted. The trees were solemnly blessed, each sapling sprinkled with holy water, and 115 years later some of the trees were still bearing fruit. Rye and buckwheat were first grown in California at Fort Ross. Barley, maize, wheat, flax, beets, potatoes, cabbage, radishes, turnips, beans, peas, garlic, hemp, pumpkins, watermelons and tobacco were also raised.

The Spaniards watched the Russians with suspicion. In 1814

an officer of the Viceroy delivered a message to Fort Ross requesting the Russians to leave Spanish soil. The following year Kuskov sailed to San Francisco and brazenly traded with the Spanish friars. The Spanish military again merely requested that he leave, so he returned to San Francisco with a larger cargo of merchandise. From time to time Spanish officials called at Fort Ross, and Kuskov discussed with them abandoning the settlement as if he were actually contemplating it. He understood that the Spaniards were satisfied merely to talk about the situation, as if it relieved them from the need for military action. Soon Kuskov was selling large quantities of iron in San Francisco, for the Spanish had no foundries or metal-working plants. The iron foundry at Ross produced more than the Russians needed, and the plows imported from Finland and Russia were superior to those the Spanish had been using. Russian bells were even ringing from the towers of the Spanish missions—some of them ring still.

Despite all this, Fort Ross was not living up to expectations. The Russians were not efficient farmers, and the small shipyard, which they had built, failed. The use of unseasoned wood made their ships unseaworthy. The Fort's population did not increase, and the area of land under cultivation was not enlarged even though Alaska was on the brink of starvation.

In 1821 the Charter of the Russian-American Company expired. In the negotiations surrounding its renewal the directors of the company protested vigorously the encroachment of foreigners on territories which had been granted to them by Paul I. Czar Alexander issued a *ukase* claiming for Russia the northwest coast as far south as 51° north latitude and prohibited all foreign ships from approaching these shores closer than one hundred miles. To enforce this decree a Russian squadron was sent to America. It was a great moment for the Russian-American Company. The Russian government had at last committed itself to supporting them. A new empire seemed in the making.

But on December 2, 1823, the United States issued the Monroe Doctrine, and American pressure became suddenly so strong that in April, 1824, the first treaty ever to be concluded between the United States and Russia was signed, placing the boundary at 54°40′ North—a designation later used in the famous American slogan, "Fifty-four-forty or fight!"

Mordvinov, the director of the Russian-American Company, protested this violation of his company's rights. He wrote, "Since the beginning of our colonization we have assumed the right to annex all peoples inhabiting the whole continent up to the Rocky Mountains, that frontier established by nature herself."

The Russian Chancellor, Count Nesselrode, replied, "To spread onward to the Rocky Mountains we have no right." Russia had abandoned her policy of territorial expansion on the North American continent, though the significance of this treaty was not fully recognized by Americans at the time. Fort Ross, now actually on American soil, became instantly an isolated settlement, and the Russian dream of having California as a province vanished.

Russia had lost her final opportunity of becoming a power in the Pacific.

the decembrists

William Pinkney of Maryland, new Minister to Russia, arrived in St. Petersburg in January, 1817. His first audience with the Emperor was cordial and at the New Year's Ball (Russian calendar) he chatted with the Empress for twenty minutes, the first time anyone below the rank of Ambassador was so honored. But he had not been in St. Petersburg long when the American Consul, J. L. Harris, got into an argument with another American, Lewis, who pulled the Consul's nose and slapped his face. Harris demanded that Lewis be arrested, but the Russian police, unlike the Philadelphia police, did not want to meddle with foreigners. They turned the matter over to Chancellor Nesselrode, who, also wanting nothing to do with it, put it in the hands of Pinkney. Pinkney, realizing that the brawl involved the dignity of his government, preferred that it be handled unofficially by the police, where it would not attract undue attention. Pinkney did not believe in Consular immunity and did not wish to establish a precedent in its favor. His position was exactly opposite that which Dashkov had taken in the Kozlov affair. Though the Chancellor assured him that Czar Alexander I wished it resolved in this way, Pinkney refused, and the Emperor was forced to retreat from his position and give tacit sanction to the conduct to which the United States had held during the Kozlov affair. Nesselrode's original proposal was unwise, since it would have set a precedent for extra-territorial courts presided over by diplomats of foreign nations. Many years later a similar type of court was imposed on China by the great powers. The Harris-Lewis affair however was quietly disposed of without diplomatic problems, and shortly afterward Pinkney requested recall on grounds of ill-health. He had been well-liked in Russia and at the birth of his daughter, Dushka, the Empress herself acted as godmother.

Pinkney was succeeded by George W. Campbell, former Tennessee Senator and Secretary of the Treasury under Monroe. Campbell was faced with a vital task. Several Spanish colonies in South America had declared their independence, and the whole of Spanish America was in a state of actual or potential insurrection. Spain wanted her colonies back. England wanted South America independent, for Spanish trade restrictions prevented British commerce in those regions. Russia sided with Spain. Alexander I felt the Holy Alliance should be used to bring the Spanish colonies into line.

Before Pinkney left Russia he reported that some sort of mediation was contemplated by the Russian government and that Russia would not be in accord with the United States. In the spring of 1818, the Portuguese Minister informed John Quincy Adams, now United States Secretary of State, that the Holy Alliance would cast its lot against the South American colonies, and Russia would be given a stronghold on the American continent. This caused grave concern in the State Department, where negotiations for the purchase of Florida were pending. Adams therefore instructed Campbell that his foremost task was to obtain accurate information on Russia's attitude toward the Spanish colonies. Campbell was advised to abandon hope for any commercial treaty with Russia, since it would add another source of friction. More important was the need for a permanent agreement regarding the northwest coast.

A dispute with England had arisen over the Columbia River, which the British claimed by virtue of the voyages of Sir Francis Drake, Captains Cook and Vancouver, and the explorations of Mackenzie. The United States based its claim on Captain Gray, Lewis and Clark explorations, and the establishment of Astoria in the northwest by John Jacob Astor. A London convention in 1818 had provided for joint occupation, with neither country yielding its claim. Canning, British Minister in Washington, and United States Secretary of State Adams had violent arguments, one of which was reported as follows:

ADAMS: Are you seriously claiming the mouth of the Columbia?
CANNING: Don't you even know we have a claim?
ADAMS: I don't know what you claim or don't claim! You claim India; you claim Africa, you claim . . .
CANNING: Perhaps a piece of the moon.
ADAMS: No, thank God, I haven't heard that yet; but there is not a spot on our habitable globe that I could affirm you do not claim . . . Keep what's yours, but leave the rest of this continent to us!

Adams, expecting serious trouble—perhaps even war—with England, wanted to reach an agreement with Russia concerning the northwest. He knew that, despite the Russian-American Company, Russia had no great interest in the North American continent. He wrote to Campbell that Russia's presence on the west coast could "never form a subject of serious differences or jarring interests." Yet he knew, too, that should England and the United States engage in a war, the Russian-American Company might take advantage of the situation.

During this period Russia was, to all intents and purposes, unrepresented in the United States. Dashkov still sulked in Philadelphia. Baron Tuyll, a Hollander in the Russian diplomatic service, contemptuous of republican government, had been appointed Minister to the United States but had refused the post. Finally, another Russian, Pierre Poletica, arrived in Washington with his credentials and asked for information regarding the pending

Spanish-American Treaty and the two Englishmen General Jackson had executed in Florida. Secretary Adams told him how matters stood with England and gave him a copy of the treaty. Under questioning, Adams stated that if Spain did not ratify the treaty before the next Session of Congress, the United States would occupy Florida. As to the Buenos Aires government, the United States would, for the moment, forbear recognition.

On June 17, 1819, Poletica made overtures to Adams in an attempt to obtain the adherence of the United States to the Holy Alliance. Emperor Alexander had, for a long time, contemplated such a move, but could not make official overtures until assurances of favorable reception were forthcoming. Poletica, realizing that American public opinion was against the Holy Alliance, assured Adams that its essential purpose was to preserve peace and had succeeded in doing so in several menacing European situations. Adams replied that it was a matter for the Senate to decide.

Although the Holy Alliance was maligned by those not in accord with it, it was far from being purely a force for repression. Nor was American opinion unanimous in condemnation of the Alliance. Fourteen organizations in the United States favored its adoption. These peace societies were represented in every New England State except Vermont, and in New York, Ohio, Indiana, and North Carolina. Noah Worcester, Pastor in the Congregational Church, at Thornton, New Hampshire, had been in direct correspondence with Emperor Alexander I.

Though John Quincy Adams wrote, concerning the Peace Society members, "If these gentlemen continue to correspond with Emperors and Kings they may find themselves corresponding with attorney-generals and juries," he did not dismiss the advantages of the Holy Alliance. A Russian invitation for the United States to join the Alliance was the most forceful recognition which could have been given by a European power to the young western republic. It would have lessened American fears of Great Britain and opened diplomatic doors in Europe which thus far had virtually remained closed. Yet for the United States to join was impossible, since it would have given tacit consent to European exploitation of North and South America. Furthermore,

opinion in Congress, led by Henry Clay, who urged immediate
recognition of the rebellious Spanish colonies, was decidedly hostile to the Holy Alliance. Clay had branded it as a sinister union
of autocracy and legitimacy to hold in subjection "eighteen million people now struggling to burst their chains."

In November, 1819, learning that England had made overtures to the United States regarding joint recognition of the Buenos
Aires Government, Poletica read to Adams a Russian reply to
questions troubling the United States.

1. Q. Had Russia any agreement with Spain?
   A. No. Special agreements were contrary to the Emperor's
      policy.

2. Q. What was Russia's attitude toward independence of the
      revolting colonies?
   A. Russia must chart her course by the requirements of
      the situation.

3. Q. In case of a Spanish-American war, would Russia remain
      neutral?
   A. War between the United States and a European nation
      could scarcely avoid becoming a general, disastrous war.

The reply to this last question was a blow to Adams. Though
it did not commit Russia to supporting Spain, it left little doubt
where Russia would stand. Fortunately the threat of immediate
war was removed by a treaty which concluded the short, bloody
Seminole War. Andrew Jackson, by the very arrogance of his campaign, raised the American flag at St. Mark and Pensacola and
stunned the Spanish. Adams, in the treaty of 1819, obtained from
Spain the cession of East and West Florida, along with "all the
rights, claims and pretensions of that power [Spain] lying north
of the 42nd parallel."

Minister Poletica, sensing that it would be impossible to draw
the United States into the Holy Alliance, bent his efforts toward
keeping America neutral. He cautioned Adams against precipitate action in Florida or any steps favoring the Buenos Aires
government. Tatischev, Russian Minister in Madrid, prodded the
Spanish government to come to an understanding with the United
States over Florida, so that negotiations in other colonies could

be conducted. In his message to Congress in March, 1820, President Monroe stated that both Russia and France were anxious for the controversy to be settled, and that, to this end, he recommended postponement of the Florida annexation until the next session.

Emperor Alexander, pleased by this, began to take a less stern attitude toward the revolting Spanish colonies. The arrival of a new Spanish minister in Washington removed some of the pressure from Poletica, and whatever hopes he might have had of persuading the United States to join the Holy Alliance were shattered when Secretary of State Adams, speaking for the Monroe Administration, declared, "The political system of the United States is essentially extra-European. To stand in firm and cautious independence from all entanglements in the European system has been a cardinal point . . . from the peace of 1783 to this day." He added that although the President was "thoroughly convinced of the benevolent and virtuous motives which led to the conception of the Holy Alliance . . . the United States will more effectively contribute to the great and sublime objects for which it was concluded by abstaining from a formal participation in it."

In June, 1822, the House of Representatives voted to establish a legation in the Republic of Colombia. Czar Alexander merely sent a note in which he stated that, with the political principles he held, he could not, under any circumstances, receive a representative from any revolutionary South American country. Poletica was removed from his post. Baron Tuyll replaced him. The Campbells, who had not been happy in Russia, having buried three of their children beneath the winter snows along the Neva, were replaced by Henry Middleton of South Carolina.

The importance of that period in Russian-American relations was that, for the first time, the focus of negotiations had centered around Washington. Russia had sent a man who, although he had failed in his objectives, had been an active diplomat. Russia had also for the first time recognized the United States as a world power.

Baron Tuyll arrived in Washington just as the situation on the west coast was reaching a climax. Alexander had issued his *ukase* claiming for Russia the northwest coast. The United States, though it had at the moment no territorial ambitions as far north as 51° latitude, was unwilling to abide by the terms of the *ukase*. Adams had already pointed out to Poletica that the Emperor had issued his declaration without first having agreed on the territorial provisions through a treaty with the United States, and that, furthermore, it denied the freedom of American ships to trade in a vast area of the Pacific. England, sensing an opportunity to get Russian support in regard to the Columbia River issue and perhaps a special trade agreement with Russian America, tried her utmost to get Russia and the United States on bad terms. England, however, dared not pursue this course too far, because she wanted American support in regard to South America.

The United States did not resort to diplomacy. President Monroe, in his message to Congress on December 2, 1823, said, "The occasion has been judged proper for asserting, as a principle in which the rights and interests of the United States are involved, that the American continents, by the free and independent condition which they have assumed and maintained, are henceforth not to be considered as subjects for future colonization by any European power." His government, he added, could not view the use of force in Spanish-America "in any other light than as a manifestation of unfriendliness toward the United States."

It has been said that the Monroe Doctrine was directed against Russia. This is a great overstatement. The Monroe Doctrine struck at all the nations of Europe who had territorial ambitions in the Americas—if it pinched the Russian boot, it tramped squarely on the feet of Spain and England. Even more important, it was a codification of the American spirit, for as the Declaration of Independence had been a political formalization of the Rights of Man, so the Monroe Doctrine expressed the rise to manhood of the American Republic.

Russia recognized the seriousness of the Doctrine. Middleton, in St. Petersburg, was quickly informed that "the Emperor had the good sense to see that his *ukase* should not be pushed too far and orders had been issued to the Russian fleet in the Pacific not to bring about any incident with American trading vessels." Pursuing this advantage, the United States, after innumerable discussions, amendments and counter-provisions, concluded a treaty with Russia in which navigation, fishing and trade rights were clearly defined and boundaries established.

The United States immediately turned its attention toward Central and South America. The backbone of Spanish domination was already broken, though Spain still held Cuba and Puerto Rico and from these islands dispatched feeble military expeditions against Colombia and Mexico. In 1825, when John Quincy Adams became President and Henry Clay Secretary of State, strife in the former Spanish colonies continued unabated. Clay wrote a long dispatch to Middleton. "I am requested by the President to instruct you to endeavor to engage the Russian government to contribute its best exertions toward terminating the existing contest between Spain and the Colonies. Russia is so situated that, whilst she will be less directly affected than other parts of Christendom, her might and her councils must have a controlling influence . . ."

Middleton presented this dispatch to Emperor Alexander, and received from Nesselrode a rather vague answer, the only clear portion of which was, "Spain would be pleased to hope that the United States, convinced of the evils and dangers that would result in Cuba and Puerto Rico from a change in government, will use their influence in defeating every enterprise against those islands."

American officials hailed this reply with joy because, for the first time, the question of legitimacy had not been mentioned. Copies of these messages were sent by Nesselrode to Peter Oubril, Russian Minister in Madrid, and a note appended stating that although Russia did not intend to exert pressure on Spain, the Emperor was willing to mediate. Spain, however, showed no willingness to mediate, and with the sad death of Alexander the matter was postponed.

It was a dark cold autumn morning, when, in his troika, the Emperor, Alexander I, decided to stop at the Alexander-Nevsky monastery. He ordered a Requiem Mass, prayed for a long time, and departed. At the last gates of St. Petersburg, he stopped his carriage, rose from his seat, and cast a melancholic look toward the city.

After a journey of nearly two weeks Alexander reached Taganrog on the shores of the Azov. He descended the River Don to the Cossack capital. In November he went into the Crimea, visited German colonists at Simferopol, stopped at Count Woronzov's beautiful palace, and finally reached Sevastopol, where he reviewed the fleet and inspected fortifications. Upon his return to Taganrog fever had begun its devastating work. Shortly thereafter he began to grow deaf. Finally erysipelas attacked him. He died on December 1, 1825. "Extreme stillness, when the news reached the north," Merezhkovsky wrote, "reigned in St. Petersburg. Everybody was silent and motionless, as if holding their breath. The theatres were closed, ladies put on mourning, requiem services were sung in the churches, and the melancholy sound of bells floated over the town . . ."

Certain legends assert that Alexander I did not die. One relates that from a local hospital the corpse of a soldier was procured to impersonate the Emperor, and that Alexander went to Siberia, where, as a hermit, he lived until his death in 1864. These legends seem to derive from the change that came about in his personal life, a tendency toward mysticism which made the last years of his political life contradictory and confused. They gained some credence when, in 1926, the Soviet Government opened his tomb and found it empty. But, regardless of speculation on this matter, which, to be seen in its proper light, must include the fact that he was aware of a plot to assassinate him, history records his death, at least in the political sense, as having occurred on December 1, 1825.

His influence on Russia and Europe had been tremendous. He had conquered Napoleon, freed Germany, saved France from a harsh treaty, granted liberal constitutions to Poland and Finland, and added Georgia and Armenia to his Empire. He had tried to arrive at a written constitution for Russia, but had never been able to set his pen or seal to it. "To explain," wrote Karpovich, "the failure of his constitutional projects on the basis of a supposed radical change in his views—a change that transformed him from a liberal to a reactionary—would be to simplify the problem." Unrest in Russia, revolutionary sparks throughout Europe, danger signals from the fate of the Spanish colonies, all these combined to make him still more cautious about reforms.

"Enough glory for Russia!" Alexander had exclaimed to a friend. "We will commit a great error if we think more glory is necessary. But when I consider how little has been done for Russia itself, a heavy load weighs on my heart."

The last blow to his liberal policies came in the fall of 1825, when a plot to depose him was made known to Alexander by John Sherwood, the son of an English mechanic. "Ah! The monsters!" Alexander exclaimed. "The ungrateful monsters! I intended nothing but their happiness. Why didn't I follow my original plan when they killed my father, and go with my wife to America, where at least we could find a happy refuge . . ."

As early as 1818, several societies in Moscow and St. Petersburg had conspired to overthrow the government and either assassinate or depose Alexander I. Among the Russian people a transformation had taken place. Russian officers and soldiers had not in vain seen Paris, where they had dwelt for two years as conquering heroes.

"From the time that Russian armies returned to their country," wrote Turgenev, "liberal ideas began to propagate themselves in Russia. Men of various ranks went back to their homes and related all they had seen in Europe."

Revolutionary talk did not become serious, however, until after the signing of the Russian-American Treaty in 1824. Mordvinov, director of the Russian-American Company, was infuriated by the "violation of the sacred rights of the company."

The leader of the revolutionary movement was Kondrati Ryleev, a young poet and writer, who, upon the death of his mother, had found his financial affairs in a muddle and had sought employment in the Russian-American Company. Ryleev, who handled the routine correspondence of the Russian America colony, had come to hate governmental control over the territorial ambitions of the colonists in Alaska and Siberia. Through correspondence he gathered a great number of adherents to his plan for freeing the Russian-American Company from the Russian government. Returning employees of the company met each other and aired their grievances in his office. The foremost of these was

Zavalishin, a Russian naval officer, who had a project which would have led to the penetration of Oregon and the annexation of California. Mordvinov, director of the Russian-American Company, had given his support to this project. But when Zavalishin had made his report to the Russian Government, he had received a stern reprimand, and Alexander I had written to Mordvinov, "Give a harsh rebuke to Ryleev for the Zavalishin report and remind him that merchants have no right to criticize diplomats. Stop him from writing those memorandums!"

In November of 1825, the Neva River flooded and caused great damage and loss of life in the St. Petersburg area. Even after the flood-waters receded, in portions of the city there was a wake of filth, disease, dissatisfaction and hunger. The voices of the poor people began to rumble, blaming the government for an act of God or an accident of nature. "All was not well at the headquarters of the Russian-American Company," wrote a contemporary. "In St. Petersburg, their main office, located at 72, Moika Quai, became the center for the dissatisfied elements of the empire."

When the news of Alexander's death reached St. Petersburg

Emperor Nicholas I

on December 9th, a crisis ensued because of a conflict of heirs. Alexander I and the Grand Dukes Constantine and Nicholas were brothers in the order of succession. Nicholas, the younger child of Paul I, had little taste for learning and was interested mainly in military matters. He was, because of being a strong one for protocol and a tough Army disciplinarian, unpopular. As a result, immediately after Alexander's death, the Russian Government both correctly and with a certain partiality, swore allegiance to Constantine. *Ukases* were signed with his name, coins were stamped with the silhouette of his head. But the Grand Duke Constantine was in Warsaw.

Days passed, and he did not arrive in St. Petersburg. There began to be an uneasiness among the people. There were rumors that Constantine had abdicated, rumors that Nicholas planned to seize control of the Government. In all fairness to Nicholas, this was untrue.

Meanwhile, the office of the Russian-American Company was being used by the Decembrist conspirators. "Here crowded meetings of the Decembrists listened to impassioned calls for the assassination of the entire Imperial family."

"During the past few days," wrote Merezhkovsky, "Ryleev had crowds of visitors from morning until night."

"I and Bestuzhev," wrote one of the conspirators, "dined often with Prokofiev. We found there Bulgarin, Gretch, Batenkov and many friends. Our host, Prokofiev, walks around the tables and pours wine in our glasses. By now, many more new visitors gather at the Russian-American Company. Kussov, mayor of St. Petersburg. Romanov, just returned from Fort Ross. Bestuzhev, who drew us a map of California. And Baron Steinhel, a friend of Ryleev."

This small group of highly educated men were divided between moderate and radical views. Some of them wanted to "liquidate" the entire Romanov Dynasty and destroy "the teachings of God." Others, especially Pestel and Ryleev, wanted strong centralized administration with no local autonomy. Pestel insisted that a despotic military regime would be required for at least eight years. He considered the Jews "exploiters of the peasants" and planned to transfer them to Palestine.

Another group supported Nikita Muraviev, who planned to limit the Emperor's powers to those of the President of the United States, and to divide Russia into independent, sovereign provinces united by a confederacy.

Despite the radical differences in their ideas and methods, these men had a unity of purpose—the downfall of the absolute authority of the Romanov Dynasty. Also, most of the conspirators were in favor of Russian expansion in the Pacific and on the North American continent, which would have caused Russian-American relations to follow a far different path than that which history has actually recorded.

Three weeks now had passed, and Constantine still did not return from Warsaw to claim his throne. Nicholas waited nervously in the palace, not wishing to take over control of the government without a public abdication on the part of the legitimate heir.

Constantine was in Warsaw as Commander-in-Chief of the Polish Army. He had divorced his first wife, a German Princess whom he had married in a miserable State-arranged affair. Later, in 1820, he had contracted a morganatic marriage with a Polish woman. He had come to feel himself more a Pole than a Russian. Long before the death of Alexander, fearing the trouble this marriage might cause in Russia, he had secretly abdicated his right to the throne. But for three weeks after the death of the Czar, he hesitated announcing such an irrevocable step; and it was this hesitation which allowed the Decembrists to complete their plans for revolution. On December 24th, his renunciation to the Accession reached Nicholas and put an end to the confusion.

Thus, paradoxically, the Decembrists were handed a ready-made torch to light the fuse. If Grand Duke Constantine had accepted the throne, the Russian Army would never have considered revolting. But with Nicholas assuming the role of Emperor, many units of the Army, especially those stationed in St. Petersburg, were willing to join the revolution.

On December 25th, the conspirators met for the last time.

Ryleev was dressed in dark brown, "with a fashionable waistcoat made of a Turkish shawl, and a tall white cravat. He was visibly excited, his eyes shone, and a feverish color in his cheeks made him look almost unwell."

The room was crowded, smoke-filled, noisy. During the next hour, in the midst of the tumult, as the conspirators began to draw a plan for action, certain words were heard with increasing frequency: *constitution, free press, equality, liberty, assassination.*

"Novgorod shall be Russia's new capital," someone shouted.

"Blood is justice!"

"The concrete and the abstract are one and the same!"

"The ultimate condition of all conditions is the unconditional!"

"For each murder and each death, a thousand new souls will feel the spirit of liberty!"

The meeting threatened to degenerate into a mere shouting of slogans.

Then Ryleev called the conspirators to silence. "These things come after we have been victorious," he said. "There will be time enough then to bring our views into accord. What we must do now is to go out into the streets and shout out against the oath of allegiance. We must shout to the regiments that Constantine has been forced to abdicate. We must lie for truth!"

There was tremendous applause. Ryleev, the poet, was spinning a web that would unify men who had no common bond except their discontent.

"When the regiments had mutinied, and the people are armed, we will lead them straight to Admiralty Square," he continued. "We must try to avoid bloodshed. But we must not be afraid to spill our blood or any other blood!"

There were more shouts of approval. While this was going on, Ryleev took Kahovsky aside and thrust a dagger into his hand. Ryleev said, "Dear friend, you are alone on earth. Kill the Czar!"

On the cold, misty morning of December 26th, Admiralty Square was deserted. The revolution had been fixed for 8 A. M. Two of the conspirators met in a little shop and watched the square through a frosted window.

"What has become of them?" asked one. "Where is Ryleev?"

"Sleeping. He always sleeps late."

"I pray he doesn't sleep too late for Russian freedom!"

By 9 A. M. the square began to be filled by soldiers, coming to take their oath to Nicholas I.

By 10 A. M. the square was crowded with soldiers and people. There was an atmosphere of tension, people pushing each other and milling about. Then the cry, "Hurrah Constantine! Long live Constantine!"

"Long live Constantine and his wife Constitution!" (There was an amusing discrepancy here in the minds of the people. Having heard so much talk from the Liberals about Constantine and their own vaunted liberal Constitution, they had naturally assumed Constitution to be the name of the wife of Constantine.)

When Nicholas I was informed that the Moscow Regiment was in revolt and already two of his generals wounded, he sent the order for his palace troops to be thrown into action.

The rebels, moving toward the Palace of the Senate, encountered General Miloradovitch, the hero of 1812, and the Governor of St. Petersburg, who had been sent by the Emperor to reason with them. General Miloradovitch was mortally wounded.

The Moscow Regiment was joined by a company of the Palace Guard and great numbers of sailors from the warships at Kronstadt.

Nicholas I revealed high personal courage by riding his horse through the enormous, surging crowds. He faced the mutinous soldiers, with their loaded muskets pointed at him, as he made repeated efforts to bring them to their senses.

In mid-afternoon Nicholas sent for reinforcements. The short winter day was fast drawing toward a close, and the Emperor knew that if the revolt was not broken before nightfall, he might lose his throne. Cannon were moved in and an order to disperse the mob given. But the soldiers refused to fire upon their own people. Finally, a young officer, whose soldiers had refused to take their stations around a cannon, manned it himself and fired three rounds.

As if by magic the crowd fled. In a few minutes the streets were empty. The revolution was over.

Metternich said, "The history of Russia begins where the novel lets off."

Of 121 conspirators, five were put to death: Ryleev, Pestel, Muraviev, Bestuzhev and Kakhovsky—who had failed in his assignment to murder Nicholas I, but killed General Miloradovitch instead. The rest of the conspirators were punished, most of them exiled to Siberia.

Ironically, Mordvinov, director of the Russian-American Company, who had helped to bring the Decembrist conspiracy about, was one of the judges who condemned them.

Thus ended the first serious attempt to destroy the autocratic Government of Russia.

always poland

In March, 1826, Henry Middleton, the American Minister to Russia, reported that Nicholas I was favorable to the course which the United States desired him to pursue in bringing Spain to recognize and accept the independence of her former colonies in Latin America. "Once internal disorders had been quelled, the Emperor would continue the work of Pacification commenced by the deceased Emperor Alexander of glorious memory."

In July Middleton renewed his pleas, and in August the Russian Foreign Office requested Oubril, the Russian Minister in Spain, to notify the Spanish Cabinet that "a truce seems to the Emperor much to be desired and for the good of Spain." But, in October, Oubril informed his Government that the message must be deferred "until a more propitious time." When Middleton heard this, he began to doubt the sincerity of Russia, though he knew that the real cause of the deadlock was the obstinacy of Spain. Spain had spent centuries building an empire, and in a few years it had been destroyed. The Spaniards were in no mood to listen to advice from any foreign source. On April 30, 1827, Middleton sadly confessed that all hope of persuading Spain "to adopt measures suggested by reason must be abandoned."

Henry Middleton lasted ten years in St. Petersburg, longer than any American Minister before or since. During his stay, Russia had retreated from its position in regard to South and Central America, had made a treaty with the United States, had, together with French and British squadrons, destroyed the Turkish Fleet at Navarino, and by the treaty of Adrianople extended her frontier to the southern estuary of the Danube.

Shortly after the inauguration of Andrew Jackson, Middleton was recalled. As he was making preparations for departure, news of revolutions in France, Belgium and Prussia alarmed St. Petersburg. The dread cholera made its appearance in many Russian cities. Then Poland embarked on a bloody war with Russia.

John Randolph, aging, quarrelsome, was appointed United States Minister to Russia by Jackson, said Edward Barrows, "partly to pay a political debt, and partly because he had been advised not to!" "Randolph," wrote an American biographer, "called President Adams a traitor, Holmes a dangerous fool, Daniel Webster a vile slanderer, Edward Livingston unfit to touch without tongs, while to Henry Clay he addressed this classic apostrophe: so brilliant! so corrupt! like a rotten mackerel in moonlight, he shines and stinks!"

Randolph was ordered to reopen the questions of a commercial treaty and maritime rights. With Russia growing stronger and less dependent on the powers of western Europe, there was reason to believe that the time was ripe. As early as September, Nicholas I had informed Krudener, the Russian Minister in Washington, that he was willing to negotiate in regard to maritime and commercial matters. "Such a treaty would give uneasy feeling to Great Britain, who reserved to herself the right to dictate maritime law. The intrepid Jackson and the faithful Van Buren, his Secretary of State, if they could secure the support of Russia, were willing to defy the mistress of the seas." "The new facilities afforded to the Russian

A tea-house in Cronstadt

Navy," wrote Van Buren, "by the Emperor's conquests in the East, must, before long, give them preponderance in the naval concerns of the world . . ."

On June 28, 1830, Randolph, aboard the 700-ton American Sloop-of-War *Concord,* under the command of Matthew Calbraith Perry, who later was to open up Japan, departed from Norfolk for Kronstadt. He took with him a supply of wine, books, firearms, ham, a barrel of bread, a coffee pot and mill, and three slaves, John, Tuba and Ebos. He also took with him young John Randolph Clay. Trouble began almost immediately. Forty-three days of storm at sea, "unprecedented tempestuous and cold weather," put Randolph in such bad humor that he began to annoy Perry. "Their cabin rang with quarrelsome dissent." When Perry found it necessary to have two of his crew flogged, Randolph was furious. He wrote to the Navy Department, "The *Concord* is a sort of hell afloat. Perry treats his men more brutally than a Virginia gentleman would dare treat his meanest slave."

The *Concord* reached Kronstadt on August 9th. "The Czar,"

wrote Chaplain Jenks, "was more than cordial and had a long discussion with Perry on matters of administration in the American
Navy. He ended the audience by suggesting that the Commodore
enter the Russian service. But Perry was anxious to get out of
his kingdom."

Shortly after his arrival, Randolph received a letter from
President Jackson. "The great and rapidly increasing influence of
Russia in the affairs of the world renders it very important that our
representative at the Court of St. Petersburg should be of highest
respectability . . . I know of no one better fitted for the station than
yourself."

Randolph gave the cold, reserved Russians a hilarious twenty-
six days. To dispel the notion that American diplomats always
wear black, like undertakers, he was attired in a gaudy full-dress
suit and carried a steel sword. "I dressed," Randolph said, "like
Mr. Madison during the late convention." Betsy Patterson Bonaparte describes how, in the palace of the Emperor, "the court
ladies laughed in describing to each other Randolph's behavior.
He, for the first time in the presence of royalty, greeted his Imperial
Majesty with the hearty salutation, 'How are you, Emperor? How
is Madam?' " It was also gossiped that Randolph, awed by the
court atmosphere, plunged to his knees before the Empress.

Randolph denied these accusations. He explained that in
advancing, one of his legs being somewhat shorter than the other,
he limped in such a manner that the Empress thought he was about
to kneel. The Emperor made a movement to prevent such a thing
and said, "No! No!" "Randolph," wrote Washington Irving, "is
too well informed on point of etiquette to have made such a
blunder. I have no doubt, however, that he left behind him the
character of a very rare bird."

The remaining three weeks Randolph spent fighting his
chronic ill-health with alcohol and drugs. He coughed, expectorated
blood, and cursed the northern city. "Heat, dust impalpable, insects
of all nauseous descriptions, gigantic as the empire they inhabit.
This is the land of Pharoah and his plagues. Nevertheless, it is
beyond doubt the most magnificent city I ever beheld."

On August 12th, Randolph, in "handsome equipage with four
or five horses," left the famous hostelry, the Demouth, and went

to call at the Ministry of Foreign Affairs to discuss a commercial treaty. He was informed that Nesselrode was ill. "My Russian campaign," he confessed, "has been a Pultowa to me, though I am not a Bonaparte, but a poor half-ruined Virginia planter."

On September 7, 1830, 26 days after he had landed on Russian soil, Randolph departed for England, leaving young John Randolph Clay to represent the United States. The shortest stay of any American Minister in Russia was over.

If Constantinople was Russia's temptation, Poland was her misfortune. From the Thirteenth Century Russia and Poland engaged in wars. By the Sixteenth Century these wars occurred with almost mathematical regularity, 1507, '12, '22, '34, '36, '61, '65 and 1580. The Polish dream of an empire that reached from sea to sea was nearly realized in 1610 when Moscow was captured and Wladislav, the Polish Prince, was made Czar of Russia. It was not until 1721, when Peter the Great created a Russian Empire, that the tide shifted. Empress Catherine shattered the Polish dream and began the partitioning of the land.

Yet, caught between Prussia and Russia, Poland, like Ireland, seemed unable to live peacefully either in captivity or in freedom. After 1772, Poles fought not only on their own soil but wherever they could face the Russians. Four divisions, 55,000 soldiers, joined Napoleon in his invasion of Russia. After Napoleon's defeat, the Vienna Congress put all that remained of Poland into Alexander's hands. He immediately granted amnesty to all who had fought with the French and in November, 1815, made a triumphant entry into Warsaw. He wore Polish orders and uniforms, visited the homes of Polish aristocrats, attended numerous balls, distributed decorations and appointed several Polish men as "Generals of His Suite."

Even as this was happening, as Alexander was giving Poland a liberal constitution and virtual freedom, the Poles began clamoring for the return of Mogilev, Podolia and Lithuania. Alexander told Czartorsky, "Don't compromise me! I'm sorry, but I can't permit you to press me for this annexation. You must be patient. It must look as if I, of my own volition, give you these provinces."

The Constitution of 1815 guaranteed Poland freedom of the

press, the abolition of confiscation of property, and the retention of the Polish language in government offices, where only Poles could occupy administrative and military posts. The right to vote was given to all males over thirty who paid taxes of not less than a hundred zloty. General Zayonchek, who had fought with Napoleon, was made Viceroy. The new Polish Constitution contained more personal and political freedoms than the Russian government had ever given to its own people. "Yet," says Karpovitch, "because of the unwillingness on the part of the Poles to give up the idea of a restored Polish empire, relations between the Russian sovereign and his Polish subjects became strained."

Nevertheless, for the first time in many years, Poland was at peace. Commerce between the two countries flourished.

When Pestel, one of the Decembrist leaders, approached influential Poles, he was told that Poland would join in the revolt only if her 1772 frontiers, including Lithuania and the Ukraine, were restored. Pestel rejected these conditions. Some few Poles did participate in the Decembrist uprising, but their efforts were

A Russian merchant family

not very energetic, and they received only the light punishment meted out to them by their own courts.

In 1829, Nicholas I went to Warsaw, took his oath in the Catholic Church, and was crowned. Until 1830, despite his personal aversion to the liberal Constitution which Poland had been granted, he conducted himself correctly and without prejudice. But the July revolution in France, when the streets were marked with blood, was the signal for a new Polish uprising. Nicholas, who hated Louis Philippe, ordered the Polish army mobilized, with the intention of sending it to France. New revolts broke out in Belgium and Italy, and the tricolor replaced the flag of the Bourbons at the French Consulate in Warsaw. On November 29th, Polish revolutionaries broke into Belvedere Palace, intending to assassinate Grand Duke Constantine, but he escaped because a Polish officer who resembled him was murdered. This war spread and lasted until the end of 1831, when Warsaw fell. Nicholas then confiscated the estates of the ringleaders and before sending them into exile in the Caucasus, told them, "Gentlemen, my brother did more for your land than you deserved."

With the escape of Polish revolutionaries abroad, there began agitation for the justice of the Polish cause. England and France had encouraged the Poles in their attempt to gain independence, and now that the war was over the clamor reached its summit— riots broke out in Paris, the windows of the Russian Embassy were shattered. Revolutionaries in all parts of Europe used the Polish situation to serve their own purposes. Another major war, formed around the pretext of a crusade to restore Polish independence, was threatening Europe.

American hopes of a commercial treaty were shattered. Young Randolph Clay made repeated visits to the Russian Foreign Office, only to be informed by Nesselrode that his attention was "entirely absorbed by the revolt in Poland." Van Buren, afraid youthful zeal might impair later chances at success, ordered Clay "to do nothing." Meanwhile, President Jackson offered the post to James Buchanan of Pennsylvania. Buchanan, ignorant of French and loath to go to a distant land, hesitated. He finally accepted and arrived in St. Petersburg on June 2, 1832.

Buchanan was at first scornful of Russian society, branding it as "having all the vices and none of the virtues of the French aristocracy." Yet, before long, he had entered Russian social life with more zest than his predecessors. He became a familiar, popular figure at diplomatic receptions, military parades and private parties. He confessed he was astonished at his success, and grudgingly admitted that the women of the upper classes were "cultivated and accomplished." But the glitter of social life did not blind him when he complained that there was "no freedom of the press and no public opinion." The peasants were ignorant barbarians, perfectly content with their lot and far too backward to be "fit for liberty."

Buchanan felt that while America was "a sealed book in regard to the Russians, the Emperor was, despite the differences in principles of government, anxious to remain on good terms with the United States, not from love, but for political considerations."

Ten days after his arrival, Buchanan visited Nesselrode and took up at once the question of a commercial treaty. The Polish rebellion had been crushed, but the Russian Government was alarmed by the violent anti-Russian feeling throughout Europe. In Turkey, Hungary, Austria and Prussia, Polish exiles were arraying themselves against Czar Nicholas. The Russian Foreign Office was fearful that a treaty might stir up more friction. Baron Krudener, Russian Envoy to the United States, who was home on leave, had met Buchanan in Washington three years before. An able, honest official, he bent his efforts toward assisting Buchanan. At first they made little progress. The thorny question of neutrality rights, "neutral goods on enemy ships are not subject to capture," and the definition of lawful blockade were objected to by the Russian government. "What will England say?" exclaimed Nesselrode. "England would have no right to object," replied Buchanan. But Nesselrode shook his head, "It would set England aflame!"

Finally, after lengthy negotiations, Buchanan received, on October 22, 1831, a note from Nesselrode informing him that the proposal for a commercial treaty had been rejected. In vain Buchanan reminded Nesselrode that the Emperor had informed the President of his willingness to conclude a treaty. Buchanan wrote home that Russia was "unwilling to recognize by Treaty any principles of public law which might be disagreeable to England. There is no doubt that all their energies for some time past have been directed in detaching England from France." Buchanan, whom one American historian characterized as "a dignified, formal, mediocre gentleman," showed perception when he reported: "Should Russia assume an attitude of defiance against England and France, it is more than probable she would agree to make a treaty with us concerning Maritime rights. But we must keep in mind that if we had such a treaty, and Russia should be engaged in war with England, upon the capture of any American vessel having Russian goods aboard, she would be the first Power to call upon us to assert those principles of Maritime law which we had thus enacted." Though clearly doubting the wisdom of a maritime treaty, Buchanan remained anxious to secure a commercial agreement.

In November, with the situation deadlocked, he obtained another interview with Nesselrode and surprised the Chancellor by pointing out that American ships carried two-thirds of all St. Petersburg's exports. He stated too that Russian exports to the United States in 1830 had amounted to $1,621,899. He made it clear that Russia had a great deal to lose.

On December 12, 1832, Nesselrode broke down and announced that Russia was willing to sign the Commercial Treaty. After discussion as to the length of duration of the treaty, in which Buchanan won his point of not putting a time limit to it, Buchanan suggested that they sign the treaty on December 18th, the Emperor's name-day. Nesselrode, always delighted by such niceties, agreed, insisting only that the treaty be kept secret because of England. But Emperor Nicholas no longer cared what England thought of a Russian-American treaty. In October, England and France had signed a pact and recognized Belgian independence, which was what he had feared, since Belgium had been part of the Netherlands, where Nicholas' sister was queen.

On December 18th, Nicholas held a gay, festive reception. The Winter Palace was filled with the elite of St. Petersburg. The Emperor, accompanied by the Empress, entered the Grand Ballroom, and the thousands of guests, in silence, made the customary curtsies. Buchanan wrote:

"The diplomatic corps, according to etiquette, were arranged in line to receive the Emperor and Empress. Mr. Bligh, the English Minister, occupied the station immediately below myself. You may judge my astonishment when the Emperor, accosting me in French, in a tone of voice that could be heard all around, said, 'I signed the order yesterday that the Treaty should be executed according to your wishes,' and immediately, turning to Mr. Bligh, asked him to be the interpreter of this information. Mr. Bligh is a most amiable man, and his astonishment and embarrassment were so striking that I felt for him most sincerely."

That same afternoon Buchanan of the United States and Nesselrode of Russia went to the Ministry of Foreign Affairs and signed the first Commercial Treaty between the two powers. It was promptly ratified by the American Senate.

Meanwhile, in the United States, where the deeds of Pulaski and Kosciusko had achieved fame, sympathy for Poland was increasing. "American newspapers, dependent on French and British sources for Russian news, printed numerous articles, some none too authentic, denouncing the Czar." While Buchanan was trying to conclude a commercial treaty, the *Washington Globe,* considered the official organ of the administration, was campaigning in defense of Polish aspirations.

The Russian government instructed Baron Osten-Sacken of the Russian Legation in Washington "not to try to fight public opinion on the Polish question." Contrary to his instructions, Osten-Sacken drew up a note of protest, more pungent than discreet, and presented it to the State Department. The arrogant note charged President Jackson with insincerity, "encouraging the abuse of Emperor Nicholas, while at the same time professing friendship for him." Jackson was tactful; hoping the inexperienced Russian diplomat would withdraw the note, he delayed two months before writing an answer. Finally, on December 4, 1832, Osten-Sacken was informed that "no further explanations can be entered into until an imputation so injurious to the reputation of the Government and respect for its Sovereign shall be withdrawn." After waiting a month for a reply, the President gave instructions to Buchanan to bring the matter to the attention of the Russian Government.

Nesselrode expressed his regrets and assured Buchanan that

Osten-Sacken would be recalled immediately. In his report to Jackson, Buchanan suggested that the editor of the *Globe* refrain from further statements about Poland. Buchanan also, his mission accomplished, requested to return home.

On August 5, 1833, Buchanan had his last audience with Nicholas. After expressing deep regret for the American's departure, the Emperor stated that he was surprised at the amount of pro-Polish agitation in the United States. "We are not propagandists," stated Buchanan. "We let other nations the task of managing their own concerns in their own manner."

"I entertain not a doubt," reported Buchanan, "that the Emperor has been treated in the Polish question with great injustice. My own conviction desires to see the independence of the brave and gallant Poles reestablished, but truth compels me to say that the cruelties of the Imperial Government toward them have been greatly exaggerated. I am more and more convinced that no other course, in the repression of a Polish revolt, could have been pursued with safety."

As the agitation in Europe reached a climax and war became probable, Livingston, the American Minister to France, stated, "In the event of war, I have thought it my duty, in discussions with the Russian Ambassador, to answer to an observation that Russian commerce would be destroyed by the blockade, that we Americans will carry on our Russian trade."

"uncle sasha"

The fate of the Decembrists cooled the territorial ambitions of the Russian-American Company. After the December revolt, the Russian government decided to make administrative changes, putting management of the company into the hands of professional navy men. Peter Chistiakov, manager of Russia's American colony, was succeeded by Baron Ferdinand Wrangel.

During the Wrangel administration, Article 4 of the 1824 Treaty expired. This article read, ". . . for a period of 10 years, citizens of either country might reciprocally frequent, without any hindrance whatever, the interior seas, gulfs, harbors and creeks for the purpose of fishing and trading." On April 17, 1834, the day that portion of the treaty expired, two American ships were ordered out of Sitka. The Captains of the ships refused, stating that they would not leave until notified by their own Government. Wrangel, on April 27th, issued formal notice forbidding American

105

and British ships to visit Russian territory north of 54°40′. This notice appeared in the *Washington Globe* on July 22nd. When the notice reached St. Petersburg, Count Kankrin, Minister of Finance, was petitioned "to urge the Government of the United States to announce publicly that Article 4 was no longer in force." Simultaneously, a warship, the *Chichagov,* was dispatched to Alaska with instructions to prevent all foreign ships from approaching Russian possessions.

The American Government instructed William Wilkins, who succeeded Buchanan, to open negotiations for the renewal of Article 4. Wilkins replied that he thought it could speedily be accomplished. He called on Nesselrode, who listened with patience, but insisted that he must consult with the Russian-American Company before entering negotiations. Two years later Wilkins returned to the United States with matters still unsettled. Not until George Dallas arrived in St. Petersburg in August, 1837, was the matter reopened, and a year later Nesselrode "invited the United States Government not to contravene the prohibitory notice."

While Nesselrode was simply avoiding the renewal of an agreement which was no longer desired by Russia, the fact that the United States, always ready to debate any abridgment of its commercial rights, should have acquiesced, can hardly be explained. Forsyth, Secretary of State, made no effort to contest the Russian declaration, and President Van Buren felt that trade in that region was "too inconsiderable to attract much attention." Nevertheless, American sea captains treated the Russian prohibition with contempt. Whalers constantly visited the Russian colony. As late as 1845 the new Russian Envoy, Bodisco, was instructed to inform Washington that "repeated encroachment by American vessels will contribute to the demoralization of the native population and provoke inevitable collisions." The President again supinely acquiesced, agreeing that the Russian cruiser patrol "cannot but contribute to keep up the excellent relations existing between the two countries."

In 1840, the Russian-American Company leased for a period of ten years a large strip of land to the Hudson Bay Company. Bodisco protested, stating that the lease would create a suspicion in the American mind that "they are being turned out from Russian

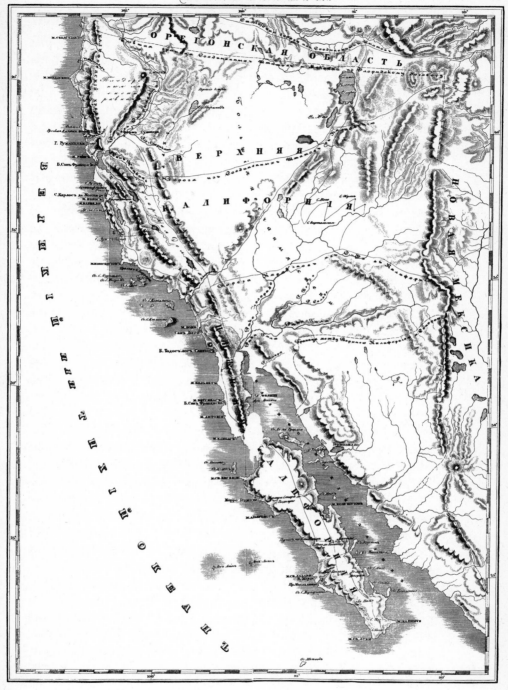

Map of Russian California

territory in order to give it to England." Nesselrode, however, was more interested in British-Russian relations and hinted that too much importance must never be given to American protests.

Behind these political maneuvers was the simple fact that time was running out for Russian America. While the United States and England were strengthening their positions, Russia had stood still. There had been too many mistakes, too many missed opportunities, too many wasted expeditions. Quietly, peacefully, the Russian outpost in California had continued its existence. Shortly before the collapse of Spanish rule in California, Yanovsky, who was now in charge of Russian America, had presented the Governor of California with a large mirror, in return for which he had received a brace of pheasants. But in 1821, when Mexico became independent, the Mexicans, as soon as they had taken over control of California, delivered an ultimatum for Fort Ross to be abandoned within six months.

Fort Ross was weak. The handful of soldiers, clad in blue and green cloth uniforms, had as small-arms a few dozen old flintlocks which Napoleon had lost during his retreat from Moscow. There were a few Indians "filled with savage pride to wear the Imperial uniforms." Hastily the Russians reinforced and repaired the stockade and twenty-nine small cannon, loaded with grapeshot, were added to the obsolete ones.

But even as the fort was strengthening its defenses, the Russian Government decided to abandon the settlement. The reasons were many. Ross had been established to provide food for Alaska, but there had not been enough farmland cultivated to make the site an agricultural success. The Russians, so few in number, were not farmers and had failed in their efforts to raise grain and cattle. Their yearly average of wheat shipped to Sitka was scarcely above twelve tons. From 1825 to 1829, the expenses to maintain Ross totalled 224,176 roubles, and the receipts for the same period were only 43,858. Baron Wrangel had made a personal investigation of Ross, and as a last desperate measure to save it had made an expedition to Mexico in an effort to purchase San Rafael and Pueblo Sonoma. The Mexicans had refused. But it was doubtful, when the Russians had not been able to exploit land already theirs, that such a purchase would have helped.

An incident with the Hudson Bay Company caused the decision. At the mouth of the Stikine River in Alaska the Russians had posted an armed ship to prevent settlers or marauders from sailing up the river. In 1834, a Hudson Bay ship asked permission to go up the river. The ship, when the request was refused, sailed off. A year later the Russian-American Company was ordered to pay 1,500,000 francs to the Hudson Bay Company. The Russian government examined the British claim and found it justified. The Russian-American Company, to escape paying this sum, leased a large portion of its northern land.

From every side pressure was increasing. The Mexicans were determined not to permit a foreign settlement near San Francisco. Americans were drifting into California in increasing numbers. The Hudson Bay Company was becoming more and more aggressive as the supply of fur-bearing animals decreased. Then came a last glimmer of hope. The Mexican Governor, Figueroa, approached Wrangel and hinted that if Russia would give formal recognition to the Mexican Republic the matter of land "could be arranged." Wrangel sailed to Mexico, crossed from Mazatlan to Vera Cruz, and reached St. Petersburg in the summer of 1836. He reported to his directors, "If we delay, the Americans will get California."

Wrangel was received by the Emperor. Instead of emphasizing the benefits to the Russian-American Company, about which he sensed the Emperor did not care, he explained the advantages Russia would obtain by recognizing the independence of Mexico. He cited Prussia, which had already made a profitable trade agreement with Mexico.

"Prussia!" said the Emperor, "Prussia put profit above honor. I live by an opposite rule."

The Emperor would listen no further. The fate of California was sealed. Even the directors of the Russian-American Company abandoned hope. "The United States waits," wrote Rotchev, the Commandant of Fort Ross, "for the right moment to annex all California." The Russian Minister of Finance was petitioned for permission to liquidate Ross Colony. The petition stated, "From a political viewpoint there is nothing but trouble. The English have strongholds right up to our frontiers. The Mexicans hold the excellent bay of San Francisco, where hordes of United States citizens

John Augustus Sutter

are settling." On April 27, 1839, the Emperor consented to the sale of Ross. Politically, only Bodisco objected, "The liquidation of Bodega and Ross will create an unfavorable impression of our strength." Bodisco was right, for with the loss of Fort Ross, the loss of Alaska became a matter of time.

Meanwhile, a man from Switzerland arrived at Sitka and called on the Russian Governor. He presented a letter, which read, "With great pleasure I introduce to your acquaintance Captain John A. Sutter, a Swiss Gentleman and a person of the first class among men, honored for his talents and his reputation . . ." It was signed by the American Consul at Honolulu, but in 1834, the Chief of Police at Berne, Switzerland, had issued a warrant for the arrest of Johann Augustus Sutter, merchant of Ruenberg, for having secretly liquidated his assets, deserted his wife and five children, and left behind a mountain of debts. He was believed to have fled to America.

Sutter had fled to America, crossed the United States to Vancouver, from whence he sailed to Hawaii, where he successfully impersonated an officer of the Swiss Guard. He made numerous friends and became a minor celebrity. He spoke often of California as "the land of opportunity." When a Mr. French, a merchant, offered him passage to Sitka, he accepted. "Ah, those days at Sitka,"

Fort Ross in the Forties

Sutter, the fraud, reminisced shortly before his death, "A magnificent reception was given me by the Authorities and Princess Menschikov. She gave me the privilege of dancing with her. There were many parties and feasts, sometimes three a week, and I made use of my knowledge of languages. With the Chief Clerk I spoke Spanish, with the storekeeper, German, with the Governor and his Lady, French." The curious fact about his statement is that the Princess Menschikov had never lived in Alaska.

Armed with a letter of introduction, and a retinue of more than a dozen servants, including two Kanaka girls, Sutter sailed to Monterey, California, where he posed as an officer of the Royal Swiss Guard of Charles X and made a profound impression on the Mexicans. Soon he was Captain John Sutter of New Helvetia on the Sacramento, lord of over 229 square miles of land, a territory ten times the size of Bermuda. Sutter became a friend of the new Commandant of Fort Ross, Alexander Rotchev, a writer, poet and translator. When Rotchev was ordered to sell Ross Colony, he approached Sutter. The Hudson Bay Company had refused a Russian offer, and Sutter himself hesitated wanting to buy only the livestock and movable property. But a letter from Governor Kuprianov made him reconsider. "We prefer," wrote Kuprianov, "the esteemed Captain to be our successor. We would rather burn all our property than sell it to the Mexicans." Eighteen months later the transaction was concluded, and, on December 13, 1841, signed in San Francisco. It read in part: "The Russian-American Company abandoning its southernmost settlements with the consent of His Majesty the Emperor of all the Russias, cedes to Monsieur Sutter all its posts at New Albion, Port Bodega and Fort Ross." Sutter promised to pay, within four years, the sum of $30,000, with a cash down payment of $2000. "Champagne flowed freely," wrote Sutter.

In December, 1841, the two hundred inhabitants of Fort Ross sailed for Alaska. For seven years the Russian government tried to collect the money Sutter owed them. Finally, in 1848, Bodisco was instructed to put pressure on the American government, which by this time was nominally occupying California. "I called on Buchanan," reported Bodisco, "and jokingly hinted that some time ago he had been very eager to get our little colony. I told him he had his chance, for a mere $30,000, to make us forfeit our rights to California. He laughed."

In January, 1849, an American named Steward, who had been appointed Russian Consul in San Francisco, pressed Sutter for payment. To his surprise, he was paid $10,000 in gold dust and the remainder in notes. No sooner had Steward converted the notes into cash than he vanished, leaving, in the words of Zollinger, "the Russian-American Company minus the cash and the Czar minus a consul." The Russian failure in California had been made complete, and Sutter's empire was trampled in the avalanche that followed the accidental discovery of gold. Sutter died in Washington in 1880, in poverty, still arguing with Congress over his rights to the ownership of California.

Though Russia had failed to build an empire in the Pacific, the efforts had not been wholly wasted. Islands in the Pacific that still bear Russian names are considerable. Lisianski, near Midway, Krusenstern, Rumiantzev, Chichagov, Kutusov and Suvorov in the Tuamotu Archipelago of the Marshalls and Gilberts, Rimsky-Korsakov and Bellingshausen, Borodino and Ponafidin south of Japan. These were but a few of the discoveries made by Russians, a feat of major proportions when it is taken into consideration that most of the voyages were begun from the most distant ports of

Europe and with a minimum of cooperation from the Government.

Russia had failed, too, in America. But while people were fleeing from all parts of Europe to America for political, economic and religious freedom, the Russians, with supposedly the most harsh government in Europe and the most tortured political and religious history, went there merely to get furs. They were probably the hardiest, fiercest people ever to land on American shores, and they braved conditions of bitter cold and hunger that other Europeans would never had survived. But they were not settlers. They did not bring their wives and children. They did not bring plows, axes, or seed. They believed that agriculture was for men who were not able to hunt. And when the sea-otter and the blue fox were gone, they boarded ships and went back home.

Pioneers in Russian-American trade were the American family of Ropes. In 1832, William Ropes, a Salem merchant, was admitted to the Guild of Russian Merchants. His ships brought Southern cotton to the factories in Narva, Riga and Revel. When mineral illuminating oil began to replace whale oil, William Ropes shipped it to Russia. Before his death, in 1859, *Ropsky kerosin* was known throughout the Empire. His son, William Hooper Ropes, settled in St. Petersburg, bought a huge dog as protection against bandits, and traveled thousands of miles by sleigh into the interior of Russia to purchase bolt-rope, crash and sheet-iron. He distributed among the peasants religious pamphlets which his brother, Joseph, a student at St. Petersburg, had translated. His home became the meeting place of Americans visiting Russia. In 1840 an American chapel was founded on land donated by Emperor Nicholas, who ordered "every courtesy extended to this foreign religious initiative." "It was a chapel of dissenters," wrote Albert Parry, "where a Mr. Ellerby preached fire-and-brimstone."

W. H. Ropes married an Englishwoman, had nine children, most of whom were born in St. Petersburg. One, Ernest Eduard, remained all his life in Russia. His oil business prospered, he became wealthy, and opened an oil refinery which he managed until his death in 1916. He was perhaps the only American citizen ever listed in the *Almanac of St. Petersburg*.

A change took place in Russian-American trade. Instead of

A Russian Cart

Derbys, Cabots, and Peabodies, names like Fenway Court and Enoch Train appeared. With the increasing speed of American ships, new products were imported by Russia, including pineapples, madeiras, marsalas, sherries, Jamaica rum, dry fruits and cigars. Displayed in shop windows, these "overseas delights" were kept bundled like babies to protect them from the rigors of the Russian climate. In 1840, the *Kamchatka,* launched by the New York firm of William Brown and decidedly the finest "war steamer" in Europe, was purchased by Russia, and arrived in Kronstadt, where it was visited by numberless Russians.

In this atmosphere George Miflin Dallas, new American Minister, arrived with his wife and two daughters. A few days after his arrival, Emperor Nicholas gave a dinner in his honor. Empress Alexandra, to whom Dallas was presented, voiced surprise that the American Government changed representatives so frequently. "I hope you will prove an exception to this practice and will be happy in Russia and stay long."

"The Empress," reported Dallas, "who spoke distinct but not handsome English, wanted to know all about our Novelist, Fenimore Cooper."

She asked Dallas about the latest work the American was writing. "He is my greatest favorite, especially *The Pioneer, The Spy,* and *Last of the Mohicans.*"

A Russian Drozhky

Dallas told her about the new novels, *The Red Rover* and *The Water Witch*.

His only recorded observation about Czar Nicholas was that he was "capable of pushing Russia to a European ascendancy."

Dallas, sensing that social position was the key to diplomatic success, rented a fine house, and, with his wife and two daughters, began to frequent the salons of the aristocracy. He attended a soirée at the richly furnished house of Count and Countess de Laval. He found de Laval a generous host. "But the Countess," wrote Dallas, "is the personification of a toadstool, fat, coarse, short and ugly." The dresses of the women he found excellent, but "some of the matrons" shocked his American notions by "a most profuse display of bust . . ."

At Nesselrode's ball he had a lengthy conversation with the Emperor and Empress. So marked was the attention the Emperor gave him that it created a sensation in that crowded, brilliant circle. "The Emperor raised his voice several keys louder and said to me, 'You are the first gentleman who has ever induced me thus publicly to speak English.'" The Empress inquired of young Queen Victoria, "I hope she will be great, for she cannot be beautiful." When, a year later, the Czarevitch, the future Alexander II, fell in love with Victoria, he was informed that "marriage between an English Queen and a future Emperor was impossible."

At a ball in the magnificent palace of Prince Belosselsky, the Emperor discussed with Dallas the possibility of Canadian independence. "On the whole," said Dallas, "England would be wise to consent to the separation."

"Then where would she get timber?"

"From Russia, of course."

Nicholas smiled wryly, and changed the subject.

"Why not send a naval squadron to visit America?" said Dallas. The Emperor said he would give it consideration, but that he was more concerned about "American accusations made against him in regard to the Polish question."

"You are so powerful," said Dallas, "you inspire jealousy."

"Yes, we are powerful," said Nicholas, "in defense, not attack."

Toward the end of his second year in Russia, Dallas admitted that he regretted leaving. He had enjoyed St. Petersburg society and his "triumphs with the ladies at cards or chess." "Nicholas," he said, "was inflexible but not cruel." He visited Admiral Krusenstern at the Naval Academy and discussed the visit to Japan which Rezanov and Krusenstern had made thirty years past. They also discussed the American Indians, with the Russian Admiral likening "the Cherokee and Creek Indians to the Circassians of the Caucasus."

Dallas called on Poletica, having made his acquaintance in Washington, but found the former diplomat "old and quarrelsome, remembering little of America and perhaps never having been its friend." He visited Prince Saltikov, the *grand seigneur* of Russia, who showed him a copy of the Declaration of Independence, with autographed signatures. But the old aristocrat was not even aware that George Washington had ever been President. It was this combination of ignorance and half-knowledge about the United States that distressed both Dallas and the Russian Foreign Office. As the Russian diplomat, Baron Brunow, stated, "It has proved very difficult to get correct ideas of the actual state of things in America."

Dallas left Russia on July 24, 1839. He took with him "a magnificent gold Snuff Box, studded with costly diamonds, a present from Emperor Nicholas to J. J. Audubon, the great ornithologist." His stay had not been noteworthy for political negotiations; but he had at least succeeded in opening a narrow door into Russian society and in correcting certain false impressions about the United States at a time when Russian-American relations, doomed until the two nations arrived at a deeper understanding of each other, had reached a stage where misinformation was more dangerous than actual ignorance.

Only here and there were there signs of clear insight into the nature and destiny of the two great lands. Shortly after the arrival of Dallas in Russia, Pushkin, under the pen name of The Reviewer, made an incisive critical report on the United States. Though his report was not complimentary, it examined American life more carefully than any Russian diplomat cared to.

The North American States have attracted the attention of the most outstanding people in Europe. America calmly follows her destiny, secure and flourishing, made strong by the peace that reigns there, proud of her institutions, and fortified by her geographical position. Recently, however, a few penetrating minds began to study the character of these institutions and their observations cast a more doubtful light on certain matters. The respect for this new nation and its laws was greatly shaken.

To our surprise, we discovered within democracy a repulsive cynicism, cruel prejudices and intolerable tyrannies. Everything noble, everything that uplifts the human soul, is being suppressed by a kind of egotism and a passion for *comfort*. The majority brazenly suppresses society. Despite the cry of liberty, the slavery of the negroes continues. Not having nobility, the snobbishness of the people is surprising. The politicians show only greed and jealousy and are ingratiating in their efforts to please the mighty voters. There are contradictions to all the established rules of society. The rich man puts on a torn coat when he goes into the street in order not to insult the proud poor; yet he secretly despises them and is despised by them. Such is the picture of the United States recently presented to us.

Pushkin went on to foretell the fate of the American Indian:

Chateaubriand and Fenimore Cooper have presented to us the Indians only from a poetical point of view. The savages in some novels resemble real savages about as much as idyllic shepherds resemble real ones. Sooner or later, by sword, fire, rum and chicanery, savagery must disappear with the approach of civilization. It is inevitable. The remnants of the ancient inhabitants of America soon will be completely exterminated. The vast plains and boundless rivers, in which the Indians procured food with arrows and nets, will be transformed into cultivated fields, studded with villages, and into commercial ports where the smoke of steamboats will be seen and the American flag will wave. Yet must I condemn the flagrant injustice and the heartlessness of the American Congress toward the Indian tribes.

But the voice of Pushkin was not heard in distant America, where such voices were needed. And it was not heard above a whisper in Russia, where such voices were also needed.

History is filled with small things which the historians tremble to record, fearing they have not sufficient importance. The animosity of nations toward each other can stem from a single battlefield, but the friendship of nations is made up of more threads and patches than all the darned socks and breeches in this world. George Dallas, on his return to America, at a Philadelphia banquet, said, "One day a lad of nineteen appeared before me with a request to see the Emperor. 'I've brought him a present all the way from America,' said the boy. 'I want to give it to him with my own hands.' When I learned what the present was, fearing to offend the Emperor, I told the boy I could not arrange the audience immediately."

"On June 26, 1838," recorded Anna Okulova, "a young American came to St. Petersburg and expressed desire to see the Emperor. He was received by Count Tchernishov, Minister of War, and General Adlerberg. 'Gentlemen,' he said to them, 'I've heard so much abuse about your Emperor that I decided with my own eyes to see the truth. I've visited a great part of Russia. I saw happy people everywhere. Therefore I came here to thank your Emperor. I am a poor man, all I can do is present him with an acorn from the tomb of George Washington. He also was a friend of humanity.'

"The Emperor," added Mlle. Okulova, "ordered the Court gardener to plant the acorn on the little island of Tsaritzin (in Peterhof) and to erect a tablet commemorating the gift."

"To my surprise," said Dallas in Philadelphia, "I learned the boy had been received by the Emperor and the Empress. According to Tom, he met the Emperor's daughter and had a wonderful time. The Czar wanted to know about American railroads and schools. The Empress wanted to know about American house-keeping. She thought there were no servants in the United States. Tom laughed and said she must have read Mrs. Trollope. After receiving a watch and a chain with a ruby, the happy boy departed . . ."

Years later, Elisabeth Karamzin, to honor the memory of her father, planted in flower-pots two acorns from the American oak at Tsaritzin. After they produced young shoots, she sent them to Ostafievo, near Moscow. In 1939, American correspondents were shown two huge trees, descendants of an oak at the grave of Washington. But the trees and the authenticity of their origin is of minor importance, for what is being recorded is the act of a young man, scarcely more than a boy, who wanted to see for himself what Russia was like. This is the kind of freedom which Soviet Russia has lost and that the United States is in danger of losing, a kind of freedom which goes beyond all formality and protocol—an expression of the Rights of Man which both Czars and Presidents were too wise not to acknowledge.

Alexander Bodisco, the Russian Minister, was one of the few diplomats who liked Washington, D. C. He was constantly forced to sympathize with the Ministers from other countries, for the disparagement of the United States Capital was a favorite pas-time of the European diplomatic circle. De Bacourt, the French Minister, complained that Washington was deserted by day and raucous by night, the time when cows, pigs and dogs prowled the streets. Bodisco suggested that it was at least sanitary, since the animals ate up all the refuse.

The various Diplomatic Corps in Washington unfortunately comprised a group of men who would never have sat at the same table with one another under ordinary circumstances. De Ba-court would cry out, "Everything about Americans revolts me . . . their opinions, their manners, their habits and their character!" Then he would lean forward and whisper, "Most Americans secretly carry pocket-daggers." Henry Fox, the British Minister, was a withered, cynical, silent man, who spent his nights at the card table; he had an unsavory reputation, the rumor being that he had been sent abroad because of gambling scandals. Martino, fat and jolly, but gluttonous at table, represented the Netherlands, while the representative from Belgium, a notorious skinflint, was noted for asking himself to dinner. On the rare occasions when he invited the Diplomatic Corps to his own Legation, he would mourn over the cost of a joint of lamb or the wasteful habits of American servants. "Uncle Sasha" Bodisco, as he was affectionately called, the most popular member of the group, had the weakness of always pretending to be much younger than he was. He used both wigs and cosmetics, and, in the presence of unmarried ladies, frequently referred to his sons and daughters as nephews and nieces. Having a considerable private fortune, a quarter of a million in American investments alone, he carried a heavier burden of diplomatic social obligation than was required of him.

Christmas night in 1839 was cold and snowy. Washington has a forlorn, inhospitable air. But the Russian Legation was a cheerful sight. Grain had been scattered over the snow for the birds. Flares were posted to mark the road for approaching carriages, and a great bonfire was burning in the street, where the coachmen would soon gather round, warm themselves, and exchange nips of brandy. Inside the Legation, logs blazed in the fireplaces. The rooms were decorated with candles and wreaths, and, of course, there was a Christmas tree.

Alexander Bodisco surveyed the preparations for the party. He had done the decorating himself because he enjoyed such things, and because, nearing sixty, he knew that the pleasure of a party was in the preparations and the anticipation. One of the rooms was stacked with gifts—toys, books, boxes of candy, bright ribbons and ivory fans—for the young guests that his sons and daughters had invited. A widower, it had been to share a sense of family with his children that he had decorated the Legation with holly, evergreens, candles and mistletoe. "Uncle Sasha" made such Christmas festivities an annual event.

That afternoon it had been called to his attention that Harriet Williams, the fifteen-year-old daughter of a clerk in the Adjutant General's Office, had not received her invitation. It would be cruel not to invite her, particularly since her name had been on the list. It would look like an intentional snub for her father. The previous year Harriet had been elected May Queen at the fashionable school of the Misses English in Georgetown. The school, displeased that the daughter of a clerk should be selected for such a high social honor, had disqualified her for academic reasons and made the award to a student of impeccable social connections. Jessie Benton, daughter of Missouri's Senator, had tried to organize a boycott of the May Day celebrations. "An unfortunate accident," Bodisco had agreed, "but at least this time it can be remedied." He sat down and wrote a personal note, apologizing for the lateness of the invitation, and asking her to be sure to attend.

Bodisco watched the carriages arrive. He could hear young laughter and shouting, and the deeper voices of the coachmen as they called to each other. Most of the young people were not ordinarily allowed to travel alone or to use the carriages, and they were enjoying their freedom. But Bodisco noticed that they became more quiet as they, in small groups, approached the Legation. When he met them at the door their faces were almost adult with gravity.

But youth is irrepressible, and soon the Legation rang with the sounds of Christmas cheer. The first hour of the party was somewhat confusing for Bodisco, who found himself trying to remember names to associate with the galaxy of new young faces. Nevertheless, he enjoyed himself far more than at the formal diplomatic dinner which had ushered in the holiday season. Remembering the late invitation to Miss Harriet Williams, he crossed the room to where his son, Waldemar, was surrounded by young ladies and asked whether she had come.

His son introduced him to a tall, poised, beautiful young woman, and Bodisco was so surprised and delighted that he found himself stammering a bit. Finally he laughed and said, "You must excuse me, Miss Williams, but I'm afraid I had imagined you were about this high." He indicated a certain height with his hand and the young woman looked down at him and smiled. Feeling that the circumstances required something further, Bodisco offered to show her about the Legation, which she accepted. He found her conversation not brilliant, but neither foolish nor timid.

Later in the evening he found himself dancing with her and talking to her a great deal more than he had intended.

A few weeks after the Christmas party, Bodisco could be seen almost every afternoon standing outside the schoolbuilding, waiting for her. He had that abstracted and foolishly enthusiastic air which can sometimes be seen in kind, elderly gentlemen. He would smile at the children as they came out of the school, but his eyes were always lifted toward the doorway, as if his smile was merely an anticipation of the pleasure he would feel when he saw Miss Williams. He would carry her books and trot along beside her, without noticing the strange looks which people cast at them. He was so short and stout beside the tall young girl, and it was a little awkward for him to match his stride with hers. He was sixty, she was fifteen, but if there was anything ridiculous in his courtship, it escaped the notice of both Harriet and Bodisco.

Bodisco's infatuation did not pass unnoticed in diplomatic circles. There was much shaking of heads and whispered jokes about his senility. De Bacourt called Bodisco a *"vilain vieillard,"* but admitted that Miss Williams "was beautiful as the devil."

If Bodisco knew the unkind remarks which were being made, he paid no attention. Less than three months after the Christmas party he made his proposal of marriage. He observed not merely the courtesy of asking Mr. Williams for his daughter's hand, but, in accordance with Russian diplomatic custom, requested permission from the Czar to marry a non-Russian. He went still further and requested formal permission from the President of the United States to take an American wife. The wedding was set for April 9th, 1842, at the bride's home in Georgetown.

Bodisco made all the arrangements himself, even such details as selecting the bridal gown and ordering ices for the reception. Part of his reason for doing this was to spare the inexperienced Harriet from undue social strain, but without doubt he enjoyed himself thoroughly. Fourteen-year-old Jessie Benton was to be the bridesmaid. Senator Henry Clay would give the bride away. Mr. Fox, the British Minister, would attend Bodisco.

All Washington was agog. Early on the morning of the wedding a crowd began to assemble outside the Williams' home. Bodisco, who gave much time to the perfection of details, rehearsed the wedding several times shortly before the actual ceremony. Despite his care, the wedding was delayed by an accident which occurred to Mr. Fox, who had spent most of the night playing cards. Already late when he tumbled out of bed, Fox had sent his servant to the livery-stable. The man returned with the news that there was not a single carriage available. It would have taken hours to reach Georgetown afoot; so, buckling on his dress sword and grabbing his ceremonial hat, Fox hurried to the livery-stable and offered to ride in anything. "Even a wagon," he said.

"They ain't nothin' with wheels on it to be had, 'less you want that there wheelbarrow."

"But I must get there!" said Fox.

"I have got one wagon. But I don't hardly think you'd want it."

"Get it out! Hitch it up!"

The crowd gathered outside the Williams' home soon saw a sight long to be remembered. Fox, attired in his splendid scarlet and gold uniform, arrived on the top of a large funeral hearse that came flying up the street toward them. A huge plume of dust stretched out behind the somber carriage, while the driver stood high on his perch and whipped the horses, while Fox shouted down at him like an admiral from the bridge of his ship.

The wedding guests included President Van Buren, Louise Morris, Henry Clay, Buchanan, Senator Benton, and "Davie" Farragut. Any fears which might have been felt by members of the wedding for the future happiness of the couple were unfounded. Alexander Bodisco was proud of his young wife, and she gave him no reason to regret his choice. He accepted the Williams' family as his own and was as indulgent with Harriet's younger brothers and sisters as he was with his own children. He won the respect and affection of everyone, including those who had considered it an "immoral" marriage. The Bodisco coach, bearing the Minister and his beautiful wife, became a familiar sight on the streets of Washington and Georgetown.

Two years after the wedding, Bodisco took Harriet to visit Russia, and she created a sensation in St. Petersburg. The gown she wore at a ball given by the Grand Duke Michael was rumored to have cost a thousand dollars. The Emperor named her "The American Swan" and ordered a distinguished court painter to do her portrait. The Emperor was godfather to their first-born. Bodisco and Harriet had seven children, the youngest, William Basil, born at their country house just outside Washington.

"Uncle Sasha" Bodisco enjoyed twelve years of extremely happy married life. One cold morning in January, 1854, he was killed when his horse shied, and he was thrown to the ground. His will read, in part, "As my dear wife will likely become a widow when it would still be convenient for her to marry again, I do wish with my whole heart that she makes a good choice. I rely on her prudence and flatter myself that she will take for a husband only a man worthy of her. I thank my dear wife for having embellished my life and wish with my whole heart that hers will continue without clouds until the last moment of her existence."

Jessie Benton, who was now Mrs. John C. Fremont, remarked at the funeral of Alexander Bodisco, "Many who had had their jest at his marriage had now only a sincere prayer for the kind old Russian Minister."

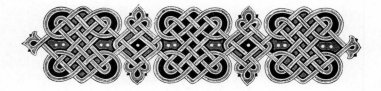

Perry's Flagship in Japan
courtesy of Arthur Walworth

on to japan!

A Russian landowner stood on a hill, his arm outstretched toward the horizon. To his son he said, "I own all that. All the land to where the earth curves away." His son replied, "Yes, Father. That is how far we must go to visit our friends and hear a bit of news from the rest of the world."

The great tracts of land that had made Russia unconquerable from the point of view of invading armies, Napoleon's not excluded, were a curse to the Russians in their efforts to unify the nation. Something had to be done about those enormous distances. Peter the Great had tried canals. Alexander I had begun the construction of a few highways. Nicholas I completed the Petersburg to Moscow highway. But more, much more, remained to be done if the Russian cities were to have commerce and communication.

125

Russian caricature showing the possible use
of the locomotive for mass-production in art

In September, 1834, Nicholas announced that he desired a railroad to connect St. Petersburg with Moscow. A young Austrian called Gerstner, who had participated in building the first railroad on the continent, was in Russia studying mines and manufacturing. He secured an audience with the Czar and outlined his plan—a rail network to connect the Volga River, Moscow, St. Petersburg, Odessa, Taganrog and the Black Sea. To finance this he suggested the formation of a joint-stock company, justifying such a monopoly because long winters and heavy snows would make railroad construction and maintenance expensive.

Kankrin, Minister of Finance, was bitterly opposed. He condemned railroads as "people riding aimlessly about the country spending money they can ill afford for a dubious thrill." He wanted high tariffs and no imports and saw railroads as a threat to his policies. He insisted that railroad building was not a government function and spoke violently against joint-stock companies.

Nicholas, torn between the need for better military and commercial transportation and the fear of financial disaster, had to compromise. As Pushkin had expressed it: "Russian roads are awful. But Russia cannot afford to risk three million rubles on an experiment." So the Czar approved merely an experimental fifteen-mile line between St. Petersburg and Pavlovsk. On Christmas Day, 1835, the company, backed by British capitalists, was given a charter.

On October 7, 1837, the first Russian railroad was opened. Gerstner imported three locomotives and the rails and carriages from England, and solved the snow problem by digging a trench on each side of the tracks, using that same dirt to raise the tracks above land level. Financially, the road was such a success that passenger fares were soon reduced to less than half that of the horse-driven stage lines.

But opposition mounted. The stage lines, which suffered from the competition, tried to prevent further expansion. Kankrin was quoting Adam Smith to prove that industrial railroads would bring economic disaster. There were the hysterical voices of those who felt moral and religious objections—a kind of opposition amply described by the single terse sentence of a Hamburg newspaper, "Many crossed themselves at the sight of those gigantic machines." Twenty years later an old woman in Ostrovsky's play *The Thunderstorm* still won applause by denouncing the railroad as "a fiery serpent which Godless city people had harnessed for the sake of speed. . . . When the serpent thought it was unobserved, it actually pawed the ground, a fact I noted from the corner of my eye."

But it was an agricultural crisis, with a resulting economic depression, that forced Nicholas to turn his eyes momentarily from the railroads. Hard times continued in Russia from 1839 to 1842, and Kankrin worsened the situation by raising the tariff on manufactured goods. Gerstner, seeing little hope of further expansion, went to America to study the railroads there, which were being built under conditions approximating those in Russia.

"The thing I want to escape from," he wrote, "is the system of England, where Stephenson's [the English inventor and founder of railways] thumb pressed upon a plan authorizes it. In the United States, no man's thumb print is better than another's. Each tries to surpass his neighbor, a rivalry out of which grows improvement. In England it is imitation; in America it is invention." Gerstner was impressed by the tendency of American railroaders to meet problems as they arose, rather than to try to foresee every contingency from the beginning. He liked, too, the refusal of

American railroaders to tolerate interference by the stockholders. "Despotism," he wrote, "is an important factor in American railway development."

Gerstner died quite suddenly in Philadelphia on April 12, 1840. Shortly after his death, a mission was sent from Russia to study the Baltimore and Ohio double-track system. Two members of this mission, Melnikov and Kraft, chose the men who were to become the true fathers of Russian railroads, Major George Whistler, and young Thomas Winans.

On February 1, 1842, Nicholas I authorized the Government to build a railroad from St. Petersburg to Moscow. That summer Major Whistler sailed for Russia and conferred with the Czar. Whistler brought his entire family, including his son, James McNeill, who was to begin his painting career at the Imperial Academy of Art.

Nicholas I, from the beginning, though not insensible to the commercial values of the railroad, had his heart set upon making it possible to transport soldiers between the two cities in one day of travel. When Gerstner had first presented a plan, Nicholas had said, "Is this the shortest possible route?"

"Not perhaps the shortest," Gerstner replied, "but the shortest commensurate with the towns that will be touched, and therefore the best possible route."

Nicholas took a pencil, bent over the map, and drew a straight line from St. Petersburg to Moscow. "That is my railroad," he said. "Build it that way."

This boldness, which could have been disastrous if the terrain between the two cities had been of a different nature, resulted in one of the world's most perfect railroads, phenomenally straight, 405 miles of rail to cross 399 air miles, meeting the modern railroad definition as "one that connects two important terminals, runs over level ground, and has no curves."

Whistler traveled by foot and on horseback over this route and reported that it was feasible. He estimated the cost at forty million dollars and construction time at seven years. His report urged that the rolling stock and machinery should be manufactured in Russia, thus avoiding excessive transportation costs and stimulating domestic industry. His recommendation of 5′5½″

gauge, however, brought a storm of protest from Russian engineers, because the Czarskoe Selo line had six-foot gauge, and because "a broad country ought to have a broad track."

Whistler's second report, devastating in its thoroughness, considered every aspect of the problem, from size and weight of the rolling stock, to the estimated speed of passenger trains. No Russian engineer dared raise his voice, and ever since Russian railroads have been constructed on a 5'5½" gauge.

Whistler then wrote to Ross Winans, to whom American railways owe more than to any other man. Winans had wandered into Baltimore to sell horses in the first year of the B&O's construction, had left off horse trading, and, among his countless achievements, had pioneered the coach with the long aisle down the middle, had planned the first eight-wheel passenger car, and had thrown out the ancient principle that the axles must move with the wheels and developed the "friction wheel" with outside bearings.

At the time Whistler wrote to Ross Winans, the latter was involved in an argument with other locomotive builders over the position of engine boilers, and had signed a contract to build twelve new locomotives. Unable to go to Russia himself, he sent his sons, Thomas and William. Whistler and the young Winans began work in 1843, using a factory at Alexandrovsky to produce machinery and locomotives. A machine shop was established at

The Russian Academy of Art

Kolpino and 2500 serfs were hired. This machine shop became as fundamental to Russian industry as Peter the Great's Naval Academy had been to Russian education. From it came the first true Russian engineers.

Ingenuity was required in getting financial backing from a Russian Government that was always in monetary distress. Whistler managed to do this, and, considering the infant stage of industry, the amount of rail equipment manufactured in Russia was extraordinary. Though the railroad was one of the most expensive ever built, costing fifty million dollars, its value to Russia, both in transportation and industrial development, was tremendous.

Whistler did not live to see the railroad completed. He died of Asiatic cholera in April, 1849, and the railroad opened on March 13, 1851, replacing four days and nights of horse-coach travel with 22 hours aboard one of the 2000 cars and 164 locomotives that the Winans* had built. Even in the years before its completion (1846-1851) half a million passengers and 13,500 tons of merchandise were transported.

Whistler's contributions to Russia, in addition to the railroad, included improvement of the fortifications and docks at Kronstadt, the construction of a great iron roof over the National Riding Academy, an iron and stone bridge over the Neva River, and a plan for the canalization of the Dvina River at Archangel. Awarded the Cross of St. Anne in 1847, no American in Russia, except possibly John Quincy Adams, was ever held in such high esteem.

England, France and Austria, frightened by the rapid rise of the Russian Empire, turned a cold shoulder to the East. Meanwhile, Russia looked more and more to America for help in technical fields of development. Steam frigates, steamers, corvettes, and war transports were ordered. The American Minister, Charles S. Todd, reported that of Russia's seventeen ships-of-the-line in the Black Sea, nearly all had been built in the New York docks

*The Winans brothers acquired a large financial interest in the Moscow Railroad, and subsequent contracts made their firm one of the wealthiest in the world. Thomas Winans married a Russian woman and returned to Baltimore, where his wife became popular through her extensive charities—during the hard winter of 1857 providing food and fuel for as many as six hundred indigent Baltimoreans a day. Today, the Winans mansion in Baltimore is called Alexandrovsky.

of Eckford and Rhoades. "The day might soon arrive," he wrote, "when the power of the U. S. and Russia, by sea and land, should be such as to command all the Nations of the Earth to be at peace."

Captain Crawford, the British Naval Attaché, after witnessing a review of the Russian Navy in the Baltic, stated, "At present we do not possess supremacy on the sea." As the Crimean War was to prove, Russia's naval power was still relatively weak, but although Crawford had exaggerated, he sensed, as all military men from this time on would, the enormous potential of both Russia and the United States.

From 1840 to 1860, American inventors, mechanics, and schemers and speculators bombarded the Imperial Chancellery and the American Legation in St. Petersburg with letters, packages and samples—plows, harrows, scythes, pitchforks, baby cradles, clocks, and treatises on alcoholism, spinal diseases, and so forth. Quincey and Abbot Lawrence, hearing of the "generosity of the Emperor," offered him a splendid investment in a Boston stock. Even the Secretary of the Treasury wanted to know if the "Emperor will consent to buy 10 million dollars worth of U. S. bonds to be issued soon." The other face of the United States was beginning to show itself, and it reached such proportions that Nicholas I was forced to issue a *ukase* forbidding "unknown persons from sending presents to members of the Imperial Government."

Yet Nicholas himself did not escape the lure of American products. When he heard of the remarkable exploits of the yacht, *America,* which had won "hands down" in competition with the entire Royal Yacht Squadron of England, he ordered an exact model of the schooner for himself. When Cornelius Vanderbilt visited St. Petersburg on his dazzling yacht *The North Star,* Nicholas ordered his naval engineers to reproduce it. The American dentist, Dr. Edward Maynard, the inventor of gold fillings, successfully repaired the Emperor's teeth and was honored with a medal. Silas Burrows tried to persuade the Russian Government to establish the magnetic telegraph throughout the Empire.

But while Russian-American relations became more complex in the fields of commerce and industrial development, diplomatic relations were being casually fulfilled by a group of Ministers who were "neither very important in themselves nor left any worth-while record of their experiences." This group, which followed Dallas, included C. C. Cambreleng (1840-41); Col. C. S. Todd (1841-46); R. I. Ingersoll (1846-48); A. P. Bagby (1849-50); and Neil S. Brown (1850-53).

Two minor events will perhaps suffice to show the level of diplomatic achievement of this period. Colonel Todd was elected a member of the Imperial Agriculture Society. One American Minister, a former Senator who was always excusing himself from keeping engagements on the grounds of "sudden indisposition," had a valet who reported to the American Consulate, "Oi'll not stay wid his igsillincy longer; oi've done wid him. This morning oi thought it was time to get his igsillincy out of bed, for he had been drunk a week and in bed most of the time . . . so oi took him by the collar, showed him his ugly face in the glass and oi said to him, says oi, 'Is thim the eyes of an invoy extryorr-rdinary and ministher plinip-oo-tentiary?' "

By the middle of the nineteenth century all the Western nations had tried, at one time or another, to open commercial relations with the Japanese. Only the Dutch, who occupied the tiny island of Deshima in Nagasaki Bay and were held in con-tempt by the caste-conscious Japanese, had been allowed to trade.

California shippers were interested primarily in the possibility of lucrative commerce, but they were also interested in getting permission for their ships to sail through Japanese territorial waters, since the archipelago stretched some nine hundred miles and interfered with the shortest routes to China. Whaling ships had long been curious about the possibilities of these Oriental waters, especially as the whale became scarce in the usual fishing grounds.

Two attempts were made by Americans to penetrate Japan in the 1840's. The Biddle expedition, consisting of two armed ships, sailed into Yedo, only to find itself surrounded by hun-dreds of small Japanese craft. No American was permitted to set foot on shore, and after ten days of futile waiting, they with-drew. In 1849, Commodore Glynn learned that sixteen American sailors had been imprisoned in Japan for nearly a year and a half. With an unarmed ship he sailed straight into Nagasaki Harbor and informed the Japanese authorities that if the sailors were not released the United States was prepared to take a terrible revenge. Two days later the seamen were delivered to Glynn— but no member of his party got ashore.

In 1851, another expedition, under the command of Commodore Aulick, set sail for the Orient. But before he could reach Japan he was ordered to hold up his expedition and await further orders. The American Government had decided that greater care should be taken both in outfitting the expedition and in choosing a commander. The choice, after a great deal of discussion, fell on Commodore Matthew C. Perry, son of Captain Christopher Perry of the Barbary expedition, and younger brother of Oliver Hazard, the hero of Lake Erie.

Perry's first act was to secure all the information he could about Japan. He knew that previous attempts to penetrate Japan had failed because of insufficient preparation and ignorance of Japanese customs. There were many books about Japan that were fairly accurate (the pre-Perry picture of Japan as a mysterious province of the moon is a convenient but false myth), but much of the printed material dated back to the Sixteenth- and Seventeenth-Century Jesuit missions. There were also men in America who had been there.

Perry therefore went to New Bedford to interview whalers and other seamen and learned a great deal from them about Japanese manners and customs. The technical information was also valuable, for although seamen might err on the legal position of the Mikado or the power of the Shogun, they would not be mistaken about tides, shoals, and the navigability of waterways. Perry's masterful handling of navigation in unchartered Eastern waters was due in part to information he acquired from these Yankee sailors.

The best book of the time on Japan was by Philipp von Siebold, a physician who had accompanied the Dutch Agent at Deshima many times into the interior, and who knew Japan better than any other European. While his book contained errors, it was Perry's most valuable source of information. Von Siebold himself offered to go with Perry on the expedition, but for reasons connected with Siebold's departure from Japan, Perry decided against it.

The Dutch had been allowed in Japan only on condition that they remain on the tiny island of Deshima. So rigorous were the Japanese in their attempt to prevent contamination of their own way of life, that the law prevented any Japanese subject from remaining on Deshima after sundown. Eventually these regulations were softened, and Dr. von Siebold made a number of friends among the more learned Japanese. From one of these friends he had received a gift, a carefully prepared map of Japan. When the Japanese authorities were informed of this there was a considerable uproar. Von Siebold managed to destroy the map and all correspondence with his Japanese friends, so as not to incriminate them. But, although he refused to admit anything under interrogation, the man who had given him the map committed hara-kiri. When it was discovered that von Siebold had also been corresponding with officials in Russia, he was expelled from Japan.

Perry therefore decided that the value of this man as an interpreter and technical advisor was not worth the risk of Japanese animosity. He took the advice and the many pamphlets which Siebold sent him, but steadily refused to take the doctor himself.

The Japanese hierarchy was in many ways not unlike that of Merovingian Gaul, the Emperor being relegated to spiritual affairs, with the Shogun a kind of all-powerful Mayor of the Palace. The confused nature of Japanese spiritual and temporal authority was a major stumbling block to a proper understanding of the country, and most historians of that period either thought along the lines of Guelph and Ghibelline or else considered *both* men to be Emperors and Japan a Dyarchy. The relationship between the rulers was of more than academic importance, for unless Perry had an accurate idea of Japanese administration, his mission would become involved in endless confusion.

Social classes in Japan presented an equally baffling problem. The first four classes corresponded to the royal ranks and the remainder to the lower estates of medieval Europe. As a sign of their semi-divinity, members of these four classes wore petticoat trousers and carried two swords. Next came the physicians, lawyers, scribes and bureaucrats. Finally, there were the merchants, the group with whom Perry and the United States had most in common.

It was difficult for the Americans to comprehend the low social position in Japan of the merchant class. They were the wealthy people of Japan, some of them owning entire towns and living in a state of luxury that only the highest of the nobility could aspire to. Yet even the lowest-ranking warrior in the Samurai caste would have disdained to soil his hands with trade; for beneath the social position of the merchants there remained only the hewers of wood and drawers of water, those most humble of laborers, and at the very bottom, those who scavenged and who buried the dead.

How to open Japan to trade (high-caste Japanese were not merely oblivious to the advantages to be gained from trade, but despised anyone even remotely connected with it) was a paradox for which Perry had to find some solution. According to his biographer, Barrows, Perry, first of all, had to "enter peaceably a nation which wanted to resist him by force. There he must negotiate on equal terms with a proud caste that disdained all foreigners as inconsequential scum. He must arrange a treaty with an unknown power that had opposed all such treaties, and this treaty must recognize the political equality of foreign merchants, a class which the Japanese higher powers felt degraded to mention."

Perry sensed that the only possibility of negotiating with the Japanese was to surround trade by Americans with all the pomp and ceremony that Orientals reserved for religious and military occasions. Instead of using force, instead of trying to frighten the Japanese or to appease them with humility, the Americans would send a trans-Pacific demi-god, enthroned in the interior of his sacred ship, and acting as the "Personal Ambassador, Lord High Admiral and Grand Panjandrum of His High Mightiness, the Exalted President of the United States of America." Perry decided he would surround his expedition and particularly his own person with all the mystery and mumbo-jumbo that he could think of. But he was careful not to let the American public get knowledge of his scheme, for fear they would destroy his mission with ridicule before it ever got out of American waters.

An impressive armada, including the *Mississippi, Susque-*

hanna, Princeton, Alleghany, Saratoga, Vandalia and *Macedonian,*
the greatest aggregation of steam vessels in any American expedition of this period, were to accompany Commodore Perry.
Knowing that an unprecedented amount of coal would be used,
he made an agreement with New York shippers Howland & Aspin-
wall to land adequate supplies of coal at Cape Town and Mauri-
tius, a precaution which later saved the expedition from disaster.

He chose dozens of gifts, mostly mechanical, including a
miniature train with a real locomotive and tracks, a complete telegraph outfit with plenty of wire and a technician to install and
operate it, and a daguerreotypist with all the necessary facilities
for making pictures. Perry had complete freedom, more than any
Naval Commander of the United States has ever had on a mission. Daniel Webster, the Secretary of State, wrote, "The success
of this expedition depends solely on whether it is in the hands of
the right man. It originated with him [Perry], and he of all others
knows best how it is to be successfully carried into effect, and
if this is so, he is the proper man to draft his instructions."

Considering the elaborate nature and far-reaching consequences of the Perry expedition, interest outside official circles
was slight, and also unfavorable. The *New York Herald* commented "Of course it's just a hydrographical survey of the Japanese
coast."

Perry's expedition had its troubles. When the time came to
leave, of the half a dozen ships he had expected, only the *Mississippi* and *Princeton* were available. At Baltimore, where he
stopped to load the presents he had selected for the Japanese,
less than half of them were ready, so he had to order them sent
on a later ship. In the Chesapeake, the *Princeton* developed such
"mechanical tantrums" that he had to put in at Norfolk, where
the difficulties were found to be so great that she had to return
to New York shipyards. Perry left orders for the *Powhatan* to
replace the *Princeton* and rendezvous near Canton.

The *Mississippi* sailed eastward to Madeira, down the African
Coast to Cape Town, and on April 6, 1852, encountered three
of the expected four ships waiting in the harbor of Macao. China
was suffering from a dynastic struggle known as the Taiping Rebellion, and strong pressure was brought on Perry to use his

American Expedition Under Perry
Landing in Japan

squadron to evacuate Americans from the danger zones. He flatly
refused to be deterred from his mission, and at Shanghai added
the *Susquehanna* and the *Caprice* to his fleet. In the Liu-Chiu
Islands he held a dress rehearsal of his plan of entrance into
Japanese waters.

It was midsummer of 1853 when he began the last lap of
his journey. On the afternoon of July 7th, Cape Idzu rose out
of the sea, and the squadron anchored for the night. On the
following morning the ships sounded their way into Yedo Bay
through a heavy mist that did not lift until they were near Uraga.
The waters were deserted, except for a few fishing vessels, which,
as the fire-breathing monsters, "the ghostly flotilla which was so
completely to upset their world," bore down upon them, scurried
out of their path. By noon the squadron was opposite the town

of Uraga, and from ashore came the sounds of war gongs, signal shots, and the cries of amazed villagers who had gathered on the banks of the harbor. Just before dropping her anchor, the *Plymouth* let out a terrific blast from her steam whistle.

In a short while the bay was swarming with small craft, some with as many as thirty Japanese looking very martial and inhospitable. The Vice-Governor of Uraga, with a Dutch interpreter, boarded the *Susquehanna* and demanded to see the Commander. He was informed that the Commander bore a personal message from the President of the United States to the Emperor of Japan, and that the Commander could give an audience only to the highest of Japanese officials, potentates of his own rank, Lord High Admiral. The Vice-Governor replied that the Americans must go to Nagasaki, the only port where foreigners could be received.

Perry had known this would happen and was determined not to make any compromise. He did not want to conduct negotiations under the eyes of the Dutch, as he would have to at Nagasaki. The Vice-Governor was therefore instructed that the Emperor's officials must come to Uraga, and, furthermore, that Japanese boats must not come near the American warships. When the Vice-Governor did not comply immediately, the guns of the *Susquehanna* were trained on several of the small craft, and the order was given again to the Japanese official. This time the Japanese officials signaled their boats to withdraw, and the Vice-Governor announced that he would consult with the Governor of Uraga.

A heavy guard was posted on the American ships during the night. The next day, while Japanese artists were making sketches of the huge warships, Governor Yezaimen, resplendent in yellow silk with gold and silver edgings, came aboard and was received by Franklin Buchanan, the Commander of Perry's flagship. The squadron, said Yezaimen, must leave Uraga immediately. The letter from the President could be delivered only at Nagasaki. The Americans replied that, if the Emperor would not come to Uraga, an armed guard would be landed and march to Yedo (Tokyo) to deliver the letter.

Governor Yezaimen was baffled. There was no precedent

for such arrogance and obstinacy. He stated that he must have further instructions from Yedo, which would require four days.

Captain Adams said, "We will wait three days, no more."

This was the first American compromise, since the distance from Uraga to Yedo was less than three hours by boat. But Perry had his reasons for allowing the Japanese time. During those three days he had small boats scouring the bay, charting it, taking soundings. The Japanese protested, but were curtly informed that it was an American law to make soundings and charts whenever a squadron was in strange waters, and Americans were bound by honor to obey the laws of their nation. The Japanese, who were not accustomed to Western manipulation of lies within the field of honor, withdrew.

On the third day, Governor Yezaimen returned and delivered a splendid talk full of equivocation, politeness, and suave misunderstandings. His talk was like a modern newspaper advertisement of Florida real estate and vacation sites, dwelling upon the advantages of Nagasaki over Uraga. After three hours of this, the Americans made their second compromise. An official was to come to Uraga, bringing formal certification of his rank, which must be equal to that of the Lord High Admiral and Personal Ambassador of the United States' President. The letter to the Japanese Emperor would then be formally delivered.

Governor Yezaimen was so pleased by this offer that he immediately cast aside his formal dignity and engaged in storytelling, drinking and gaiety with the Americans. He was astonishingly well-informed about matters outside Japan, knowing of the plans for building a canal at Panama, showing intimate knowledge of the recent Mexican War and the acquisition of California, and able to point out the location of such cities as New York and Washington. Though he had never seen steam engines as large as those on the *Susquehanna,* he understood their principle of operation. But, willing as he was to reveal his knowledge of the outside world, he remained silent about Japan.

All that night and the next day, the sounds of hammering and of movement ashore continued as pavilions were constructed and screens stretched along the roadway. At four the following afternoon Yezaimen came aboard the *Susquehanna* and announced that the delivery of the letter could take place. Above the village flags and streamers were flying. While military bands played aboard the *Susquehanna* and *Mississippi* and thousands of natives in gay dress stood on the shores, fifteen boats carrying one hundred marines and two hundred sailors in parade uniforms were lowered into the bay. Halfway between the ships and the shore the small boats hove-to while the guns of the warships boomed a salute to their Commander. Commodore Perry appeared, a tall, impressive man, standing at the gangway of the *Susquehanna* flanked by two enormous negroes with shining black skin. In front of him were two young Midshipmen in blue uniforms carrying rosewood boxes with silk tassels and gold seals. Perry was not a welcome visitor, possibly not even a respected one, but he was making certain that the Japanese would not dare to treat him like a Dutchman groveling for trade.

When Commodore Perry stepped ashore, the sailors and marines had formed an armed lane, and the procession marched toward the pavilion, where a crimson carpet was spread. Perry walked across it. Two of Japan's highest and most noble Princes rose ceremoniously to receive him. Perry made a deep bow. The rosewood boxes, one containing the Commodore's credentials, and the other, the letter from the President, were given to the Japanese. In turn, Prince Toda presented his credentials and a message for Perry. From that moment on the two Princes sat in absolute and impenetrable silence. Perry also sat in silence. All his careful preparations had overlooked the simple matter of how one withdraws from a ceremonial meeting, and how one overcomes the poise within the silent and unmoving men of the Orient.

When the silence became unbearable, Perry stated that he was departing for Liu-Chiu of the Okinawa group of islands, and Canton, but would return to Japan in the spring for the Emperor's reply to the President's letter.

Prince Toda inquired whether he would return with all four ships.

"Oh, probably many more," said Perry. "These are but a small part of the squadron under my command."

Then Perry made a blunder. "I am forced to return to China, because of a revolution there."

"What revolution?" snapped the Japanese interpreter.

"The Taiping affair. A revolt against the government . . ."

The interpreter, without even transmitting the message to his superiors, said acidly, "This is no time to talk about revolutions!"

A few days later the American squadron put to sea. Despite the mistakes which he had made, Perry had, without bloodshed, forced the Japanese to receive foreigners on terms of equality. He had placed the Emperor in a position where it would be impossible to ignore the United States, and had forced him to make a decision on a matter which he had hitherto disdained to consider. The squadron sailed to the Bonin Islands, and, although the British had a vague claim to the islands, Perry decided they would make a good coaling station and hoisted the American flag.

In February, 1854, with a larger fleet, Perry returned to Japan, and, after a massive display of power, concluded a treaty on March 31, 1854, which opened the ports of Shimoda and Hakodate to United States trade. Despite the great credit which Perry deserves, he could not have succeeded had the times not been ripe, for the Japanese by 1852 realized that isolation was no longer possible.

The history of Japanese-American relations owes an even greater debt to Townsend Harris, the first American Consul to Japan, who by 1859 had negotiated the Commercial Treaties, the basis of all American-Japanese relations for many years. Commodore Perry won the respect of the Japanese, but it was Harris who won their confidence.

While Perry was interviewing old sailors in New Bedford, an expedition was being prepared by the Russian government under Rear-Admiral Putiatin, with the purpose (Perry himself believed) of either forestalling the Americans, or, in case of American success, of reaping some commercial benefit. "It can be suspected," stated Perry's official report, "that Russia hoped a conflict might develop between the U. S. and the Japanese. In that case Russia had the choice of mediating or openly siding with Japan in order to demand commercial concessions as a reward."

Russian access to the Pacific depended on a weak Japan, or, if Japan were strong, on her friendship. The enormous Russian interests in Siberia and Alaska prevented indifference to anything that concerned Japan. The fact that the Americans and Russians arrived in Japan within a month of each other hints at more than mere coincidence and lends weight to the possibility that Dr. von Siebold had been a Russian agent. Nevertheless, the Putiatin expedition had been under discussion for at least five years before the Perry mission was authorized. One sure fact is that news of the organization of Perry's expedition hurried up the Russians into sending their own.

Ever since the failure of Rezanov to open Japan to Russian trade, the idea of establishing another mission there had stirred Russian interest. In 1843, at the end of the Anglo-Chinese Opium War, Russia began to fear that the treaty signed by China would so increase British influence that Russia might be frozen out of the Far East. Admiral Putiatin suggested that a naval expedition be sent to China to secure concessions and to investigate the possibility of maritime trade to supplement the overland trade through Kiakhta. The expedition should also make explorations along the Siberian coast, particularly near the mouth of the Amur. Kankrin, the Russian Minister of Finance, replied that reasons of state forbade any such expedition, hinting that an exploration of the Amur without Chinese permission might cause China to shut off the Kiakhta trade. The Russian-American Company, however, was instructed to make "unofficial" investigations of the Amur basin, and when it reported irresponsibly enough that the Amur was not navigable and the region unsuited for future expansion, the entire matter was temporarily dropped.

In 1847 Nevelsky discovered that the Russian-American Company had actually submitted its report without making any investigation at all. He appealed to Nicholas Muraviev, the new Governor of the Far East Territory, and was allowed to explore the Amur area. Nevelsky reported that Sakhalin was an island, not a peninsula as had always been thought, and that the Amur flowed through two broad estuaries, one into the Tartar Strait and the other into the Sea of Japan. From talking with the natives, Nevelsky discovered that they paid no taxes to the Chinese government and had no connection with it. Nevelsky promptly raised the Russian flag over the Amur, an act which nearly led to his court-martial, until Czar Nicholas I announced that wherever the Russian flag had once been raised it must never be furled.

Admiral Putiatin now pressed strongly for a naval expedition to delimit the Russo-Japanese boundary in Sakhalin. He was instructed to outfit the frigate *Pallada,* to purchase a small vessel in England, and rely on ships already at Far Eastern stations for the rest of his squadron. His destination, however, was still China, and exactly when Putiatin decided to sail to Japan is not clear. Putiatin states in his report that he first learned of the Perry expedition when he reached the Cape Verde Islands. But it must be remembered that Putiatin had already opened the gates to Russian-Persian trade and that, before going on this new mission, he was promoted to Vice-Admiral.

Russia wanted to get to Japan before the Perry expedition. That much is obvious. In June, 1852, Captain Lindenberg of the Russian-American Company, was instructed to make contact with Japan. His ship, the *Menshikov,* was not allowed to put into harbor.

A further proof that the Putiatin expedition had Japan as its final objective was the presence of Ivan Goncharov, the novelist, aboard the *Pallada.* Grand Duke Constantine, hearing that Goncharov had expressed an interest in Japan, arranged for him to go with Putiatin as a sort of reporter, and to write articles to increase the popularity of the Navy. Goncharov, whose interest in Japan was of the armchair esthetic variety, could have wished on himself no worse punishment than a trip around the world on a sailing ship; but Grand Ducal requests are not easily or safely refused, and he went "as a sort of reluctant Homer."

Goncharov, however, not merely provided an excellent account of the voyage, but was apparently a source of much amusement to the Russian Naval officers, who jokingly assured him that his instinctive fear of cannibals would never be tested because the *Pallada* was too unseaworthy to ever get as far as the Pacific Ocean. Little did they know how close to the truth they were.

The *Pallada* barely got to England, where, storm-battered, it put into drydock for extensive repairs. Terrible gales off the Cape of Good Hope and a hurricane in the China Sea followed, and the threatened outbreak of the Crimean War added new

danger to the mission. While Perry had been able to keep to a
fairly close schedule on his voyage, Putiatin, who had only sailing ships, knew that it would be impossible to plan any exact
time for accomplishing his task. When, after purchasing the *Vostok*
in England, his aide wrote that the two ships were to meet at
such and such a place and such and such a time "without fail,"
Putiatin added, "Of course there can be no such thing as 'without
fail,' but we will try."

Putiatin, whose ragged and weatherbeaten squadron eventually consisted of the *Pallada, Vostok,* and the corvette *Olivutz,*
obtained a supply of canned goods in the Bonin Islands, then
headed straight for Nagasaki, the port associated with centuries
of Western subservience to Japanese wishes.

The contrast between Perry and Putiatin is marked. Putiatin
knew almost nothing about the Japanese, and his manner was,
ironically, like that of a small businessman from an American
midwest town. The Japanese met his frank, bluff ways with a
smile, good-natured contempt, and endless negotiations. Russian
requests were ignored.

Russian Naval Officers in Japan

Goncharov recorded the typical Japanese answer to a question when he inquired how many people lived in Nagasaki. "It is not possible to say," replied the Japanese official, beaming. "Some days more, some days less. I hope you can understand that it all depends on the people who die and the people who are born, and who comes into the city, and who goes out of it. Yes?"

And these were the sort of replies that Putiatin received in his efforts to negotiate a treaty. At one such meeting, Putiatin delivered a lecture on the advantages of window glass, instead of the paper which the Japanese used to cover their windows. "We will bring you glass, and you can give us salt, of which you have so much more than you need." When the Japanese gentleman smiled, Putiatin, encouraged, added, "You use all your labor in cultivating rice. We could bring you rice from Java and you could give us some of the minerals in which you are so abundant. Life would be so much easier for your people."

It sounded very good, the Japanese gentleman admitted, but personally his entire attention was centered on the Russian clock which had been given to him the day before. "Would Putiatin be so kind as to explain the workings of the astronomical dial and the thermometer?"

This kind of resistance, perfect courtesy which simply refused to deal with matters of trade, baffled Putiatin. But behind it was the extremely clever Japanese mind, which knew that Japan was in a geographical position of extreme importance to Russia, and knew, too, that Russia was a serious threat to Japanese independence. As Goncharov summarized it, "Should they let us in or not? Since admission is forbidden but refusal so difficult, they try to be sly. They tell us, for example, that we have eaten all the pigs in Nagasaki, and there will soon be no more fresh meat. So the next day they charge us an exorbitant price for ducks. But we are patient, we pay their price, so what are they to do? Isolation is no longer their salvation, for it has stopped their progess . . . But who will they choose? Those shrewd, tireless traders, the Americans? Here we are, a handful of Russians and the Russian bayonet already shining in the Japanese sun. Already the Japanese perceive the writing on the wall. If they do not open to us, then it must be to the Americans, or if not to them, to the next who come."

Putiatin remained in Nagasaki a month before delivering his official letter from Nesselrode, and two months more after it had been delivered. Perry had accomplished more in ten days. Upon his return to Shanghai, where Putiatin learned that a Russo-Turkish war was practically inevitable, he decided to approach Perry with a proposition to join forces. This was on November 12, 1853, eighteen days before the Russian squadron in the Black Sea destroyed the Turkish Fleet at Sinop. Perry civilly, but decidedly, rejected the proposal. "Inconsistent," he wrote, "with our policy of abstaining from all alliances with foreign powers. Such cooperation cannot advance the interest of the United States, however it might benefit the Russian Emperor . . ."

Putiatin had no choice but to return alone to Japan. In December, after sending Lieutenant Crown to Russia to get further instructions in case of war, he returned to Nagasaki and found the Japanese a great deal more interested in Perry's activities than in the Russians'. He remained a little over a month, but with no success, except for a favorable exchange of gifts, clocks, pocket watches, vases, mirrors, thermometers, compasses, rugs and other household goods, in return for Japanese silk, sabres, pipes, lacquered boxes, and fans.

In Manila, the Russian squadron encountered a French warship, and there was a strained air about the meeting, both the Russians and the French fearing that war had begun and that the other might have definite news of it. When Putiatin heard that an English squadron was expected, he decided to get out of Manila. The decks of the Russian warships were readied for action, and the *Pallada,* which by now was almost unseaworthy, was prepared for scuttling in the event of armed action.

In Manila, Putiatin also heard news of the American success in Japan. The English-language newspapers stated that Perry had signed a treaty with Japan opening three ports to American commerce. Goncharov said it might be true, but he doubted it.

In March, 1854, as Russian troops crossed the Danube, Putiatin left Manila, determined to make one more effort to obtain a treaty with Japan and then to head for the safety of Siberian waters. The Russians spent Easter in Nagasaki, and the crews exchanged gifts of painted eggs which had been obtained from the

Japanese. A few days later Japanese officials began to show interest in what the Russians had been doing since they left Japan. "We stopped at Bataan," Putiatin informed them.

Maps were brought out. The Japanese studied them and said nothing.

"I could see," wrote Goncharov, "that they were very much put out by our visit to Bataan. It aroused their suspicions and their ancient hatred of the Spanish . . ."

Putiatin, without a treaty, sailed for Siberia. On May 29th, the *Vostok* was encountered, and her Captain reported that Russia was at war with Turkey and that relations with England and France were strained. A few days later when the bleak, desolate coast of Siberia at the mouth of the Amur was sighted, Goncharov pleaded to be released from his mission. Putiatin, who had been informed that a powerful Anglo-French squadron was at large in the Pacific, ready to strike at the Russians, and realizing that a civilian would be a hindrance in case of war, put Goncharov ashore.

The frigate *Diana* brought the long expected news that Russia was at war with England and France. Putiatin decided to dismantle the *Pallada* and transfer her crew to this new frigate. He decided that he would conclude a treaty with Japan at all costs, and, after scuttling the old ship in Tartary Strait, he sailed for Osaka, where he hoped to strike at "the nerve center of Japan." This time, imitating Perry, he paid no attention to Japanese protests, and demanded that negotiations be opened at once.

But on December 23, 1854, the day negotiations were to have been opened, an earthquake shook the whole coast of Japan, causing damage in Yedo (Tokyo), great ruin at Simodo, and the utter destruction of Osaka. The *Diana* was rocked by huge tidal waves, her masts shattered and rudder torn away. A storm that lasted for days followed, and the Russians were forced to abandon the ship and go ashore in Heda Bay. With the aid of many Japanese small boats, Putiatin tried to drag the *Diana* into the more sheltered waters of the bay; but when a white cloud, the sign of a new storm approaching, swept down from the summit of Mt. Fujiyama, the Japanese boats fled, and the *Diana* sank.

Putiatin would not give up. While his sailors were constructing a new schooner, the *Heda,* he had endless meetings with Japanese

officials, and finally, on February 7, 1855, concluded a treaty by
which Japan opened to Russia the ports of Simodo, Hakodate, and
Nagasaki. Japan also ceded Urup, an island in the Kuriles, to
Russia, and permitted the northern part of Sakhalin to remain
under Russian administration. It was an odd twist of fate that
gave Putiatin his hour of glory at the moment when his naval
force was shattered and his hands empty of gifts.

On March 15th, the *U.S.S. Powhatan* arrived at Simodo and
furnished the Russians with food and provisions, as well as information about the movements of British and French warships. Since
the *Heda* was too small to transport all the Russians, many of them
were given passage aboard the American schooner. Putiatin,
aboard his tiny Russian schooner, reached the Amur, after a narrow escape with a British warship. For four months he and his
crew trudged across Siberia. Finally reaching St. Petersburg, he
was made a Count. No man was more deserving.

By 1858, Putiatin was once more in the Far East, negotiating
a treaty with China, a tireless, jolly fellow who won by persistence
what he failed to accomplish with diplomacy. Though it is doubtful
whether or not he would have been able to conclude a treaty with
Japan had not Perry already opened the doors, one can feel certain
that no man would have tried more persistently.

CRIMEAN WAR

"What the Russian War was about, nobody knows to this day, but we all felt very much outraged at the time," a British Naval officer wrote.

The Crimean War was murky and inglorious both in political and military spheres. Men died by the thousands of cholera and the only reputations to be enhanced were those of Tennyson and Florence Nightingale.

Bismarck once remarked that Russia, to a soldier, was like a featherbed—easy to get into but hard to get out of. In September, 1854, Allied forces landed in the Crimea, and after victories at Balaklava and Inkerman, the besieged city of Sevastopol was finally captured in the following year. But the victory was hollow, since the Allied forces found themselves in a ruined, disease-ridden city, surrounded by deserts and empty wasteland,

149

several thousand miles from the heart of Russia. Mark Twain, who visited Sevastopol in 1867, wrote, "Not one solitary house escaped unscathed—not one remained habitable even. Such utter and complete ruin one could hardly conceive . . ."

Warfare was not confined to the Crimea. In the Arctic, British ships bombarded Kola, and in the White Sea, the Solovetsky monastery. Anglo-French squadrons attempted an invasion at Petropavlovsk, Siberia, and blockaded the Alaskan coast. The Aland Islands were seized and Finnish coastal villages destroyed. Yet, despite the almost global proportions of the war, and the enormous casualties, Russia was never seriously threatened, and by the time it was over nearly everyone was in agreement that it had been "much ado about nothing."

In the United States, the Crimean War attracted unusual attention, partly because of the religious-crusade banners which tried to drape the carnage with an air of holiness. Any war in which Great Britain was involved during the Nineteenth Century found the Americans cheering the other side. Added to memories of the War of Independence and the War of 1812 were new elements of Anglophobia, the thousands of Irish immigrants who were swarming to America.

The United States was peculiarly susceptible to military enthusiasm. Only eight years had passed since the siege of Chapultepec, and the fall of Mexico City had ended a war too soon for most Americans, leaving their militant patriotism still unquenched. They were eager readers—so great was their interest in the Crimean War that in 1855 one publisher brought out a periodical devoted to it, *War News,* a sixteen-page weekly.

A portion of the press was at first sympathetic to the Allied cause. But pro-Russianism soon swept the nation, brought on by a combination of factors. Southerners felt a natural affinity for Russia because of the similarities of their agrarian problems. In February, 1855, when Senator Cass of Michigan made an anti-Russian speech in the Senate, William C. Dix retorted, "In all her Southern advances Russia has touched desolation with the wand of energy, and it has brought forth fruit an hundred fold; she has made waste places bright and waving with ripened grain . . . Let

The Bombardment of Sevastopol in 1855

England first come with clean hands before making such a charge. To a strange point, indeed, events have come, if English aggrandizement the world over is alone the work of Divine Providence, and the growth of any other nation the unpardonable sin of international law!"

One cause of American pro-Russianism was the widespread, and very vocal anti-Catholicism of the period. An example of this is to be found in the books and articles of Charles Boynton, a Cincinnati clergyman who blamed Papal machinations for all the ills and evils that beset mankind. In the Polish rebellion of 1832, Boynton insisted that Nicholas I was "merely defending his home from the intrigues of a spy, the Pope," and warned America that all Roman Catholics should be deported. After the outbreak of the Crimean War, Boynton warned that an Allied victory would mean a Popish victory, and systematic destruction of all Protestant missionary activity.

Probably the sanest judgments of the war written in the United States were those by Thomas Dorr, a far-sighted man who was beginning to be worried about the future of the American Union. He regarded a republic as the highest form of government, but the most difficult to maintain. Sensing the dangers of unending territorial expansion, he bitterly opposed the policy of Manifest Destiny, and cited as examples the Romany Republic and the medieval city of Novgorod. "With Russian expansion," he warned, "all appearances of liberty have shrunk up and evaporated."

America stood at that same crossroad, and the dissolution of the Union or any attempt to preserve it by force of arms would result in another illustration of the rule that republics, unless carefully watched, turn into vigorous, centralized states, with the center uniting in itself the powers of the Federal and the State Governments. Negro slavery, to Dorr, was not important enough to be worth the risk of dissolution, which would eventually lead to strong central power and the rise of an empire. "Of those who say that unless Negro slavery in the South be instantly abolished, the Union ought to fall, we may ask what will then be the probable condition of the white men of this continent?"

Dorr's predictions were shrewd. He foresaw the time when China and Japan would be Anglicized or Americanized, perhaps a combination of the two. The Australian archipelago would become a federal republic. England would ultimately take Egypt, for she had to have it to protect her Indian trade, and France would secure the rest of North Africa. The Russian pan-Slav dream was a movement similar to that of Manifest Destiny in the United States.

Dorr put little confidence in Nicholas' outspoken affection for the American democracy. "His tolerance is evidently caused by distance and a desire to propitiate a nation, which he has the wisdom to foresee, will soon rival his own in territory and population, with elements of greater physical and political strength."

Despite pro-Russian sympathy, no American seriously expected the United States to enter the war. Ivan Golovin, former official of the Russian Ministry, and perhaps the first political Russian exile in America, sensed that United States sympathy was of "a harmless sort." He predicted that the Yankees would sell gunpowder to both sides, whatever their inner feelings might be.

Of the Americans actually involved in the war, most of them cheerfully transported munitions to the French and British, and would have been happy to do the same for the Russians had the geographical situation been reversed. Several American physicians and surgeons did serve with the Russian Army. Samuel Colt visited Russia, and shortly thereafter a Russian officer, who was disguised as Colt's valet, went to New York and successfully stored 50,000 muskets in cotton bales and took them back to Russia. But more frequently American traders and shipmasters took the course of least resistance, as did Captain John Codman on the *William Penn,* hiring out to the French and the Turks, preferring the latter because they paid more and were careless about receipts. Codman reported, "No one seemed to care for the Turks; for their ignoble retreat at Balaklava they were heartily despised by their friends as well as by their enemies . . . I have actually seen a mule and a Turk harnessed together to a cart, and a Frenchman riding upon it and whipping up the team." When Sevastopol finally fell, the city was sacked and the loot divided two-thirds to the French and one-third to the English. "The Turks got nothing, it being supposed that they owed the whole of their share in gratitude!"

Despite the amoral attitude of American commerce, there was a strong belief in the Russian Army that the United States contemplated direct action in the war. Tolstoy, in his "Sevastopol Tales," describes a conversation in which both Russian soldiers and sailors were convinced that the Grand Duke Constantine would bring the American Navy to assist the besieged defenders. But although Russian officials encouraged this belief, the most that was hoped, by Stoekl and Catacazy, Russia's diplomatic representatives in Washington, was to persuade the United States to outfit ships that would operate under the American flag.

Bodisco died in 1854, while Stoekl was enroute with supplies to Honolulu and the Bonin Islands to help the Putiatin expedition in its quest of a trade agreement with Japan. Upon his return to Washington, Stoekl took charge of the Legation, moving with extreme caution in diplomatic affairs, since he felt it was preferable to keep the United States friendly rather than to risk incurring disfavor by pressing too hard for assistance.

Catacazy, however, was more adventurous, and suggested to Nesselrode that an American ship be hired to transport a Russian cargo openly to a Russian port. Whether or not the ship reached port, the result would be favorable to Russia, for a British seizure would arouse ire in Washington. American diplomats were already angered by a speech of Lord Clarendon in the House of Commons, which caused President Pierce to remark in his Report to Congress, "We desire most sincerely to remain neutral, but God alone knows whether it is possible."

Stoekl, however, who felt that an Anglo-American war was likely, insisted that it was better to remain friendly than to gamble on petty gains through using the American flag to cover Russian cargoes. Russia's policy, he pointed out, must be circumspect. Sooner or later America would be drawn into the war, though she would hold off as long as possible, because of her present trade advantages. But American greed would push her into armed conflict—her eyes were already on Hawaii (then the Sandwich Islands), on Mexican territory, and on Canada, which most Americans considered to be rightfully theirs anyway. This report so impressed Czar Nicholas that he instructed Stoekl to use his own judgment in American affairs.

Marcy, United States Secretary of State, soon began to make overtures that convinced Stoekl he had correctly interpreted the American scene. In October, Marcy inquired how Russia would regard American annexation of the Hawaiian Islands, and Stoekl replied that he thought it would be a very fine thing. A few months later Marcy inquired how Russia would feel if the United States began trade negotiations with Persia. Russia would be delighted, said Stoekl, and the more trade the Americans obtained the better, since it would supplant British trade.

Sensing the danger that the war would bring to the Alaskan colony, so isolated from the Russian Empire, Stoekl had a scheme to protect it and bring pressure on British possessions in the Pacific. He proposed to have ships fitted out in California, with crews predominantly American, and to sail the ships to Sitka and offer the American sailors the chance of becoming temporary Russian subjects. But Nesselrode promptly refused to give his permission, on the grounds that it was a violation of International Law.

Then, just before the Christmas holidays of 1854, the British passed the Foreign Enlistment Act, and Stoekl immediately informed Marcy that Russia would now be justified in arming privateers and making foreign enlistments. Nesselrode again overrode him, pointing out that the privateers would endanger Alaska by using it as a base, and that for them to operate from Siberian ports would render them ineffective in the Pacific. Moreover, Great Britain was already in trouble over her Foreign Enlistment Act, as Mr. Crampton, British Chargé d'Affaires, had already been expelled from Washington for soliciting the enlistment of British subjects while on United States soil.

Nesselrode had, meanwhile, been carrying out his own plan to protect Alaska, by simply letting it be known that he was considering the idea of selling it to the United States. To prevent this, the Hudson Bay Company was authorized by the British Government to conclude a Treaty of Neutrality with the Russian-American Company. In the course of the war there were several violations of this treaty, but Alaska was nevertheless safeguarded from invasion.

Stoekl had been prompted to take diplomatic risks because he was losing hope of American participation in the war. He had learned by this time that the American politicians were using the Allied menace as a vote-getter among the Irish and anti-Catholics, but that Congress had no desire to get into a war. *The London Times* stated bluntly that pro-Russian sympathy in the United States was the result of the "ranting and vindictive fury of Irish rebels," and of American greed for Cuba and Santo Domingo. The United States was warned that "the fleet that can winter in the Baltic can summer in the Gulf of Mexico."

A few American politicians favored active support of Russia. Senator Gwin of California, lawyer and doctor, who had served Mississippi as a Congressman before making the trek to California, was an ardent Southerner and slavery advocate. He hoped to see California divided into two states, the southern half to be admitted as a slave state. In his campaign for reelection in 1855, he chose the Crimean War as a campaign issue, and ardently assured Stoekl that California could furnish the Russians with the fastest clippers and most daring seamen to be found anywhere in the world. Beverly C. Sanders, San Francisco merchant, offered his steamers—at a price. One enthusiastic supporter

offered Stoekl the services of 300 Kentucky Riflemen. An Oregon-
ian, Simon Marye, offered to drive the Hudson Bay Company from
Vancouver Island. A strange offer from a man who signed himself
Amicus asked authority to go to Europe to start a world revolution, to enlist Kossuth and Mazzini, and use the ambivalence of
the liberals to link their cause with that of the anti-liberal Nicholas
I. An Austrian immigrant, Franz Poulet, enlisted a large number
of recruits for Russian service. But when he was later arrested
for stealing spoons, it was discovered that he had used the enlistment racket to extort money from people, and then used this same
list of recruits as subscribers for a German-language newspaper
in Philadelphia in order to encourage advertisers to buy space in
the paper. This same man, who called himself "Col. Burgthal, late
of the Royal Hungarian Army," promised to deliver six million
German votes to George Dallas for President.

In the midst of such extravagant and untrustworthy proposals
and of confused political manipulations, it was difficult for Stoekl
to keep on a steady course. Toward the end of the War, in desperation, he finally overstepped the legal limits by ordering a war
steamer in New York to be used in the Pacific. The *S. S. America,*
flying the American flag, but with a Russian crew, headed for
Cape Horn. A British vessel tried to seize it at Rio de Janeiro, but
was bluntly informed that seizure would incur the risk of war with
the United States.

When Secretary Marcy was informed, he replied that there
was no need to worry until the British made an official complaint,
"In which case we will tell them frankly that it ill becomes them,
who have received so much help from American citizens, to complain because the Russians had a steamer built in this country."
The British chose to ignore the matter.

Despite the pro-Russian sentiment both among the American
people and in the American Government, the actual aid given
to Russia was very slight. Most important was the United States'
forcing Great Britain to acknowledge that neutral shipping was
not to be interfered with. Although this was done, not for Russia,
but for the benefit of American shipowners and commercial houses,
it was of inestimable aid to the Russians in obtaining supplies for
the prosecution of the war. The Russian merchant ships in Ameri-

can waters were interned—but authorities permitted their sale. British recruiting in the United States was forbidden. Spain was prevented from joining the coalition against Russia. Spain had offered to throw in her lot, in return for a guarantee of Cuba from the Allied Powers; but the uncompromising attitude of the American Government made France and England hesitate to pledge themselves to the defense of any Spanish possession in the New World. As a result of American firmness, a pleased Czar Nicholas announced that whatever attitude the United States chose to assume toward Cuba in the future, would be, as far as Russia was concerned, the right attitude.

The Crimean War brought increased trade between Russia and the United States. Following the death of Nicholas I, and after the Treaty of Paris, the United States made overtures to the new Foreign Minister, Prince Gorchakov, for trading rights on Sakhalin Island and the Amur region. The Americans were assured that they would be given every facility for trading. The new Emperor of Russia offered to arrange a direct Entente with Washington for parallel action in the Far East, with the result that Russian Admiral Putiatin and William Reed, the American Envoy to China, worked hand in hand in Chinese affairs.

All the criticism originally distributed among Nicholas I, Metternich and Castlereagh settled finally upon the shoulders of Czar Nicholas. Only Pushkin earlier made a partial defense of the Russian Emperor when he stated that while Nicholas had a great deal of the drill sergeant in him, he also possessed something of Peter the Great. Nicholas I was a conservative at a time when the world was spinning a dream of a golden age of liberalism.

His reign began with the Decembrist revolution and ended in the disastrous Crimean War. For this he earned the reputation of being "the *gendarme* of Europe." Born the year that Napoleon took command of the Army of Italy, the first twenty-one years of his life had been a period of incessant war and bloodshed, and the Decembrist revolt had warned him of what would happen if he did not rule with an iron hand. His faith shattered by the dubious loyalty of the Russian aristocracy, he had turned to men of the lower classes for his advisors and Ministers. Against his own family, his wrath was immediate and his punishment severe. "Always act," Nicholas told his children, his voice filled with bitterness, "so that people will forgive you for being Grand Dukes."

He founded the hated Third Section of the police to deal with political crime, something for which he had no patience and no forgiveness. He sarcastically instructed the director of that dreaded police group, "Understand, Benckendorf, this handkerchief which I now present you must be used to dry the tears of those unhappy people the law cannot help!" He was both a dictatorial and paternalistic man, devoted to the Russian cause and to the best interests of his country as he saw them. But it was during his iron-fisted rule, by subjecting the press, the universities, and the government itself to the scrutiny of his Secret Police, that the seeds of the revolts of 1905 and 1917 were sewn.

Yet, as one examines the rulers of that period in Europe, Nicholas I seems to have had good cause for feeling that the world could stand some stronger discipline. In France, Charles X had revealed his uncanny ability never to keep a promise. Spain had Ferdinand VII, who spent his years of exile embroidering an altarpiece for a shrine. In England, the profligate George IV had done everything possible since succeeding his misguided father to besmirch the concept of royalty.

Within Russia, meanwhile, Nicholas had brought about several important changes. He decreed that serfs could not be exiled to Siberia without due process of law, and that families could not be separated. He entrusted Speranski with the codification of the Russian laws, and for the first time these mysteries of two centuries of Russian autocratic whim were made clear and concise. It is only by contrast with the widespread liberal movement in western Europe, by his refusal to join the liberal parade, that Nicholas became branded as a tyrant with medieval ideologies. For Nicholas I followed, deliberately and with conviction, in the path of his ancestors. And, had Russia been victorious in the Crimean War, the judgment of historians might have taken on a different light.

At the beginning of the Siege of Sevastopol the defenders had decided that the best means of preventing Allied entrance into the

The letter of Capt. Pestchouroff to Col. Gowen regarding the latter's claims

harbor was to sink vessels across the channel. During the war nearly eighty vessels were sunk, many of them to escape capture, since the Russian Fleet did not dare contest the combined British-French-Turkish naval forces.

After the war the Russian Government wished to raise these vessels because they were a threat to Crimean shipping. So anxious to clear the harbor were the Russians that they were willing to give up not only half the value of the vessels recovered, but to furnish the gunpowder, chains, and whatever else might be needed.

Raising a ship is simple in theory—just hitch something to it and lift. But practical difficulties make the task almost insuperable. The English, French, and German engineers who were consulted said without hesitation that raising them was impossible, the ships would just have to rot away or be eaten by *teredo* worms.

Stoekl, however, had heard of an American army engineer, Colonel Gowen, who had raised the *U.S.S. Missouri,* sunk off Gibraltar in 1845. He urged Gowen to go to Russia and submit a proposal to the Grand Duke Constantine. Gowen, however, went first to Sevastopol to investigate, and became convinced that he could handle the job. His first contract with the Russian Government would simply have given him half of the value of the vessels recovered. But Gowen was a gambler. He made a second contract in which he would receive the total value of all of the ships, except the *Vladimir* and *Turk,* but guaranteed to remove three vessels which were causing particular obstruction by a given date, and if the three ships were not cleared by that time to pay 500 rubles a week on each of them until they were raised. Furthermore, he guaranteed to clear the entire harbor by April 1, 1862. Failure to do so would mean forfeiture of all the machinery that Gowen was bringing to Sevastopol.

Gowen began work on a small ship and promptly ran into difficulty. His plan was to use four floating caissons, two on each side fore and aft, with chains to be slipped under the ship's keel. The sunken ship would then be raised by steam winches. Aware that the weight of the ship would tend to draw the caissons together, he counted on anchors to hold them. But not only did the anchors fail—the utmost pull of steamers of 700 horsepower were unable to hold the caissons apart. So work was suspended until two more caissons could be constructed.

Gowen had to go several hundred miles inland for his materials. The new caissons were made of wood, with a covering of zinc for the submerged portions, with six watertight compartments braced and trussed with timbers to give the greatest possible strength and buoyancy. To raise ships of less than 1000 tons these caissons remained on the surface of the sea, but for battleships, which in some cases displaced 5000 tons, they were submerged and then raised by pumping the water out of the compartments. These caissons were forerunners of the modern floating drydock.

Since there were no chains in existence that could stand the strain Gowen proposed to put on them, he ordered the English firm of Brown, Lennox and Company to make chains, each link weighing a hundred pounds, with only $\frac{1}{16}$ inch play between the links. The English firm telegraphed Gowen that he must have made a mistake in his instructions. They had never heard of such a chain, and it was not feasible. Gowen replied that he wanted the chains made exactly as he had already specified.

Slinging the ships, embedded deep in mud and silt, was extremely difficult. Stretching chains through port-holes failed, because as soon as the chains were taut, they cut right through the wooden sides of the ships. Boring holes through the hull below the orlop decks produced an identical failure. So, channels had to be dredged beneath the ships, and the chains passed underneath the keels, an operation which was both hazardous and time consuming.

Once Gowen has solved these problems, work moved along swiftly. The first three ships were not raised in time to avoid a penalty amounting to 27,000 rubles. General-Admiral of the Navy, the Grand Duke Constantine (the younger brother of Alexander II), was so pleased at the progress being made in the harbor that he told Gowen to forget about the fines, and in addition offered to purchase the salvaged steamer *Elborous* for an additional 27,000 rubles.

"I returned to Sevastopol and received the money I had previously paid for fines," wrote Gowen. "Four weeks afterward I received a letter-demanding that I return to the Government 8200 rubles. I refused. When they paid me for the *Elborous,* they retained from it the 8200 rubles. I wrote several letters to the Minister of Marine and the Grand Duke Constantine, but never received a reply."

One of the communications, written when the harbor had been cleared, is as follows:
"His Majesty the Emperor thanked me for what I had done and said it was a species of Engineering that had no parallel. I had raised and removed over seventy vessels. My machinery and materials had cost me over 900,000 rubles. I therefore requested Him to forego the forfeiture clause in my contract. He replied that he would assist me, and gave orders for a commission to report upon the harbor and value my machinery and pay me money for it. The Grand Duke Constantine gave the same orders.

"The commission valued my machinery at 355,000 rubles, and reported the harbor clear for all practical purposes. Admiral Glazenapp recommended that I be paid in Government bonds. In St. Petersburg, the Minister of Marine said he could not pay me in bonds, and hardly knew from what appropriation he could take so large a sum. He inquired if I would like to receive it in ten installments covering ten years. No, I said, I want it all.

"Well, he said, you shall have it. You go and travel abroad for a month, then come back and I will have all your money ready for you.

Original handwritten letter
of Colonel Gowen to Admiral Lessovsky

"He then asked me how I had been used in the country. Quite well, I replied, with but one exception, eight gun boats, my private property, that the Port Authorities had prevented my selling for 16,000 rubles. He said, Write out your complaint and send it to me and I will send it to the Minister of Justice.

"On my return a month afterwards, I called upon him. He said, Why did you make that complaint? I fear now I shall have great difficulty in getting your money.

"He asked me if I would withdraw the complaint if I were paid the 16,000 rubles. I told him that I would. He paid me. I gave him a receipt. He told me I would never receive another ruble.

"I proceeded to Warsaw, saw the Grand Duke Constantine. [Now the Viceroy of Poland.] He told me he was sorry but that he had nothing to do with the Marine Department."

After other complications and a fruitless search for a responsible Government official who would hear his case, Gowen was forced to make a second appeal to the Grand Duke in his effort to recover the value of his machinery—355,000 rubles:

"The Grand Duke said to me: Gowen, I had a higher opinion of you than any foreigner who came to this country, but I regret much that

SCHEDULE of the RUSSIAN FLEET sunk in Sevastopol Harbour in 1854 and 1855, and Raised and Cleared by COLONEL JOHN S. GOWEN during 1858—59—60—61—62.

No.	CLASS.	NAME.	Guns	Launched	Sunk	Raised or Cleared	No.	CLASS.	NAME.	Guns	Launched	Sunk	Raised or Cleared
1	Corvette	Pyllade and Merchant Vessel	18	1840	1854	*1859—60	38	Cutter	Poepeshnoï		1835	1855	*1858
2	Frigate	Seizopols	60	1841	1854	*1860—61		(Lay in Sivernia (North) Bay.)					
3	Line of Battle Ship.	Ouriel	84	1840	1854	*1859—61	39	G. Brig.	Nearcue	12	1840	1855	Rsd. by Govnt.
4	Ditto	Three Saints	120	1834	1854	*1859—61	40	Ditto	Argonaut	12	1838	1855	Mrch. 18 1859
5	Ditto	Selafail	84	1840	1854	*1859—61	41	Ditto	Endymion	12	1839	1855	Mrch. 19 1859
6	Ditto	Varna	84	1842	1854	*1858—61	42	M. V.	Merchant Vessel			1855	not found
7	Ditto	Siliatria	84	1835	1854	*1858—61	43	G. Brig.	Jason	12	1850	1855	Rsd. by Govnt.
8	Ditto	Gavriel	84	1839	1854	*1858—61		(All lay in Karabelnia Creek.)					
9	Frigate	Flora	44	1839	1854	*1859—61	44	Transport	Liman		1850	1855	May 10 1859
(Nos. 1 to 9 sunk in the outer Line between Forts Constantine and Alexander.)							45	G. Brig.	Ptolemy	12	1845	1855	Feb. 5 1859
10	Frigate	Media	60	1843	1855	*1859—62	46	Transport	Kishinev		1851	1855	*1858
11	Ditto	Messemoria	60	1840	1855	*1859—62	47	Schooner	Smelai	16	1839	1855	July 30 1858
12	Line of Battle Ship.	Rostislav	84	1844	1855	*1858	48		Hospital Ship			1855	*1858
13	Ditto	Twelve Apostles	120	1841	1855	*1860—6.	49		Dredging Machine		1855		*1858
14	Ditto	Sviatoslav	84	1841	1855	*1859—62	50		Merchant Vessel		1855		*1858
15	Frigate	Kagoul	60	1843	1855	*1859—62	51		Prison Block Ship		1855		*1858
(Nos. 10 to 15 sunk in 1st inner Line between Forts Michael and Nicholas.)							52		Floating Light Ship		1855		*1858
16	Line of Battle Ship.	Maria	84	1853	1855	*1860—62	53		Lighter		1855		*1858
17	Ditto	Chesma	84	1849	1855	*1860—62	54-6		3 Prison Block Ships		1855		*1858
18	Ditto	Kraboü	84	1847	1855	*1859—60	57		Caisson (Dockgate)		1855		*1858
19	Ditto	Constantine	120	1852	1855	*1858—60	58		Floating Bath		1855		*1858
20	Ditto	Paris	120	1849	1855	*1858—59		(All sunk in South Bay.)					
21	Transport	Gagra and Merchant Vessel		1841	1855	*1858	59		Merchant Vessel		1855		Broken up
(Nos. 16 to 21 sunk in 2nd inner Line between Forts Michael and Nicholas.)							60		Ditto		1855		Broken up
22	Frigate	Koolevchi	60	1847	1855	July 7 1860	61		Ditto		1855		Broken up
(Lay in Mid Channel (Main Bay) and lower Masts above water.)								(Sunk between Fort Paul and Careening Bay).					
23	Man of War	Sagoodül	84	1843	1855	*1858—60	62	Brigantine	Ingone		1837	1855	
(Lay in Main Bay abreast and close to Fort Paul.)							63	Transport	Kouban	350 t	1837	1855	Nov. 1859
24	Corvette	Calypso	18	1845	1855	March 9 1859	64	Ditto	Kinburn	Sch.	1837	1855	
(Lay in South Bay, off the Old Admiralty.)								(Sunk in Careening Bay.)					
25	Frigate	Karvarna	56	1845	1855	*1858—59	65		Merchant Vessel		1855		Broken up
26	War Steamer	Elborous, Iron		1848	1855	April 30 1860	66-9		4 Ditto		1855		Broken up
27	Ditto	Danube, Iron		1851	1855	¼ Septr. 1855 ½ March 1860	70		Ditto		1855		Broken up
28	Ditto	Bessarabia		1843	1855	Feby. 30 1860	71-4		4 Ditto		1855		Broken up
29	Ditto	Gromonozets		1843	1855	March 5 1860		(Sunk in Main Bay, towards Inkerman.)					
30	Ditto	Odessa		1843	1855	April 14 1860	75	War Steamer	Granoë		1843	1855	Aug. 31 1858
31	Schooner	Lastouchka	16	1838	1855	*1859		(Sunk at Sivernia (Main Bay) near the Chesma.)					
32	War Steamer	Crimea		1843	1855	Dec. 20 1859	76	Corvette	Oreste	18	1836	1854	1860
33	Corvette	Andromache	18	1841	1855	*1858—59		(Sunk in Quarantine Bay.)					
34	War Steamer	Turk		1843	1855	July 31 1858		(Cask floating over Boom across Main Bay.)					
35	Cutter	Strella		1835	1855	July 25 1858	77	Yacht	Parijanka		1849	1855	*1859
(Nos. 25 to 35 sunk in Sivernia (North Bay) Main Harbour.)								(Sunk in Sivernia Bay, in shore.)					
36	War Steamer	Vladimir		1848	1855	Aug. 17 1860	78	Transport	Berezan		1851	1855	*1858—61
(Lay in Main Bay astern of the Koolefchi.)													
37	G. Brig.	Æneas	16	1842	1855	Sept. 30 1858							

mers & Ships with the dates attached were raised whole & lifted by Floating Docks.
(*) Denotes all those Cleared and removed by Blasting.

List of Russian Ships Raised by Colonel Gowen

you should come to me a second time for your pay. The Minister of Marine says you have been paid. Whom shall I believe, a Minister of the Crown whom I have known since I was a boy? Or you?

"I replied that if I had been paid, there was a receipt for the money.

"He said, Do you think I would doubt the word of a Minister of the Crown? This audience is at an end!"

Fourteen years later Gowen was still attempting to resolve the issue:

New York, March 14, 1876
"I have waited these long years hoping that the Russian Government would pay me ... do justice to me in a matter in which I spent six years of my life and my entire fortune."

Russia cannot be defended for her conduct in the Gowen case. But her machinations were due to neither internal corruption in the Russian Government, nor from any desire to cheat an individual of his rightful money. The constant shortage of funds of the Russian Government, the simple fact that so little money was available to pay for the countless things which Russia desperately needed, forced Russian officials to seek every opportunity, every minor loophole, to avoid not merely actual payment, but the embarrassment of not being able to pay.

Conversely, though one cannot help feeling sorry for Gowen, he was naive to the extreme and had no business entering into such a dangerous and unnecessary gamble. He lost, and, with the exception of a relatively minor item, he was never paid.

During the Crimean War, Alaska became a territory impossible for Russia to protect against British naval power. Kostromitinov, the San Francisco agent of the Russian-American Company, devised a scheme which would involve the transfer of all Russian interests in Alaska to an organization called the American-Russian Commercial Company, incorporated in California. Senator Gwin of California, however, quickly pointed out to Russian Minister Stoekl that Great Britain would not be misled by the "sale," and would refuse to recognize it.

This new scheme, which Stoekl quickly disposed of, became a straw in the wind that produced many odd results. The American newspapers heard rumors of the transaction and reported that there was talk of Russia's selling Alaska. Portions of the press which were hostile began to play up the story as proof of Russian bankruptcy. These rumors persisted until finally the United States Secretary of State, Marcy, thinking that perhaps Russia did wish to sell Alaska, approached Stoekl, who made a flat denial.

Stoekl wrote Chancellor Gorchakov that while he hoped the Americans would forget the incident, he was doubtful that they would. Once the idea of securing more land was planted in the American mind, it became irremovable and indestructible.

The directors of the Russian-American Company were aware of the danger to Alaska. British seizure of the territory would be a breach of the Monroe Doctrine, but it was doubtful that such a consideration would halt the British, or that the United States could prevent it. The directors therefore appealed to the Emperor to contact the Hudson Bay Company to see if both companies could not agree to mutual neutrality.

Meanwhile, officials of the Hudson Bay Company had been worried by the reports in American newspapers of the possible sale of Alaska. Fearing the Americans as neighbors much more than the Russians, and, knowing that refusal to grant neutrality would probably bring about United States possession of Alaska, the Hudson Bay officials embraced the offer from St. Petersburg. Thus, for a time, the Alaskan problem was solved.

But Alaska continued to be an object of concern to both St. Petersburg and Washington—the latter wanting to buy it, and some Russians wanting to sell it. Leader of this Russian group was the Grand Duke Constantine, who saw that, as the fur trade diminished, the Russian-American Company would face bankruptcy unless the Government extended a helping hand. Constantine realized that the Crimean War had not settled matters in Europe, and that another clash with England would be forthcoming. The strain on the Russian navy and military to keep Alaska protected would jeopardize any Russian war effort in Europe. He therefore submitted, in 1857, a memorandum to Chancellor Gorchakov urging the sale of Alaska to the United States.

It is important to remember that the traditional Russian policy of expansion was through acquisition of land on the heartland continent of Eur-Asia. Constantine was following that precedent. Gorchakov, however, was very cool to the idea of selling Alaska; but he could hardly ignore the Emperor's brother, so he asked Baron Wrangel, the former Governor of Russian America, to make an appraisal of the territory. Wrangel estimated the value of the Russian-American Company at a little more than $5,000,000.

In Washington, Stoekl was constantly being badgered with the problems of the Russian-American Company. He was even more concerned about the future. European standards of distance could not be applied to the Far West of the United States, where colonization of the Oregon Territory was going ahead rapidly and the American hunger for expansion had not yet been appeased. Stoekl was firmly convinced—as were most Americans—that the United States would eventually annex Canada. He foresaw an era when Alaska would cause "embarrassment and bickering" between the United States and Russia.

Having worked diligently to develop a Russian-American Entente, he could not believe that Alaska was important enough to Russia to risk American enmity. Indeed, the crisis was already at hand, because the Russian-American Company, worried about American penetration, had refused to allow American companies to send traders to Alaska. Since the Russian-American Company had offices in San Francisco and freedom to trade along the California coast, the Americans had a grievance which could lead to serious difficulties.

Stoekl therefore sent a memorandum to the Grand Duke Constantine, stating his fears of future entanglements. Constantine promptly reiterated his demands that Chancellor Gorchakov do something about selling Alaska. The Chancellor slyly replied that he believed the initiative must come from the United States, and that he would instruct Stoekl to be prepared to listen to any offer to purchase Alaska. Since the charter of the Russian-American Company would not expire until 1861, there were still three years before anything decisive could be done anyway.

The United States was busy digesting the vast territories in the West. The American eyes that looked northward toward Alaska were like those of a child gazing at a horizon of cookies and candies. The United States itself was beginning to feel violent disunity over matters of State's Rights and negro bondage. The Mormons were causing trouble by their unwillingness to permit other settlers free passage through their territory. Not long after Constantine received Stoekl's memorandum, the United States was shocked by the Mountain Meadows Massacre in which wagon trains from Arkansas were attacked by the Mormons and all but seventeen children out of the entire 120 settlers were murdered. President Buchanan dispatched the Second Calvalry under Colonel "Joe" Johnston to establish order in the Mormon country, while Brigham Young announced flatly that he would not allow troops to enter the desert country.

This brought another headache to Stoekl; for the Mormons had also hinted that they might be willing, under favorable circumstances, to withdraw from American soil and migrate to Alaska. Stoekl promptly asked Buchanan whether the Mormons would migrate as colonists or as conquerors, to which the President replied that he did not know and did not care—he would be so happy to get rid of them.

The Mormon threat came to nothing, but it was another of the many worries that made Stoekl eager to listen to any American proposition to purchase Alaska. In January, 1860, California Senator Gwin called at the Russian Legation and announced that President Buchanan was interested in Alaska, but he warned Stoekl that all negotiations would have to be kept secret and carried on only through the Assistant Secretary of State. President Buchanan did not want the adamantly opposed Secretary Case to know about the negotiations. Gwin believed the President was willing to go as high as $5,000,000. Since this figure matched Baron Wrangel's estimate of the value of Alaska, Stoekl was indeed interested. Furthermore, the Russian-American Company was in grave financial difficulties; its shares were now selling well below their value at the time of the appraisal.

The declining fur trade had forced the Russian-American Company into new ventures. An attempt to sell Alaskan lumber had resulted in disaster. The Russians also lost money in a desperate scheme to sell Alaskan ice in California. Ironically, and as an indication of the poor management of Russian business ventures, at this same time a New England Yankee was making a fortune transporting Massachusetts' ice to India. A Soviet historian summed up the situation: "In the first period, up to 1821, there were a lot of furs, but no buyers. In the second period, up to 1838, there were more buyers and less furs. From 1838 to 1860 the cash box was empty."

Then came the ominous rumblings from extremists of both the North and South. There was "Bleeding Kansas," the "Underground Railroad," the Abolitionists. An uneasy calm before the storm set in as both sides sat back to digest the impossible Missouri Compromise. Senator Gwin's offer to purchase Alaska was forgotten. Although the Grand Duke Constantine continued to press for the disposal of Alaska, the impending Civil War, then the War itself with its mounting financial pressures, erased all American interest in territorial expansion, while the North and the South concentrated on one thing—how best to chop each other up.

"seichas!"

On the eve of the Civil War, if the Russians had wished to ally themselves with the people most akin to themselves in political theory and social institutions, they would have chosen the Secession States. Remarkable similarities existed between the Russians and the Southerners in the United States. The descriptions of life in *Anna Karenina* and *War and Peace* cannot fail to impress a Southerner with their approximation to *ante bellum* life below the Ohio. And a Russian reading today the recaptured flavor of the Southland in Stark Young or George Washington Cable, or even the sentimental novels of Augusta Evans, feels the same nostalgia that grips an expatriate from Kentucky or the Mississippi delta.

In Russian art, most of all in Russian music, foreigners have found the expression of a sad and disconsolate race. "Russians," wrote the Grand Duchess Marie, "pass quickly from the highest

168

enthusiasm to complete dejection and mistrust. They go the whole way, forgetting all moods preceding and opposite."

But does Russian music contain any songs of greater sadness than *Massa's in the Cold, Cold Ground* or *Nellie Was a Lady?* Or the chants sung by negroes in bondage, *Deep River* and *Goin' Home?* The gay, rollicking Russian *Trepak* is mirrored by *Turkey in the Straw* and *Old Dan Tucker*. The Cossacks who fled from serfdom to the Turkish frontier and the steppes of Central Asia gave us gay melodies, and the Southerners who went into Indian country and the Far West sang of Barbara Allen and Lord Lovel. The world has grown familiar with the magnificent *a capella* of the Kedroff Quartet and Serge Jaroff's Don Cossack Chorus. But this kind of singing had long been known to Americans in the rich harmonies of groups like the Fiske Jubilee Singers.

America has had as much and as great folk-music as Russia or any other country. The ballads of the Texas plains, the mountain music of Virginia and the Ozarks, the songs of the Mississippi, the negro spirituals, were only a part of the American scene. But where the native melodies of Slavic countries had been founded on a bedrock of time, American songs sprang from ephemeral epochs, banners of sound flung recklessly into the sky by a nation of people who were too busy to listen. One wonders whether American music, no matter how high its quality, will ever hold in the hearts of its people the place reserved among Russians for the *1812 Overture* or the *Marche Slave*. Respect for America's music has been increasing daily with the influx of foreigners who were among the first to applaud it. New citizens have simply made America aware of her inherent musical strength. It is not difficult to understand, therefore, why *Porgy and Bess* was written by George Gershwin, a Jew, the *American Negro Suite* by a Dane, and the *New World Symphony,* with the somber dignity of its *Largo* movement, by a Czech.

The Russian and the Southerner had much in common. It was no coincidence that the favorite author of Czar Nicholas I, Sir Walter Scott, was also the novelist most widely read in America. De la Rochefoucauld found in the South "a taste for reading more prevalent among gentlemen of the first class than in any other part of America." One needs only to read Turgenev to

A Russian Village in Central Russia

realize that the same sort of comparison applied to the Russian aristocracy, who were among the most insatiable readers in Europe. Both in Russia and in the South, gracious living meant not only the cultivation of the mind, but also the cultivation of manners. Mark Twain found among Russians the same innate courtesy that he recognized among the Southern planter class. "The French are polite," he wrote, "but it is often mere ceremonious politeness. A Russian imbues his polite things with a heartiness, both of phrase and expression, that compels belief in his sincerity." What appealed to Mark Twain most about Russia was the spacious life of her country gentlemen, so reminiscent of home. Russians had a hospitality as proverbial throughout Europe as that of the South throughout the United States.

Both had a passionate concern with good food and good conversation, beautiful women, and fine horses. Even Russian architecture affected a colonial style somewhat similar to the American. There was a country estate near Novgorod, with its wooded mansion and wide lawns, strikingly like plantations on the James or the lower Yazoo Mississippi. Save for the language and the colored servants, a Russian dining south of the Ohio

"Tea drinkers" in Russia
in the 1860s

could have considered himself in the predominately Russian atmosphere of Lake Ilmen.

Even the languages themselves developed similar methods of expression which reflect the leisurely life of those spacious days. Ask a Russian today who has spent part of his life on a great estate any question involving the passage of time, and, whether prince or peasant, he will reply, *"Seichas!"* The Russian-English dictionary will define this as "immediately." Colloquially, it means nothing of the kind. It has the precise meaning of "Directly!" when spoken by an American Southerner, meaning in half an hour, half a day, or perhaps next week. For neither the Southerner nor the Russian have the slightest conception of the value which the grim world of commerce has placed on punctuality.

In one regard, however, Russians and Southerners of the time differed. A Russian aristocrat was born, lived, and usually died on the same estate, and Russian manor houses were seldom sold. In the old South, prevailing belief notwithstanding, it was rare for a plantation to remain more than one generation in the same family. The effects of tobacco and cotton crops upon the soil caused the planters to move on. Southern belief in the hereditary concept of estates began generally in the era following the Civil

War when the planters had to remain on the same land because they could find no buyers. Washington was born at Bridges Creek in Westmoreland County, but his name is associated with Mount Vernon. Robert E. Lee was not born at Arlington but at Stratford. Jefferson Davis was born at Fairview, Kentucky. How long has it been since Rosewall was occupied by a Page, Westover by a Byrd, or Brandon-on-the-James by a Harrison? In actual fact the South was one of the most peripatetic civilizations ever known, unmatched for its roving nature until the automobile spread this tendency across the whole continent.

Despite this particular difference, the plantation and the Russian manor house produced a people alike in their vices and virtues. The men of each were impetuous and daring, willing to stake everything at cards, on a horse, or in a duel. Scarcely a Southern family existed that could not name at least one member fallen on the field of honor. In Russia, two of her greatest poets, Pushkin and Lermontov, met death under these circumstances. Russian gentlemen, bred in the traditions of a land gentry, possessed no ability to conserve themselves physically or financially. The penniless Russian nobleman became as proverbial as the bankrupt American planter, yet he somehow managed to hold onto his land. In good years the Southern planters would invest all their capital in additional slaves, and if the next season brought no market for cotton or tobacco, slaves and plantation and all fell under the auctioneer's hammer. In Russia, similarly, two-thirds of all private serfs were heavily mortgaged.

In the institution of labor in bondage these two peoples came closest together, yet neither recognized the essential identity of the two systems. Russians were horrified by slavery in the United States, comparing it unfavorably to their own benevolent system in which the serfs could not be beaten to death or separated from their families. Yet, in truth, save for the color line, there was little difference.

Publication of Stowe's *Uncle Tom's Cabin* and Turgenev's *Sportsman's Sketches* in 1852 brought both systems to the attention of the world. Mrs. Stowe's work created much more of a sensation, however, even in Russia.

Since so much blame has been heaped on Russia and the

United States in regard to slavery, it is worthwhile to remind the reader that white serfdom existed in almost every nation until the Nineteenth Century. The French Revolution of 1789 brought it to an end in France, and between 1807 and 1816 provided impetus for similar reforms in Spain, in southern Italy, and in most of Germany. In the remainder of Germany and the Hapsburg dominions, serfdom was abolished by the Revolution of 1848. Remnants of serfdom in America were not abolished until 1833, when the Patroon System in New York State finally ended. As for slavery, the British Empire abolished it in 1833, the French colonies in 1848, and the Dutch East Indies between 1859 and 1869. It continued in the Argentine until 1853; Venezuela, 1854; Peru, 1856; and in Brazil until 1881.

Legally, there were important differences between serfdom and slavery, but in practice they were much the same. In Russia the protective statutes that benefited the serfs had been unenforced for decades. In America the slave laws were harsh, but common sense and humanity had modified them. American law stated: "No slave has any right that a white man is bound to respect." The Russian law stated: "The serf has no property rights which can be effectively defended against his master." Obviously, there were cases of brutality to negroes in America, but everyone who has read *The Brothers Karamazov* will also recall the story of the serf child torn to shreds by hounds loosed by the master who had seen the child throw a stone at them.

Literature has emphasized one basic evil of the Russian system not present to any extent in America. Russian novels are filled with absentee landlords who left the management of their estates to brutal German overseers.

In *Anna Karenina,* Levin was an exception with his love for the land, working side by side with his peasants in the fields. Vronsky enjoyed rural life, but it was only an interlude between the years in St. Petersburg and the Turkish war. Old Prince Bolkonsky, in *War and Peace,* lived on the land because he was too cantankerous to live anywhere else. Still, the importance of absentee landlords was overemphasized, and in Russia estates with the landlords highly interested and personally directing their activities were fact far more than fiction.

In the American South, absenteeism was practically non-existent. There were few large cities and few enough enticements. Periodic visits to such centers as Richmond, Atlanta, Montgomery, were a late development in the plantation system. Wherever absenteeism existed at all, it was a matter of health, not pleasure, in the malarial sections of Louisiana and South Carolina. Charleston alone could be compared with St. Petersburg or Moscow as a center of social life. In 1790, with a population of 15,000, only half of whom were white. Charleston boasted a "semi-public library, thriving bookstores, excellent newspapers, mantua makers and milliners in touch with the latest Paris fashions, a thronged race course, dancing assemblies, and easy-mannered men's clubs." Also, there were a good many so-called "Boston clubs," where planters could indulge themselves, at cards or other games.

Without doubt, Southerners had reason to be angered by Abolitionist propaganda, which, for example, pictured Charleston as inhabited by lustful, brutish men, a mosquito-bitten filthy place where women flailed negroes in public. Albert Beveridge, while research on his biography of Lincoln was in progress, wrote, "The Northern atmosphere in which I was brought up was well-nigh lurid; and the things about the South that all of us were told by the politicians, and which all of us took for granted, formed a very tissue of hatred." After reading a piece of Abolitionist propaganda, Senator Beveridge remarked, "If I had lived in the South, and had a wife, a mother, sister or sweetheart, and anyone had sent such an infamous thing to me, I would have felt like taking the first train north, shooting the wretch, and taking the consequences."

In Russia, Tolstoy had a similar great awakening when he investigated Russian social history before writing *War and Peace*. When he received countless letters criticizing him for not portraying the brutality and cruelty of that period, in 1869 he wrote an appendix for *War and Peace* (for obvious reasons omitted from the Soviet edition, but also strangely omitted from English translations). In this epilogue Tolstoy states that he had not included the stories of serfdom and wife-beating usually associated with the period before the liberation for a very good reason: "In studying letters, memoirs, and old mementos I failed to find these horrors, this lawlessness and brutality, in any significant degree. I can still find them today, or at any time, if I look for them!"

But aside from all moral issues, slavery and serfdom were wasteful institutions in an era when profits were becoming the sole ambition of the rising bourgeoisie. From the day that the Mississippi planter found that he could hire Irish immigrants more cheaply than he could provide for his own slaves, slavery was doomed. And when Russian landowners found that free serfs would work for less than it cost them to support them, serfdom was doomed. Thus, the two systems were destroyed because they were no longer economically feasible. The pity of it is that the humanitarian idealism which first prompted the drive toward Abolition, was, particularly in the United States, twisted by extremists of both sides into a kind of propaganda that brought about a hatred and bitterness that still smolders in many hearts.

Russia had never known a "color line." On the shores of the Black Sea, in the Georgian principality of Abkhazia, colored people, descendants of Africans, had settled in the Eighteenth Century. By 1861, they wore Georgian dress, spoke a Georgian dialect, and were members of the Russian Orthodox Church. They were free men with full rights and privileges.

Peter the Great once received as a gift a young "Abyssinian" whom he named Hannibal. Peter had the child baptized and stood as his Godfather. Hannibal later became a General in the Imperial Army. He was an ancestor of Pushkin, whose daughter married into the Royal Family of Nassau and in turn the ancestors of the family of Milford-Haven. Hannibal's son became an Admiral in the Imperial Navy.

From that time on wealthy Russian families began to take young negro boys into their households. Family portraits of Russian aristocracy often included a colorfully dressed negro. In St. Petersburg, giant negroes in Oriental costumes guarded the Emperor's audience chamber. General Cassius Clay, the American Minister to Russia in the eighteen sixties, remarked that the "Nubians were so black that charcoal would have made a white mark on them." Andrew D. White, on the occasion of the wedding of the Grand Duchess Xenia in 1894, with Peterhof Palace crowded to capacity, attempted to slip outside to get a breath of

Russian sketch of Ira Aldridge,
the American negro actor

air. Unable to find a door through which he could make an inconspicuous exit, he was amazed to find himself confronted by a Tennessee negro of the palace guard, who said, "If you please, suh, you kin git out de crowd, suh, troo dis yeah doah!"

Colored circus and cabaret performers, actors, boxers, jockeys and trainers, all from America, flocked to Russia, flourished there, and left numerous *café-au-lait* descendants. A prime example of the success of an American negro in Russia was Ira Aldridge, the great Shakespearean actor, who, after playing in London at Covent Garden, made a tour of Russia, appearing in St. Petersburg, Moscow, Novgorod, Odessa, and Kiev. After his performance of *Othello,* St. Petersburg students unhitched the horses from his carriage and pulled his carriage through the streets themselves—the greatest compliment a Russian can give to an actor. He then married a Swedish lady, Countess Amanda Pauline Brandt, became an honorary member of the Imperial Dramatic Society of Riga, and was decorated by the Czar. His other honors included a gold medal from Kaiser Wilhelm of Prussia.

Minister Clay made the following report:

"I could not apply in the usual way to have Captain Chester, a colored American citizen, presented to His Imperial Majesty, as there was no precedent, and I did not know how His Imperial Majesty would be disposed to act. . . . The Emperor sent an invitation to Captain Chester to assist in the review of the Imperial Guard, which he did, riding around with His Imperial Majesty's Staff, and taking lunch at the winter-palace with the Staff Officers and a portion of the Imperial Family. . . . I have made these facts known to you, as I regard the affair of some importance. We have four million of colored citizens. They are with us, and of us, for good or evil. I think it is the duty of all good citizens to try to elevate the African race in America and inspire them with all possible self-respect; and prepare them for the ultimate influence which they must sooner or later have upon the political and economic interests of the United States."

It was not until after the Civil War that American negroes began to appear in any numbers in Russia. The Fiske Singers delighted St. Petersburg audiences in 1895. Allie Burgoyne, remembered by New York theater-goers for her role in *Blessed Event,* went to Russia in 1902 as a dancer, and studied dramatic acting in St. Petersburg. Georgette Harvey of the New York stage appeared in St. Petersburg in 1914, where she played at the famous cabaret Villa Rodé. After the revolution in 1918, as scores of Russian exiles swarmed into western Europe, among them appeared several negroes who were Russian subjects, yet descendants of American negroes, and with odd names such as Misha Smith, Tania Johnston, and Sasha Bruce.

Nor were they all entertainers and servants. Two famous Moscow restaurants, the Yar and the Aquarium, were owned by a man called Thomas, another negro who married a Russian. Michael Egypteos, in 1862, entered the Naval Technical College of Kronstadt, and reached high rank. The Imperial Navy owed him a great deal, for he supervised the construction of many warships.

Mention is made of these negroes not to try to make the reader feel that there were a great many of them in Russia, but to make it more apparent as to why the Russians could neither understand nor have any sympathy for slavery. It was incomprehensible to them that men should remain in bondage simply because of the darkness of their skins or a presumed difference in blood. And it was because of this, for all their similarity, that the Russian noble and the Southern planter could never come to any real understanding. This fact alone may also underlie the reason why slavery presented a more serious problem to America than serfdom to Russia.

Although there were many more Russian serfs than American slaves, the political organization of the United States also permitted a wider range of difficulties. While Alexander II in Russia had merely to make the decision to free the serfs and appoint a commission to study the best means of accomplishing it, republican America cast thousands of conflicting voices into the arena, and, as is too often the case among men who cannot reach prompt agreement, their tempers began to flare. The prediction of Metternich that Government on the American pattern meant a perpetual tour-de-force seemed to ring with truth.

Political parties were crumbling and new alignments were being formed. Among these new groups was one calling itself the Republican Party, and in 1854 it won a staggering victory in the Congressional Election. During this period of confusion only the radicals knew what they wanted. The confusion of the Conservatives was shown in a letter written by Lincoln, still an obscure Illinois lawyer, in which he stated that he did not know what he was politically. He had always regarded himself as a Whig, but he was being labeled as an Abolitionist, despite the fact that he had never favored Abolition. He opposed the extension of slavery, but he had repeatedly denounced the Abolitionists as demagogues. Of one thing he was certain, he was not a member of the Know-Nothing group. "As a nation we began by declaring that all men are created equal. We now practically read it, All men are created equal except negroes. When the Know-Nothings get control it will read, 'All men are created equal except negroes and foreigners and Catholics,' " wrote Lincoln. "When it comes to this, I shall prefer emigrating to some country where they make no pretense of loving liberty—to Russia, for instance, where despotism can be taken pure, and without the base alloy of hypocrisy."

That Lincoln understood the determination of the South to hold to its position was revealed when he wrote, "After freeing ourselves from King George, we announced the principle of

equality for all. But now, when we are fully fed and have no fear of being made slaves again ourselves, we have become so greedy to be masters that we declare the very reverse of this doctrine to be true. . . . The Czar of Russia would be readier to take off his crown and declare all his subjects free, than our American gentlemen would be to set the slaves at liberty."

Though both of Lincoln's remarks reveal an uncomplimentary attitude toward Russia and the Russian Emperor, at this very moment Alexander II was choosing the path of emancipation that Lincoln was to take unwillingly a few years later. For although Alexander did not take off his crown, he did declare all his subjects free, and did it honestly, paying the masters for their serfs, and without bloodshed anywhere in the vast empire.

On March 3, 1861, the bells of every church in the Russian Empire proclaimed the signing of the Emperor's Edict of Emancipation, after five years of consultation, investigation, and compromise. Twenty-six million men were given their freedom.

Speaking in Washington a year and a half later, General Cassius Clay, American Minister to Russia, thrilled an audience with his description of that event: "I think I can say without implication of profanity or want of reverence that since the days of Christ Himself, such a happy and glorious privilege has not been reserved to any other man to do that amount of good, and no man has ever more gallantly or nobly done it than Alexander II of Russia."

When Alexander signed the Edict of Emancipation, the American Union was already dissolved. For a month Jefferson Davis had been President of the Confederacy. War was not always regarded as inevitable, and many men felt that if war was the only way to preserve the Union it would be wisest to bid the South a reluctant Godspeed. More and more forts and arsenals were going over to the hands of the Secessionists, and the South was strengthening its position. The President would not act and the President-Elect could not.

Fort Sumter, however, under the command of Major Robert Anderson, refused to recognize the Confederate Government at Montgomery. In March the new President, Abraham Lincoln, was inaugurated and spoke of compromise, but the South refused. March faded into April, with food and munitions at Fort Sumter dwindling. Then early one morning a shell from Fort Johnson looped high over Charleston Harbor and fell on the ramparts of Sumter. As Fort Moultrie joined in the bombardment, Major Anderson gave the order to return their fire, and the Civil War had begun.

CHAPTER TWELVE

RUSSIAN-AMERICAN "entente"

Stoekl, the Russian Minister in Washington, two days before the secession of Georgia, sent a dispatch to his Government. "Great Britain," he wrote, "seems about to enjoy a stroke of fortune rare in history. She alone will profit by the destruction of the United States, for it will be fatal to the rest of the world." Stoekl, concerned for still more personal reasons, since his wife was an American, skated close to the edge of diplomatic impudence by pleading with the Southern leaders to compromise. But after the attack on Sumter he followed a rigid line of fidelity to the Lincoln government, breaking off all correspondence with his many Southern friends.

Alexander II and Chancellor Gorchakov were firm in their belief that the Union must be preserved. Gorchakov dispatched a plea to the North, through Stoekl, in an attempt to prevent the destruction of institutions which had been able to reconcile union and liberty. "The struggle dare neither be indefinitely prolonged nor lead to the total destruction of one of the parties. Sooner or later it will be necessary to come to some settlement. The American nation would, then, give proof of high political wisdom in seeking in common such a settlement."

Another dispatch from Gorchakov to Stoekl states even more clearly the firmness of the Russian intention not to see the Union permanently dissolved. This dispatch, which Stoekl read to Secretary Seward, was made public in a speech in Boston by Edward Everett. "The American Union is not merely, in our eyes, an element essential to the universal equilibrium. It constitutes also a nation to which our August Emperor and all Russia have pledged the most friendly interest. These two countries, placed at the extremities of the two worlds, and both in the ascending scale of their development, appear called to a natural community of interests and sympathies of which they have already given mutual proofs to each other."

In 1862, when Colonel de Arnaud, one of the Russian Lafayettes who fought on the Northern side, was interviewed by

Chancellor Prince Gorchakov

Chancellor Gorchakov, he admitted that he did not believe the United States had sufficient naval power to maintain a blockade of the South. "If they haven't, we have!" said Gorchakov. "The Emperor will not permit anyone to interfere with this blockade, even if he has another war!"

But while the Civil War was to forge bonds that would practically amount to an Entente between Russia and the United States, England and France were seeking means to aid the Confederacy so that the Union would be permanently smashed. France was the most insistent on intervention, but the bitterness of England was even greater than the opportunism in the hearts of the French. The hostility of the English stunned young Henry Adams when he arrived in London in 1861: "No one in England—literally no one—doubted that Jefferson Davis had made or would make a nation, and nearly all were glad of it."

Five years earlier an article in the *Edinburgh Review* had summarized the attitude of the English. "The evil passions which *Uncle Tom's Cabin* gratified in England were not hatred of slavery, but national jealousy and national vanity. We have long been smarting under the conceit of America—we are tired of hearing her boast that she is the freest and most enlightened country that the world has ever seen. Our clergy hate her voluntary system—our Tories hate her democrats—our Whigs hate her parvenues—our Radicals hate her litigiousness, her insolence, and her ambition. All parties hailed Mrs. Stowe as a revolter from the enemy."

The London *Times* was soon urging support for the Southerners who "have gallantly strived so long for their liberties against a mongrel race of plunderers and oppressors." *Punch* was printing anti-Union cartoons. The *Morning Post* professed itself "shocked at the inhumanity of the North." The Queen and the Prince Consort and the Duke of Argyll were not unfavorable to the North, but the Parliament was outspokenly pro-Union, led by the old war-horse, Lord Palmerston, the Prime Minister. Metternich had once called Palmerston "the most interventionist of statesmen," and Palmerston, now 77, was still at it. His attitude was that if the American Union were destroyed, Britain would be residuary legatee for American trade; but a victory for democracy in America would strengthen the hand of the democratizers in England. He did not shrink even from war, though he voiced it inversely, as is the habit of politicians. "I fear," he wrote, "that from foolish and incalculating arrogance and self-sufficiency, or from personal calculations, Mr. Seward may bring on a war with us."

In France, Napoleon III wanted to see the Union broken because it would fit in with his plans for an Empire in the New World, or at least something that would compensate for the loss of the Louisiana Territory by his uncle. Even twenty years earlier, in the days of the July Monarchy, when John Quincy Adams had outraged Southern sensibilities by presenting Abolitionist petitions in the House of Representatives, Monsieur De Bacourt, the French Minister to Washington, had rejoiced at the possibility of the Union being smashed. "For my part," he added, "I am delighted with all this mischief."

Napoleon III once actually outlined his plans in the presence of a Professor of the University of Virginia. These were to establish a French Gibraltar at Key West, to seize Florida, Louisiana, and the Gulf Coast, and to bring the Mexican Empire under French domination.

The Mexican venture was the first step in his plans. In 1859, Mexican exiles had asked Archduke Maximilian to become a candidate for the throne, but he had refused. After the outbreak of the Civil War, Napoleon's insistence and Archduchess Charlotte's enthusiasm broke Maximilian's resistance, and in 1863 he accepted.

The choice of Maximilian was one of Napoleon's frequent errors in judgment. To begin with, Maximilian's gentlemanly assets—generosity, bravery, and good-will—were insufficient. Mexico was a land in which the pistol and the machete were being used to solve all political, personal and philosophical problems. Any ordinary soldier on the spot would have considered the invasion of Mexico and the occupation of Mexico to be horses of two widely different colors; and besides, Maximilian was not even of the stuff from which conquerors are made.

Whether a Mexican Empire under Maximilian was necessarily a bad idea is another matter. American historians have generally assumed so. In fact, they have almost unanimously applauded its destruction. But it is hard to believe that such a monarchy could have been any more chaotic than the seventy-five years of military dictatorships and revolutions that took place instead.

At the outbreak of the Civil War, a considerable number of young Russians offered their military services to Lincoln and the Union. Among them was Prince Alexander Eristov from Caucasian Georgia, great-uncle of the author of this book. Prince Eristov, whose English was imperfect, when called upon to explain why he had chosen to fight with the Union forces, took a peach between his fingers: "Like this the peach is so beautiful," he said, "and its skin with all those little hairs is protection in the severest weather." Breaking the peach in half, he added, holding the two pieces far apart, "But like this, it can withstand nothing! The peach will wither, it will turn ugly inside. Do not, I beg you, let your country be happened to like a peach." Then, a moment later, sighing, he said, "Georgia is so famous for his peaches." He meant of course his native Caucasian Georgia.

Another Russian who served with the Union Army was Ivan Turchaninov, graduate of the Imperial Artillery School, and a veteran of the Hungarian Campaign and the Crimean War. Having come to the United States several years before the outbreak of the Civil War, he had won a reputation for his outstanding engineering services to the Illinois Central Railroad. He may have even been acquainted with Lincoln, then an attorney for the Illinois Central. Turchaninov—or John Turchin, as he signed himself in America—became a Colonel in the 19th Illinois Volunteers, serving in Missouri, Alabama 'and Kentucky. He participated in the battle of Chickamauga and in 1862 was raised to the rank of Brigadier.

Colonel Charles Arnaud joined the forces of General Fremont. He was wounded and returned to Russia in February, 1862.

But while individual Russians were contributing their services to the United States military, a more important contribution was being made on the diplomatic front. It is difficult to estimate the restraining effect which the Russians had upon the British

and French, particularly in that darkest hour of the Union cause. The French Minister in Washington wanted to extend full recognition to the Confederacy, and urged the British and Russian Ministers to join him, but Stoekl told him that Russia recognized and would continue to recognize only one Government in America and that he would have no intercourse or connection with the seceding States.

Realizing the possibility that the Confederacy itself would approach him to find out on what terms Russia would extend recognition, Stoekl felt he needed a statement of policy by a higher official of the Russian Government. Gorchakov sent the following: "We shall not recognize the Southern Confederacy until it shall have regularized its position in respect to the Northern Republic by establishment of diplomatic relations of a permanent character." That statement clearly allowed recognition only if the South came back into the Union, or if the Union itself acknowledged the independence of the Southern States.

Stoekl performed a great many services for the United States which were not required of him. He saved Seward from a serious blunder. In 1856, the United States had refused to adhere to a provision of the Treaty of Paris which would have outlawed privateers, because in the event of war with England, the United States would have been helpless without privateers. Russia had supported the American position. But with the outbreak of the Civil War, the South stood a good chance of breaking the blockade with privateers which the United States itself had wanted legalized. So Seward informed Great Britain, France, and Russia that the United States now was willing to accept the privateer provision in the Treaty. Britain and France refused.

Chancellor Gorchakov then suggested that the anti-privateering clause be put into a separate Russian-American treaty, to which Seward agreed. This treaty was drafted and already before the Russian Senate when Stoekl arranged a hurried conference with Seward. "In the case of war between the United States and France or England," asked Stoekl, "would the United States use privateers?"

"Yes, as a matter of course," replied Seward.

"But Russia controls the north Pacific ports. We should have to seize your ships there as pirates."

The Treaty was immediately dropped, and Seward thanked Stoekl warmly.

These acts of friendship do not imply that there was sympathy on either side for the political institutions of the other. Nations make treaties of alliance or develop ententes because they share a dislike for some other nation, not because either feels the other has achieved the best possible way of life. Americans did not like Russian autocracy any better than they ever had, and Russians regarded American democracy with as much skepticism as before.

Stoekl, for example, believed that the industrial and financial power which the United States had achieved in less than a century had come about in spite of their wasteful form of government. He felt that America's industrial progress had been matched by an equally rapid moral decline. "The sole fruit of the republican institutions has been demagogy, venality, party intrigues, and the struggle among themselves of greedy and ambitious politicians.

This war was not inevitable, but a direct result of democratic structure. Whichever side wins, there must be a revaluation of American values after the war is over, and out of that revaluation there will surely develop reorganization along aristocratic lines."

This belief in the bankruptcy of American ideals was common throughout Europe. Long before the Civil War gave American philosophy its ultimate test, European rulers felt that the Republic had survived so long only because it had never met serious opposition. In 1854, Prince de Rohan Soubise asked Andrew White if George Washington had left descendants. "No," said White. The old Prince then urged that a collateral branch of the Washington family be sought out. "You cannot escape it," the Prince said. "No nation can get along for any considerable time without a Monarch."

But skepticism of American democracy did not prevent Russia from lending her support to the United States. Russian Chancellor Gorchakov wrote, "In spite of the diversity of their constitutions and their interests, Providence seems to urge the United States to draw closer the traditional bond as the basis and very condition of their political existence. In any event, the sacrifices they might impose upon themselves to maintain it are not to be compared with those which dissolution would bring. United they perfect themselves; separated they are paralyzed."

But when the War dragged on, draining the strength of both the North and the South, with unabated ferocity and neither side showed any will to compromise, Gorchakov began to worry. Even an eventual Northern victory would leave the United States too weak to stand as a threat to England. Since that was the main purpose of Russian support, Gorchakov decided to personally urge the United States Government to bring the war to an end. He had a long talk with Bayard Taylor, then Secretary of the American Legation in Russia.

"Your situation is getting worse and worse. The chances of the Union are growing more and more desperate," said Gorchakov. "Can you find *no* basis of arrangement before your strength is so exhausted that you must lose for many years to come your position in the world?"

"The revolt *must* be crushed. Nothing short of that will suffice," replied Taylor. "The South cannot hold out. We are bound to win."

"It's not that," said Gorchakov. "It's the fury that seems to possess both sides . . . the growth of enmities making the gulf continually wider between the two sections. Southern separation, and I fear it must come, will be considered by Russia as the greatest possible misfortune."

When Taylor remained silent, the Chancellor, revealing the pressure which his stand in regard to non-recognition of the Confederacy had thrust upon him, said, "Russia alone has stood by you. We will continue to stand by you, but we are very, *very* anxious that some means should be adopted . . . that *any* course should be pursued . . . which will prevent the division that now seems inevitable!"

"Your Excellency," Taylor insisted, "my government cannot, without disgrace and ruin, accept the only terms which the rebels would offer. Not, at least, until our strength has been tried and has failed."

Gorchakov sighed. "Well, you know where Russia stands. We desire, above all things, the maintenance of the American Union. Russia has declared her position and will maintain it. Proposals are being made to Russia to join in some plan of interference. She will refuse any invitation of that kind. Russia will occupy the same position as at the beginning of the struggle . . . you may rely on it, *she will not change*. But I cannot express to you how profound an anxiety we feel . . . how serious are our fears!"

This Russian-American Entente was never embodied in a formal treaty, but it became as binding upon both sides as if it had been formally ratified by the Senates of the two countries. The Entente is gone now, the friendship has been forgotten, but at one time it was accepted as a basic assumption by the statesmen of all countries. In orienting their policies towards Russia and the United States, other governments accepted the Entente as axiomatic during the middle half of the Nineteenth Century, just as their successors took account of Bismarck's Dual Alliance in dealing with Germany and Austria.

Despair hung over the North American Union in the spring of 1863. Hope of preserving the Union was at its lowest ebb. The ten months that followed the Second Battle of Bull Run were so discouraging and disastrous that thousands of loyal Unionists felt that an end might as well be made at once. Hope rose only to be shattered as victories and defeats followed each other with annoying impartiality. One Northern commander after another took the field, only to be outmatched by General Lee. Malvern, Shiloh, Antietam, Fredericksburg—the list seemed endless. After two years of heartbreaking effort, Lee and his soldiers in gray still lay safely behind the Rappahannock, and the Confederate Congress dreamed on in Richmond.

On the sea the situation was no better. Southern raiders had sunk nearly a thousand Northern vessels and destroyed shipping valued at twenty million dollars. The raiders would dart out like mosquitoes, then disappear. Still more raiders were being built for the Confederacy in European ports; British shipyards echoed to the hammers that forged successors to the *Alabama*. At Toulon, under the benevolently Southern eyes of Napoleon III, more ships were being constructed. At Nantes and Bordeaux the keels of corvettes were prepared for an all too familiar "unknown buyer."

The North had been disunited at the outbreak of the war. To be sure, Lincoln's *Emancipation Proclamation* of January, 1863, had changed the war from a sectional conflict into a struggle to uphold a principle. Union soldiers were now singing Julia Ward Howe's stirring *Battle Hymn of the Republic*. But there had never developed in the Union ranks that unity of purpose which had always animated the South. Neither slogans nor banners, nor even the grave speeches of Lincoln, could change the fact that it was the Southerners who were fighting a holy war in defense of their liberties and their firesides.

The Northern armies had nothing to show for two years of bloodshed which had wet the earth from the Atlantic to the Midwest. When Lee threatened to invade the Northern States. Baltimore was joyous, Philadelphia paralyzed, and New York City ready to secede. Every city between New York and Washington felt itself at the mercy of Southern cavalry.

Bitterness and hatred assailed Lincoln from every quarter.

He was blamed for the war, for the defeats, and for the empty National Treasury. When Lincoln invited the Republican Speaker of the House to a social function, Mr. Wade replied insultingly, "Are the President and Mrs. Lincoln aware that there is a civil war? If they are not, Mr. and Mrs. Wade are, and decline to participate in feasting and dancing."

In July, 1863, riots broke out in New York City over the Conscription Laws, and within two days a thousand soldiers and civilians—many of them negroes who had been lynched—lay dead in the streets. Property worth $1,500,000 was in ruins.

Secretary Seward was informed that French troops in Mexico were pressing northward. At about the same time came news that a British regiment, to the spirited strains of *Dixie,* had landed in Canada. Two European powers seemed ready to attack—one from the north, the other from the south. *Harper's Weekly* reported:

"The month of September is the time fixed upon for the departure of the rebel ironclads from British ports. We trust that long before they can threaten us, a sufficient number of the monitors will be released from their present work in the South to enable our government to station several of them in each of our great harbors."

Two weeks later, *Harper's Weekly* said:

"The British have launched another pirate. Her commander is a southerner, but her crew, like herself, are British. It is suggested that she will come to New York and bombard the city. We deem it very likely."

Europe was beginning to stir at this same hour. Russia was forced to turn her attention to another Polish revolution. Besides this, the Russians were keeping a wary eye on the Schleswig-Holstein business, an affair so complicated that British Prime Minister Palmerston stated, "Only three men ever understood it fully; one was Prince Albert, who is dead; the second is a professor, but he is insane; and the third is myself, but I have forgotten it." At any rate, in 1863 Denmark and Schleswig-Holstein drew up a joint Constitution, which the German Diet declared a violation of Protocol. In January, 1864, Prussia and Austria declared war on Denmark.

The Polish revolution presented no great danger to the Russian Empire, but it placed the Russian Diplomatic Corps in a

Emperor Alexander II

difficult position, now faced as they were with their own private civil war. Britain and France were delighted and promptly began using Poland as a part of their strategy. Czar Alexander II was showered with Machiavellian offers of mediation, which would have been tantamount to giving Poland independence. In an effort to drive a wedge into the Russian-American Entente, the United States was even asked to join Britain and France in a demonstration against Russia. The United States Secretary of State, Seward, firmly rejected this invitation. "In regard to Russia, the case is a plain one. She has our friendship in preference to any other European power, simply because she always wishes us well and leaves us to conduct our affairs as we think best."

On May 11, 1863, Gorchakov notified Washington that Emperor Alexander II "appreciated the firmness with which the Government of the United States maintains the principle of non-intervention, the meaning of which in these days is so often perverted . . ."

The United States people sympathized with the Poles, but were too deeply involved in their own civil strife to have strong feelings about any European revolution. Editors on the Union side pointed out that a European revolution would affect Napo-

The Russian Steam Frigate *Oslyabia* in New York Harbor

leon III and hoped that the troubles in Poland might remove the spotlight of attention from the American Civil War and cause the withdrawal of European aid to the Confederacy. English and French intervention on behalf of the South was so imminent that Lincoln delivered the preliminary proclamation of Emancipation with one eye cocked toward Europe, hoping to win favor for his cause by this act. Nor was the situation purely one of fear on the part of the United States, because Americans were so angry over the cleverly timed violation of the Monroe Doctrine by Napoleon III that only the dire demands of the Civil War prevented a force of Union soldiers from invading Mexico.

Then, on September 11, 1863, a Russian steam frigate, the *Oslyabia,* slipped into New York Harbor, and anchored near several British and French warships. Being the first Russian warship ever to enter New York Harbor, there was considerable speculation as to the reason for her presence. The *Herald* suggested that her commander, Captain Butakov, had been sent to inspect the *Monitor.* Interest and curiosity increased when it was announced that Mrs. Lincoln intended to pay a visit to the *Oslyabia.* No First Lady had ever set foot on a foreign warship. The newspapers devoted columns to the description of her entertainment

American guests aboard the Russian Frigate *Oslyabia*

aboard and to the toasts which were drunk to the health of Czar Alexander II and the President of the United States, as the *New York Herald* reported, "Toasts that will be heard with dismay in the palaces and aristocratic halls of Europe."

The *Richmond Examiner* reported sarcastically:

"A health being drunk by the wife of an Illinois lawyer should convulse with fear the people of Europe! Plain Mrs. Lincoln . . . appendant to that extraordinary freak of nature, the President of the United States, she can not only distinguish herself by the resplendent tints of her silks and possession of her jewels, but she can frighten the world! . . . The Czar emancipates the serfs from their bondage of centuries and puts forth the whole strength of his Empire to enslave the Poles. Lincoln proclaims freedom to the African, and strives at the same time to subjugate freeborn Americans. In this striking coincidence a similarity of character and feeling is denoted!"

After Mrs. Lincoln's visit, rumors spread in New York that the presence of the warship was the first step toward Russian intervention on the Union side. Newspaper editors cautiously pointed out that there was no basis in fact for these rumors. Then another rumor began to gain credence among more gullible New Yorkers, a report that somewhere out beyond the Narrows the entire Russian Fleet was waiting for favorable weather to enter the harbor.

Russian Sailors from the Russian Frigate *Oslyabia*

Little attention was given to these rumors at first, but when a dense fog continued for days to paralyze New York shipping, and the *Oslyabia* still showed no signs of preparation for putting out to sea, the dock area became charged with excitement. The five thousand French and British sailors then in port were officially ordered restricted to shipboard, and all shore leave for officers was temporarily cancelled. Meanwhile, hasty communications were taking place between the European capitals and their Washington representatives.

On September 23, the *New York Herald* reported, "Two large steam frigates, probably Russian, are lying off Stonington, Connecticut." (Actually, Lessovsky, the Commander of the Fleet, having been at sea for two months, put in first at Stonington to find out if war had been declared. He was happy to find that it had not.)

On the 24th of September, a wind at last swept the fog from the harbor, and the entire bay could be seen in rare clarity, revealing the anxious presence of the British *Nile* and *Immortality,* a number of French gunboats, a solitary Spanish frigate, and, of course, the mysterious Russian. There were no signs of unusual activity on the *Oslyabia.* Far out at sea two black marks could be seen, evidently smoke. Then two ships came into view and were identified as corvettes. As they came abreast of Fort Columbus (now Fort Jay, Governor's Island), their sides billowed white smoke, and thousands of people who lined the Battery heard the rumble of cannon. The guns on Fort Columbus returned the salute, as the Russian corvettes, their brightwork flashing in the sunlight, slid gaily toward their anchorage.

Fort Columbus and the ships themselves were still saluting as the *Vitiaz* and *Variag* swept up the channel, their decks lined with officers and men shouting and waving their caps. Squarely in front of the Battery, the blue St. Andrew's Cross (on the jacket of the book) was lowered smartly from the mast of the *Vitiaz,* with the Stars and Stripes hoisted in its place. The ships steamed on into the North River, where they anchored.

New York was in an uproar when next day two more Russian ships, the *Alexander Nevsky* and the *Peresviet,* both brand new, steamed down Long Island Sound and anchored in Flushing Bay. The *Nevsky,* Flagship of Admiral Lessovsky, was the largest ship that had ever passed through Hell Gate.

A new rumor spread that Admiral Lessovsky bore sealed orders from Emperor Alexander II, to be opened only in event of a war between the United States and a European power. "Sealed Orders," was the phrase on everyone's lips. Then, by overland telegraph came the news, startling even Lessovsky himself, that

Admiral Lessovsky

yet another Russian squadron had arrived, this time in San Francisco.

Across the length and breadth of the Union, news of the arrival of not one but two Russian Fleets brought complete delight and jubilation. Years later Myron Herrick recalled the scene from his childhood when his mother had clasped him to her, saying "Myron! Myron! We're saved! The Russians have come." President Lincoln, in his Thanksgiving Proclamation, which was to set a precedent for that annual event, spoke of "God's bounties of so extraordinary a nature that they cannot fail to penetrate and soften the heart."

The Federal Arsenal and the Brooklyn Navy Yard were placed at the disposal of the Russians. Delegations by the score came to welcome them, and along the Battery hundreds of the curious and unofficial hovered. Admiral Lessovsky was a frequent visitor at the apartment of Admiral David Farragut in the Astor House. Friends since they had met as young officers in the Mediterranean, they discussed the Civil War and the troubled state of Europe. Farragut asked bluntly why Lessovsky was in New York when affairs in Europe were so unsettled. "I am here," Lessovsky replied, "under sealed orders. They can be opened only in a contingency which has not yet occurred."

The official reception of the Russians was postponed until the steam clipper, *Almaz,* which had been delayed, arrived in

THE NEW ALLIANCE CEMENTED

Russia and the United States Fraternizing.

Reception by Our City Authorities to the Russian Naval Officers.

An Enthusiastic Popular Demonstration.

The Russian Cross Mingling Its Folds with the Stars and Stripes.

VISIT TO THE FLEET.

Presentation of the Resolutions of the Common Council and Speech of Admiral Lisovski.

RETURN TO PORT.

MILITARY AND OFFICIAL RECEPTION.

Grand Display in Fifth Avenue and Broadway,

DINNER TO THE RUSSIAN OFFICERS.

Grand Entertainment at the Metropolitan Hotel.

Speeches of Admiral Lisovski, of the Russian Navy; Admiral Farragut, of the American Navy; General Walbridge and Hon. Hendricks B. Wright, M. C., of Pennsylvania.

Letters from Mayor Opdyke, Admiral Paulding and General Canby.

Sympathy Between Russia and the United States,
&c.,   &c.,   &c.

Admiral Lisovski and the officers of the Russian fleet now in our harbor were entertained last evening at the Metropolitan Hotel, the host being Mr. James B. Eads, of St. Louis, a gentleman who has been extensively engaged in building iron-clad gunboats for our government. There were some thirty of the Russian officers present, all resplendent in handsome uniforms, and many of them wearing the cross of St. Stanislaus and other decorations. Our own navy was represented by the gallant Admiral Farragut (in plain clothes), Commodore Bradford, Chief Engineer Stimers and Naval Constructor Delano. Brigadier General Van Vliet represented the army. The national government was represented by Mr. Collector Barney. The municipal government had no representative present; but the letter from Mayor Opdyke will explain why. The community at large was well represented by the Hon. Hendricks B. Wright, member of Congress from Pennsylvania; the Hon. Hiram Walbridge, formerly member of Congress from this city, and other citizens. Altogether there were some eighty per-

Headlines, New York Herald of September 29, 1863 and October 2, 1863

New York. On the first day of November a committee of Aldermen and Councilmen from the Common Council, with the band of the *U.S.S. North Carolina*, crowded aboard the yacht *Andrews.* As the yacht skirted Governor's Island and approached the Russian Flagship, the band burst into the Imperial Anthem, *God Save the Czar.* In the rigging of the *Nevsky* were hundreds of white-capped sailors who cheered as the American flag was run up the mast. The *Nevsky's* band struck up *Yankee Doodle,* which they thought was the United States national anthem, and the entire Russian squadron fired a twenty-one-gun salute.

One newspaperman, who was more interested in the *Nevsky* than in the ceremonies, reported that she carried fifty cannon, more than seven hundred officers and men, and that the cannon

Reception of Committee aboard the Flagship *Alexander Nevsky*

bore the markings of a Pittsburgh foundry. After the "Resolutions" of the Councilmen were read, and the Russian Admiral had
made a formal acceptance of the honors bestowed, stewards came
in with bottles of champagne on massive silver trays. "I propose
a toast in which you will all heartily join," Lessovsky said. "To
the man to whom you have entrusted the future of your country . . . the President of the United States."

When the ceremonies ended, the Councilmen, with a number of Russian officers, boarded the *Andrews* to make their official
entrance into New York City at the 23rd Street dock. On shore,
the Second Marine Brigade met them with a thundering rifle and
cannon salute, and the procession proceeded downtown along
Fifth Avenue toward City Hall, over a route draped with flags
and gaily colored bunting, through Fourteenth Street and over to

Broadway. In front of Tiffany's, Ball & Black's, and Lord & Taylor's, were Russian emblems and flags, which the visitors noted with delight. At City Hall, the Russians entered the reviewing stand while their cavalry escort clattered by, the Sixty-Ninth Infantry bringing up the rear to the tune of a Russian popular song from *L'Etoile du Nord*. The Russian visitors were amazed that so many troops could still be found in New York City in the midst of a war.

In the days and weeks that followed, hundreds of delegations and invitations were presented to the visitors. Social leaders fought to have them attend all kinds of affairs. Lessovsky and his Senior Officers exhausted themselves receiving committees and attending public functions, because he felt it was his duty to make a favorable impression and to become acquainted with as large a segment of the American public as possible. Fortunately, Lessovsky and a number of his echelon spoke English.

The Procession of Russian Visitors through Broadway

At a dinner given by James B. Eads, the famous inventor and manufacturer of ironclads, the Russians were shown a model of the new revolving turret which was to be installed on the *Milwaukee* and *Winnebago*. The Russians were particularly impressed by a new steam device for elevating and depressing these guns, which permitted the removal of many vulnerable portholes. At the dinner Lessovsky asked permission to express his "homage to Admiral Farragut, who has filled the world with the renown of American arms, and who is familiar to his countrymen as 'that brave old salamander.' "

Then General Walbridge rose to return the compliment:

"Four empires continue to struggle for supremacy. Russia, representing one-seventh of the earth and dominating the Eastern Hemisphere. America representing the Western Hemisphere. England and France, though animated by different convictions, have struggled to suppress the rising greatness of these two nations . . . England for the purpose of pursuing a commercial policy, France for the purpose of impressing her moral greatness on the world. In the struggle of Russia in 1854 against France and England, the sympathies of our people were with Russia!"

There were deafening shouts of approbation. Walbridge then made a few comments on Peter the Great, and concluded:

"It is just, it is proper, that now, when we are struggling for our existence, Russia should come gallantly to our rescue . . . Providence has decreed that there shall be two great Hemispheres, the Eastern and the Western. The one shall be represented by Russia, the other by the United States!"

That was pretty strong stuff for an official representative of the United States Army, and he was speaking of nations with whom his government was presumably at peace. It was a strange kind of "private" dinner. Foreigners had been shown technical secrets of the United States Navy, and its ranking Admiral had been one of the speakers. But General Walbridge must have startled even the Russians when he announced that the Russian Fleet had been sent to New York so that at a given signal "they could sweep the commerce of France and England from the seas."

But if Lessovsky was surprised, he did not show it. He rose and delivered a masterpiece of ambiguity:

"There is no middle ground! I hope the present circumstances will end peacefully, but let happen what will, we are ready for any sacrifice. Just as we could see Moscow burned, so shall we not shrink from the burning of St. Petersburg if necessary!"

A few days later the streets of New York were again empty of all French and British sailors.

Admiral Lessovsky and Captains of the Russian Ships

Editorial comment on the visit of the Russian Fleet continued. The *New York Sun* stated, "If France should enter into a war with us, Russia might act as a counterweight in the scales." The *Post* welcomed the Russian Fleet as "evidence of the friendly feeling of the Czar and the people of Russia at a moment when other Governments of Europe have been in accord with a desperate band of traitors and rebels seeking to destroy our Union." The *Tribune* took this occasion to be historically philosophical, pointing out the similarity of the social experiments that were going on in Russia and the United States, and the similar problems of government, both nations consisting of large stretches of territory and tremendous, growing populations. The *Herald* went further, stating, "We have ever liked the Russians. In the fate of their great Empire we see a reflection of our own march to power. Should France and Russia go to war, the Czar would find then as now a refuge for his vessels in our harbors . . . Perhaps it is even time to abandon our traditional policy of isolationism and meet the hostile alliance of western Europe by an alliance with Russia."

Cartoon from Harper's Weekly of 1863

Only the *Journal of Commerce* remained cautious. "To be sure, Russia has been friendly to us and the two nations have an affinity of interests in the Pacific. Yet we must make no distinctions in our friendship. Russia is embroiled in Europe, and we are restrained by the Monroe Doctrine. Inconsiderate friendship is sometimes as bad as open enmity!" And in the Midwest, the *Missouri Republican* warned, "The pale ghost of Poland's murdered liberty will someday haunt America! By and by we will doubtless all wear Russian beards, Russian overcoats, and Russian pants; our wives will wear Russian petticoats, and our innocent children will receive daily lessons in the Russian system of government, by due application of the lash!"

The London *Times* explained that the reason British and French sailors were being kept off the streets of New York was

The Great Russian Ball at The Academy of Music, November 5, 1863

because "the French and English do not wish to play second fiddle where the Russians are being 'lionized.' The enlisted men are not allowed on shore because Americans are enticing them into entering their service. The sailors are invited into taverns, get free drinks, and then are offered such advantageous terms that they cannot resist temptation, and desert from their respective ships."

British cartoons pictured President Lincoln as an uncouth, ragged, slouched figure against the background of a ruined nation, trying vainly to "hold a candle" to the complacent, powerful Russian Bear. The caption of one such cartoon in *Punch* read, "We Air in the same fix, I calculate. You with your Poles, with southern rebels, I, who spurn my rule and my revenge defy." Even an American in London, Henry Ward Beecher, a staunch defender of the Northern cause, denounced as "monstrous the flirtations of America with powdered and whiskered foreigners."

On the night of November fifth the Academy of Music on Fourteenth Street in New York was the scene of such lavishness as perhaps its walls had never before enclosed. Although Admiral Lessovsky had protested against such extravagance as a ball would entail at a time when money was sorely needed for the prosecution of the war, the plans had gone ahead. At the entrance a magenta carpet had been laid, and on either side of the central door a bronze statue holding a flambeau. The tremendous candelabra had been converted to gas light, and from them came great waves of heat. The walls were covered with white tapestry, decorated with golden tassels, and in one corner stood an enormous shield bearing the Russian Coat-of-Arms, and in the opposite a similar shield of the American Eagle. At one end of the hall was a huge model of the *General-Admiral,* the new Russian frigate which had been launched in the United States in 1858. There was also a "quiet little temple where guests could partake of the cup that cheers."

The costumes of the American ladies were voluminous and the ladies themselves buxom and determined. One Russian officer wrote home that if Russian girls ever manifested a small portion of the interest shown by the American beauties, there would not be a bachelor in the whole Empire. "The women wore buttons from the coats of Russian officers, and blue and white ribbons in the form of a St. Andrew's Cross. There were cockades from Naval caps and anchors taken from Midshipmen's caps."

Every conceivable fabric and color seemed to be present—

lavender velvet, rose-colored silk, blue tarlatan with puffs, gold-embroidered satin, and white corded silk with empress scarves. One imposing dowager had a headdress of white roses and black lace barbes, topped by a large green bug. Two sisters appeared in identical dresses of pink moiré and point d'Angleterre lace showered with diamond powder. "They *all* wore diamonds," stated the *Herald*.

Theodore Roosevelt, the Chairman—whose son was one day to denounce the Russian-American Entente—had arranged an impressive program of music, leaning rather heavily toward the Viennese. Many of the composers are now forgotten: Helmsmuller, Grafulla, Gungl, and Tucker who is remembered for his *Sweet Genevieve.* The particular selection from *Martha* that was played was not recorded in the press, but it is safe to assume that it was *The Last Rose of Summer,* the most popular operatic number of that period.

A supper from Delmonico's was served in Irving Hall, which had been temporarily joined to the Academy of Music by a gay canopy. Food was plentiful, frequently disguised and decorated with figures of Peter the Great, George Washington, Lincoln, and Alexander II made out of sugar and cake, as well as frosted statues, Greek temples, eagles, lions, and Dianas. The New York *World,* with a statistical turn of mind, perhaps best indicates the lavishness of the occasion—12,000 oysters, 1200 game birds, 250 turkeys, 400 chickens, twelve monster salmon of thirty pounds each, and a thousand pounds of steak. Not to mention desserts, *pieces montées,* a hundred pyramids of pastry, a thousand large loaves of bread, and 3500 bottles of wine.

"The Ball is over, the music hushed," *Harper's Weekly* commented, "the dances ended, the wine drunk, the costly laces and diamonds put back to their places. And now that the signs of revel are dying out it occurs to us that we have a headache, and we are saying wisely to each other that the ball was not, after all, so very sensible a thing; and that when our brothers and our sons are dying on battlefields, it is hardly decent for us here to be dancing and making merry."

The *World* decried New York's persistent lack of good taste in overdoing everything. The *Journal of Commerce* somberly accused, "About the same time that people honored the Russians with music and dancing, men, women and children perished under the sharp hand of despotism in Poland, because they had dreams of liberty. So the world rolls. While the sun shines on one side it is dark on the other. We hope that the people who were guilty of the folly of last night's affair will now permit the Russian bear to gnaw his paws in peace."

But the most bitter turnabout came in the *Herald*, which a few weeks before had urged an alliance between Russia and the United States. "Russia sends her Navy here to keep it safe in the event of war with France, but we doubt if she would send it here if we needed it to aid us in fighting England. Her Navy in fact is not worth sending. One of our ironsides could blow it out of the water, with all the barbarians aboard, in a couple of hours . . ."

Admiral Lessovsky had tried to prevent the ball for exactly these reasons. But even he must have been surprised at the suddenness with which the New York press reversed itself, with the excessive enthusiasm and puritanical remorse which has always characterized American journalism. The problems of international friendship are clearly exposed in this single event, for there was no direction which Lessovsky could have chosen which would not have had the same results. To refuse to attend the ball would have embittered New Yorkers against the Russians, and perhaps the Admiral would even have been rebuked by his own ministers in Washington and St. Petersburg. And the ball had been wonderful, with the Russian officers conducting themselves in a manner which should have endeared them to the American people.

Lessovsky learned from one of his officers why the *New York Herald* had reversed its policy. "The wife of the *Herald's* editor visited without warning our frigate *Alexander Nevsky* on the day that a reception, also *ex tempore*, was being given to school children and their teachers. Under such conditions one officer can hardly properly entertain each individual. Nevertheless this American editor's wife was offended because she had not received attention in preference to all the others, and a few days later we Russians, who had previously been treated by the *Herald* as friends, became 'barbarians.' "

The Russians did not remain in New York very long after

the ball. Their next excursion was to Washington to pay their respects to President Lincoln. Many of the younger officers took this opportunity to visit Annapolis and inspect the Naval Academy, then less than twenty years old. The Russian Government had instructed Lessovsky to ascertain the size and number of warships which England and France had in the Western Hemisphere, and to inquire how large a force the United States could bring to bear in event of a general war. After meetings with the United States Secretary of State, Cabinet Members, and the Secretary of the Navy, the Russian Fleet sailed for Havana and Cartagena, while the *Variag* and *Almaz* returned to New York.

After returning from this southern cruise, having determined French and British Naval strength in the South Atlantic, the Russian Fleet remained in America until the summer of 1864, when Lessovsky received orders from St. Petersburg to return. Only the *Nevsky* was to remain in New York. By this time the outcome of the Civil War was no longer in doubt, and the threat of war between Russia and the Anglo-French alliance had vanished. General Grant was driving steadily towards a final

William H. Seward and the Diplomatic Corps at Trenton Falls, New Jersey

crushing blow, and the French and British Governments were showing signs of wanting to keep clear of the conflict. Spain was still embittered, but the Spanish had so fallen from their position of strength in the New World that no one paid much attention to them.

The American attitude toward the Russian Fleet had somewhat settled. There were no more gigantic balls in New York, but there were no more bitter editorials in the newspapers either. The Russian officers made a number of private excursions, particularly one to Niagara Falls. One of the young Midshipmen who made this excursion was Rimsky-Korsakov, who also attended the American premiére of Gounod's *Faust*. Admiral Lessovsky's last public appearance was at a banquet in Boston, where the Mayor —whose name was Lincoln—gave him an enthusiastic welcome. "The Russians," Mayor Lincoln said, "did not bring arms or munitions of war. They brought more than these, the kindly sentiment of international brotherhood."

Nations do not ordinarily act from altruistic motives. Russia did not send fleets to New York and San Francisco because she loved America. But the presence of those fleets was, nevertheless, a compelling proof of Russia's attitude towards European intervention.

The reasons for the dispatch of the Russian fleets to the United States are complicated. In simplest terms, Russia feared a war which the Polish revolt might set off. The Polish revolt, which began within the borders of the Kingdom of Poland, spread over the whole western region of Poland proper. Yet at no time was the revolt itself a serious menace to the Russian Empire. Russia was mostly worried about the safety of her Fleet, which could be bottled up in the Black Sea and the Baltic by France and England.

The Polish uprising was a minority revolt, obtaining little support from the peasants or the Roman Catholics. Although not particularly affectionate toward Russia, the Catholics knew that the Polish nobility would rule with an iron hand.

General Count Berg, the Russian Viceroy, placed Warsaw under martial law on January 22, 1863. Great Britain and France, sensing an opportunity to embarrass Russia, presented a joint note to Gorchakov urging an international conference. Nearly every European state except Prussia was marshalled into line. Then, on March 2, 1863, Britain's Lord John Russell demanded that Russia give Poland a constitution and extend amnesty to the revolution-ists. Chancellor Gorchakov refused.

The French and British were involved in a complicated maneuver. Not merely the Polish revolt, but the American Civil War and the tag end of the Crimean War were inextricably mixed. Napoleon III, who felt that France had not been given all she was entitled to in the Peace of Paris that settled the Crimean War, saw an opportunity of playing off Russia against England, and, at the same time, of gaining tacit English consent to his dream of an empire in Mexico, the very thought of which made Britons shudder. Great Britain had an objective clearer than France's but the road she had to pursue was winding and devious. First of all, she wanted to maintain a treaty that irritated Napoleon, and, further, the destruction of the American Union. It had also always been a cardinal point in British policy to keep Russia weakened by internal strife.

The Poles, who believed that France and Great Britain would eventually force a settlement favorable to them, resorted to des-perate guerilla warfare. Lord Lyons, the British Minister to Wash-ington, urged his Government to act or to withdraw; for England's wavering attitude was doing the Poles no service. Another British note was presented Russia and a conference was urged. Gorchakov replied that Russia was willing to recognize that Poland was not the concern of Russia alone, since Prussia and Austria also held parts of that former Kingdom. But under no circumstances would negotiations be undertaken with Great Britain or France, who had no concern in the affairs of eastern Europe.

Since the English could not hope to get Bismarck to support them, they had no recourse except to back down or to go to war. Britain, annoyed by Napoleon's persistence about readjusting old treaties, announced that, while she demanded an international congress to settle the Polish question, that congress must concern itself with Poland alone. This confused matters even more, since the sole claim the Western Powers had to interfere in Poland lay in a provision of the Treaty of Vienna. Thus, Russia decided it was time to prepare for a possible war, and removed her fleet.

Russia had fifteen capital ships in active service. Eleven more were under construction, but none of these would be ready for service in time. Except for the frigate, *Oslyabia,* which was in the Mediterranean, the Fleet was harbored in the Baltic. The Pacific Squadron was stationed at Petropavlovsk. On June 9, 1863, a week after General Lee with a veteran army 25,000 strong crossed the Potomac and invaded the North, Admiral Melikhov, sensing that the Russian Fleet would be at the mercy of England in the event of war, submitted a plan whereby it could be used advantageously against British and French shipping. However, Admiral Krabbe, the Minister of Marine, did not at this time take action.

War fever was mounting. The Russian Army was one and a half million strong, and in Poland 120,000 rebellious soldiers waited in readiness. Shore batteries were being installed along the Baltic and fortifications along the approaches to St. Petersburg. Exiled Poles in England and Sweden were preparing to smuggle arms and ammunition into Poland. An obscure German called Karl Marx, in cooperation with Polish patriots and covertly supported by the British, had purchased arms and smuggled them in English ship-bottoms into the Baltic. The Anarchist, Michael Bakunin, who had managed to escape from exile in Siberia and had appeared in San Francisco in 1861, was now in London with his friends, Hertzen and Ogarev. A report was received that Lapinsky, a Pole, was outfitting several privateers with the intention of inflicting "a mortal blow to Russian shipping."

Admiral Krabbe, after a meeting with his officers, in which it was decided that the only effective resistance Russian ships could offer was through privateering, raiding the shipping lines of the French and British in the Atlantic, re-studied the Melikhov report and was convinced that the immediate dispatch of the entire Baltic Squadron to America; "to the only friendly country," was the best solution. At a conference with Alexander II he pointed out that the Confederate States, with inadequately armed privateers, had demoralized Atlantic shipping. A well-equipped Russian Fleet could cause even more damage to British shipping. "Further, I am of the opinion that the appearance of a Russian Naval Squadron in the Atlantic would carry more weight in the diplomatic discussions now taking place, than can any armaments of land forces, which would be of a defensive nature only when opposed to England."

Krabbe insisted, however, that Great Britain must be kept in ignorance of such a move until it had been carried out. Not only would the surprise effect be greater, but prior knowledge might cause England to try to prevent the Fleet from making an Atlantic crossing and thereby precipitate war. Alexander II decided the plan was feasible and ordered preparations for immediate departure. Command of the Squadron was offered to a veteran naval officer, Admiral Unkovsky, who, feeling that he was too old for such a task, recommended Lessovsky, whose knowledge of English and whose recent visit to the United States in 1861 made him the best qualified.

The only problem was the position of the *Oslyabia* in the Mediterranean, which had to be ordered to proceed to New York independently. The officers of the *Oslyabia* were instructed to spread rumors that her destination was the Siberian coast, and on the night of August 21, the ship quietly left the Port of Cadiz.

The Baltic Fleet entered the Atlantic on a course well north of the Orkney Islands, a maneuver which was carried out so smoothly that the British Admiralty were hard put to believe the first reports of its arrival in New York. Since the ships were heavily laden with supplies, leaving little space for coal, most of the Atlantic voyage was made under sail, which also served to eliminate the tell-tale smoke and further preserve secrecy. In addition to having an English teacher aboard each ship, money for wages and other expenses for two years was kept aboard the ships.

There is no written record that the Lincoln Administration expected the Russians. From the memoirs of certain Cabinet members, it seems that the appearance of the Russian Fleet was a great surprise to them as it was to the private citizens. A recent Soviet publication of documents reveals the plans for the expedition were not only specifically kept from the sharp ears of the American Minister, General Clay, but even from the Russian Ministry of Foreign Affairs. Not until July 23, 1863, did Chan-

The Invitation of the Mayor and the City Council of Baltimore
to Admiral Farragut and the Officers of the Russian Frigates

cellor Gorchakov, at the request of Admiral Krabbe, send a dispatch to Stoekl "to ascertain the attitude of the Federal government in case Russian ships arrive into American ports for the purpose of repairs and taking on supplies." Stoekl never knew of the impending arrival of the Russians until informed in the middle of August by Captain Crown, who was secretly sent ahead of the Fleet.* On September 23, 1863, Stoekl wrote to Chancellor Gorchakov that the Federal Government had granted permission to Lessovsky to anchor in American waters, and enclosed a letter from the Secretary of the Navy, Gideon Welles, placing the Brooklyn Navy Yard at the disposal of the Russian Fleet.

It is safe to presume that the arrival of the Russian Fleet was therefore unannounced to the United States Government. John W. Foster, later Secretary of State, asserted that the Fleet came "without any previous notice." If any man in the American

---

*Captain Crown was the grandson of an Englishman who entered Russian Naval Service during Catherine the Great's reign. Captain Crown was chosen for the mission because he knew America well and spoke English. As an officer of Admiral Putiatin's expedition to Japan, he visited the United States in 1853, returning to New York in 1857, where he supervised the construction of several warships.

Government did have secret information, it was Seward, who habitually conducted all his negotiations direct with Stoekl, the Russian Minister at Washington.

But whether or not Seward, and perhaps President Lincoln, knew of the proposed visit and its object, it is certain that no one else had an inkling of the plans. Except for the commanders, none of the men on the Russian ships knew their destination until they were beyond the Danish Great Belt Channel in the Kattegat. The purpose of the voyage was to escape blockade in the Baltic Sea in the event of a war with England and France, and, by basing the warships on a friendly shore, to be able to inflict heavy damage to enemy commerce. In the words of Professor Golder, "The Russian Fleet was not ordered to America for our benefit, but this should not blind us to the fact that we did profit by the event."* Certainly the arrival of the Russians was most timely, since the tide was turning in the favor of the North with the battle of Gettysburg, July 1st-3rd, and the fall of Vicksburg on July 4th. This meant that the English and the French had to decide upon intervention and be quick about it. The Russian Fleet caused them a moment of uneasy reflection at the very instant when any hesitation on their part meant sure defeat for the Confederacy.

The report of the Russian Ministry of Marine to Alexander II contained the following: "This sudden appearance of Russia's Naval squadrons in the ports of the American Union was the more impressive because no one expected anything of the kind, coming at the very moment when an alliance was on the eve of being concluded between two of the greatest maritime Powers."

While New York was seething with excitement over the arrival of the Lessovsky Squadron, another Fleet, under the command of Admiral Popov, was steaming toward San Francisco.

Admiral Popov was one of the saltiest men who ever strode

---

*The secret orders to Lessovsky from the Minister of Marine, Admiral Krabbe are printed in the Appendix. One paragraph of these orders reads: "The aim of the undertaking of the squadron entrusted to your leadership in the event of a war at present forseen with the western powers is to act with all the possible means available to you against our opponents, inflicting by means of separate cruisers the most painful damage and loss to the commerce of the enemy, or making attacks with the entire squadron on the weak and poorly protected places of the colonies of the enemy."

Admiral Krabbe

a bridge or cursed a landlubber. A competent naval officer, he got along famously with his superior, the Grand Duke Constantine. But he despised the Minister of Marine, Admiral Krabbe, who had risen to his high-ranking position without going to sea as often as he should. Popov, who privately expressed the opinion that Krabbe would get seasick crossing the Gulf of Finland, disliked brass-hats in general and Krabbe in particular.

His Fleet had returned from a South Seas expedition and was waiting in Nagasaki for further orders, when Admiral Popov suddenly decided that there were too many "doddering old women" among the officers on his ships. He made a clean sweep of all the old officers and promoted new ones to their posts, an unprecedented act which became known in naval circles as the "Nagasaki Razgrom" ("the Nagasaki Purge").

When newspapers arrived from Hong Kong, and Popov became aware of the seriousness of the situation in Europe, he called a council of his commanding officers. "If there's a war," he said, "these God-damned Englishmen will get the news before we do. The Chinese waters are packed with their filthy ships, and we wouldn't stand a chance. All because we've got numbskulls like Krabbe in the Admiralty!"

Popov glared at the officers, as if daring them to challenge his statement. "I want every ship ready to sail at dawn," he continued. "All bills on shore must be paid, all business attended to. I have no doubt that war will soon be declared, and we're not going to get caught here, Admiralty or no Admiralty!"

The captain of one of the ships suggested that it would be better to await orders from St. Petersburg.

Popov replied, "Any officer who finds it impossible to follow my instructions will be released immediately. The squadron will get under way at dawn."

Popov had decided upon his destination. He was sailing to San Francisco, a port that he knew well. There were no facilities in Chinese or Japanese ports for providing his six ships with ammunition and provisions. If he took the fleet to Siberia, it would be cut off from the Pacific trade lines. He knew of the strained relations between the United States and the powers of Western Europe, and was familiar with the California coast. "With the help of God," he wrote, "I hope to be in a position to cause much damage to the enemy before we are scratched off the register of ships."

If the arrival of the Lessovsky Squadron in New York was a surprise to the American Government, the arrival of the Fleet in San Francisco was a surprise to the Russian Government itself. Admiral Popov, in less than twenty-four hours, had arrived at the very same decision which the Russian Government had required nearly a year to make. His arrival so smartly on the heels of the Baltic Fleet's grand entrance into New York harbor must have added to the consternation of the British and French.

While there was no gala reception for the Russians in California such as there had been in New York due to the suddenness of their arrival, the three principal newspapers, the *Morning Call, Evening Bulletin,* and *Daily Alta California* were filled with articles about the Russian visitors. Much nonsense was printed about Russian life, anecdotes were fabricated about important Russian personages, and Russian history was sweetened into something that would please Americans. One newspaper, the *News-Letter,* which had a Southern editor, referred to the Russian ships as "dung-barges," and to the Russian consul, Mr. Kostromitinov, as "Contra-Costa Meat-Enough." The Southern editor stated that the Russians refused to make the proper social distinctions in San Francisco, allowing themselves to be entertained in taverns by ruffians and harlots.

The El Dorado of San Francisco

Admiral Popov himself was amazed at the changes that had taken place in San Francisco. In a glowing report to St. Petersburg, he wrote, "Such a miracle could only have been produced by men with no wealth. Rich men would never have had the energy to begin, much less to bring to consummation such an exploit."

The feverish energy of the Californians bewildered the Russians. Everything was done at a sort of telegramatic tempo, as if speech cost so much a word. Even children playing in the streets had a restlessness and feverishness about them. At one of the theatres, the Bella Union, people threw eggs, apples, and softer fruit at the actors, and there was usually a fist-fight before the evening was over, which the Americans seemed to enjoy more than they did the stage performance.

On another occasion, invited to see Lotta Crabtree, "America's première actress," the Russian officers entered the theatre, wearing their dress uniforms. They found themselves in the midst of a raucous crowd of men who spat on the floor, propped their feet on top of the chair backs, and who, when the actress appeared on the stage, threw coins at her. "What an insult!" said one Russian officer. "Is there nothing sacred to these Americans?"

But the Russian officers were amazed to see that Lotta smiled at her audience and blew kisses at them, and frequently interrupted her performance by stooping to pick up the coins which had been tossed on the stage.

Three weeks after the arrival of the Russian Fleet, a fire broke out in San Francisco. The Russian sailors helped to bring it under control and to save the furnishings in several houses. One unfortunate incident occurred. however, when several Russian sailors, attempting to save a piano, threw it out of a second-story window onto a cobblestone street. The opinion of the owner of the house was never recorded.

One Russian sailor, Kovshikov, an incorrigible drunkard, went ashore one evening and never returned to his ship. For weeks the police and harbor authorities of San Francisco conducted a futile search, and Kovshikov was finally listed as a deserter. Two days before the Russian Fleet sailed into the Pacific, he reappeared, his clothes in tatters, exhausted, and crying with relief at having found his countrymen. He told a tale of visiting a saloon, of being approached by three men who bought him a considerable quantity of whiskey. The next thing he could remember was finding himself aboard a strange merchant vessel which had already put to sea. He learned, to his horror, that the ship was bound for Africa. Later in the afternoon he saw a ship on the horizon that appeared to be bound eastward, and, more than an hour later, when he was certain the ship would pass near him, he jumped overboard. Fortunately, he was spotted in the water, and was taken aboard and given passage into San Francisco.

The Russians were entertained at a dance held in the Town Hall. Tickets were sold at a hundred dollars apiece "so housemaids, laundresses and men-servants could not attend." By the middle of the evening, however, it became evident that the Americans preferred wine to song. Even the musicians abandoned their instruments and joined in the drinking bout. "I suspect," wrote a Russian officer, "that the difficulty was mainly the result of the fact that San Francisco ladies are uncommonly poor in their dancing."

Another dance was held in honor of the Russians by the Montgomery Guard, San Francisco's militia. A Russian officer wrote home "There were no drunkards and most of the American ladies could dance. But what strange people are these Americans! When we entered the ballroom it was absolutely dark, and then suddenly the room was flooded with light, revealing hundreds of canary birds in gilt cages. While the dance music was playing, you could hear all those birds squalling at the top of their voices!"

Few Americans visited the Russian ships, despite the invitations that were extended. Newspaper reporters came aboard the *Abrek* on a few occasions, and of course there were merchants, and several Chinese laundrymen who wished to suggest the excellence of their establishments. The Russians were so pleased with a Dr. Chapka, who had none of the rudeness which they found in most Californians, that they made him their guest-of-honor— until San Franciscan port authorities informed the Russians that Dr. Chapka was "a sort of male mid-wife, with a most unsavory reputation."

These incidents and minor events have been mentioned in an effort to show why the Russians never formed a clear or accurate picture of the United States. Yet, in another sense, they were the first Russians on American soil to come into contact with a wide stratum of life in the American vein.

While the officers and crews of the Russian squadron were spending as much time as possible ashore, Admiral Popov was champing at the bit. Many Russians expected war, but Popov was one of the few Naval officers who wanted it. The kind of man he was is shown by the fact that in 1895, when more than seventy years old, he re-entered the Imperial Naval Academy for "further instruction in methods of naval warfare."

At the time of the arrival of the Russian squadron, San Francisco was being defended by a solitary American gunboat. A few weeks later the gunboat was sunk, leaving the city with no protection, since the shore batteries were inadequate to repel an attack from the sea. There were rumors that Confederate privateers, the *Alabama* and the *Sumter,* were lurking off the California coast. Admiral Popov, when informed of this, issued instructions that the following message should be sent to any Confederate ship that was sighted by the Russians. "All ships of this Squadron of His Excellency Commander-in-Chief Rear-Admiral Popov are bound to assist the authorities of every place where friendship is offered to them in all measures deemed necessary by the local authorities to repel any attempt against the security of the place."

Popov further instructed his captains that at the first indications of hostility, the Russian ships were to open fire. By this simple expedient Popov had taken upon himself the right to protect the entire California coast.

This act by Admiral Popov promptly involved him in difficulties with his own Government, because he sent copies of this order to Stoekl in Washington and to Krabbe in St. Petersburg. Stoekl hastily informed Popov that Russia did not recognize the Confederate Government, and therefore the Civil War must remain an American domestic problem. Popov must please not intervene. "Even if Confederate ships do attack, it is your duty to be strictly neutral. If, however, a privateer should slip past the forts and threaten San Francisco itself, you would have the right, solely on humanitarian grounds, and not out of any political consideration, to make your influence felt for averting the consequences of such an act. It is to be hoped that you would not fail to produce the desired effect without resorting to force, and without involving Russian diplomacy in complications that your Excellency would, surely, want to avoid."

Chancellor Gorchakov replied more succinctly. "Russia is strictly neutral. I must withhold my approval of Admiral Popov's proposal."

Late in March, 1864, Popov was given orders to remove his ships from American waters, which suggests that the Russian Government was still somewhat concerned as to whether Popov would hold to a policy of neutrality.

Many of the Russians regretted leaving the shore of California. Several of the officers had fallen in love with American women, and in the diary of one of them was the following entry, written a few days after the ships had sailed into the Pacific: "Farewell. Young love is short. The heart is like a lamp. In port the heart burns with an intense flame, but at sea the light of that lamp grows dimmer until is disappears like vapor on a sunny day. Whoever says we love but once in a lifetime has never lived on the drifting sea."

The Steam Frigate *Alexander Nevsky* in the Dry Dock at Kronstadt in 1865

Upon the return of the Russian Fleet to its homeland in 1864, a delegation, led by Admiral Lessovsky, called on the American Minister to thank him "for the cordial and brilliant reception which was extended to the Russian flag by the government and the people of the United States." Lessovsky concluded, "That the day is not distant when your country, now passing through the school of adversity, shall be happily united, is the earnest prayer of ourselves and of all generous Russians."

Cassius Clay, in his acceptance of this honor, made a remark which is possibly difficult for modern Americans to understand, but which was, in his own time, the foundation of American doctrine:

"Though one Government be autocratic and the other republican, no necessary antagonism results from such difference of form. Although we are not prepared to go as far as Pope—'Let fools forms of government contest, What's best administered, is best'—yet we Americans of all people are the least inclined to propagandize because we are eminently practical. We know that political institutions grow. They are not made. Since the time of Catherine II we have been friends, because it was in our interest to be so. But allow me to say, Admiral, that the enthusiasm with which you have been received in America sprang from no such cold calculations. It was based on a higher principle than interest—sentiments yet nobler than the gratitude which we owed your Emperor for his friendship in our hour of trial and misfortune—it came as a common cause in the advancement of humanity."

holy russia

Through all the centuries of man's recorded history, religion has played an important, frequently predominant factor in the relations between peoples of different races and nationalities. Thus, although in the diplomatic field Russia and the United States had been drawing into accord since the beginning of the Nineteenth Century, the average American citizen felt little sympathy for Russia until the Crimean War. Much of this sympathy sprang from Protestants in the United States who, as the Catholic population began to grow, revealed their resentment by siding with anyone or any nation which stood firmly against the Roman Catholic Church. From this came the first strong emotional ties with the Russians, who, together with a smaller but powerful Lutheran movement in Germany, formed the eastern wall against Roman Catholicism.

Historically, interest in the Eastern Church began in the era of Peter the Great. Exactly what Peter the Great's views on religion were is difficult to determine, and his frequent profane ribaldries concerning the Church and the Priesthood suggest that he was contemptuous of both. But, as a public spectacle and as a support of the throne, he undoubtedly saw their utility and values.

Peter was not however a man who cared much for rituals, and there is reason to believe that his personal taste was for the simplest possible form of Church service. This would explain his interest in the Society of Friends, for he attended several Quaker meetings while he was in England. He was impressed with William Penn, but at no time revealed serious intentions beyond curiosity. The only probable result of his associations with the Quakers was an increased ire against powerful, pretentious churchmen. He therefore allowed the Patriarchate to lapse upon the death of Patriarch Adrian, and established a council to superintend Church affairs. Unlike Henry VIII, he had no interest in theology and never attempted to make himself *summus episcopus,* but he intended to keep the reins of Church policy in his own hands. He negotiated with Constantinople for recognition of his newly established Holy Synod. This act brought the Church within the control of the State and caused the downfall of the Patriarchate in all the countries of eastern Europe.

But although he broke the political power of the Eastern Church, it was the tolerance and favor which Peter the Great showed to the Scots, of whom he had a great many in his service, that provided the first link between western Europe and the Eastern Church. The Scots were interested in bringing themselves into the Orthodox Church, probably for political and business, as well as religious, reasons. Furthermore, Scottish guardsmen in the Palace wanted to be able to take the Sacrament in the Russian church, having no church of their own to attend. The Patriarch of Constantinople, however, who considered them thrice schismatical, if not thrice heretical—they had broken away from the Church of England, which was in schism with Rome, which in turn was in schism with Orthodoxy—would not study their case. But at the request of Peter the Great, the Russian Synod opened correspondence with the leading churchmen of Scotland, and this early exchange of doctrine became the basis of religious communication between western and eastern Europe.

To complete the cycle, it was Peter the Great who organized the Bering Expeditions, which eventually led to the establishment of the first Orthodox Church on American soil.

Father Veniaminov was the son of a poor peasant who made a meager living by sweeping, dusting, ringing the bell, and gathering wood to warm a village church. Veniaminov entered a monastery to become a priest, without knowing how to read or write. In 1778, as a missionary priest, he went to the Alaskan colony. During the next sixteen years, this remarkable man, of humble origin, not only performed his regular duties for the Russian colonists, but he created the Aleut alphabet, composed a grammar, and translated the Holy Scriptures and other books into Aleutian. It is without doubt a result of the efforts of Father Veniaminov that the Alaskan population today still remains faithful to the Orthodox Church. In 1794, as a result of his urgent letters, the

The Russian Cathedral of St. Michael in Sitka

Russian Church, Sitka, Alaska.

Holy Synod decided to send a Bishop to the Alaskan colony. While at sea, the ship that was bearing the Bishop to his new post sank, and everyone aboard was lost. Veniaminov was appointed Bishop. Five years later he was raised to Archbishopric rank. He spent another ten years in Alaska, trying not merely to instruct the Aleuts in the Orthodox Faith, but to bring them into unity with the Russian colonists.

When Metropolitan Philaret died, Father Veniaminov was appointed his successor, the highest religious position in all Russia. Ironically, he left Alaska for his new post, unaware that his adopted land had been sold to the United States.

During his lifetime, and in the years that followed, more and more Russians drifted southward to take part in the settlement of California. Excepting the tiny church at Fort Ross, which fell into disuse after the sale of the fort and the surrounding lands, there was no church in all that part of the world which the Russians could attend. Thus, the growing Russian population in California obliged the Russians to approach the Protestant Episcopal Church and ask for the right to take Communion in its churches. Protestant Episcopalians, having the American equivalent of the Anglican Communion, seemed most nearly in harmony with Russian Orthodoxy.

The Anglican San Francisco clergy were perfectly willing to grant the request, but stated that such permission exceeded their authority and must be referred to the whole Church. In 1862,

Palm Sunday in St. Petersburg

the General Conference took up the question and appointed a Russo-Greek Committee to study the possibility of inter-communion between the Anglican and Orthodox Churches. Chairman of this Committee was the Right Reverend William DeLancy, Bishop of New York, and the Secretary was John Freeman Young. Probably the Committee would have gone no further than to make an intellectual investigation and then drop the matter, had it not been for the arrival of the Russian Fleet and the excitement that followed. Orthodox chaplains were entertained by the American clergy, many matters were discussed, and Bishop DeLancy offered the Russian priests their choice of any of the sixty churches in his diocese in which to hold services for the Russian sailors. Much of the discussion concerned the *Shorter Catechism,* written by the aged and beloved Metropolitan Philaret of Moscow, which had been translated into English and was frequently used by Episcopal clergymen in teaching children the essentials of church doctrine.

As a direct result of these meetings with the Russian chaplains, the Russo-Greek Committee decided to send John Freeman Young to Russia to study Orthodoxy and investigate the possibility of inter-communion. In April, 1864, Young arrived in St. Petersburg. Young summarized the purpose of his visit as follows: "The end contemplated by the movement of the American Church is the attainment of more accurate knowledge of the Orthodox Eastern Church than we are yet in possession of, making known to her Hierarchy at the same time, as opportunities may serve, our well-established claims to recognition as an integral portion of the *One, Holy, Catholic and Apostolic Church;* having in view (should it appear feasible and desirable when we come to know each other better) such mutual recognition of Orders and Sacraments, as will allow members of the Anglo-American Communion to avail themselves of the offices of the Eastern Church, with the consent of its Bishops and clergy, without renouncing the communion of their own church, and to permit members of the Eastern Church, with like consent, to avail themselves of the ministrations of the Anglo-American Church."

Reverend Young was cordially, but somewhat apprehensively received. Russian prelates had not forgotten the persistence of the

Englishman, Mr. Palmer, who had made a similar mission in 1840. The position of Young, however, differed from that of Palmer, in that Palmer had come as a private individual, whereas Young was the delegate of a recognized branch of the Apostolic Church—a branch regarded by the Russians as heretical and schismatical but nevertheless one of the recognized independent national churches of Christendom. The letters Young bore were the first sent to any of the Eastern Churches by any of the Western Churches, relative to reunion, since the great schism of the Eleventh Century.*

Upon arriving in St. Petersburg, Young went to call on Prince Urussov, the Synod Secretary, who urged him to proceed to Moscow, the Russian Rome. Young did this. After his arrival in Moscow, he went to call on Bishop Leonid, who could speak English. The Bishop, who had been a classmate of Admiral Lessovsky at the Naval Academy, had difficulty in understanding Young, for long disuse of his English had left it rusty, and "because the English language as spoken in America has been changed into some peculiar provincial dialect." Young presented the letters he had brought from the United States, signed by seven of the forty Bishops of the Episcopal Church. Oddly, every one of the seven Bishops, except the Bishop of Michigan, was from the Atlantic Seaboard, although the original purpose of the Delegation had been the problem of Russians stranded on the Pacific Coast.

---

*The English had long recognized the value and need of a reunion of the Western and Eastern Churches. Birkbeck wrote, "Before there can be any question of reunion between the Churches, the close relation between Russian national and religious aspirations must be realized and appreciated by English Churchmen; and that, rather than abuse Russia for having solved the most difficult question of the age, and indeed of all ages—viz. the reconciliation of the secular and religious aspirations of nations, in a manner which has resulted in their being able to work together to the preeminent advantage of both Church and State—we Englishmen, whatever the political difficulties which they may have with her—and I do not deny that these are from time to time anything but insignificant, though perhaps this need not be so forever—have no wish whatever to see Russia under an infidel government, or that her Church should lose its influence in directing her destinies."

Palmer had been refused admission to the Sacraments in Russia as an Anglican, the reason given being "that it was impossible for an individual, whether priest or layman, to be in union at the same time with two Churches which were not in union with one another."

The letters expressed the desire of the American Church for peace and union with the Orthodox Communion. They wished an exchange of views, and hoped to obtain permission to send young men to Russia to study the language and the religion for the purpose of translating some of the principal works of the Russian Church.

The Metropolitan Philaret received Mr. Young and had several lengthy conversations with him. The American came to an impossible barrier at the outset when the validity of the 49 Articles of the Church of England came up. Young called them "merely an historical fact," to which Philaret replied that that might be true for the American Church, but it was certainly not true of the English.

"The most important people of the English Church think the same way," said Young.

"That means that the Articles have lost their importance," agreed Metropolitan Philaret. "But they, nevertheless," remain the law. And they are too intolerant on the doctrine of the Eastern Church where it is not in agreement with the Western Church." Philaret was alluding to the ostensible, though perhaps not essential cause of the schism of the Greek and Roman Church—the procession of the Holy Ghost, which Byzantium said the Catholics had changed by the addition of Filioque (. . . and the Son) after the words, "who proceedeth from the Father."

Young was not inclined to fight for Filioque. The American Church was willing to omit ". . . and the Son" from the Nicene Creed, but such an omission would require time, because people were unprepared for it.

"If the Americans can simply drop a portion of the Nicene Creed, I would be tempted to suspect that it hints at a lack of depth in the beliefs of the Americans," said Philaret. "Probably the American Church does not cling very firmly to its church forms because they are not very ancient. They only date from the separation from Rome. The Russian people, on the other hand, have maintained their forms for nine hundred years. It would be difficult for them to accept calmly the idea of union with a church having different forms." Philaret then added, "The Russian Church has a Mother, and in some ways rather a severe Mother. For example, we Russians are willing to tolerate baptism by immersion, but the Greek Church will not tolerate it. So the Russian Church must be prudent."

"Two enlightened men like ourselves," continued Philaret, "might arrive at an agreement regarding principle and fundamental questions. But the Church—and I am sure it is true in America too—does not consist solely of learned and enlightened men. The mass of people—in both countries—might not understand and therefore create difficulties."

As an example of the kind of misunderstandings which could arise, Philaret mentioned the *ikons*. Young condemned them as mere pictures which encouraged idolatry. Philaret smiled. "You see, to a Russian, *ikons* are the object of pious veneration but never of adoration."

Before Young terminated his conferences with the Metropolitan, an agreement was reached. The establishment of immediate relations between the two clergies was undesirable. Private correspondence might, however, be initiated, and doctrinal questions could be advanced for written discussion. The American Liturgy would be translated and printed in Russia, but not by the official Russian Synod press.

An important part of Young's mission was concerned with the availability of the Sacrament to Russian immigrants in America. Young felt that if inter-communion could not be arranged, and Philaret assured him that it was not at present possible, the only other solution was the establishment of Russian churches in the United States. Philaret suggested that Young had best confer with the Metropolitan Isidor in St. Petersburg. So, on his return to St. Petersburg, Young met with Isidor, explaining that he felt the first church should be erected in New York, that the building should be beautiful, and that the priest must be both a scholar and a man of pleasant and agreeable manners, because in the United States, unlike Russia, the clergy ranked with the best families. Without good manners and the gift of eloquence, a Russian priest might find himself unwelcome in New York.

After Young had departed for the United States, Metropolitan Isidor conferred with Philaret, stating that he was not sure a church in New York would be desirable. Isidor shrewdly suspected that American enthusiasm for Orthodoxy was less than Young had claimed. Furthermore, Russia must not give the impression of proselytism. Orthodoxy sought no converts. If a church were to be built, the place was in Washington, near the Russian Legation. (Most of the members of the Legation at that time were not Orthodox. The late Bodisco and Stoekl were both Lutherans.)

"A church is needed most in California," continued Isidor. "But who would give us the money? The government will not pay for it. The Holy Synod has nothing to give. Prince Gorchakov can be asked for anything except money. But if we were to build near the Legation in Washington, we could approach the Emperor himself!"

But the more Philaret considered a site, the more he became convinced that New York was the most favorable spot in the eastern United States.

It was not until after the sale of Alaska, when by a *ukase* of Alexander II—almost certainly instigated by Metropolitan Veniaminov— the Russian Church received for its maintenance $72,000 a year, one percent of the sale price of Alaska, that money was available for these projects. This annual sum became the financial basis for the Russian Church in the United States until the 1917 Revolution. Negotiations were underway for the construction of a Russian Church in San Francisco by 1869, and soon afterward came the announcement that a church would be built in New York City, whose priest would be American-born Reverend Nicholas Bjerring, a former professor at the Roman Catholic Academy in Baltimore.

Bjerring, whose small but graceful church was located at 951 Second Avenue, died in 1880. Soon thereafter a larger church appeared downtown near Eighth Street. The Russian Church in America grew rapidly. At the threshold of the Twentieth Century a beautiful Byzantine cathedral arose on 97th Street, off Fifth Avenue. On February 29, 1917, two weeks before the Revolution, the Russian Cathedral Choir sang at the White House and was warmly applauded by President Wilson.

Today every State in the United States and in Canada possesses at least one Russian church. By 1957, there were at least three hundred Russian churches with congregations numbering

400,000 people. Four generations have now knelt on American soil to worship and to hear the Slavonic words of the Orthodox Liturgy—whose beautiful music, due to the great musicians who all wrote Liturgical music in Russia, may have been partly responsible for the hold on all Russians of the Russian Church, and for its consequent power.

An American, by the name of Cyrus W. Field, unconsciously helped the sale of Alaska. His failure with the Atlantic cable, in 1858, brought together three men, Jeptha Homer Wade, a daguerreotypist; Hiram Sibley, a former shoemaker who had become President of the Western Union Telegraph Company; and Percy Collins, acting United States Agent in Siberia. They conceived a plan to link Russia with America via Alaska and build a 16,000 mile telegraph line from New York to Paris. The line would run from San Francisco to Alaska, cross the Bering Straits to Siberia, and join the trans-Siberian lines.

Hiram Sibley made the arrangements with the British, Russian and American governments. The United States released Captain Charles Bulkeley from his Army duties to supervise the work, and young Robert Kennicott, already famous for his explorations in Alaska and the Yukon, was obtained as geographical adviser from the Smithsonian Institute.

On July 8, 1865, twenty-four vessels departed from San Francisco. This expedition of ships, dog-sleds, and canoe parties explored 6,000 miles around the North Pacific, mapping, charting, and setting up telegraph poles. The Stanovoi littoral in Siberia sweeps upward into rugged crags that tower 6,000 feet above the sea. Investigation disclosed that the narrowest part of the Bering Strait was, unfortunately, not a feasible place to lay a cable, so a point further south was chosen where the distance was nearly four hundred miles across.

Robert Kennicott died of a heart attack at Nulato on the Yukon, less than a year after the expedition had reached the Arctic. It was not Kennicott's death which halted the expedition, but news that an Atlantic cable had been successfully stretched from Ireland to Newfoundland. By March, 1866, the Collins Overland Telegraph decided that there was no longer a need for their line.

But in distant Siberia, George Kennan, who was superintendent of the Kamchatka Division, did not get word to suspend operations until 1868. Along the land route on both the Siberian and Alaskan shores the telegraph poles still stand, gaunt reminders of the attempt to join the American and Russian empires by telegraph.

There was sadness in many diplomatic quarters when it was learned that the telegraph line was being abandoned. "I would not have the Atlantic cable become dumb again to secure the success of your enterprise," United States Secretary of State Seward wrote to Hiram Sibley, "but I must confess to a profound disappointment in the suspension of the enterprise." The Russian Marine Ministry, which was always encountering difficulties in communication with the Pacific Squadron and with Alaska, was also deeply disappointed.

All projects since that time to link America with Russia have been unsuccessful. At the end of the Nineteenth Century a plan was submitted to the Russian Embassy in Washington to bore a tunnel under the Bering Straits. In 1901 a company was formed to build a railroad across the Straits. All these projects failed.

The doomed telegraph project stimulated American interest in Alaska and provided extensive geographical knowledge of the Arctic. One American in particular, Seward, a man of keen but sometimes wayward imagination, who, during the Civil War, had urged Lincoln to declare war on England and France because he felt it would reunite the country, fixed his eyes upon Alaska and vowed that he would do everything within his power to make that vast territory fly the Stars and Stripes. As early as September, 1860, he had declared in St. Paul, Minnesota, "I see the Russians establishing seaports and towns and fortifications on the verge of this continent, and I can say, 'Go on, build your outposts all along the coast, even to the Arctic Ocean; they will yet become the outposts of my own country!' "

The Russian Minister, Stoekl, left the United States, he thought forever, and arrived in St. Petersburg, where he was approached by the Grand Duke Constantine. The Russian-American Company was in such desperate straits that it had been forced to sublet its chartered privileges to the Hudson Bay Company.

Grand-Admiral
The Grand Duke Constantine

Stoekl told them bluntly that he believed Russia had made a serious error by not selling Alaska in 1858. He was not even sure the United States would still be interested, the aftermath of the Civil War having, for the time being, dampened enthusiasm for territorial expansion. At a conference with the Emperor, a decision was made to sell Alaska. Alexander II asked Stoekl to return to the United States and conduct the sale. He was told not to accept less than $5,000,000. Those were his complete instructions.

Stoekl arrived in New York on February 1, 1867, where he was stricken ill and in bed for six weeks. The time was not wasted, however, as he used it to drop hints and spread rumors that Russia was considering the sale of Alaska. He was aided by several other events. For nearly a year pressure had been exerted on the Johnson Administration by the Pacific Coast settlements to secure trading rights in Alaska, or, failing in that, to purchase the territory. Also, a group of Californians, aware that the Russian-American Company lease would expire in June, 1867, had conceived the idea of forming a company to take over the charter on a twenty-five year lease. Moreover, the citizens of the Washington Territory had requested the United States government to attempt to obtain Alaskan fishing rights and privileges for them.

Secretary Seward took up the various proposals with Stoekl. Stoekl replied that the Russian Government must refuse them. "Very well," said Seward. "Will Russia sell the whole territory?"

"Such a solution might offer advantages to both Russia and the United States," replied Stoekl.

Seward announced that he would take the matter up with President Johnson.

The President, who was not enthusiastic, agreed to leave the matter to his Cabinet. On their urgent advice, he authorized Seward to negotiate. A few days later Seward and Stoekl met and proceeded directly to the matter of price. Seward offered five million, which Stoekl refused. "Five and a half million," said Seward. "That's our final offer!"

"I'm afraid I couldn't consider less than seven million," replied Stoekl, who later that same day made out a report to his government that negotiations had begun and that he had high hopes of obtaining $6,000,000, a million more than he had been instructed to obtain.

But as Seward continued to reveal eagerness in subsequent interviews, Stoekl decided he could risk holding to his $7,000,000 declaration. Seward came up to it, a little at a time, complaining bitterly that he was exceeding his instructions and would probably never be able to get it approved by Congress. Stoekl was aware that there was truth in this, because Seward was regarded as a crack-pot by many Senators and Representatives. He cautioned Seward, therefore, that if they did reach an agreement, it would be better to have a member of the Senate claim the initiative for having made the purchase. Congress would then be more kindly disposed. Seward, however, refused to consider such a thing. It was his duty as United States Secretary of State to carry out the negotiations, and he had no intention of being stripped of the honor of presenting the Nation with a new important territory.

The next day, Stoekl cabled the joyful news to St. Petersburg that the United States had agreed to pay seven million dollars. Chancellor Gorchakov, seeing that the United States was anxious to acquire Alaska, or at least that Seward was, decided to try to tempt the United States Government into taking over the debts of the Russian-American Company, to have the money deposited in London, and to pay the incidental gold-exchange fees.

But this time Seward balked. Seven million had been the price, and the United States had met it. "I consider the price too high as it is," said Seward. "I have gone far beyond the wishes of my Government in order to prevent unnecessary bickering. But I will not for one moment entertain any suggestion of taking over the obligations incurred by the chartered company. And my Government will not clear the transaction in London. We had our bellyfull of London in the late war."

Stoekl, who personally felt that his task of trying to wheedle a few more concessions was unpleasant and unfair, agreed to drop these. Seward then admitted that there might be some justice in the Russian Government's objection to paying exchange fees, and said that his government would add a couple of hundred thousand dollars to cover it. Thus the final figure of $7,200,000 was reached, the price for Alaska "free and unencumbered by any reservations, franchises, etc."

It is small wonder that the world, to this day, believes that when the United States deals with European diplomats it is like a sheep going to the shearing. It may seem strange in the light of Alaska's present value that there could have been so much discussion over the purchase of a vast land at two cents an acre— though no one then knew the actual acreage of Alaska. But it was really much more strange that Congress ratified the purchase, and in four hurried days. The ratification of "Seward's Icebox" took place in a kind of hands-thrown-in-the-air manner, with Congress playing the role of a resigned father paying the gambling bills of an irresponsible son.

Actually, Alaska was nearly as indefensible in American hands as it had been in Russian hands. It could not be reached by land without crossing foreign territory, and British naval power was in a position, in the event of a war, to wrest it from the United States. The Russian Empire had learned, by hard experience, that *expansion must come by overland conquest* (an interesting thought when one considers the burgeoning Chinese

New Archangel in the 1860's (Sitka)

population today, the fact that the yellow race is Russia's historical enemy, and the only one to outnumber her, man for man). Yet, the new American empire, which until this moment had also confined her growth to lands that bordered upon her own territories, had now embarked upon approximately the same precarious course that Russia had decided to abandon.

Most Americans feel that the Russians were "out-foxed," that they did not have accurate knowledge of the wealth of Alaska. The fact is that both the Russian Government and the directors of the Russian-American Company were aware of the extreme richness of Alaskan mineral deposits.

As early as 1848 a mining engineer by the name of Doroshin had discovered deposits there of limestone, marble, graphite, coal, and gold. In 1855, a vein of gold was opened and a small shipment sent to San Francisco. But the Russians had no way of exploiting these resources. Having at their disposal insufficient ships, money, and trained engineers, both the Russian Government and the Russian-American Company had no choice but to remain silent about their Alaskan treasure trove, any hint of which would "bring not only an army of foreigners with shovels, but an army of enemy soldiers." Had Alaska still been a possession of Russia at the time of the Klondike gold-rush, the horde of Americans who swept north would have either driven the Russians out or caused such friction as to make a war inevitable between the two countries.

A Soviet Marxist historian analyzes the situation fairly accurately: "The Czar of Russia knew perfectly well what he was selling, and the U. S. knew just as well what they were buying." This should perhaps be amended by adding that at least those Americans who wanted to buy Alaska knew what they were buying.

Seward and Stoekl reached an agreement just as Congress was on the verge of its annual spring recess. Seward, who knew that on such occasions Congress was prone to passing bills and treaties which they did not like in order to get away from frenetic Washington, was so anxious to have the sale ratified by the Emperor and ready for Congress at this propitious moment, that he told Stoekl to cable the draft of the treaty to St. Petersburg at America's expense, a mere $9000. On Friday evening, March 29th, Stoekl went to Mr. Seward's residence where he found him playing whist with his family.

"I have a dispatch from my government," he said. "The Emperor gives his consent. Tomorrow, if you like, I will come to the Department."

"Tomorrow?" said Seward. "Why wait until tomorrow?"

"But the Department is closed. You have no clerks, and my secretaries are scattered about town."

Seward called for his hat and coat. "You muster your Legation," he said. "You'll find me waiting at the Department at midnight!"

At four o'clock on the morning of March 30, 1867, the treaty lay on Mr. Seward's desk—signed, sealed, and ready for delivery to the Senate.

The Senate at first refused to have anything to do with a measure sponsored by the Johnson Administration. It required all the power and prestige that Senator Sumner possessed to keep the debate open until there was some chance of success. Sumner personally did not care about Alaska, but as Chairman of the Senate Foreign Relations Committee, he supported the purchase partly for Seward's sake, and partly to cement Russian-American relations. Then, as the pressure mounted, Sumner finally urged

Stoekl to withdraw the treaty. He feared that it would not be approved and that it might cause political damage to his own career. Stoekl refused. "The honor of the United States is involved, for it was not Russia who took the initiative," said Stoekl. "Refusal of the Senate to ratify a treaty which my Government made in good faith can only be regarded as an insult."

Sumner returned in despair to the floor of the Senate. Then, without warning, the Senate opposition vanished, and the treaty was ratified on April 4th by the comfortable majority of 37 to 2. This feat of magic has always been graciously attributed to Sumner's oratorical powers. But in 1912 Professor William A. Dunning accidentally discovered among the papers of President Johnson a memorandum that quoted Seward to the effect that the Russian Envoy, Stoekl, had paid fairly large sums to important Washington figures—to Thaddeus Stevens, $10,000; to Nathaniel Banks, Chairman of the House Foreign Relations Committee, $8000; to John Farney, $30,000; to R. J. Walker and F. P. Stanton, $20,000 each.

Other evidence reveals that Stoekl reported to his Government that the greater part of the $200,000 which had been added to the sale price of Alaska had been used for "secret expenses." Also, Riggs Bank paid to Mr. Stoekl during this crucial period various sums in gold—$26,000; $18,000; $35,000; $45,000; and $41,000. In his request to be transferred, Stoekl wrote, "I urgently need a rest. Do not tell me to stay here in Washington because there is no other post to give me. Give me a chance to breathe for a while an atmosphere purer than that of Washington—and after that do whatever you wish with me."

In the House of Representatives, where no one knew anything about Alaska and no one wanted to, the margin of approval of the purchase was narrower. One Congressman made the comment, "That Alaska was created for *some* purpose I have little doubt. But our information is so limited that conjectures can assign *no* use to it, unless it is to demonstrate the folly which those in authority are capable of in the acquisition of useless territory." Another quoted the comment of Captain Gordon, "I would not give the most barren hills of Scotland for all I see around me."

Despite opposition in the Senate and the House, in the press and public opinion, ratification came with unparalleled speed. Little more than a fortnight passed between the first Stoekl-Seward interview and the final action of Congress. In its celerity this peaceful exchange of territory is without parallel in history. It was the first considerable part of the vast Russian Empire ever to be alienated permanently and voluntarily. Moreover, it was the first acceptance of sovereignty by the United States over any territory separated geographically from the rest of the nation. Without doubt, had it not been the current belief of most Congressmen that Canada, too, would soon be annexed, the treaty would never have been ratified.

No one understood the tremendous change in American foreign policy that the acquisition of Alaska portended. From this moment on, American hands stretched farther and farther beyond their native shores—Hawaii, the Phillipines, the Canal Zone, the Virgin Islands, Guam, Puerto Rico, Yap and other bits here and there, until finally the United States even laid claim to part of Antarctica.

Senator Sumner, on the floor of the Senate, when asked why Russia wanted to sell, said that he had no information, but that he recalled Napoleon's reasons for selling Louisiana: "Napoleon, first, needed money for his Treasury. Secondly, he was unwilling to leave this distant, unguarded territory a prey to Great Britain. Thirdly, he was glad 'to establish forever the power of the United States and give to England a maritime rival destined to humble her pride.'"

In the case of Russia, however, the reasons for sale belong in a different order: (1) unguarded territory; (2) to establish United States power; (3) need of money. The usual explanation that Russia sold Alaska because of dire financial difficulty contains only a few grains of truth. Even the Soviet Marxist historians discount it, pointing out that Russia could have gotten twice that sum from Great Britain. Moreover, seven million dollars could hardly save a nation whose yearly expenses amounted to more than three hundred million dollars. Of that seven million, the Russian-American Company received $700,000. $72,000 a year was sent to build and maintain the Russian Church in the United States, and $1,000,000 was used to liquidate maritime debts.

From the viewpoint of the Grand Duke Constantine, the sale was effected to relieve the Russian Government of the burden of having to underwrite the ever-increasing deficits of the Russian-American Company.

Besides this, the analogy of the sale of Alaska to Napoleon's sale of Louisiana was not a true one. Napoleon was an expert dealer in miscellaneous real estate, who viewed the world as an enormous chess game—give a piece here to get an advantage there. Russian policy had been announced in the proud words of Nicholas I, "Where the Russian flag has once been raised it must never be lowered." Russian policy contained the same stubborn pride expressed by Franz Joseph of Austria when faced with the loss of Venice, "If we must lose it, then let us lose it with honor like soldiers, and not like tradesmen."

Only the firmness and absolute power of Alexander II made possible the peaceful sale of Alaska. There was bitter opposition in Russia, particularly within the Russian-American Company. Admiral Zavoiko, the hero of Petropavlovsk, was obliged to retire from service and was banished to his estate for his refusal, as a director of the Company, to sign the release papers. The last Governor of Alaska, Prince Maxutov, was equally adamant. Baron Theodore Osten-Sacken, Russian Consul General in New York, protested the decision of the Emperor. The Russian press was indignant.

Indeed, it was a remarkable transaction—a nation that did not want to sell, selling to a nation that did not want to buy. Yet with this single event, the balance of power triangle of Russia, Britain, and the United States in the Pacific was destroyed, and overnight the United States assumed the paramount strategic position, the full significance of which may not even now be realized.

It was on a cool, misty day in the October of 1867 that the actual transfer took place in New Archangel—soon to be Russian Archangel no more but American Sitka. In the harbor three American vessels answered the salute of the guns on Castle Hill as the United States Marines stood at attention before Baranov's Castle. High overhead the blue and white St. Andrew's Cross began dropping gently down the Standard. It was almost down when it fouled in the halyards, and a Marine had to climb hastily up and disengage it. For one moment more it floated free over the farthest outpost of Russia before it was caught up and flung to the people below.

It fell into the arms of lovely Princess Maxutov, the Governor's wife, and she wept softly as she clutched the lowered standard and watched the Stars and Stripes climb steadily up. From the ships in the harbor came another salute, echoing again and again among the islands and channels until it died away over the broad Pacific.

In exactly the same year elsewhere in the world there occurred an extraordinary coincidence. At the very time that Russia sold out and withdrew from the Pacific, a new era began in Japan with the abolition of the Shogunate, an era destined to make Japan the economic and military power in the Pacific.

CHAPTER FOURTEEN

"VA-ET-VIENT"

In the 1860's and 1870's Russian interest in and knowledge of the United States increased. American writers and poets became more popular and widely read than ever before. In addition to Poe and Fenimore Cooper, these decades brought into Russia the works of Washington Irving, Emerson, Longfellow, Whitman, Hawthorne, Lowell, Holmes, and Bret Harte. Enthusiasm for American adventure novels was particularly high. It did not matter that Cooper and Mayne Reid (whom the Russians believed to be American) wrote of lands that had never existed inhabited by Indians resembling Rousseau's Noble Savage. To small Russian boys America became the land of freedom and excitement; they visualized the stamp of buffalo feet and the smoke from Indian tepees; they dreamed alternately of going to the Caucasus to fight the Turks and to America to fight the Indians; their minds pictured America as a land of gold nuggets, wagon trains, ivory bones, pirates, savages, and the outlaw's pistol.

"Like most Russian boys," wrote Grand Duke Alexander, "I contemplated running away to America, and I learned the names of the states, the principal cities and rivers, so I would not get lost when I arrived there."

The urge to "run away to America" was not confined to Russian boys. To Russian men the United States was a kind of sanctuary, a land to which they could flee if life became too difficult. The United States was a sort of daydream, an escape from the tedium of daily life, and from the small personal failures which men in all lands and all times suffer.

There is a strong probability that more educated Russians of the pre-1917 vintage than educated New Yorkers have read the whole of Mark Twain. Life on the Mississippi with its beloved stern-wheelers reminded Russians of life along their own Volga. Turgenev praised the Americans "as the greatest poets of our time—not the poetry of words, but of action." He sensed there was a poetry in "getting ready to dig through the Panama Isthmus" and in laying the electric telegraph across the ocean. He was intrigued by the activities of Phineas T. Barnum. Among the American writers, however, only Whitman and Hawthorne impressed him, for the rest "simply copied English literature." When Henry Holt, the American editor and publisher, broke the deplorable American habit of not paying the author for translations of his work and sent Turgenev a check for his American edition, Turgenev called Holt, "A Phoenix of a publisher."

"In a little seaside town," wrote Baron Roman Rosen, "where I went to school, an American Consulate had just been established and the Consul had raised a mast from which waved the Stars and Stripes. After school, I used to steal away every now and then and run to the American Consulate and take off my cap to the flag that represented to my boyish mind an emblem, of what I could not exactly define, but I felt it deeply . . ."

Yet, despite the "dream" which the United States had come to represent to many Russians, and despite the fact that men like Chekhov, Tolstoy, and Turgenev dreamt of and planned their coming to America, few Russians did. Between 1851 and 1861 an average of only sixteen hundred and twenty Russian subjects annually entered the United States. Although by the year 1870 this figure had increased to three thousand a year, most of these were Poles, German-Russians, and Jews, rather than Slavs.

The Russians who did come to America were a new kind of Russian. Kourbsky and Machtet went to Kansas and tried to organize a utopian colony along communistic lines. They failed and returned to Russia disillusioned. Nikolai Geins emigrated to America and unsuccessfully tried his hand at organizing communistic colonies in the West. Nikolai Chaikovski, who was later disgusted by the Reds in the Russian Revolution, going over to the Whites to head their anti-Bolshevik Government in Archangel, joined Geins in this project. Everywhere the seeds of revolution were being sown and tested, often unknown to the very men who were sowing them.

But while the Russians who came to the United States were still few in number, more and more Americans visited Russia. Many of these Americans were non-professional travelers and tourists whose interest had been awakened by the visit of the Russian Fleet and by the abolition of serfdom. Gustavus Fox speaks of a "numerous colony of English and American residents in Moscow." Bostonians in particular, who had fanned-out all over the whole world—including Alaska, Hawaii, China, Japan, and India—made their homes in the Russian Empire. Aside from the Winans and the Ropes, the names Young, Colt, Roberts, Appleton, Longfellow, Curtin, and Coffin became familiar to Russians. Old Anson Burlingame, whom Lincoln had appointed Minister to China and who had been so beloved by the Chinese that they appointed him Chinese Ambassador to the European Powers and the United States, actually died in St. Petersburg. Admiral Farragut arrived at Kronstadt in 1867 with his squadron and was royally received.

The American tradition of a European "grand tour" for the young men of quality had been initiated by George Ticknor. Following in his wake were many others, a number of whom obtained degrees at German universities. Before the Civil War, their interest had been confined to western Europe, but strained American relations with the French had caused increasing numbers of them to visit Germany and Russia. During the reign of Alexander I only four Americans published records of their travels in Russia.

Admiral Farragut's Squadron in Russia in 1867

The reign of Nicholas I saw 15 books written by Americans on Russia. By the end of the reign of Alexander II, 72 Americans had written their impressions.

Among the more important reports was a book by General McClellan on the Crimean War. George Kennan, who worked on the telegraph in Siberia, left interesting records. Mark Twain's *Innocents Abroad* contains excellent passages. The contribution of Eugene Schuyler, who translated Turgenev's *Fathers and Sons* and Tolstoy's *The Cossacks,* was considerable.

Nathan Appleton contributed much to Russian-American friendship. Whenever the American press or public opinion became violently anti-Russian, he would take up his pen. In 1904, when Americans were looking with aversion towards Russia, he published the diaries and notes of his visit in 1868.

But while Americans in increasing numbers went to Russia and formed a wide range of impressions, none of them sensed the undercurrent in St. Petersburg, the signs of incipient revolt. They had no background or point of origin from which to compare. A strident tone had crept into Russian voices, and strange words of a new dialectic.

Admiral Farragut

St. Petersburg was one of the most frenzied places in the world in the 1860's. This was the heyday of a revolutionary called Lavrov and his violent Historical Letters. And this was the decade of extravagant philanthropic ventures, of the supposed release of the individual from all restraint and obligation. The death knell of man's courtesy to man was being rung; extremism and exaggeration in all things became the vogue, while the Narodniki stated bluntly that "a shoemaker who makes a good pair of shoes is a greater man than Shakespeare, because the world must have shoes and can get along very well without poetry."

There were similarities between this era of Russian history and the post-1918 Jazz Age in Greenwich Village. Russian women bobbed their hair, smoked cigarettes, and talked metaphysics. Young Russian men let their hair grow long and argued Hegel. But the similarities were of a superficial nature. Dostoevski was not writing a detective story or even a psychological novel in *Crime and Punishment*. He was unfolding the tragic failure of Nihilism as a way of life and the ruin which it could bring to Russian youth.

By 1870, the violence of the revolutionary movement, still in its infancy, stirred Dostoevski to expose and prophesy in a novel the danger of Nihilism to the social fabric of the world.

This book, *The Possessed,* so little read in the United States, anticipated not merely the Russian revolution, but the destructive power of the human intellect and of human idealism when it cannot find spiritual values.

It is not surprising that the Americans knew nothing of all this. They prepared, as they always prepared for their trips to Russia, by reading Théophile Gautier's recommended *Voyage en Russie.* Even the Russians themselves, outside of student circles, recognized the hand that wrote upon the wall. No one but the Terrorists themselves expected an attempt to be made on the life of Alexander II, just as no one but John Wilkes Booth and his conspiratorial associates had dreamt that President Lincoln would be assassinated.

Alexander II had been, probably, the most beloved ruler in Russian history. The reforms and accomplishments of his reign were numberless. Yet Alexander II, the Emancipator, was to be stalked for years by assassins who bore him no personal hatred or animosity, who merely wanted to destroy the "symbol" of good government in the way that effigies are hanged or burned. This same mad reasoning was to become world-wide by the end of the century, when terrorists struck down an American President, an Austrian Empress, an Italian King, and a President of France. This kind of reasoning justified the bombing of a parliament "because there is no such thing as an innocent Bourgeois." This kind of reasoning caused the Russian plotters to choose the first anniversary of Lincoln's death for their attempt. They were stymied because the difference in Russian and American calendars would not allow the date to have significance in both nations!

Ossip Komissarov, who had been emancipated by the Emperor's Edict, migrated from his native town of Kostroma to St. Petersburg. He found work as a journeyman capmaker. Late that winter, when the Petersburg climate was at its worst, he was taken ill. It was the middle of April before he was able to be up and about, and, being a pious young man, his first thought was to go to a church to give thanks for his recovery.

With legs unsteady from weeks of disuse, he trudged toward a little log cabin chapel on an island in the Neva. As is so often the case with a man who has been bedridden for some time his eyes seemed attracted by everything that moved and every glint of light. The sky was vast and overwhelming. When he arrived at the river bank, he found the bridge gone. Park officials, seeing that a thaw was about to set in, and, fearing high water, had dismantled the little foot bridge to keep it from being washed away. There was ice on the river, but it did not look safe to walk on.

Ossip reluctantly left the river and moved on along the Palace Quay. His thoughts were never recorded, but were probably of no great consequence. As he drew near the Summer Garden, he saw a carriage embellished with the Imperial Arms and hurried forward to see if he could get a glimpse of the important personages who were about to enter the carriage. A crowd had gathered, and Ossip, being rather small, could not get close enough to see. The pushing and jostling was tiring to the capmaker, who had not yet regained his health, and he was about to turn away when he noticed a burly, broad-shouldered man methodically pushing forward through the crowd. Ossip ran and got behind him and soon had a good view of the carriage.

In the carriage, two men in uniform and two women were chatting. Ossip recognized the Emperor. He did not know who the others were (the Duke and Duchess of Leuchtenberg and Princess Marie of Baden, the ladies both daughters of the Emperor). The Emperor began to put on an overcoat. Ossip was watching these proceedings, when his attention was attracted by the big man whom he had followed through the crowd. The man took a pistol from his coat pocket, raised his arm, and took careful aim at the Emperor. There was a loud report. Ossip found himself, the pistol almost against his face, being pushed and shoved. The bullet had flown harmlessly into the air. Ossip had unconsciously managed to heave the man's arm upward, and then, fearing he might get shot himself, had simply hung onto the man's arm.

The assassin, and perhaps Ossip, would have been gravely mauled if the police had not intervened. The Emperor remained standing beside his carriage until the man had been bound, then strode over to him.

The Kazan Cathedral

"Who are you?" asked Czar Alexander II, using the familiar thou.

"A Russian!" replied the man.

"A Russian? And you want to kill me? Why?"

"Because you have betrayed us. You have cheated us of our land. The freedom you gave us was worthless!" *

The Emperor gave orders to General Todleben that the man who had saved him, Ossip, should be taken to the Winter Palace. Then the Emperor instructed the carriage driver to go directly to the Kazan Cathedral, where he gave thanks for his escape.

When Alexander II learned that Ossip was from Kostroma, the birthplace of Susanin, who had saved the life of the first Romanov Czar (Michael), he made the poor capmaker into a hereditary nobleman, and as a special mark of Imperial favor, added Kostromskoy to his name. With his new name and his new fortune, Ossip vanished from the pages of history.

President Johnson sent a formal message to the Emperor congratulating him on his miraculous escape. Feeling this was not enough, since other nations had also done this, the House and Senate passed, and the President signed, a Joint Resolution congratulating the Russian *people* on the escape of their Emperor. It was an act unique in American history. Never before had the

*Police investigation revealed that the man was Dimitri Karakzov, moderately wealthy, and a member of a Nihilist revolutionary group.

Gustavus Fox,
Assistant Secretary
of the Navy, 1861-1866

American Republic sent any message to a foreign nation that indicated personal feeling for the sovereign. The United States had always adhered to the policy that since kings and emperors existed they had to be recognized, but only with grim, impersonal formality.

The bearer chosen for the message was Gustavus Fox, Assistant Secretary of the Navy. Mr. Fox announced to the surprised nation—indeed the world—that he would cross the Atlantic in the *Miantonomoh,* an ironclad of the monitor type. The seaworthiness of the *Monitor* had been demonstrated in shallow coastal waters, but few believed that it could, with its low decks, make a trans-Atlantic voyage.

The passage from Newfoundland to Queenstown was not merely successful, but uneventful. It took eleven days. The London *Times* reported that the strange ship stood not a foot above the water's edge and that a man standing on deck looked as if he was standing in the sea. "The royal visitors at Sheerness on Saturday saw an extraordinary, and—we wish we could not feel it—portentous spectacle. They saw something between a ship and a diving-bell . . . the Romans would have called it a tortoise . . .

almost invisible, but what there was of it ugly, invulnerable and irresistible. Round this fearful invention were moored scores of big ships. These ships form a considerable part of the navy of this great maritime power, and there was not one of them that the foreigner could not have sent to the bottom in five minutes, had his errand not been peaceful. The wolf was in the fold, and the whole flock was at his mercy."

In France the *Miantonomoh* was less feared, for the French did not have all their blue chips riding upon the fortunes of the sea. But Napoleon III showed considerable interest in the *Miantonomoh* and asked Mr. Fox many questions regarding the construction and principles of operation. Mr. Fox was present at a historic moment, though he did not then know it. For while Fox and Napoleon III were chatting, a telegram was brought to the Emperor. That telegram had been dispatched from Prussian Headquarters in Bohemia, announcing that the Austrians were retreating in disorder after a decisive battle near the village of Sadowa. It was a stinging diplomatic defeat for France, and made inevitable a Franco-Prussian War. As the *Miantonomoh* signaled a new age in sea power, so the mighty Krupp guns signaled a rising power in Europe which would soon be thundering before the gates of Paris. Small wonder that Napoleon III became distracted in his conversation and soon excused himself.

Fox and his entourage received a warm welcome in Russia. Two lines of Russian ships escorted the *Miantonomoh* across the Gulf of Finland. At the harbor approaches of Kronstadt the fortresses boomed salutes, and the quiet blue waters were filled with cat-boats and yachts. From a chartered steamer crammed with passengers a band began to play *Hail, Columbia*. Admiral Lessovsky, now Commandant of Kronstadt, boarded the *Miantonomoh* to welcome the Americans.

RESOLUTION OF CONGRESS PRESENTED PERSONALLY
TO THE EMPEROR OF RUSSIA AT ONE TODAY.
FOX
ST. PETERSBURG, WEDNESDAY
AUGUST 8, 1866

This was the first cablegram ever sent from Russia to the United States over the transatlantic telegraph.

Alexander II sent the following message to the President of the United States: "This mark of sympathy has touched me deeply. It is not merely personal to me, it is a new attestation of the sentiments which unite the American nation to Russia. The two peoples find in their past no recollections of old grievances, but, on the contrary, memorials of amicable treatment. It is with great satisfaction that I see these bonds continually strengthening. I have communicated my sentiments to Mr. Fox, and I pray you to express them to Congress and to the American people."

Prince Gorchakov reported to Stoekl in Washington: "The Emperor has been most favorably impressed with Mr. Fox. The tact with which he has acquitted himself of his mission has been highly appreciated in our official circles. It would have been difficult to commit to better hands the measure of cordial courtesy prescribed by Congress."

With the formal portion of his duties concluded, Fox made a tour of Russia that was a succession of banquets and feasts. He became an authority on *zakuski, ukha, borshtch, koulebiaka, pirozhki,* and other Russian delicacies. He sat before piles of sturgeon, grouse, quail, snipe stuffed with truffles, and his path was lighted by bowl after bowl of flaming rum. "I was like a bee wandering among flowers," Fox reported. "But the striking feature of our visit was the spontaneous reception everywhere accorded to us by the people themselves. The flag of the United States has been shown and honored for a thousand miles in the interior of Russia, and our national airs have become familiar to her people."

At Kostroma people threw their coats on the road for the Americans to walk across. In the center of this ancient city, in Susanin Square, the Americans stood before the magnificent monument with the statues of Michael, the first Romanov Czar, and Ivan Susanin, the peasant who had saved his life.

On a cold, snowy night in the winter of 1613, Susanin had climbed out of bed and lighted a candle. At the door he found himself staring into the faces of a group of military officers who told him that they were enroute from Moscow with important dispatches for the Czar. But in the deep snow they had lost their way. Susanin, detecting the Polish accent in their speech, and knowing that the regular couriers traveled singly or in pairs, told the officers that he would take them to the Czar's lodgings, but that it was quite some distance. He invited them to refresh and warm themselves while he dressed.

Then Susanin went into the other room, woke his wife, and told her to hurry to Czar Michael's residence and warn the guard. He let her out through the window, then dressed, trying to calm himself, aware that if the officers were actually on a mission with important dispatches, he would probably be thrown in jail.

He went into the main room, built the fire, offered the suspected Polish officers bread and drink, and delayed them on one pretext after another as long as he dared. Finally they lost patience and forced him to lead them through the snow; but instead of going in the direction of the Czar's lodgings, he led them deep into the forest where they became lost. His murdered body was found there in the snow.

Mr. Fox's tour continued on in lavish style. Since Americans were not permitted by their own Government to receive decorations from foreign nations, Czar Alexander II presented him with a handsome snuffbox studded with twenty-six diamonds. Honorary citizenship, which in Russia meant "honorable citizen of the town" and required unanimous consent of the City Council, was bestowed on Fox in St. Petersburg, Moscow, Kronstadt, Korcheva, and Kostroma. From Michael Pogodin, the son of a serf who had risen by his own efforts to become a successful publisher and professor of Russian History at the University of Moscow, Fox received an autographed letter of Peter the Great, a poem by Derzhavin, a letter by Pushkin, a letter by Zhukovsky (author of the words of the Russian national hymn), a handwritten fragment by Gogol, a poem, *The First Snow,* by Countess Rostopchin, a facsimile of Karamzin's *History of Russia,* and a fragment in the handwriting of Safaric, the great Slavic philologist. These gifts were placed in the archives of the United States State Department.

Because he had been invited to attend special military maneuvers given in his honor, a privilege usually reserved for visiting royalty, Fox returned the honor in the only manner in his power. For technical reasons the Navy Department had forbidden the firing of the great 15-inch Dahlgren guns. But Fox ordered that when the Emperor inspected the *Miantonomoh* the guns should be fired in his honor.

One of Fox's last acts was the presentation to the Empress Marie of a thousand silver rubles to be dispensed in any charitable enterprise that she wished. It was a return gesture. Admiral Lessovsky had done the same for American charity in 1863.

The last function Fox attended was a dinner given by the Aristocrat's Club of St. Petersburg, where he read a poem which Oliver Wendell Holmes had written in honor of the visit:

> *A nation's love in tears and smiles*
> *We bear across the sea;*
> *O Neva of the Hundred Isles*
> *We moor our hearts in thee!*

The first demonstration of the importance of armor plate in naval warfare had been the destruction of the Turkish fleet at Sinope in 1853 by inferior but armored Russian squadrons. The unhappy experiences of the British and French fleets before Sevastopol had further emphasized the importance of armor. The western European powers had begun experiments with ironclad vessels.

But it had not been until the *Virginia* entered Hampton Roads, destroying the hapless Union vessels, that frigates were swept into oblivion. Wood was banished from the sea, at least in every military sense. No naval authority in the world could refute the evidence of that single naval engagement.

Before naval men had begun to digest the full implications of that event, John Ericsson's strange new ship had appeared. The *Monitor* was not important to naval history because it defeated the *Virginia*. There is some doubt whether the *Monitor*, without the tactical advantage of surprise, would have been the victor in that classic sea battle. The important contributions of the *Monitor* to naval warfare were the movable turret, which allowed the gun to track its target without the ship having to get into a broadside firing position; the development of a ship which sat so low in the water and exposed so small a surface area that it was extremely difficult to hit; and a ship which prepared human imagination for the possibility, providing certain technical problems could be overcome, of developing a boat that could travel underwater.

Not all of these things were immediately realized. Nevertheless, the influence of the Monitor-type vessel on the navies of Europe was extraordinary. Russia had immediately begun construction of a fleet of Monitors and by the time of Fox's visit possessed the largest Monitor squadron in the world. During the 1870's, it was not Prussia that Great Britain feared as a naval power, but Russia. Under the leadership of peppery old Admiral Popov, the almost defunct Russian Navy had shaped up into a major striking force. The gigantic *Peter the Great,* which was under construction at the time of Fox's visit, was unquestionably the most powerful ship of its time.

Popov was willing to try anything that would give Russia naval supremacy. Since he realized that such supremacy required inventive genius, and Russia's shipyards could never hope to compete with Britain's, in production, Popov then made what was perhaps the most amusing blunder in the history of naval development. He built two ships, experimentally, which he called "popovkas," based on the *Monitor,* but perfectly round. It was his belief that the circular shape would permit quick maneuvering. Unfortunately, it prevented any maneuvering at all. The old Admiral persuaded the Empress Marie to take a short cruise on one of them, but she got so violently seasick that the cruise was cancelled. Then, shortly after this, one of the "popovkas" got caught in an eddy in the Dneiper River and spun round and round. It was carried, helpless, down the river and dumped into the Black Sea. There the crew was rescued ignominiously by a more orthodox ship. That ended the "popovka" experiments in the Russian Navy.

The American Civil War had been important not only for the development of ironclads, but for the enormous increase in the use of steam to propel ships of war that it had stimulated. There resulted a wild confusion among the admiralties of western Europe as to whether future warships should be rigged with sail or equipped with coal bunkers. After the Civil War, the navies of the world became a hodge-podge of every conceivable type of floating ship. No one knew what to build. There had never been a full-scale sea battle between two fleets of ironclad ships, and naval authorities did not know whether to build small fast ships of high maneuverability, or heavy-tonnage ships with more firepower but clumsy and slow movement. Almost all the experience of centuries under sail, except for basic battle tactics, had to be cast aside or at least reconsidered in the light of the new technological developments.

With the publication of Admiral Mahan's famous book, *The Influence of Sea Power on History,* both Great Britain and Germany chose the battleship as the champion of their navies, and with good reason. By 1890, Germany had become the main threat to English domination of the sea, and with the launching of England's *H.M.S. Dreadnought* in 1905, the supremacy of the battleship over any lighter vessel was assured.

While the United States was not able to keep pace with Great Britain in shipbuilding, western Europe still feared American ingenuity and technology. It can with some degree of truth be asserted that from the last years of the Civil War on, the United States had the potential of becoming the greatest maritime power in the world.

CHAPTER FIFTEEN

GRAND DUKE ALEXIS

The most widespread corruption in American history took place during the Grant Administration. Grant could not conceive of refusing a job to a friend, and could not understand anyone who would be so unmannerly as to bring ethical considerations into a matter involving a favor. This was not cynicism, but a belief so deeply engrained in Grant that he objected to Civil Service because it would not do his bidding. It was "impolite," he said. With a President who held such beliefs, corruption was inevitable.

The *Crédit Mobilier*, which involved a large part of Congress in bribery and impeachment trials, was an ambitious fraud. The Internal Revenue Bureau, according to the *Nation*, was "one of the greatest sinks of corruption to be found in any nation on earth." One-fourth of the national revenue was regularly stolen. To make matters worse, the men in office were not merely knaves, but also incompetents. Senator Butler of Massachusetts, known as "Spoon" Butler in the South because of his weakness for stealing the movable property of Louisiana Confederates, approached Hamilton Fish with a scheme to form a syndicate to purchase the three northern States of Mexico. Then they were to bribe Congress to purchase this new territory at, of course, an exorbitant price.

The newspapers rebuked the politicians for appointing men of "doubtful" reputations to key posts. This was an unnecessary kindness—the reputations of most of the appointees were not at all *doubtful*. The Grant Administration resembled the rutting season among animals, "with the decencies and amenities of civilization entirely forgotten." As Minister to Belgium, Grant chose J. Russell Jones, his neighbor in Galena, Illinois, "the most elegant gentleman who ever presided over a livery-stable." Jones happened to be the uncle of Babcock, Grant's private secretary, who was indicted in the Whiskey Ring scandal. The "fire and brimstone" Methodist whom President Grant tried to send as American Minister to Brazil was too much even for the Senate, which was not usually particular about such matters.

John Lothrop Motley was dismissed as Minister to Great Britain, because he had incurred Grant's dislike. The President, to his surprise, had difficulty finding a successor. The *New York World* ran a want ad on the front page:

WANTED: A respectable man willing to be Minister to England. He must smoke, must not part his hair in the middle or write books, and must have contributed to the savior of the republic either a house, a farm, a cottage, a span of fast horses, or a pair of shirt studs.

Allan Nevins called the Perkins claim "perhaps the most malodorous of the many claims upon which lobbyists, shysters, and political harpies fed." Captain Benjamin Perkins, a buccaneer and blockade-runner, had supposedly made a contract with Stoekl, the Russian Minister, to supply Russia with 150 tons of gunpowder. He also contracted, a year later, in 1856, with Captain Otto Lilienfeldt, a Russian agent, to deliver 35,000 muskets to Sevastopol. The arms and powder, according to Captain Perkins, had been delivered to the Russians, but he was unable to collect. The Russian Government insisted that it knew of no such contracts, and demanded to see them before paying the claim.

During the Buchanan Administration the State Department asked the Russian Government to submit the matter to a Court of Arbitration. Chancellor Gorchakov refused, stating that the claim was fraudulent. During the Civil War, Seward took up the matter again, stating that Perkins' claims were not destroyed by the refusal of the Russian Government to recognize them. Gorchakov replied angrily that Russia would go to war before she paid a kopeck.

The wretched Perkins claim continued to reappear at inopportune times. There was little doubt that it was fraudulent. When the Russian Government asked for copies of the contracts, Captain Perkins admitted that there had been nothing in writing. Secretary Seward, however, perhaps because he could not believe in a fraud of such magnitude, or because he was familiar with the Gowen case, in which Russia had been at fault, took the claim seriously.

When Grant became President, he pushed the claim assiduously, particularly after the Perkins' heirs retained Grant's wife's two brothers as legal counsel. The old Captain was dead by this time, but his widow had hired Joseph B. Stewart, an able lawyer, though notorious for his connections with dubious ventures. Thus, when Frederick Dent and Judge Louis Dent, the President's brothers-in-law, obtained the help of "Spoon" Butler and General N. P. Banks, they formed a rather potent political coalition, and Grant demanded that Hamilton Fish, Secretary of State, do something about the claim.

Hamilton Fish stood out as a man of honesty and competence in Grant's cabinet, not because he was outstanding in virtue, but more like a one-eyed man in a kingdom of the blind. Fish apparently thought the claim was fraudulent. But political pressure forced him to press the claim anyway. The Perkins affair became entangled with the sale of Alaska when the House refused to vote an appropriation to pay for Alaska until the Russian Government settled the claims of all American citizens. Stoekl, who had worked so hard to make the sale of Alaska, gave up in despair. He wrote to his government that, as far as he was concerned, "if the United States were unwilling to pay for Alaska, they could have it without paying . . ."

Alexander II replied: "Please, please do not mention a single word about cession without compensation. I feel it is imprudent to expose American cupidity to temptation."

The Russian Government was disturbed by the inactivity of the American Congress. Alaska had been formally turned over to American possession in October, 1867, and was not paid for until, a full year later, Stoekl decided to send a number of "gifts" to key men in Congress. Robert Walker was given such a present. Hamilton Fish refused, but allowed his law partner to accept it. Thus Stoekl had to bribe Congressmen into buying Alaska, and then had to bribe them into paying for it! There can be little doubt why European nations remained skeptical about the democratic processes of government in America!

Shortly after Stoekl left the United States, a new Minister arrived to represent the Russian government, Constantine Catacazy. He was no stranger to Washington, having served as secretary to the Russian Minister twenty years earlier, when he had been involved in a romantic scandal.

Catacazy had been First Secretary of the Russian Legation in Rio de Janeiro. The Kingdom of Naples was at that time represented in Brazil by a Prince of great wealth and great age, with a wife who was young and pretty. One day the Princess vanished, and for a week the old Prince fumed and raged, declaring that she had been kidnapped. Don Pedro's court was in an uproar. Then the Princess was found, living happily in a honeymoon cottage on the outskirts of Rio, with Catacazy. The Russian Government hastily recalled the young Secretary and re-assigned him to Washington, where he arrived arm-in-arm with his gay Princess.

The ladies of Washington had decided not to receive "Madame la Princesse," and Catacazy had rented a cottage in Bladenburg to eliminate problems of protocol.

But now, twenty years later, the old Neapolitan Prince was dead, and "Madame la Princesse" was the wife of the Russian Minister. If the wives of American politicians snubbed her, it would cause complications between the United States and Russia.

No sooner did Catacazy arrive in Washington than Secre-

tary Fish pressed him for a settlement of the Perkins claim. Fish
had been given copies of two letters, one supposedly from Russia,
which stated that Gorchakov had resigned as Foreign Minister
and had been replaced by a Count Ignatiev. The letter stated that
Count Ignatiev had censured Catacazy for his inaction in regard
to the Perkins claim. The second letter was supposed to be Catacazy's reply, a violent denunciation of President Grant and Secretary Fish as being crookedly involved in the Perkins affair. These
letters had been given to Fish by Joseph Stewart, the attorney of
the Perkins claimants.

When Fish demanded an explanation from Catacazy, the
Russian Minister denied that he had written the letter and called
it "a clumsy forgery." He denied also that Chancellor Gorchakov
had been replaced (he had not been replaced). Next, an article
appeared in the *Washington National Republican,* "An Administration Organ of disreputable tone," edited by W. J. Murtagh,
who was said to be financially interested in the Perkins claim.
The article was a vicious attack on Catacazy.

The Russian Minister replied by printing a series of letters
which he and General Cassius Clay had written to each other.
Fish, outraged at this violation of good taste, sent a stern note
to the Russian Legation asking whether the letters had been published with official sanction. Catacazy replied that he had had
the honor of publishing them himself, in his official capacity.

Fish then wrote to Mr. Curtin, United States Minister in
Russia, asking him to inform the Russian Government that Washington officially condemned Catacazy's act as "most unwise, im-
politic, and indecorous."

Fish was justified in this action. Catacazy's publication of
official correspondence was a violation of accepted European diplomatic procedure. But as an individual who found himself being
slandered, yet shackled by his official position and by rules which
did not bind his opponents (opponents who were being aided by
important members of the American Government), his act was
understandable. From this moment on, however, Catacazy can
hardly be defended for his personal or official actions, even though
the Grant era was indeed one of those "times that try men's souls."

About the middle of the Nineteenth Century the United

States was constantly finding itself outraged by Europeans, but Americans were amazed that any other country could feel outraged. Congress was a sounding board for vicious and splenetic attacks on European government, society, and morals, while the slightest hint of criticism from abroad found the American nation in an uproar. "We air a great nation, and we must be cracked up!" was the American attitude. Daniel Webster, as Secretary of State, sent out diplomatic dispatches that read like election-time stump speeches. Replying to a courteous note from Austria protesting American support of Austrian rebels, Mr. Webster stated that Austrian sensibilities had no right to be wounded because American support of democratic principles had given the United States a territory beside which Hapsburg possessions were "a patch on the earth's surface."

Later, President Grant thrived upon the well-established American tradition of righteous smugness. He had little right. Battle tactics may have been his forte, but his second Inaugural Speech was an appalling array of clichés, shallow thinking, and bad grammar. Even Hamilton Fish, the best man in the Cabinet, was guilty of disregarding the rules of international diplomacy, but he could speak. Deserving of praise for his settlement of the *Alabama* claims against Great Britain, he nevertheless nearly wrecked negotiations by adding a claim of fantastic proportions for their prolongation of the Civil War—an addition of eight billion dollars. Gladstone remarked that the conduct of the American Government in the *Alabama* negotiations was the most disreputable he had ever known in diplomatic affairs.

Meanwhile, the Russian Minister was riding toward defeat. From the moment that he crossed swords with Hamilton Fish, Fish began gathering information. Before he was through, he had an imposing dossier. From a newspaperman he learned that Catacazy had possibly cheated his own government, buying New York real estate for the erection of the Russian Orthodox Church for $17,000 but charging the Russian government $20,000. From the Marquis de Chambrun, the French Minister, came the information, paid for by Fish, that the letters involving General Clay had been forged by Catacazy.

Documents forged in Legations are, of course, not unknown.

Messrs. Hartwig and Forgach won reputations for themselves along these lines early in the Twentieth Century. Since the First World War, forged documents have played an important role in the activities of some foreign representatives. But in the Catacazy case, the French Minister was a most peculiar person from whom to secure authentic information. It is difficult to imagine M. Chambrun, a loyal Frenchman, trying to pour oil into the creaking Russian-American machinery. He would much more likely have tossed in a cupful of sand.

Catacazy was infuriated. He "chattered about the forgeries all over Washington," dragged them into the conversation at every dinner and ball that he attended, until his hosts and hostesses were heartily sick of it. Fish soon heard that "the Minister was spreading slanderous tales about him and the President." Then, from Andrew Curtin in St. Petersburg, Fish learned that Catacazy had reported to Prince Gorchakov that President Grant had stated the United States would send gunboats to the Black Sea in event of an Anglo-Russian war, provided Russia supported the American demands on Great Britain for the huge *Alabama* claims.

Grant denied any such conversation. He said it was a lie.

There can be no positive knowledge of who was the liar in this particular case. Without doubt, Catacazy was a habitual liar. Grant was not, in the technical sense, a habitual liar; but he was capable of telling lies, and, also, he often made spur-of-the-moment declarations that caused his Cabinet great difficulties, and which could only be resolved by denying them. Andrew Johnson had called him a liar, and in consequence the incoming and outgoing Presidents had ridden to the Inauguration in separate carriages.

Catacazy blew the lid off the affair with an interview published in the Cincinnati *Commercial* on February 26, 1871, entitled, *Reported Trouble Between President Grant and the Russian Minister*. In this article he was reported as having said that the Perkins claim smelled, and he accused members of the President's entourage and immediate family of having private interests in the claim.

When Fish called on Catacazy, the Russian Minister admitted giving the interview. But when Fish read to him portions of the article, Catacazy protested that he had not made those statements. There is some probability, seeing that Catacazy had readily admitted giving an interview, that the reporter of the Cincinnati *Commercial,* a newspaper violently against the Grant Administration, had made Catacazy's statements more bald and condemnatory. On the other hand, diplomats sometimes forget how words, hastily uttered, can look on a printed page.

Oddly, however, this article did not arouse much attention in the American newspapers. They were full of other matters, the Ku-Klux outrages, Horace Greeley's political ambitions, railroad building, and political corruption at the ward and precinct level. Moreover, the fact that anti-Grant papers did not use this matter as a stick with which to beat the Administration was in itself a severe condemnation of Catacazy's reliability.

Not until May, 1871, when talk had begun of a possible visit to the United States by one of the Russian Grand Dukes, did the New York papers begin publishing accounts of the "feud" between Catacazy and the Grant Administration. The *Tribune* made a short, accurate resumé of the Perkins claim, stating the known facts without speculating. Several weeks later, the United States Government announced that the Law Officer of the Department of State would shortly make a report on the claim. This report by one E. Peshine Smith declared that the Perkins heirs could not collect on the gunpowder allegedly purchased through Mr. Stoekl, but could collect on the muskets allegedly contracted for by Captain Lilienfeldt—because Russia did admit the authority of Lilienfeldt to make contracts. Smith therefore believed the claimants entitled to the sum of $295,000, plus interest since July 1, 1856.

If Mr. Fish thought this compromise would please both sides, he was soon disillusioned. The Perkins heirs growled for gunpowder money. Catacazy declared that his government would not pay a cent of such a fraudulent claim. Then there appeared an anonymous letter, probably written by Catacazy, in the *Evening Post.* This letter stated that "the most disreputable men in America" were behind the Perkins claim:

"Whatever the American Minister of State may choose to say at this juncture it is, nevertheless, an incontrovertible fact that when the subject of Perkins' fraud was first introduced between us he not only exhibited a great aversion to introduce the matter, but distinctly gave me to understand he had no confidence in the validity of the claim, and even referred me to his son-in-law, a lawyer of eminence in New York, as an advisor to assist me in getting up evidence necessary to defeat the schemes of the unprincipled speculators. It was only at a very late period that Mr. Fish, who is a very weak and vacillating man, evinced a disposition to change his tactics by addressing a note to this Imperial Legation, daring to propose arbitration in regard to a matter which a few weeks before he had pronounced unworthy of serious consideration. In view of the original attitude of the Minister of State, an attitude maintained in the course of many interviews, during which he gave indications of unbounded sympathy to the arguments advanced by the unworthy representative of His Majesty, this late communication from the foreign office may be looked upon as a piece of sublime impertinence, and as such I have purposely abstained from replying to it."

Hamilton Fish, after the publication of this letter, informed the Russian Government that their representative in the United States must be replaced. Chancellor Gorchakov agreed, but requested that Catacazy be allowed to remain until after the visit of Grand Duke Alexis.

Someone in the State Department let the newspapers know that Catacazy would be recalled. The last weeks of the Russian Minister's stay in Washington were made as unpleasant as possible for him by the victorious State Department. As one instance of the pressure that was put on him, he was informed that when he presented the Russian Grand Duke to the President, he must read a set speech of one line which the State Department would hand to him at the time of the presentation. He must, furthermore, make no attempt to shake hands with the President, for if he did, Grant would publicly snub him.

Before Catacazy left the United States, he had one last row with Hamilton Fish. Catacazy had threatened to sue the New York *World* for libel concerning his alleged purchase of church lots in New York. Fish ordered him to drop libel proceedings, and under tremendous diplomatic pressure, Catacazy gave in. So the affair ended, an unsavory episode from beginning to end. The American political situation during the Grant Administration was a quicksand into which Catacazy had fallen, but he might at least have protected his own integrity instead of lying. He had doomed his own diplomatic career, and after his return to Russia was "dismissed without petition."

Incidentally, the Perkins claimants never did collect.

During the 1870's mankind was once more on the march. The world was undergoing a rebirth. Throughout Protestant countries, violent anti-Catholic feeling was manifest; and with the recent Vatican decrees of Papal Infallibility and Immaculate Conception, Roman Catholics everywhere found themselves on the defensive. The Holy See was reported to be planning to re-establish itself in France, to counter the move by which the Kingdom of Italy had broken the temporal sovereignty of the Pope. The seeds of *Kulturkampf* were already evident in Germany. This was the year of the Paris *Commune,* when the Government of National Defense tried to set up a communistic republic, a precursor to the rise of Bolshevik power in Russia. Hysteria was in the air whenever the word "communism" was mentioned. A Berlin dispatch stated that a general strike of workers was being organized throughout the world.

A kind of extraordinary intransigence was flourishing in America. Perhaps at no time in history did Americans bear themselves with greater arrogance. They had recently completed a victorious war and were by no means averse to entering another war to "make the world safe for republics." Washington had sent the Napoleonic legions scuttling out of Mexico, and if Great Britain dared to show much belligerence, the Stars and Stripes would soon be flying over Canada.

The hatred for England and all things English was extraordinary. The American press wrote of the Mother Country with a bitterness that was almost unbelievable. It was not hysteria— hysteria is necessarily a thing of the moment. It was a bitter and sustained hatred. For the crowned heads of Europe, Americans had no use whatever. The single exception was the German Emperor, for whom the American people had a wholesome respect—the same kind of respect that Americans still have for German military prowess, despite two wars in which Germans and Americans have clashed with bitter fury.

Oddly, as American hatred of the British Monarchy was at its peak, the English themselves were seeking means to modify their outmoded system of government.

Sir Charles Dilke was pressing his plans to turn the English Monarchy into a republic.

Bradlaugh was hailed in London in the autumn of 1871 as the "coming Cromwell."

Queen Victoria, after a prolonged illness, was reported to be hopelessly insane.

"Loyalty is gone in England," *Harper's Weekly* announced.

The London *Morning Post* was forced to issue an official denial of the Queen's insanity.

At Newcastle, Sir Charles inflamed the citizens with an impassioned attack on Monarchy.

At Birmingham, Auberon Herbert was attacking the hereditary principle.

However much Americans rejoiced at troubles in England and elsewhere, all was not well in the United States. The Chicago Fire and the terrible drought that preceded it were perhaps Acts of God, but the scandals of the Grant Administration and the viciousness of the Tweed Ring in New York—a stepladder of political corruption that extended from the White House down to the meanest ward—hardly afforded Americans the right to jeer at the great Tichborne Trial then in progress in England.

In the West, fierce battles were raging in the Utah Territory, where the Mormons were using the best tools at hand—ambush and massacre. In Arizona another stagecoach was robbed—six killed and the rest wounded—an ordinary occurrence. In the South, the papers were full of negro lynchings, and insurrections as a result of the carpetbag regime. Southeastern Arkansas was but one of many sections where race riots and black uprisings had been put down with a heavy hand by exasperated Southerners. In South Carolina nine counties were under martial law enforced by United States troops. Montgomery Blair, the Postmaster General in Lincoln's Cabinet, said that while he was glad the negroes had been freed, there was grave doubt that their lives had been bettered.

Communism had come to America. The activities of the

Société Internationale were being viewed with profound alarm. In Boston, Wendell Phillips was crying out, "What is to be done for the toiling masses?" in speeches interlarded with the Marxisms that have become clichés in our own generation. A New York paper under the headline, "A Startling Story," reported that the Chicago Fire had been set by communists.

It was into this turbulent atmosphere that the Grand Duke Alexis, the son of Czar Alexander II, entered on November 20, 1871. New York elections had just taken place. "Throw the scoundrels out" was the cry, and the Tweed Ring had been smashed. Another source of consternation was the Grand Duke himself, already overdue ten days. A Russian flag had been hoisted over the Astor House as early as November 11th. The press had begun to express deep concern for his safety, but storms at sea and fogs along the American coast had twice caused the *Svetlana* to heave to. When he did finally arrive amid a flurry of extras, newsboys rushed up and down Broadway and the Bowery proclaiming his safe arrival.

Captain Hopkins, whose pilot boat towed the *Svetlana* into the harbor, rather sheepishly inquired of one of the Russian sailors if he could get a glimpse of the Grand Duke. "He's right over there," the sailor told him.

"What? That young fellow with the black cap and brass buttons?" asked Hopkins. "Why, he was on watch when I went down the channel to give you a tow. He's no royalty! No more'n I am."

When the Russian sailor explained that the Grand Duke ranked as a Lieutenant in the Navy and had to stand watches the same as other ship's officers, Captain Hopkins snorted. "Heck, if he ain't no different than other folks, if he ain't got a bodyguard and a special cabin and all that, what's he a Grand Duke for?"

This was the reaction of the first American to see the Grand Duke.

Heavy rain began to fall before the *Svetlana* anchored. The officials who went out in the *Mary Powell* to greet the Grand Duke had become drenched and presented a sorry and shivering spectacle. This group consisted of Catacazy, Generals MacDowell and Ingalls, Samuel Morse (who had cleverly worn boots), and

Reception of the Grand Duke Alexis on board the *Mary Powell*

Miss Roosevelt. After one look at the welcoming Americans, Grand Duke Alexis thanked them warmly for coming, but the weather was much too bad for an open air reception, didn't they think? He was quite willing to have it postponed.

On Tuesday morning, November 21, 1871, a great crowd gathered at Pier 39, North River, to watch the festivities. The band of the 21st Regiment entertained and Major General Dix made a long speech on Russian-American friendship. Alexis, dressed in a black uniform with a cocked hat and sword, wearing across his breast the light-blue ribbon of St. Andrew, and two sparkling decorations, acknowledged the welcome and was taken to his carriage.

The procession moved up Broadway, preceded by military bands and National Guardsmen. The Trinity Church chimes thundered the Russion national hymn, *God Save the Czar*—the tune of which is identical with *God, the All-Terrible,* one of the most beautiful in the Christian hymnal. Grace Church, despite the cold weather, had an enormous floral display. The Astor House, draped in blue and white bunting, bore a sign:

GRAND DUKE ALEXIS
SON OF A NOBLE FATHER
REPRESENTATIVE OF THIS NATION'S
DEARLY CHERISHED ALLY

Reception of the Grand Duke Alexis in New York

At the Clarendon Hotel where the reception was, he got out of the carriage with great difficulty, so many thousands of people were lining the streets. He was even requested to stand a moment on the balcony, and this astonished him most of all. Alexis realized then to his amazement that Americans, scornful of all forms of monarchy, show more enthusiasm for royalty than Europeans do. Later on, he went to the Russian Orthodox Chapel, where he was welcomed by Father Bjerring with a blessing and the traditional bread and salt.

The following day the Grand Duke left for Washington. In Philadelphia he bowed from the observation platform of the *Ruby,* his private railroad car, to the people who had gathered in the station. At Baltimore there were no crowds, because a German salesman, "a fat man with a carpet bag" had decoyed everyone away, having been mistaken for the Grand Duke.

At Washington no representative of the American Government whatsoever met Alexis. This was but the first of several bunglings by the inept Grant authorities. At no time during the visit of the Grand Duke was the President intentionally rude, but Grant's profound ignorance of the amenities of diplomatic procedure, or even rank disinterest, his lack of proper advisors in matters of protocol, and his open rancor toward Catacazy, was a source of constant friction. Yet in 1878, when ex-President Grant visited Russia, he wrote, "The Emperor approached me and taking me by the hand led me to a seat, after which we had a talk of some twenty minutes or more. There is no doubt but the United States stands very high in the estimation of the Russians."

A cheerful welcome awaited Alexis at the Russian Legation. There were even bonfires in the street to warm the crowd that had gathered outside to see the Grand Duke. The following day, Alexis met Grant, an interview of some fifteen minutes, in which Grant was quite brusque. Although the Grand Duke gave no outward sign that the reception was not all he could desire, he reported to his father, the Emperor, that he was sorry for American manners if President Grant was a fair sample.

Czar Alexander II decided he would show his disapproval of Grant's action, but in a manner that was diplomatically courteous. At the next reception in the Winter Palace, upon the arrival of the American Minister, both the Emperor and Empress stepped immediately out of the receiving line and greeted him with warmth. "We have heard from our son of the splendor of the reception he met with from the American *people*. I want you to express to *them* our appreciation."

Andrew Curtin replied uneasily, "I will transmit your message to the President."

"No!" said the Emperor. "Not to the President. Only to the American people!"

Unfortunately, President Grant was not the kind of man who would alter his ways. Courtesy and diplomatic propriety were not likely to rub off on his sleeve no matter how frequently he encountered them. Several years later, in England, having taken notice that his hosts wore colored ribbons across their breasts, Grant appeared at a reception by the Duke of Devonshire wearing a broad red ribbon across his breast lettered in gold with the names of his military victories. One puzzled Englishman inquired whether the United States had noble orders similar to that of the Garter or the Bath.

The Grand Duke Alexis decided not to remain in Washington, and returned to New York, where he received a cablegram from his father, instructing him not to return to Russia after the American tour was completed, but to continue around the world

by way of Cape Horn, Japan, and China. This confirmed what
Alexis had suspected. At the time of his departure to America, he
had been in love with his mother's Lady-in-Waiting, Alexandra
Zhukovskaya, daughter of the famous Russian poet. Alexis had
insisted on marrying her against the wishes of his parents. He
understood now that the tour was being used as a means of
separating him from Alexandra. He cabled his father, pleading
that he be allowed to return to Russia.

"To China the squadron must go!" replied Alexander II,
"and fulfill my wish!"

The young Alexis was kept occupied in New York by such
entertainments as reviewing the fire department, the water works,
and the police department. Everywhere he went in America,
Mayors and Burgesses insisted that he inspect their water works.
At the opera he heard Christine Nilsson sing the role of Mar-
guerite in *Faust*. New York merchants were selling clothing pat-
terned after his. Chefs named dishes after him, while the more
elegant bars featured "Alexis cocktails." One enterprising shoe-
shine boy had a sign advertising "a genuine Alexis polish."

A magnificent ball was given in his honor at the Brooklyn
Academy of Music. Brooklyn Heights was in its heyday. Though
he was a handsome young man, the American public was frequently disappointed by his modest attire. He assumed that, the
United States being a republic, the American people would resent
pomp or display, whereas they expected him to be decked out
as gaudily as a minstrel show. As a result, most of the young
ladies fixed their attention on the gorgeous scarlet uniform
embroidered in gold and the sheepskin dolman trimmed with
sable which was being worn by an accompanying officer of the
Russian Hussar Guard. He was the luckiest of all.

M. Jullien had composed a special *"Polonaise de Reception"*
for the ball, and Alexis danced this with Mrs. Hoffman, the
Governor's wife. For the second dance, he honored the daughter
of Professor Morse. From then on, through the twenty dances, he
danced with everyone presented to him. An indifferent dancer,
he attempted to use this opportunity to talk to various Americans,
assuming that French was as widely spoken in American social
circles as it was in St. Petersburg. He quickly found out that the

American women, and men, for that matter, who could speak French, were few and far between.

The day after Thanksgiving he made an excursion to West Point, and returned that evening to attend *Mignon*. A few days later there was a presentation to Alexis of an oil painting of Admiral Farragut. The New York portion of the tour ended with a dinner at Delmonico's with the New York Yacht Club.

Philadelphia greeted Alexis with tours of more navy yards and, of course, the water works. Alexis showed considerable interest, however, in the Baldwin Locomotive Works. He visited Independence Hall and Girard College, where a corps of cadets passed in review and the Russian National Anthem was sung.

At Bridgeport, Connecticut, he paid a special visit to the Union Metallic Cartridge Company, which had just been given a large order for revolver cartridges by the Russian Government. He also stopped at the Smith & Wesson plant in Springfield, also under contract, to inspect the revolvers for the above bullets. A great crowd awaited his arrival in Boston, and Bowdoin Square was jammed with people in front of the Revere House. At the Charlestown Navy Yard he witnessed the demonstration of a torpedo—that is, he saw the torpedo fired. It turned out to be a dud. A ball was given in his honor at the Boston Theatre, resplendent with attendants in powdered wigs and wearing the livery of English footmen. Some Boston ladies objected to Alexis' habit of thrusting his hands in his trousers pockets. The Grand Duke, of course, said he was "greatly pleased" with Boston, causing one New York reporter to remark that if he was telling the truth, he was the only non-Bostonian alive to possess such an opinion.

At Harvard, the Grand Duke was called an imposter by President Charles N. Eliot, through an unfortunate misunderstanding. Dr. Eliot, hearing of the proposed visit by Alexis, insisted that no special preparations were to be made and that classes would be conducted as usual. A group of students decided to play a prank on the President of the College. All during the morning of the proposed visit, empty hacks drove up to the President's residence. The drivers knocked on the door and announced the Grand Duke's arrival. After the President had gone outside to meet an empty carriage some forty times he became furious. When

"The Russian Bear and
the American Dears"

a caterer arrived with several waiters and informed Dr. Eliot that he had with him linen and silverplate to serve 125 guests, and that the food would arrive shortly, the President protested wildly that he had not summoned a caterer.

When the Grand Duke Alexis did arrive, modestly dressed, looking much like a student, Dr. Eliot, by this time frantic, suspected still another hoax and ordered the young man to go away "before I call the police." Not until members of the Grand Duke's suite protested, and Dr. Eliot ran and looked at a recent photograph of Alexis in *Harper's,* did he realize his error.

After these matters had been straightened out, the tour was uneventful, and it remains unrecorded whether Dr. Eliot discovered the students who had put him in such an embarrassing position.

One of the more pleasant moments of the tour was an excursion to Lowell, Massachusetts, where the Grand Duke visited his friend, Mr. Gustavus Fox, former Assistant Secretary of the Navy.

No prominent figure could visit Boston during this period without suffering at least one evening of speech-making and poetizing. The proud leaders of the "Athens of America" ranted and versified at a banquet in honor of Alexis. Oliver Wendell Holmes hurriedly had constructed a poem in honor of Alexis' visit. The poem was then sung by schoolchildren! Considering the circumstances, it was not too bad a poem, and had the lines:

> "Throbbing and warm are the hearts that remember,
> Who was our friend, when the world was our foe."

But the speech by Robert Winthrop was so devastating both in the savor with which it was delivered and the richness of its content that the remaining speakers were rather limp before they began. His words shall not be quoted here because it was the longest speech the Grand Duke had ever heard, and one of the longest if not loftiest ever recorded after an American dinner. Henry Wadsworth Longfellow, hardly short of wind himself, was apparently struck dumb, for he merely rose, gazed at Mr. Winthrop, waggled his beard, and sat back down again.

Dr. Eliot—it having been required since time immemorial that college presidents remain impervious to both the content and duration of all oratorical display—managed to talk some thirty minutes.

Reverend Phillips Brooks, by making use of those labyrinths of Biblical analogy which are reserved to the clergy, was able to speak for twenty minutes without repeating his predecessors. Although his glittering eye bespoke an inner spiritual urge to make it outwardly plain to Mr. Winthrop and others as to who, truly, was the possessor of oratorical supremacy, his Christian charity bade him forbear.

Others who spoke at this Boston marathon included Gustavus Fox and Richard Henry Dana, Jr. James Russell Lowell managed in a single speech to quote Swift, D'Alembert, Cervantes, and Madame de Staël . . . "not the famous Baroness, but the infamous baroness who preceded her." He remarked that when Russia sold Alaska to the United States, "She made us keeper of her seals, if I may say so."

Mr. Catacazy, aware that everyone present knew he was being ousted as the Russian Minister, spoke briefly. "If the goddess of diplomacy could be sculptured," he said, smiling, "I would present her in a dark robe with a finger pressed on her lips. More than anybody else, I should adopt that attitude, and wrap myself as close as possible, and put my finger on my lip as tight as possible." Then, with his eyes serious, he said, "God is my witness that I have done everything in the power of my feeble intelligence to obey the orders of my Sovereign. If I have not succeeded completely in this task it has not been for want of desire."

The Grand Duke's visit to Canada was dampened by the grave illness of the Prince of Wales. Yet the Canadians were in many ways more thoughtful than the Americans, arranging both sleigh rides and ice skating for the young Alexis. In Ottawa a reception was given in his honor by the Governor General at Rideau Hall.

Returning to the United States by way of Niagara, Alexis saw the falls spewing and hurling great chunks of ice into the river below. His special train was met in Buffalo by former United States President Millard Fillmore, who had disappeared into political obscurity since the election of 1856, when, as a Whig and Know-Nothing candidate, he had carried only one State, Maryland. In Buffalo, the Grand Duke was shown one of the giant grain elevators unloading corn from boats and reloading it on trains.

Icy weather greeted Alexis in Cleveland, but it did not prevent one of the largest popular demonstrations that he witnessed. Only the threatening bayonets of the Cleveland Grays were finally able to open a passageway through the crowds. Here he visited the vast Newburg iron foundries.

As the tour moved westward, Alexis became deeply impressed with the United States. Chicago and St. Louis surprised him with their size and bustling energy. In Chicago he toured the stockyards and saw mass production methods of butchering hogs. He was taken to see portions of the city that had been devastated by the Great Fire. At the University of Chicago (not the university of today, which was founded in 1893, but a small college that had been established by Stephen A. Douglas), he peered through a telescope supposedly the most powerful in the world.

In Milwaukee, the Grand Duke found a great number of people who could speak Russian. Former Senator Doolittle made the chief speech at a banquet in the Plankinton House. "We speak sometimes boastingly of our act of Emancipation," said the Senator, "of our giving freedom to four million slaves. Let me remind you that Emperor Alexander in 1861 set free twenty-three million serfs. Our emancipation came in blood, his came in peace. He gave liberty and land, freedom and homes. He abolished flogging in the army and opened the avenues of promotion to the common soldier. He abolished uniforms and arms for University students, allowing them to remain civilians. His last reform is what all true Americans feel to be the bulwark of civil liberty— the right to trial by jury."

In Saint Louis, the Grand Duke was stunned by the size and potency of the Mississippi River. He was awed by the stupendous bridge that was under construction. The next day, he was met by a deputation of Creek Indians. Buffalo Bill offered Alexis his services as a scout on a hunting trip into the West, and the young Grand Duke spent an evening sharing a bottle of whiskey with the Westerner.

Nonetheless, Alexis was thoroughly confused about the nature of American civil and political life. He could not understand why a people who professed their devotion to a republican form of government should be so interested in a royal personage. In Europe, liberal thinking and democratic conduct toward ordinary people was a luxury that only those in the highest social strata could afford. Alexis was beginning to feel that American democracy was a hoax, that Americans did not actually believe in it, and that the so-called American aristocracy had an insufficient heritage. In fact, it was still far too young and *nouveau* to be accurately classified.

It was no small shock to Alexis, therefore, when, having occasion to order a suit of clothes, he found that the tailor who came to measure him was one of the members of the committee at the ball which had been given in the Grand Duke's honor the previous evening. This was almost too much for Alexis, for he did not know how he was supposed to behave toward this tailor. It was an outrage to the young Russian's sense of decorum. The tailor, beaming, chatting familiarly, was unaware of any tension, because, from his point of view, he was doing the Grand Duke the greatest honor in his power, taking the measurements himself instead of sending an employee. After reflecting on this incident, Alexis decided that democracy did after all exist in the United

States, but that it was a devilish system of society for a person of royal blood to become involved in.

On January 13, 1872, the Grand Duke awoke to find himself on the Western plains near Fort McPherson. There he found a hunting party awaiting him, Buffalo Bill in white buckskins, scarcely thirty years old and already famous; Texas Jack Omohundro, famous Indian scout and guide; and handsome young General Custer, who was to perish a few years later at the Little Big Horn. Spotted Tail and his Sioux braves rounded out the hunting party.

Tens of thousands of placid buffalo still roamed the plains. Not many miles away, the Kansas-Pacific Railway was being pushed beyond Denver. Camp Alexis, named after him, was located on Red Willow Creek some fifty miles out of North Platte, and the party traveled there by wagon and horseback. There was snow on the ground, and tents were pitched, and the Second Cavalry joined them as a military escort. Alexis was a fine rider and soon became a first-rate buffalo hunter. The first day out he brought down an enormous buffalo cow and a small bull.

The Indians interested Alexis enormously. He marveled at one young brave, barely eighteen, who brought down four buffalo in a short ride, using only arrows for weapons. At night Spotted Tail's braves sang war songs and danced around the campfire. After the feasting was over the Indian women carefully gathered up the scraps of food and carried them away in their blankets. It was a treat for them, for these were a nomadic people who had to make their living from the plains. The hunting trip lasted only a week, and it was with keen regret that Alexis left the camp, and went on to Denver.

Denver was much quieter than Dodge City or Tombstone or other Western towns famed for their lawlessness. The Mexican section had nothing more to offer than an occasional knife fight and a plentitude of brothels. Holliday Street offered similar entertainment, but with some refinement. The Grand Duke, however, was permitted to visit the water works, the mines, and the legislature. Although it was time to return eastward, Alexis was determined to have another hunt, and so the party moved on to Kit Carson, Colorado. Don Miguel Otero, head of the famous commission firm of Otero, Sellar & Co., who had refused Lincoln's offer to be the American Minister to Spain, hastily set up a camp.

The hunting in this area was dangerous, since the terrain often forced the wounded buffalo to turn and charge their attackers. The Grand Duke had one narrow escape, having emptied his revolver into an enormous, shaggy-headed bull, only to see the enraged animal paw the ground, and then, with a furious roar, head straight toward him. He swung his horse deftly out of the way, avoiding an impact that would have pitched both his horse and himself to the ground. He galloped toward General Custer, leaning out of his saddle to take the outstretched gun. On the second encounter he killed the bull buffalo. The head of this bull, his greatest trophy, was shipped back to Russia.

Then came the return eastward: Topeka, Jefferson City, St. Louis, and into the South, an area of the nation that he had been looking forward to visiting. He was anxious to see how much destruction there had been in the South.

One of the things that impressed him most was Kentucky's Mammoth Cave, for he had never been in a cave, and he was surprised at the clean smell of the air and the sharpness of the winds that moved through the narrow passages. In Memphis he commented on the beauty of the women. There he visited a cotton gin, several cotton warehouses, and the jail.

In his conversations with negroes he discovered that many of them felt gratitude toward their former masters. Some were even sorrowful at having been freed. He noticed too that the negroes seemed both bewildered by and fearful of their freedom. Alexis understood those feelings, for he had seen them among the serfs who had been freed by his father.

From Memphis to New Orleans he traveled on a sidewheeler, the *James Howard*. He arrived in the early morning of Mardi Gras and was made a member of King Comus' court. He attended a performance of *The Little Detective,* starring Lotta Crabtree, a lady whom the Russians had applauded in San Francisco in 1863. Then news arrived that the *Svetlana* was anchored off Pensacola. The visit was cut short, and on February 23, 1872, Alexis left the hospitable shores of the United States.

He had not been really happy in America, but the reasons

were of a highly personal nature — those of a young man separated from and denied the woman of his choice. In leaving the United States, he still faced three more years of exile from his native land. Even if, deep in his heart, there had not been the sadness of knowing that his father, for reasons of state, would never allow him to marry Alexandra, there was now a monotony about his life. Consider his predicament on tour after tour of foreign lands, of performing in every city and town a role longer in duration than that of any actor, a role that had begun with his birth and would end only mercifully with his death.

But there is some ray of sunshine to the young man's story. Although Alexis was not permitted to make a formal marriage with Alexandra, they did find each other once again and had a child—a boy, who, in 1884, was given the title of Count Alexis Belevsky.

CHAPTER SIXTEEN

"PROSTOR"

The historical development of both Russia and the United States followed lines laid down by the logic of geography. The American Republic began as a handful of colonies scattered along the Atlantic Seaboard. After winning their independence, these colonies proceeded to send pioneers pushing westward across the plains for thousands of miles until the continent was spanned.

Russia's march to the Pacific was accomplished in the same manner.

Neither the majority of Americans nor the Russians waited to settle in the middle territories. California's admission to the Union in 1850 found her separated from her nearest sister State by many a mile, as Nikolayevsk-on-Amur was an outpost far removed from the mother country.

Russian expansion began with Ivan IV and the establishment of the Czardom of Moscow. Holding high the cross of Dmitri Donskoy and shouting, "Lord! In Thy Name we go forth!" Ivan's warriors stormed the walls of Kazan. Taking the city and its adjacent lands, they found themselves the heirs to a vast territory beyond. For Kazan is situated astride the Volga near its junction with the turbulent Kama, and commands the river routes and roads to the north, east, and south, as St. Louis controls the Mississippi, the Missouri, and the road to the American West.

Ivan's warriors moved rapidly down the Volga to seize the Khanate of Astrakhan, the Volga delta, and a stretch of Caspian seacoast. These conquests, together with the final pacification of Novgorod, were comparable in Russian history to American acquisition of the Ohio country. When Czar Michael added to Russia the region between the Volga and the Ural Rivers, he rounded off the country somewhat as the cession of Florida by Spain rounded off the United States to the southeast. In strategic value the Volga-Ural area was less like Florida than perhaps the Gadsden Purchase inland; for the Floridas completed the vital gap in the American seacoast. Florida's annexation gave America contiguous maritime control from Maine to New Orleans. Conversely, the Russian Caspian was nothing more than a land-locked sea.

Throughout history, Russia's need was an outlet to the sea. The conquest of Novgorod brought access to the White Sea for that portion of the year when it was not ice-bound. But the long, disastrous Livonian Wars of Ivan IV had failed to break through to the Baltic. Since the Caspian was useless, the Baltic unobtainable, and the White Sea of limited value, the Russians drove toward the warm waters of the south. In three militant waves and a century of time the Russians reached the Black Sea. The geographic comparison in the United States was the Louisiana Purchase.

But here again, as with the Atlantic seacoast, geography was a friend to the United States and a foe to Russia. For the Black Sea emptied through a narrow channel held by a strong nation, Turkey. The Russia equivalent of New Orleans, Constantinople, lay beyond her grasp. The United States would have faced an analogous situation if the Gulf of Mexico had had only a narrow exit. Mexico would then have become a land of many American wars, as bitter as those between Russia and Turkey. But since the Gulf of Mexico was open to the Atlantic and the Caribbean, the United States contented herself with the annexation of Texas, New Mexico, Colorado, Arizona, Nevada, and California. And although the Mexicans never fought back with such vigor as the Turks, it is significant that the United States prudently kept its greatest army post in San Antonio.

Despite vast territorial expansion, Russia would have remained a landbound country had Peter the Great not finally broken through to the Baltic. Even then Peter had to construct the great city of St. Petersburg upon a treacherous swampland if he was to achieve any strategic advantages from such conquest. In a world composed of far more ocean than land, the Russian Empire, through the will of one man, finally found its outlet to the sea.

On the borders of Europe and in the Caucasian highlands Russia conquered alien populations, but elsewhere her annexations were achieved mainly by colonization. The trail-breakers were the Cossacks, like the American frontiersmen, a social and not an ethnic group. Both of them got pretty mixed about in time, the Cossacks mating with Tartars, Kirghiz, and other Mongoloid peoples, and the American hunters and fur-trappers with Indians; but in the beginning they were men fleeing from dissatisfaction at home—fugitives, bankrupts, or simply men who were tired of civilization.

At first the Frontier lay right at Moscow's door, but it was steadily pushed back. Beyond the Ukraine, the Russian pioneers came upon new lands where the very names they gave indicate colonialism—"New Muscovy," "New Russia," etc. The colonial character of these lands was emphasized by Leroy-Beaulieu when he declared that "Russia is a colonial country, a fact which should not for a moment be lost sight of. Russia is a colony one or two centuries old." In the opening pages of his monumental history, he wrote, "Colonialism is the fundamental fact of Russian history."

It was this characteristic that Russia shared with the United States and with no other modern power. The dates of settlements in New Russia are a striking example of Russian-American parallel development. Rostov-on-Don was founded in the same decade as

Harrodsburg and Boonesboro. Ekaterinoslav was settled within two years of Ohio's Marietta. Nikolaev and Cincinnati were born the same year, and Odessa, the capital of New Russia, in the year that Ohio entered the Union.

Colonialism must not be confused with provincialism. England is provincial outside of London, France outside of Paris, but here the movement of population has been from the provinces toward the metropolitan centers. In Russia and the United States the movement was continuously away from the established centers and toward the frontiers. The United States moved steadily westward, while the main Russian movement was southward and eastward from Moscow.

Colonialism tends to develop a strange mixture of shamefaced inferiority and brazen arrogance. Thus, when the Russian or the American meets the older civilizations of Europe, this inferiority complex becomes a national characteristic for which the Russians have coined the word *samooplevanie*—"spitting on oneself." It is exemplified too in the eclecticism of New York and St. Petersburg architecture, in the hordes of American tourists who besieged post-war Paris, in the little sign that hung at the entrance to the Summer Garden in St. Petersburg: "People in Russian clothes will not be admitted." Sinclair Lewis's *Main Street* and Ivan Goncharov's *Oblomov* are literary examples of this self-castigation, not merely by individuals, but by the national characteristics of an entire people. It was this same sort of feeling, expressed in the blunt aggressiveness which is the opposite side of the coin, that inspired Mark Twain to blow out a candle when he was told that it had been burning for hundreds of years, and to badger an Italian guide by denying any knowledge of Columbus.

Colonialism manifested itself most noticeably in the American West and the Russian East. While the ruins of Kazan were still smoldering, the Cossacks were on their way eastward, not as soldiers, but as free souls like the American pioneers. Later, others went as agents of the great merchant family, the Stroganovs, just as some American frontiersmen were trappers for Astor's American Fur Company. Tobolsk was founded in 1587, Tomsk in 1604, Yeniseisk in 1618, and Yakutsk far up the Lena river in 1632. Four years later, the Cossacks reached the Sea of Okhotsk, and strung out behind them for four thousand miles was a line of isolated settlements that would become Siberia's Omahas, Denvers, and Salt Lake Cities. Behind them, too, lay hecatombs of natives, for the Cossacks had Jim Bridger's attitude towards the Tunguses, Samoyeds, Yakuts, Kalmucks, Buryats, Chukchees, and dozens of other Mongolian tribes. In their wake came the same kind of people who followed the Jim Bridgers of America—fur-trappers, hunters, gold-seekers, all types of prospectors, soldiers to build and defend the forts and keep the roads open, and officials to collect taxes and give a bare suggestion of administrative unity to the sprawling empire.

There was one factor in the Russian exodus that never existed in the American West—unwilling migrants in convict trains, a steady trickle for hundreds of years which rose in times of stress to a pouring stream. But the total migration of convicts has received far more fame than its numbers justify. Many contemporary Siberians have convict origins, but they no more account for the bulk of Siberia than Oglethorpe's American settlers account for the bulk of colonial Georgia. Like the westward movement which populated Kansas, Siberia was mainly settled by peasants and serfs in search of open lands. Siberia is sparsely settled, even by the broad standards of European Russia, but then so is Kansas by the standards of Massachusetts. In Siberia the population was held in check by governmental control of migration, for migratory peasants were untaxed peasants, and the greater the number that moved to Siberia, the harder the tax problem became. During the 1860's, less than ten thousand free colonists crossed the Urals. Not until the development of the Trans-Siberian Railway did mass migration begin.

Americans compare this situation unfavorably with their own free development of the frontier where "the weak died on the way and the cowards never started." But strong men died too, and many others returned in despair. The free road of the pioneers did not often lead to prosperous old age. During the first half of the 1880's, covered wagons pushed across the Mississippi bearing slogans like "Kansas or bust!" painted on their sides. The end of the decade saw many of these pioneers heading eastward again with such sorrowful slogans as "In God we trusted and in Kansas

Travel in Siberia

we busted!" One scholar estimated that half the population of western Kansas migrated eastward again, and he mentioned twenty towns left without a single inhabitant. In 1891 alone, 18,000 covered wagons recrossed the Mississippi, fleeing before the collapse of the land boom. The freeholders who remained were free in name only, because tremendous mortgages had reduced their equities until they were hardly above the status of Russian serfs.

Russian restrictions were undoubtedly harsh and injudicious, but wild encouragement of the movement west in America left lasting scars.

In the United States the popular mind recognizes catch-all words denoting such areas as the North, South, or the Midwest, but these are largely fictitious divisions. The Civil War emphasized the line between the two chief zones, the one predominantly a New England culture, the other Virginian-Carolinian. But both these areas were zones of external colonization. The New England pattern spread into Ohio, Illinois, and Kansas, while the Virginian movement went into Kentucky, Arkansas, and Texas. But as these two streams moved westward, there began to be cross-currents and eddies, until they fused into a generalized American pattern. Despite scattered settlements which clung to their cultural origins, American regions are, in a very real sense, hardly more than geographical expressions, and contain fewer cultural and linguistic differences than are to be found in a hundred-mile trip through Germany or Italy.

The same was true of Russia—aside from areas which were not Russian in the sense that Puerto Rico was not American. In Russia there existed the northern Muscovite (Moscow) and southern Kievan (Kiev) cultural patterns. As these two centers expanded to the Russian East, different as they were, they tended to fuse although the numerical superiority of the Muscovites predominated. In both the United States and Russia, the differences in the two cultures became fleeting and superficial: linguistically a half-dozen vowels lengthened or shortened, the stress or elision of a consonant or two, and a few words with meaning peculiar to a particular region. The fusion in both countries was a consequence of the rapidity with which the frontier was pushed back. The American West and Siberia were voids to be filled, and the actual filling process was so rapid that there was no time for regional cultures to develop. The frontier became a melting pot, an area so active that there was little time for racial or ethnic pride to develop.

Siberia, like the American West, was a land of farms. There were no manorial estates, and the aristocracy was represented only by a smattering of army officers and Government officials. The people had to work together to raise their barns, protect themselves from marauding natives, and harvest their crops. Peter the Great's Table of Ranks was as useless as John Locke's Grand Model. Independence and isolation instilled a tendency to make and execute one's own laws. A rough, drumhead justice was prevalent on both frontiers. Acts harmful to the community or to a member of the community were punished with speed and dispatch, and the evildoer was buried, and the earth grassed above his grave in the time it requires a modern judge to set a date for a trial.

This does not mean that Russia and the United States had a

corner on the frontier complex all to themselves. The frontier has played a vital role in the development of most countries. Much of the European Middle Ages can be understood only by reference to the frontier conditions that prevailed. But its role in the development of Russia and the United States was of greater importance than elsewhere, because their frontiers extended over such vast areas and because their emergence from the frontier period has been so recent. Its tremendous importance in the national development of two world powers was not even realized until the frontiers had all but disappeared.

Looked at from Washington or St. Petersburg, the mere task of traversing so much territory was appalling. The task of civilizing and integrating these vast spaces into a unified nation was a job that staggered the imagination. Henry Adams found the America of the Sixties crude in comparison with England and France, but looking back after forty years he was amazed that it had been no cruder than it was. "Doubtless the country needed ornament— needed it very badly indeed—but it needed energy still more, and capital most of all, for its supply was ridiculously out of proportion to its wants. On the new scale of power, merely to make the continent habitable for civilized people would require an outlay of money that would have bankrupted the world."

Vast as America was, Siberia was vaster. Rude and uncivilized as the West was, the Russian East was ruder and more uncivilized, with a harsher climate and more rigorous physical demands. America was so big that seventy-two warring sects could set up Utopias from New Harmony to the Great Salt Lake and not interfere with each other. America was so big that communities could be mislaid and forgotten for years. In Siberia a community could get mislaid for three centuries. On April 19, 1931, The New York Herald Tribune reported the finding of a village of five hundred souls on the Indigirka River in northern Siberia whose ancestors had settled there during the reign of Ivan the Terrible. When archaeologists discovered them, they were speaking a language that no living Russian had ever heard and that had been seen only in old documents and literary histories.

But vast as Siberia and America were, each was somehow conquered and, in part at least, civilized. In Henry Adams' day the Pony Express had already reached the outermost parts of the land, and in Siberia the Imperial Russian Post linked the scattered settlements from the Urals to the Amur. With the coming of the railroad, the American and Russian Empires were developed at a rate that would have astonished the very men who had first dreamed of them. Thus, while the frontiers vanished, it was not before illimitable space, the birthright of both Russians and Americans, had colored their lives and their ways of thinking. In Old Russia, a word was often heard that expressed this feeling— *prostor*. It is a word not easily translated, for there are other words for "distance" and "vastness." *Prostor* is immeasurable distance, vastness beyond statistical measurement, mile upon mile of rolling plain and steppe that flow beyond the curvature of the horizon, beyond and below the edges of the earth. Americans have no word for it, but Westerners have that feeling—it makes them throw their arms wide when they think of it.

The significance of this heritage is greater than commonly thought. It has influenced the national character of both Americans and Russians, endowing them with a love of vastness for its own sake. It is exemplified in America's constant references to her supposedly inexhaustible natural resources and her boundless wealth, in her tall tales of the frontier, in the sagas of Paul Bunyan, and the magnificent lies of Mark Twain. It is found in the skyscraper, in the wild buyings and sellings of the stockmarket, in the American adoration of the home run in baseball and the forty-yard pass in football. And in Russia it was reflected in the insistence of the Russian engineers that their railroad tracks must have a wider gauge than elsewhere because "Russia is so much bigger." It was exemplified in the reports of Russian resources, always more optimistic than they should have been. *War and Peace* is only one of the easier examples of its effect upon Russian literature, of the need not merely to show the workings of the human heart, but to reveal its true proportions in regard to space and time.

When Mark Twain traveled in Russia, Baron Ungern-Sternberg, Minister of Railways, felt the need to overwhelm him with statistics. When Twain remained unimpressed, the Baron, desperately searching for some way to show the vastness of Russian enterprise, said that there were 10,000 convicts working on the railway gradings and right-of-ways. The American sized him up for a moment and blandly replied that in the United States there were 80,000 convicts working on the railways, and that each one of the convicts was under a sentence of death for first-degree murder! "That closed *him* out," Mark Twain said happily.

This common passion for vast concepts influenced the national policies of both nations and became one of their most characteristic political expressions. Russia and America were big, each a world within itself, and each thought of itself in hemispheric terms. No other nations ever developed theories of splendid isolationism like the Monroe Doctrine or Slavophilism, or global notions like Pan-Americanism and Pan-Slavism.

"The Monroe Doctrine," wrote Henry Steele Commager, "had its philosophical roots in a notion that there was a difference between the American and European sphere, between the New World, young, healthy, moral, and the Old, decadent and decayed." Slavophilism was based on a belief in the uniqueness of the Slavic culture and that between the Russian and the European there was a gap that could not and should not be bridged. Pan-Slavism and Pan-Americanism are not as easy to determine in all their protean manifestations, but they had more in common than a Greek prefix. The Monroe Doctrine and Slavophilism are used with aggressive, rather than defensive, impetus. Even in their milder aspects they seem to the western European like "nationalism gone wild," to use the expressive phrase of William L. Langer. And they are related to the frontier feeling of space unlimited, to the frustration of both Americans and Russians when they found themselves at the end of the line, standing on the shores of the Pacific, with nothing but an ocean and some scattered islands before them. They are expressions of the idea that here are worlds so rich and so inexhaustible in their own resources that they can prosper without other lands or other cultures. In our own times, that basic feeling has been changed into another and less fortunate belief by both Russians and Americans—a belief that here are two nations so rich and so inexhaustible in their own resources that no other lands or cultures can prosper without their guidance.

Aside from military and political necessities, in the light of this fundamental urge in the Russian and American peoples, it becomes clear why both nations place such emphasis upon developing gigantic bombs, intercontinental missiles, and upon hurling satellites into the far reaches of the sky. Aside from the conflict of Marxist doctrines with American concepts of free-enterprise, it becomes clear why today Russia and the United States, not like David and Goliath, but like Goliath and Goliath, stand apart flexing their muscles at each other.

In the stress and tensions of our age, we tend to forget that, regardless of the forms of government in Russia and the United States, two nations with such deep feelings of *prostor* could not have avoided coming to an impasse. Only a man or woman ignorant of the facts can seriously believe that the overthrow of the Communist regime will provide a permanent solution to a problem that goes even deeper than antagonistic forms of government. The tragedy of the downfall of the Czars and the rise of Communism is that today the creed of the present Soviet Government does not countenance any serious effort to arrive at a solution with other points of view. As a result, the United States, which had begun to relinquish its feelings of *prostor,* is now forced to recharge itself with that aggressiveness in order to insure its continued existence.

CHAPTER SEVENTEEN

RUMBLINGS

During the Sixties and Seventies the Russian people became interested in the fate of their Slavic brothers in the Balkans. This developed into Pan-Slavism, a belief in the essential unity of all Slavs. In 1870 and 1871, Fadejev and Danilevsky wrote two political books that inflamed all Russians. These books discussed the plight of their racial kinsmen in the Balkans—*An Opinion on the Eastern Question* and *Russia and Europe*. Thus, when trouble broke out in the Balkans in 1875, the Russians were in no mood to indulge in what Pan-Slavist leaders called "insane pacifism."

The trouble started in Bosnia, that unhappy land which was to be the focus of a much greater conflagration in 1914. During the summer of 1875, Bosnian and Herzegovinian peasants revolted. Soon after this, the Bulgarians rose up against their Turkish masters. The Turks put down the rebellion with ruthless severity. Stories of massacres began to seep out of the Balkans. Russian Pan-Slavists went wild at the thought of their Slavic kinsmen being slaughtered by the Turks. Alexander II, however, opposed Russian intervention, feeling that Russia had had her fingers burned too often in the Balkans. He declared that he wanted the Turks disciplined, but only by a concerted action of all the major powers of Europe. But with the tremendous pressure of public opinion against him, as well as that of most of the Military and Government, Alexander II knew that if the Balkans continued in a troubled state, he would be forced to acquiesce in military action.

The British Government, under the strong hand of Disraeli, repeatedly denied the atrocity stories until an American, Eugene Schuyler, accompanied by MacGahan of the New York *Herald* and Schneider of the *Kölnische Zeitung,* made an extended tour through the devastated districts. The stories he brought back of civilians massacred, arms hacked off, and children spitted on scimitars, caused a sensation in Europe and America not unlike the stories of German atrocities in Belgium during World War I. Figures of the number massacred ranged from 15,000 to 100,000, but Schuyler himself thought they were around 30,000.

Gladstone promptly used Schuyler's report to denounce Disraeli and the British Ambassador, as well as the Turks. He urged England and Russia to join together to cleanse the terrorized provinces. "Let the Turks now carry away their abuses in the only possible manner, namely, by carrying off themselves from the provinces they have despoiled, one and all, bag and baggage!" Even Stratford de Redcliffe, who had been largely responsible for British support of the Turks in the Crimean War, wrote, "That Turkey is weak, fanatical, and misgoverned no one can honestly deny." But Disraeli remained silent and calm, biding his time until the first enthusiasm of the British people had worn off. Then he gradually steered England back to its anti-Russian position.

On the eve of the Eastern crisis, the Russian army was comparatively strong. Since the Crimean War it had been completely reorganized and equipped with modern guns, mostly purchased in the United States. The new reforms of Czar Alexander II had rejuvenated the spirits of the soldiers. The Navy, however, particularly the Black Sea Fleet, was weak. By the Treaty of Paris in 1855, Russia had lost all its naval power in the Black Sea. Repeal of the Treaty, in 1871, had given Russia only a few years to recover her naval strength. In the Baltic, however, Russia had twenty-nine battleships, twenty of which were ironclads. In addition, there were a dozen or so steam clippers and corvettes, some even equipped with torpedoes. Since the Black Sea Fleet was powerless to engage in naval operations against Turkey, it was decided to transfer ships from the Baltic into the Mediterranean to sever the Turkish lines of communication.

In March, 1876, Russian naval forces appeared in the Bay of Smyrna. Then, in May, England ordered her fleet to proceed to Besika Bay, just outside the Dardanelles, announcing it as a precautionary measure "against spread of fanaticism from the Balkans to Constantinople." On the surface everything was peaceful, officers of British and Russian ships inviting each other to dinners, and festivities being held in Smyrna after the arrival of the Russian-born Duchess of Edinburgh. But it was by this time obvious that if Russia fought Turkey, she could count England among her enemies. The Russian naval strategy had to be altered quickly, otherwise the Russian Fleet in the Mediterranean would be destroyed and the Baltic Fleet left insufficiently protected.

Admiral Lessovsky, now head of the Ministry of Marine, reported, "Russia faces the similar situation of thirteen years ago. England must be restrained from joining Turkey. Why not apply the old, but successful *Alabama* remedy?"

In November, 1876, Nicholas Shishkin, the new Russian Minister in Washington, received a cable: "Are there any traces in the Russian Legation of the plans worked out by the fleet during its stay in the United States? If so, the Legation will prepare a report based on these documents."

Shishkin, unable to locate the documents, contacted Captain Leonid Semetchkin, who had been an aide to Admiral Lessovsky and the representative of the Ministry of Marine at the Philadelphia Centennial Exhibition. Between them, they prepared a lengthy report based on the plans used in 1863. Lessovsky obtained

Emperor Alexander II, his daughter the Duchess of Edinburgh,
with her husband and the Grand Duke Alexis, her brother

the permission of Alexander II, and ordered the Commander of
the Naval Squadron stationed at Smyrna to remove from those
waters without creating suspicion.

Admiral Butakov, learning that the Duchess of Edinburgh,
the daughter of the Czar, was planning to return to Malta, asked
and obtained permission from the Ministry of Marine to escort
the former Russian Grand Duchess. Accordingly, all ships under
his command put to sea. Once in the open Mediterranean, he
ordered the Squadron to disperse and put into various Italian and
Spanish ports, the ships to rendezvous later in mid-Atlantic.

In the middle of January, 1877, they entered the harbor of
Norfolk, Virginia. The Squadron consisted of the *Svetlana,* now
commanded by the Grand Duke Alexis, the *Kreiser, Askold,* and
Bogatir. The young Grand Duke Constantine, the nephew of the
Czar, was also present. Good news awaited the Russians, for
three ships of the Pacific Squadron were already in San Francisco.
The newspapers reported that the Grand Duke Alexis "looked the
same, but with his whiskers somewhat larger." After a short stay
at Norfolk, the ships were again dispersed to various ports:
Charleston, Port Royal, and Philadelphia. On March 23rd, they
rejoined in New York, where they once again found hospitality,
though they could not help noticing that there had been a change

in the American attitude; but then, the Civil War was over, the note of tragedy was gone from the American scene.

Early in 1877, the London *Times* announced that a large shipment of Peabody-Martinis and Winchester rifles were to be transported to Turkey. The Russian Fleet prepared to intercept the cargoes, but the United States informed the Russian Minister in Washington that any such action would endanger the privilege of the Russian ships to remain in American waters. St. Petersburg protested, but for them the first round had been clearly lost.

Despite this, the appearance of Russian ships in American waters once again caused, or coincided with, a decision of the British Government to take a more conciliatory attitude towards Russia. On the day after the Russian ships entered Norfolk, Lord Salisbury pressed Turkey to accept the Russian demands. When the Turks rejected this, he closed the conference.

On February 26, 1877, the British Cabinet announced that it was recalling its fleet since "necessity does not warrant their presence any more." When England finally declared her neutrality, the Russian squadrons were recalled to home ports. "It is clear enough," wrote Lord Salisbury, "that the traditional Palmerston policy is at an end. We have not the power, even if we have the wish, to give back any of the revolted districts in the Balkans to the Turkish government. I deplored the Crimean War and I heartily wish the Turks were out of Europe."

The actual attitude of the British Cabinet on the eve of the war declared by Russia against Turkey is revealed in several memoranda. "Opinion of our military advisers," wrote Lord Beaconsfield to Queen Victoria, "is that in 14 or 15 weeks after the passage of the Prut, the Russians might arrive at Constantinople. The question submitted to the [British] Cabinet was: were we to act and if so, how? After a discussion of more than two hours the Cabinet agreed we must act, but how and when was not decided. It will be impossible for us to occupy the Dardanelles without finding ourselves eventually in conflict with the Russians or the Turks; and we have not the command of the sea which would permit us to despatch a Military Expedition from home, as we did in the Crimean War, without convoy."

The Russians had obtained their objective; England was

remaining neutral. On April 16th, a Russian magazine declared: "In the Bosphorus suddenly appeared four American frigates. The arrival of the squadron was explained as protection given to American citizens residing in Constantinople. The above fact, as well as the warm reception shown in America to the Russian squadron, will no doubt induce many people in England to ponder on the serious consequences which would result if the British Squadron now in Malta again proceeds to the Dardanelles."

The declaration of war against Turkey was issued on April 27, 1877. The war was hard and bloody, but short. By January, 1878, the Russians had seized the key fortress of Kars. In the middle of a severe winter, Russian troops crossed the Balkans and captured Adrianople, opening the road to Constantinople. Again, English war fever began to mount, shown by the following ballad of the time:

> *We don't want to fight, but, by Jingo, if we do*
> *We'll show the Russian Czar*
> *The kind of lads we are*
> *And the Russians shall not have Constantinople.*

A war with England almost came early in February, 1878, when the British Cabinet ordered a squadron to enter the Sea of Marmora "to protect British subjects in Constantinople." Shortly afterward, Disraeli announced that 7000 troops were being sent from India to Malta.

The Russian Government began to search for some means of prosecuting a war at sea. Captain Semetchkin was ordered to investigate the possibility of buying, equipping, and arming cruisers in the United States. His report so enthused the Minister of Finance that he told the Emperor he thought money was available for twenty ships; but this was soon reduced to twelve, and finally to four. Semetchkin, far from discouraged, said he thought this number would be sufficient, since he was counting more on the political rather than the military effect of the purchases.

This "mysterious expedition" has usually been considered by historians as a highly secret undertaking. Actually, it was conducted with the flair, drama, and exaggeration of ham actors on a stage. Semetchkin worked swiftly. He conferred with the Emperor on April 8th. Five days later a contingent of sixty officers and 600 seamen were aboard a German liner chartered from the Hamburg-American Line. The destination of the voyage was an obscure fishing village and summer resort called Southwest Harbor, Maine. The 600 seamen had been provided with passports identifying them as bakers, gardeners, carpenters, waiters, and coachmen. In the Cabin section were sixty "passengers" coming to America on a visit.

The arrival of the *Cimbria* stirred a great deal of excitement in Southwest Harbor. Few ships the size of the *Cimbria* had ever entered port there. A customs officer boarded her and inquired her purpose, to which Commander Grippenberg, in civilian clothes, replied that the passengers were all emigrants from Russia who were desirous of finding shelter in hospitable America. The customs officer stated that he would have to contact his superiors, but that in the meantime the passengers were at liberty to come ashore. "Only please don't bring wine or other intoxicants ashore," he said. "The State of Maine does not permit the importation of liquor."

Shortly after this, Southwest Harbor was buzzing with the news that "the foreigner had just sent a message all in numbers."

The local telegraph operator, who had never had so much attention focused on him before, reported:

"Just figgers, so help me! Had 'em arranged in groups like 89502 and so on. Didn't mean nothing! I told him he couldn't send no such queer message because it might not be the law and besides I wouldn't know what to charge him for it. And where do you think it was going? To *Rooshy!*"

Shortly afterward a United States naval schooner arrived from Boston, but the customs officials aboard the schooner made no attempt to investigate the *Cimbria* until instructions arrived from Washington. Then there was an official investigation of the ship. "Mr." Grippenberg introduced himself to the Americans as having been appointed by the Russian Government to see that the emigrants were comfortably settled in the United States. The customs officials conveniently overlooked the trunks filled with Russian naval uniforms, the marine swords with Imperial eagles

on their hilts. They accepted Grippenberg's invitation to lunch
and shortly thereafter departed.

The "secret" entry of Russian agents was a hoax. The Russians couldn't have gotten more publicity with a press agent.
Within forty-eight hours of the arrival of the *Cimbria,* the Associated Press, on information obtained from the German Captain
of the ship, printed a detailed account of how the ship had been
chartered by agents of the Russian Government. "The gentleman
in charge," added the Associated Press reporter, "has the bearing of a naval officer." The *World* and the *Tribune* printed similar
dispatches, and the *Tribune* added that one of the officers had
been recognized as a former member of the Grand Duke Alexis'
suite. "It would be rash to assume that the Russians are going to
outfit privateers, though if such should prove to be the case Russia
could certainly do immense damage to British shipping."

Seven days after the *Cimbria* had sailed, the American Minister in St. Petersburg cabled his Secretary of State: "Learn good
authority steamer left Port Baltic Saturday with 66 officers 600
sailors Russian Navy to man three steamers built at Philadelphia." His letter the following day stated, "I know of no reason
why Russia or any other power should not build war vessels in
the United States if it sees fit, but in view of the present threatening relations between Russia and Great Britain, I have thought
you might wish to be advised of this circumstance and have therefore telegraphed you."

The Russians had taken no chances that the news would not
leak out. Their intention was not a secret operation, but one
which by being publicized as secret would make it seem larger
and more threatening in magnitude. The game was played to the
hilt. The Russian Minister was on his way to New York on a
matter of great urgency. Bodisco, the Consul, was suddenly
stricken ill, so the Russian Legation could make no comment to
reporters. The British Vice Consul told reporters testily that he
knew nothing about the *Cimbria.* The Canadians were alarmed,
regarding it as no accident that Southwest Harbor, so near the
Canadian border, had been chosen. One Canadian report stated
that the Russians were planning to join the recent Fenian anti-
British activities against Canada. The British Consul at Portland

hastened to Southwest Harbor but was not permitted to board the *Cimbria* or talk to the Russians. He protested that the American Government should have a cutter on duty watching the Russians. In Dublin, where the Irish hotspurs were delighted over the possible troubles of the British, a cartoon depicted the British consul seated on a lonely rock, gazing with fear at the *Cimbria*.

Semetchkin arrived in New York and got in touch with Wharton Barker of Philadelphia, whom he entrusted with the purchase of the ships which were to be armed and used as privateers. The role of Wharton Barker was kept secret in order to prevent the British from interfering or making competitive bids on the ships which the Russians had chosen. Semetchkin was well aware that publicity of an extravagant nature would sow the seeds of suspicion over a wide area and thus provide cover for his operations. He therefore let it become public knowledge that there were a number of Russian agents engaged in purchasing privateers.

By this time London was astir. The London *Times* reported that "there are grounds for belief that the passengers of the *Cimbria* are a regularly organized crew for several cruisers." The British Naval Attaché in Washington was sent to Southwest Harbor to investigate. The British Consul in Philadelphia reported that he knew of "several Russian agents" who were engaged in the purchase of the American Steamship Line. In Philadelphia and Baltimore Russian agents were rumored to be negotiating with the shipyards. Two agents had been seen in Washington attending Senate debates. A German vessel was reported to have arrived in New York with more Russian emigrants. Ship brokers were in a flurry of activity, attempting to make contact with the reported agents. Several of the principal American ship brokers had to call on the police for protection from a horde of shysters who descended upon them with claims of having influence with or an "inside track" to the Russians.

Two days after Semetchkin arrived in New York, the newspapers reported that the *State of California* had been sold by Cramp's Shipyards in Philadelphia, "presumably to Russian agents." Semetchkin refused to interview reporters, but let it be known that "at the proper time" the *State of California* would be turned over to Russia.

Nicholas Shishkin, the Russian Minister, was harried from pillar to post by reporters, the British Minister, and the American Secretary of State. He repeated again and again that he knew nothing about Semetchkin's activities. Finally he packed his bags and went to Niagara Falls where he spent the summer.

The position of the British Minister, Sir Edward Thornton, was even more difficult, since he was obliged to protest, yet could not point to any actual contravention of international law by the Russians. Shortly after the New York papers announced the sale of the *State of California,* in reply to a protest by the British Minister, Mr. Evarts, the United States Secretary of State, said, "Surely Sir Edward has no objection to the purchase of vessels of mercantile build in time of peace." When the British Minister later protested unofficially that the *Europe* and *Asia* were being armed by the Russians, Evarts replied, "There is no law that forbids such a proceeding in time of peace."

In all, the Russians purchased three ships, the *State of California,* for $400,000 (the British attempted to halt this sale by offering $600,000), the *Columbus,* called by the London *Times* "the swiftest coasting vessel in the American merchant service," and the *Saratoga.* The Russians also ordered a sister ship to the *Columbus,* the *Zabiaka,* from the Philadelphia shipyards. The Russians, again through the legal assistance of Wharton Barker, next established an American shipping firm, manned by the Russian emigrants, with its trade lines theoretically between California and Alaska.

The ethics of this transfer were undoubtedly questionable, but they left England without diplomatic recourse. Since the aim of the Russian Government was to avoid war with England, and since the whole thing was a psychological bluff, aimed at warning Britain what could happen if Russia were to buy a whole fleet of armed cruisers, the tactics of Semetchkin were probably, in a limited sense, virtuous. Having no big stick to wield, as Teddy Roosevelt was later to do, Semetchkin made an awful lot of noise with a matchstick. If Semetchkin had merely come to the United States and purchased four merchant ships, he would barely have gotten a paragraph in any newspaper. But by clouding his mission with ominous, well-publicized secrecy, changing his sailors into civilians with passports, landing them at an obscure port where they were bound to attract attention, he made a sizeable mountain out of his mole-hill. He used every trick of publicity: messages in code, rumored agents, and perhaps the most effective method of all in handling the press, one that would allow their speculations to run riot—"no comment" and "out-of-town."

The actual effectiveness of the operation is difficult to evaluate. Peace with England, the real objective, was obtained, but whether these activities had much to do with it is doubtful. Certainly the British Admiralty was not frightened. Even Semetchkin had never counted on that. But he had hoped to upset the British Diplomatic Corps and Parliament; and, although he succeeded in the former, the British Parliament remained relatively calm. The British have been an excitable people throughout history, though generally this has never been recognized because of the outward calmness and poise of their Diplomatic Corps. But the British have, on the other hand, a profound indifference to "stunts," perhaps because they utilized such methods of bluffing so frequently themselves. Semetchkin's "secret" mission would undoubtedly have had a greater effect upon the American Government, had the roles been reversed. One of the peculiar traits of a republican form of government in which a great deal of emphasis is placed on the politics of elections is its tendency to minimize major catastrophes and to magnify the minute and unusual.

Actually, the major decision as to whether England was to remain at peace with Russia rested with Austro-Hungary and Germany. When Austro-Hungary decided that she was not getting a fair share of the Turkish spoils, she demanded a recount. Russia, in no position to carry on a long war with Turkey, much less with a major military power, decided to negotiate. The Congress of Berlin saved the peace of Europe, though largely at the expense of Russia.

The four ships which Semetchkin had so extravagantly purchased sailed quietly back to Russia, where they were incorporated in the Imperial Navy.

The people of Russia, having no yardstick to guide them, found the actions of the Nihilists a sad puzzle. Non-Russians

The Arrest of a Revolutionary (1917)

developed the comfortable fiction of the melancholy Russian soul as an explanation, but this convenient bit of brainwork did not satisfy the multitude of Russians who did not find themselves possessed of such a soul. And the difficulty in understanding the Nihilists was equalled by the difficulty in dealing with them, for their movements lacked central control, and their target was the destruction of any part of established society. In Turgenev's *Fathers and Sons* and Dostoevski's *Letters from the Underground* and *House of the Dead,* the background of these strange individuals was pictured with terrifying simplicity.

Many of the Nihilists were pious young men, an attribute not incomprehensible because they were Russians. Like Savonarola and Torquemada, they had chosen their own particular solution for the ills that beset the world and united to pursue their course no matter what the consequences. When men are fanatical enough and their aim inflexible enough, the end result, no matter how fine the original intention, is evil. The Savonarolas and Torquemadas in their zeal to save men's souls, and now the Nihilists, became perpetrators of sustained madness.

Nihilism began as a literary movement and underwent two distinct phases. The first phase has a long name in Russian that can only be translated with difficulty into English; because this name also describes an American political movement of a quite different nature—Populism. The Russian Populists had the admirable aim of educating the newly enfranchised peasants and an unselfish belief that those who had acquired an education should share it with their less fortunate brothers. The Emperor had emancipated the peasants' bodies, and the young Nihilist students of the universities would now emancipate their minds.

American humor, while making much of the country bumpkin who comes to the city and promptly buys the Brooklyn Bridge, has much less frequently mentioned the city slicker who goes into the country and finds himself no match for the farmer's shrewdness. It was this same kind of innate shrewdness in the Russian peasants that made them regard the Populists with suspicion and distrust. The Russian peasants, like the American negro, had serious reservations about anyone trying to give them anything. The Populists, who in their delusions of grandeur believed their role to be messianic, found that their efforts were not meeting with success because the peasants continued to cling tenaciously to their pre-Emancipation status of social order. Thus the Populists became convinced that the human soul could never be emancipated until the existing social order had been destroyed. At this moment the second phase went into effect: the Nihilists were born, and the history of Russia and of the world took a new turn, with sideroads leading to strange and terrible conclusions.

With this new frame of mind, it became possible for a small band of Nihilists to dedicate themselves to the single task of taking the life of Alexander II. They pursued him relentlessly for fifteen years, merely because he was the symbol of the existing state of society. The very hideousness of the Nihilists' actions lies in their impersonal attitude and in the fact that they did not have any plan to either overthrow the Government or to establish themselves in power. It was this negative approach, a dedication to the destruction of all objects of Russian veneration, that made them distinct from any previous revolutionary group. Even the Decembrists had acted in a positive spirit of rebellion, with the definite intention of taking over control of the Government and a motivation of exact and particular grievances. The Decembrists themselves would have been appalled at the very idea of ruthless intellectual vandalism.

Only when the Nihilists are seen in that light can one comprehend that on the very day the fatal bomb was thrown, Alexander II had initialled the draft of the most liberal Constitution in Russian history. The very irony of it!—Alexander II affixed his mark to Russian freedom in the morning, and was murdered in the afternoon.

Historians have been guilty of propagating the popular notion that tyrants suffer violent deaths by assassination. In the true history of the world more Lincolns and Alexanders have met this fate than all the Caesars. Tyrants never forget to shield themselves behind armor. But those great and affectionate rulers who truly love humanity forget that a man's sense of injustice is not confined to the actual years of his oppression.

Cassius Clay wrote, "Nihilism, the human language has not invented a term of greater infamy. Murder is terrible enough; war sufficiently horrible; but what shall be said of those who reduce crime to a system which perpetuates revenge, and carries the evils of war from the military into every household? The Nihilists are sowing dragon's teeth that soon will spring up into legions of armed men. This is that fatal disease, under various systems and many names, which comes at last to every nation, and which, if not sternly and heroically resisted, ends in death."

The United States Senate passed a unanimous resolution denouncing the assassin, and the New York State Assembly ordered the flags of the State to be flown at half-mast. American newspapers wrote tributes to the "White Czar." But one New York paper also reported that "nearly a dozen members of the *Société des Refugiés de la Commune* met on Houston Street to arrange the commemoration of the 10th anniversary of the Commune in Paris. They also drank beer and discussed the assassination of the Czar, which they highly approved. . . ." That same evening in Washington, the Russian Minister was obliged to give members of the Diplomatic Corps "a good lecture," because they had attended a dance instead of the Memorial Service for the Czar.

The United States and the nations of western Europe did not understand that the Nihilists had spawned a movement which was to claim, under various names and guises, the whole world as its stage. By the end of the century the western world was to feel the brunt of this same madness. Nihilism soon was to be transformed into a professional cult bearing the sinister name of Anarchism. Michael Bakunin became the prophet of this philosophy of terror which was to claim, in turn, the lives of United States President Garfield, King Humbert of Italy, President Carnot of France, Empress Elizabeth of Austria, President McKinley of the United States, the Shah of Persia, the Sultan of Turkey, and many other lesser rulers.

The last years of Czar Alexander II marked the birth of Russian industrial and scientific enterprise. "Like a sponge," wrote V. N. Ipatiev, the famous chemist, "Russia began to absorb the advancements in science made in the West." In 1874, A. N. Lodygin made the first electric lamps with which the harbor and bridges of St. Petersburg were illuminated. In 1876, Paul Yablochkov invented an electric candle. In 1877, A. T. Mozhaisky built a flying-machine with a propeller. This same year the Kronstadt Naval Base conducted tests with a submarine. The American telephone system appeared in Russia in 1881 (in St. Petersburg, Moscow, Riga, Odessa, and Warsaw) and in the following year James Seymour, Jr., an early associate of Edison, strung a telephone line from the Emperor's Gatchina Palace to St. Petersburg, a distance of 21 miles. Toward the end of the century, Alexander Popov was a pioneer in wireless communications, and Marconi openly acknowledged the pioneer work of this Russian.

There were signs, too, that Russia was becoming aware of her enormous natural resources. In 1864, Russia had imported 30,000 tons of American oil. By 1872, imports had increased to 300,000 tons. But after Dimitri Mendeleyev went to Pennsylvania and studied American methods, the Caucasian oil fields were reorganized, their output of 30,000 tons in 1870 increased to two million tons by 1885. Oil, which had originally come only from the Baku region, began to pour in from the Kuban, Georgian, and Transcaucasian areas, and Russian output soon reached an annual volume of ten million tons.

Russia was on the march. Though still trailing the powers

of western Europe, though plagued by costly wars, robbed of the fruits of her victory over Turkey, and suffering from internal unrest, the Russian Empire in population, general wealth, and industrial expansion had risen to new heights. The balance of power was shifting in Europe. The Peace Treaty of Berlin, which had ended the Russo-Turkish War, had revealed Bismarck, "that honest broker," to Russian eyes as an enemy and a betrayer. As German and Austrian military power increased at an alarming rate, Russia and France finally cast aside their long history of animosity and formed an Entente.

Immediately after the assassination of his father, Alexander III cancelled the proposed liberal Constitution, and announced that he had no intention of surrendering the autocratic power which he had inherited. He believed that the salvation of Russia required elimination of liberal ideas. Russia was to have a single nationality, a single national church, a single national language, and a single absolute ruler.

His reign was devoted to these principles, and his concentration never lost its sharp focus upon his objective of re-unifying Russia. Although he hated the Germans, he deliberately avoided trouble with Bismarck and all the other European nations. Under his strict, harsh rule the Polish, Finnish, and German educational institutions in Russia were restricted, and the Jewish people were driven from pillar to post. But it was also under his rule that Russia made her greatest economic and industrial advances, the full impact of which is only now being realized. But for the Communist Revolution, Old Russia would have been in a strong financial and industrial position today.

The assassination of Alexander II had another important effect upon the world, and upon America in particular. It marked the beginning of the end of Russian-American friendship. Outwardly, for a time, there was no break in relations. An American Naval squadron visited Kronstadt in 1879, and Rear-Admiral Thomas Selfridge was shown the Russian system of minelaying. That same year, the *U.S.S. Wyoming* was the first foreign warship allowed into the Black Sea ports.

In December, the crew of the Russian frigate *Minin* landed

in Alexandria, Egypt, at the request of Commander Henry Gorringe, U.S.N., to aid in the removal of "Cleopatra's Needle," the obelisk that now stands in New York's Central Park.

In 1882, the survivors of the ill-fated *Jeanette* of the de Long Expedition were rescued by Russians and taken to St. Petersburg, where they became the guests of Alexander III.

In the Russian-American entertainment world there was greater activity than ever before. Clara Louise Kellogg, Lillian Nordica, and Sybil Anderson made appearances at the Imperial Theatre and the Marinski Opera. In 1891, Peter Tchaikovsky went to the United States.

Despite these cordial events, however, Russia and the United States were drifting apart. Czar Alexander III, who had seen his father attacked eight times by assassins, made a determined effort to suppress the revolutionaries and the liberal atmosphere in which Nihilism best germinated. His discarding of his father's liberal Constitution and the return of power into the hands of the Russian nobility was one factor in the coolness which began to creep into Russian-American relations. But the two principal causes were the persecution of the Jews in Russia and a book by George Kennan, *Siberia and the Exile System,* published in 1891.

The power of the printed word to shape the attitudes of men and of nations is something of which historians often lose sight. The tremendous influence of Aristotle upon the entire structure of western civilization has, of course, been recognized. The number of philosophers whose ideas have influenced governments and peoples are too numerous to recite, but much less recognition has been given to the importance of two other forms of the printed word—that voluminous mass of Governmental reports which every nation in the world compiles and upon which the decisions for Governmental action are based, and the "reports to the public-at-large," which have come to be lumped under that spacious category known as non-fiction.

The Kennan Report was of this last type. It branded Russia with a scar that has never been removed, just as *Uncle Tom's Cabin* left the South with a wound that has never entirely healed. Overnight, friendship between Russia and the United States vanished. Americans cried out against a Government which could

penalize men in such a terrible fashion. Teddy Roosevelt read the
Kennan report with as much anger as anyone, and much of his
inimical attitude towards the Russian Government during the
critical years of 1904 and 1905 can be traced directly to this
source.

As a result of this book, Imperial Russia is still regarded by
Americans as a "cesspool of iniquity." Every Russian word that
has found its way into English has been flavored with odious
semantic overtones—*Czar* has come to mean an arbitrary dictator; *Pogrom* has come to mean a bloody massacre.

The damage has been done. There is little point in denouncing Mr. Kennan or his book. The Siberian exile system was in
many respects a bad system. Mankind has never devised a truly
satisfactory penal system, and in this regard mankind never will
succeed until it finds an absolute concept of justice to take the
place of sophistry. One cannot help wishing that Mr. Kennan had
been able to keep out of his report such passages as his description of the boundary stone between Russia and Siberia:

No other spot between St. Petersburg and the Pacific is more full of
painful suggestions, and none has for the traveler a more melancholy
interest than the little opening in the forest where stands this grief-
consecrated pillar. Here hundreds of thousands of exiled human beings
. . . have for the last time, looked backward with love and grief at their
native land, and then, with tear-blurred eyes and heavy hearts, they
have marched away into Siberia to meet the unknown hardships and
privations of a new life.

Torn from its context, this passage could describe the hardy
pioneers who were marching, undaunted, toward the frontier. It is
a passage worthy of the Pilgrims on the Mayflower or the men
and women crossing Cumberland Gap. Mr. Kennan knew very
well that relatively few of the men sent to Siberia were political
exiles, that 87% of them were criminals. It cannot be sufficiently
emphasized that these people had been convicted of crimes pun-
ishable by the severest penalties of law in any country in the
world. Is it preferable to behead murderers as they do in France,
hang, gas, or electrocute them as they do in the United States,
or exile them to Siberia?—for in Russia there was no capital
punishment for murder.

Exile has always seemed to most Americans a terrible fate similar to that of *The Man Without a Country*. Americans have an unconscionable fear of loneliness and isolation, that darker side of *prostor*. For the freedoms of unlimited land and sky require both solitude and self-dependence. Americans are a gregarious people. Had not the Russians also been sensitive to exile as a terrible form of punishment, Siberia could never have been effectively used as a penal colony.

It must be remembered that the Old Testament of the Bible contains hundreds of examples of exile as a form of punishment against offenders of the laws of God and Man. It must also be remembered that exile was used in the hope of purifying the offender's mind and soul, not to destroy his body and life.

While most Americans condemn Siberian exile, they forget that their own Sing-Sing and Alcatraz are also forms of punishment. The kind of isolation that the American prison represents is one which masses together evils of assorted kinds, in turn represented by the assorted prisoners. Each criminal lives not only with his own particular offense, but is exposed to the further evils of others of which he may have never dreamed; he finds himself in a university of crimes. This may account for the fact that crime in Russia was much more incidental and individual than in the United States, where it became a syndicated profession.

Substitute for Siberia some sparsely populated western state and the essence of the exile system becomes clearer. Who can doubt that a convict in Leavenworth would prefer a barren Dakota village where his family could join him, and where, if he were so minded, he could write articles denouncing the American Government for his fate.

In his biography of Lenin, Valeriu Marku describes the clean little room in a peasant's house, lined with books, where Lenin and his fiancée, Nadezhda Krupskaya, could look from the window "out on the spellbound steppe which no footfall, no sound, seemed to awaken. The far mountains of Mongolia shimmered white and seemed on winter mornings and summer days to suffer from excess of light." In this pleasant, simple cottage, Lenin was free to write his chief scientific work, *The Development of Capitalism in Rus-*

sia, which he published in 1899, while still in exile. Here, too, he corresponded with his friends in Russia. Far from hampering his work, the Imperial Government would seem almost to have encouraged it. Mme. Krupskaya, in her memoirs, revealed that Lenin received Government financial aid, with which he was able not only to rent a house, cover his living expenses and employ servants, but to go hunting and fishing and make excursions into the interior.

Many of the specific instances of the cruelty and maltreatment of convicts which Mr. Kennan pointed out in his book were probably true. But the criminals who were sentenced to salt mines and gold mines were guilty of the foulest crimes against humanity including murder. The salt mines of Siberia were no worse than the American coal mines in which the Kansan prisoners worked in the 1880's. It must be kept in mind that Kennan wrote his book to horrify the American public. He succeeded. He utilized the phenomenon of subjective experience that allows a writer to describe an act or event more vividly than one can experience it.

Kennan was particularly condemnatory of Russian censorship. He did not understand that although the Russian laws of censorship were strict, they were seldom enforced. In his book Kennan mentioned Dostoevski's moving account of his life in exile as having been recently published in the Tiflis newspaper *Kavkaz.* To illustrate cruelty to a criminal, Kennan took his story from "a fairly accurate account published in the *Siberian Gazette* at Tomsk." In relation to this "censorship," Senator Beveridge asked Tolstoy how he dared to attack the government the way he was doing. Tolstoy, amazed, replied, "Why should I not say what I think?"

The object of this discussion of the Kennan report is not to discredit either Russian or American laws and prison systems. The true sorrow is that friendly relations between these two nations could be broken by one fell swoop of the pen. But, perhaps, Mr. Kennan had merely stumbled upon the real difficulty, the one that had stood in the way of Russian-American friendship from the beginning—the profound ignorance of the Americans and the Russians of each other's values, ideas, beliefs, and cultural heritage. A whole century of diplomatic effort had never

Reception of the American "Russian Relief Committee"
in Russia in May, 1892

even approached the frontiers of the real barrier that existed
between these two nations.

Old Russia had never bothered to resort to the power of
official propaganda. Even at this crucial hour, when Americans
were raging against "a barbarian penal system," and when Peter
Botkin, a young Russian diplomat, tried to show the unfairness
of Kennan's book by publishing his own views in several American magazines, the Russian Minister to the United States, Prince
Cantacuzene, wrote to Peter Botkin, "What is the matter with you?
Are you crazy? No, we Russians have not yet come to the point
where we must defend our country on the pages of magazines or
by making lecture tours." Botkin was promptly transferred to a
post outside the United States.

Kennan continued on his triumphant lecture tour of America, "clad in a prisoner's garb and iron chains at his feet and
with a magic lantern for illustration, uttering the most impossible
nonsense about Russia, and hardly believing it himself."

But Americans are a strange people, for at the same time
that their hearts darkened toward the Russian government, they
opened their purses to the suffering Russian people. In the Volga
region a famine broke out, the result of poor crops the previous

year, and when reports of the famine reached America, there was at once a popular response to help the stricken Russians. Besides money contributions, the American people dispatched four shiploads of provisions and clothing to Russia, with safeguards for their equitable distribution.

The Russian government tried hard to deal with the famine. In the first half of 1892 the sum of $100,000,000 was spent on relief. But the major problem was transportation of such large quantities of materials. Tolstoy, never one to praise the Americans, on viewing the arrival of one of the American relief ships, remarked to Frances Reeves, who was the official American representative of the Russian Relief Committee, "The time seems to have come when the Fatherhood of God and the brotherhood of men are being universally acknowledged." Over 77 million dollars in relief funds was raised in America, the first such aid that Russia ever received from a foreign nation.

The following year, as the Chicago World's Fair was about to open, ships from Great Britain, France, Germany, Italy, Russia, Austria, and the Argentine were represented in a brilliant International Naval Review. During this visit, Russian Envoy Cantacuzene presented gifts to all the American Relief Commissioners, especially honoring Rudolph Blankenburg. "Your gracious help for Russia proves that your city is rightfully named Philadelphia—Brotherly Love."

In the dawn of the Twentieth Century, impoverished European aristocrats flocked across the Atlantic to regild the family coat-of-arms by making Yankee dollar marriages. Dukes, Counts, and Princes, including such names as Marlborough, Manchester, Roxburgh, Talleyrand, and Murat, found brides among the Vanderbilts, Goulds, Stewarts, Goelets, and Zimmermans.

Russians, however, remained faithful to their traditions. Though exposed to the captivating charms of American women visiting in Europe, there was never a vogue for the *mariage de convenance*. The Russian usually managed to love within his own caste and in his native land. From 1776 to 1917, only twenty-seven Russians married American women, while three Americans took Russian wives. Only two of the American women were wealthy, Miss Beale, of Washington, and Miss Whitehouse, of Newport. Not until the Communist Revolution stripped the Russian aristocracy of their possessions and sent them into exile did a Grand Duke, a Royal Princess, a Prince, two lesser Princesses, and a diplomat, within a decade, cast their lots with the heirs of leading families in the United States.

The infrequency of Russian-American marriages was an indication of the lack of personal contact between the two peoples. Though history emphatically proves that international marriages are not a solution to international affairs, and sometimes actually complicate existing problems, there can be no doubt that such marriages, particularly among Royalty and the aristocracy, added value, prestige, and important sources of arbitration to the European diplomatic corps. In such a situation, the United States, having no such ties, was at a disadvantage. The ease with which the Treaty of Commerce with Russia was repudiated would hardly have been possible if, for instance, a blood relationship had existed between President Taft and the Russian aristocracy.

Because there were so few marriages and romantic affairs between Russians and Americans, undue attention was often focused upon them, particularly if any shadow of scandal was involved. Thus Bodisco, aged 56, had set tongues wagging with his marriage to sixteen-year-old Harriet Williams. Kozlov's visit to a servant girl's bed had resulted in political and legal difficulties. Even the Catacazy involvement in the Perkins claim had a portion of its origins and distrusts in a romantic but unconventional affair. Vera Olcott, the "Aphrodite in Ermine," just before the First World War, armed with a toothbrush and a talent for dancing, permitted her friendship to become the object of a toss of a coin between Grand Duke Boris and her future husband, Count Alexis Zarnekau, grandson of Nicholas I, and great-great-grandson of Catherine the Great.

But it was Hattie Ely, a lady from Pennsylvania, who was destined to shake the Russian Empire, as Mrs. Simpson later rocked Great Britain. The daughter of a Philadelphia clergyman, Hattie, at the age of sixteen, eloped with a stranger she met on a train. He was Calvin Blackford, a drunkard and consumptive, who coughed himself to death, but not before Hattie had been

Grand Duke Nicholas, the son of Grand Duke Constantine

sufficiently embittered to little mourn the loss of her sickly child
by him. Returning to Philadelphia, she met a wealthy Texan,
George Madison, became his mistress, and moved into a flat west
of Broad Street. Soon she was seen in the company of other men,
and changed her residence to a mansion facing fashionable Ritten-
house Square. It was rumored that she encouraged men to play
cards and kept a Chinese bowl filled with silver dollars, which
luckless gamblers were free to use, provided of course they
returned the money with suitable gifts.

Philadelphia would not long tolerate such activities, especially since pretentious Hattie had the unfortunate habit of enter-
taining her guests with readings of English poetry and French
literature. A whispering campaign ensued, and men became cautious. It was improper to be seen entering or leaving her mansion.
Hattie decided there were places where her talents would find
more appreciation. She left.

In Paris she changed her name to Fanny Lear and became
the mistress of the Duke of Bodenbach. She soon learned that,
if she expected to rise on the European social ladder, her liaisons
must be conducted like a series of marriages, with intensity and
faithfulness. Meanwhile, the Franco-Prussian War, putting a temporary end to the glittering Parisian social life of the *demimon-
daines,* was a disaster for Hattie. Unwilling to remain in Paris in the
vain hope that the French aristocracy would again find leisure
to restore the *salon* and *soirée* atmosphere, she decided to try

St. Petersburg. There she met and fascinated the Grand Duke Nicholas, nephew of the Czar.

A novel, *The Scandalous Mrs. Blackford,* depicted this as an enchanted, bewildered love affair. The facts indicate Hattie was a clever, shrewd woman who knew how to acquire what she wanted. As the mistress of a Grand Duke, and now at last having reached the top of the ladder, it was typical of Hattie to attempt to crown her achievement by becoming his wife. Nicholas, however, whose passions were short and violent, would not have considered marriage if the Russian Government had not brought strong pressure to bear upon him. A perverse and obstinate man, he became determined to have her.

The situation was complex. Nicholas, the son of the Grand Duke Constantine, was a figure around whom a struggle for the throne might evolve. Government officials, searching for a means to discredit Nicholas, saw their opportunity. The more they insisted that he give her up, the wilder and more rash he became. His gifts to Hattie were out of proportion with those usually accorded a mistress. During the summer maneuvers of the Imperial Guard, Hattie, disguised as an aide-de-camp, was smuggled into his quarters. In Italy a nude marble statue was made of her, which Nicholas proudly displayed to his friends.

But if her Grand Duke did not see the handwriting on the wall, Hattie did. She took the precaution of placing the jewels he had given her within the walls of the American Legation. Shortly afterward, Nicholas was ordered to serve with the military in Asia, and it was from there that he wrote her a letter full of foreboding and loneliness. "There is reason to think that if death separates us, it should be through me. But I get such forebodings about your safety. Without you my life is like a soulless machine that has no reason to function. I value only you in this false world." Against orders, the Grand Duke suddenly returned. He and Hattie hastened to Vienna, where their attempt to marry was thwarted by the arrival of his furious father. Then, shortly after their return to Russia, the Grand Duke was arrested and charged with the theft of his mother's jewels.

The next day Marshall Jewell, the American Minister, sent a note to General Trepov, the head of the St. Petersburg Police.

"The Minister Plenipotentiary of the United States has the honor to say that the apartment of Mrs. Blackford, an American citizen, was entered this afternoon by the police. The apartment was searched and many objects removed. Mrs. Blackford was arrested. The Envoy hopes the General will inform him—tonight, if possible—as to why the police have arrested her, of what crime she is being accused, and where she is at present. The Envoy does not wish to hinder the administration of justice, but he assumes that Mrs. Blackford will not be deprived of the due protection of law."

General Trepov replied, "Mrs. Blackford has been transferred with all due care and attention to a place where she will not lack for anything, and where she will be in good health and in the best of spirits."

Hattie refused to surrender the jewels. Whether the Grand Duke had taken them without her knowledge, whether they had planned the theft together, to provide money for their escape, her refusal to return the jewels ruined any possibility of keeping the scandal either secret or moderate in its consequences. The entire Diplomatic Corps in Russia followed the case. Eugene Schuyler, the Secretary of the American Legation and a friend of Hattie's, was involved in the correspondence.

Finally, to avoid legal technicalities, which included not merely the American citizenship of Hattie, and the hot jewels in the custody of the American Legation, but also a document written by the Grand Duke promising Hattie an excellent settlement, the Russians offered fifty thousand rubles for their return. There was also the sordid matter of the private love letters which the Grand Duke had written to Hattie, and which the Imperial Family did not want to become public.

The matter was handled with dispatch. The Grand Duke was sent into exile, with Hattie and her considerable fortune being bundled off to Paris, nevermore to return to Russia. News of the scandal, however, spread far and wide, providing fodder for the gathering anti-Czarist and revolutionary groups. For his pains in defending the rights of an American, Minister Jewell was recalled from his post by the United States Government.

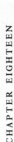

a friendship cools

"The crazy Nihilist who hurled a bomb at Czar Alexander II was the ultimate creator of New York's Ghetto and the man who added three million Jews to the American population. For the direct result of that act was to put the reactionary party in power in Russia," wrote Burton J. Hendrich.

The first large wave of Russian immigration to the United States began in 1881 and increased in a geometrical progression. Russian-American relations were faced with a new problem and one that caused a great amount of friction. From 1882 to 1890, over 200,000 Russian Jews arrived in the United States, and in the next ten years more than 1,500,000 followed them. The great majority of these came from the Polish provinces of the Russian Empire. Poor and uneducated, they had a difficult time adjusting themselves to the ways of American life.

To understand the causes of this mass emigration, one must return to the year 1016, when, after fifty years of conquest, the

Khazar Kingdom was vanquished by the Russians. Christianity became the State Religion of Russia, and the spirit of religious tolerance, which had existed for centuries, began to give way to enmity. For, although the Orthodox Church was powerful in Russia, it never ceased to look upon the Jewish faith as a dangerous rival.

Yet despite this, the position of the Jews in Russia until the 16th century was better than anywhere in western Europe. The Jews of Russia were free men. During the Middle Ages, when there were Jewish ghettos in other parts of Europe, there was no segregation in Russia. In 1478 Ivan III brought to Moscow two Jewish rabbis, who were so effective in gaining converts to their cause that for a time almost the entire Government consisted of Jewish sympathizers. The Orthodox Church finally succeeded in suppressing this movement, and, fearful that it might revive, put great pressure on the Russian government to establish a fixed policy which would not permit Jews to enter Russian territory. By 1727 this policy was supplemented by a decree that stated, "All Jews found to be residing in the Ukraine shall be forthwith expelled beyond the frontier."

In 1795, the partition of Poland added nearly a million Jews to the Russian population. Catherine II, to prevent their spreading through her Empire, permitted the Jews to retain their former rights only while they remained in the territory in which they had been living at the time of the partition. This was the official edict of the so-called *Jewish Pale*.

It must be emphasized, however, that the Jewish people were forced to live under severe restrictions, not because of prejudice on racial grounds, but because of the Jewish religion. The moment a Jew embraced any other religion, Orthodox, Lutheran, Catholic, or Moslem, every restriction was removed.

"Empress Catherine," wrote Bromberg, a Russian-Jewish historian, "approached the Jewish question with the tolerant ideas prevalent in that age of enlightenment, and the only reason that kept her from granting the Jews equal rights with the Christian population was her fear of making a radical change in the domestic policy."

Her son, Paul, gave the Jews of Courland municipal rights

and opposed the expulsion of them from Kamenetz-Podolsk and Kiev. He also severely reprimanded a judge who had refused, in a murder case, to accept a Jewish witness, and would not allow the Jewish sect of Hassidism to be molested.

Alexander I ordered the formation of a "Committee for the Welfare of the Jews." Some members of this committee advocated complete and immediate equality and others recommended gradual transition. Finally, in 1804, a decree was issued which for a time thereafter constituted the fundamental rights of Russian Jews, allowing them for the first time to settle in the rich and fertile areas along the Black Sea.

The recruiting law of 1827, under Nicholas I, which both permitted and obligated Jews to serve in the Russian military, was intended to help bring the Jews out of their seclusion and into the social fabric of the country. But this measure was carried out by the military in a brutal fashion, creating hatred and distrust among the Jews.

By 1840, the Jewish State Schools had been established.

The accession of Czar Alexander II aroused hope among the Jews, particularly after the liberation of the serfs in 1861. It must be pointed out that the Jews, though shorn of equal rights, had never known actual serfdom. The Alexander II era of liberalism caused increased contact between the Russians and the Jews. Scores of Jewish youths entered the Russian schools. Jewish newspapers and magazines sprang up, and many Jews were accepted into the Civil Service. In 1879, all Jews holding diplomas of higher education were granted the right to domicile anywhere in the Empire. Yet the stringent quota system for admission into the Russian universities was allowed to remain.

Presently, Jews began entering the revolutionary movement, slowly at first, then in considerable numbers. One of the first to be executed for terrorist activities was Solomon Wittenberg. Nearly fifteen Jews played important roles in the revolutionary "Land and Freedom" party. Two Jewish women were also involved. Among the terrorists who relentlessly pursued Alexander II were four Jews, and of those sentenced to die for the assassination of the Czar was a woman called Hessie Helfman, whose sentence was commuted to hard labor.

"Steerage" by Alfred Stieglitz,
courtesy Philadelphia Museum of Art

"It was in the organizational phases of revolutionary activity," wrote Rabbi Louis Greenberg, "for which the Jews were much more suited, that they were most successful." The Rabbinic Seminary at Vilno was the cradle of Jewish Socialist propaganda. "The Jewish revolutionaries, whose ultimate aim was the solution of the Jewish problem," Greenberg wrote, "by their increased activities in the late Seventies complicated the Jewish situation and added another vexing problem to those already in existence."

It must be pointed out that during the entire Nineteenth Century only 73 persons were put to death by the Russian Government and law forces. This was probably the smallest number in any major country in the world, and yet the Russians were called "barbarians." It must not be forgotten that capital punishment for all crimes except political terrorism and assassination had been abolished since the middle of the Eighteenth Century.

After the assassination of Alexander II, however, there was a violent reaction against the Jews. In a series of pogroms from 1881 to 1905 more than 500 Jews were murdered. One of the curious facts about these pogroms was the issuing of a proclamation by a revolutionary party called "The People's Freedom," urging its members to attack landowners and Jews. There is considerable evidence that the revolutionaries were responsible for stirring up a great deal of the anti-Jewish feeling in order to create disturbances that would ferment their own cause. Although it is a poor policy at best to defend one wrong by contrasting it with another, it is a fact that during this same period in the United States, 3,334 people were lynched, and of this figure 1,156 were white. The point in making the comparison is not to defend pogroms, but to show that in Russia, even in this period of anger and recrimination, they were not as widespread as has generally been assumed.

When, with the accession of Alexander III a new rash of pogroms began and repressive measures against the Jews were instituted by the Government, the only solution for the Jews was to flee to foreign lands. Most of them chose America, where they believed that sympathy for their situation might be found. Hordes of refugees from across the Atlantic began to descend upon New York, where they may have found themselves better off than in Russia, but far from welcome.

"Almost immediately," wrote Andrew Dixon White (U. S. Minister to Russia, 1892-1894), "difficulties arose between the two countries." Because of the absence of modern quota laws, the United States, which could not refuse the Jews entrance because of its liberal Constitution, put pressure on the Russian government to pursue a liberal policy with regard to Jewish people. The Americans stressed the humanitarian side of the question; but it was also the only way to prevent hordes of Jews from entering the United States in inabsorbable numbers.

The Russian government paid no heed to the American pressure. "It was the same old story," confessed Ambassador White. "Emigrants from the Russian Empire, most of them extremely undesirable, had gone to the United States, stayed just long enough to secure naturalization, had indeed in some cases secured it fraudulently before they had stayed the full time; and then, having returned to Russia, were trying to exercise the rights and evade the duties of both countries."

It was the Jews who returned to Russia with American naturalization papers, claiming under them privileges of American citizenship that brought the situation to a head. Russia, like many other countries, did not recognize the right of its subjects to forswear allegiance without the official permission of its government. Besides, many Jews who had emigrated to the United States were army deserters and revolutionaries. When Russian consular officials began to refuse these former Russian subjects visas, the Russians were accused of discrimination on religious grounds.

On Easter Sunday in 1903, anti-Jewish riots took place in Kishenev. Forty-seven people were killed. A wave of condemnation swept the entire world and particularly the United States, where almost a million Russian Jews were residing. In the month of April, 77 public meetings were held in fifty American towns. Eighty newspapers wrote 151 editorials on the subject, and President Roosevelt received 363 addresses, 107 letters and 24 petitions. The New York *Times* and the Philadelphia *Public Ledger* condemned the Russian government as one which "could no longer be called civilized." Hearst demanded an "immediate protest" by the State Department.

John W. Riddle, acting as *chargé d'affaires* in St. Petersburg during the absence of Ambassador McCormick, attempted to present to the Russian Minister a petition signed by "a large number of citizens of the U. S.," and was notified that the Russian government could not receive such a petition. Again, when the Russian statesman, Count Witte, was negotiating the Peace of Portsmouth in 1905, he was presented a memorial, signed by Jacob Schiff, Isaac Seligman, Oscar Straus, Adolph Lewisohn and Adolph Kraus, American citizens of German extraction, who pleaded for civil equality to be granted to the Russian Jews. While admitting that among the ranks of "those who in Russia are seeking to undermine Governmental authority there are a considerable number of Jews," this memorial insisted that the majority of the Jewish population was "on the whole, law abiding."

President William Howard Taft

On August 3, 1905, Simon Wolf, chairman of the Delegates on Civil Rights of the American Hebrew Congregation, wrote to Count Witte, "Throw the pale open, let the Jew go where he will as other citizens do, and Russia will win the appreciation of the whole world. Russia needs money and friends. The Jews of the World control much of the first and would make a magnificent army of the latter. There is no use disguising the fact that in the U. S. especially, the Jews form an important factor in the formation of public opinion and in the control of the finances. We do not hate Russia, we do not wish her destruction, but you must admit that blood is thicker than water . . ."

Simon Wolf wrote also to the first Russian Ambassador to Washington, Count Arthur Cassini, "Do not forget that Ireland's cause is fought in the U. S. In the same spirit, the exiled Russian Jews are the storm petrels of ultimate revolution in Russia. Why not free them now and prevent that revolution?" This threat was not an empty one, because a large group of these Jewish exiles returned to Russia shortly after the revolution of 1917 and became important adherents of the Bolshevik regime. Morris Hilquit once remarked, "To be a Soviet Commissar, one must first have swept the office floors of the *Novyi Mir* (a radical Russian-language newspaper in New York)."

American public opinion became solidly anti-Russian, particularly after the Revolution of 1905 was unsuccessful. By 1908 the platform of the National Convention contained a demand for equal treatment of American Jews in Russia. In the summer of 1909, a conference was held at the White House between President Taft; the Secretary of State; the new American Ambassador to Russia, W. W. Rockhill; and several members of the American Jewish Committee. The passport situation was discussed, but nothing definite decided. After many inconclusive meetings, on February 8, 1911, President Taft made it known to a large number of Jewish leaders, "The United States has no international right to object to any nation's excluding any of our people, assuming that there is nothing of a Treaty obligation between us. I would be willing to take this drastic step [abrogate the Treaty of 1832] and sacrifice the interests that it certainly will sacrifice if I was not convinced . . . that instead of benefiting anything, it would accomplish nothing at all."

President Taft pointed out that American business with Russia amounted to about a hundred million dollars (Singer sewing machines, McCormick threshing machines, and life insurance companies representing $60,000,000 of this amount), and that repudiation of the treaty would put these enterprises at the mercy of the Russians.

Mr. Schiff, the chief spokesman for the Jewish Committee, replied to the President, "You said that you are not prepared to permit the commercial relations of ninety-eight million American people to suffer because two million American citizens feel their rights are being infringed upon. . . . We feel deeply mortified. . . . You have failed us and there is nothing left to us now but to put our case before the American people directly."

As the delegates left the White House, Mr. Schiff, with the remark, "This means war!" wrote out a check for $25,000 to start a campaign to bring about the abrogation of the Commercial Treaty of 1832. In that moment the fate of the Treaty was decided. Conferences with Senators and Representatives took place and pressure was brought to bear from all sides. On December 13, 1911, Congress directed the President to notify the government of Russia of the intention of the American Government to terminate the Treaty of 1832 on January 1, 1913. The resolution passed the House by 30 to 1, with 87 abstentions. The only dissenting vote was that of George Malby of New York.

This was the strongest rebuke that the United States had ever given to Russia. Realizing this, and realizing too that the efforts of eighty years were about to be wiped off the boards, United States Secretary of State Knox sent a telegram to Ambassador Guild, urging him to inform the Russian government that the House had already passed a resolution abrogating the Treaty. To forestall Senate passage of the resolution, it was in the best diplomatic interests of both nations to simultaneously terminate the Treaty. Knox urged Guild to impress upon the Russians the American willingness to negotiate a new treaty as soon as the present storm clouds had passed over.

The Russian Foreign Minister, Sazonov, angrily replied, "Russia takes the ground that no self-respecting nation can act under pressure from abroad to change her treatment of the Jews within her borders. Russia's experience has been that the presence of Jews within her borders is a perpetual menace not only to the integrity of the country, but to law and order." Then he added, "While Russia cannot abandon her restrictions on Jews, we are prepared to consider an arrangement by which the U.S. might transfer *all* Jews from Russia to the U. S."

Ambassador Guild dodged this by mentioning American willingness to negotiate a new treaty.

"Never another treaty!" replied Sazonov.

In his report to the Secretary of State, Guild wrote, "It was not your suggestion that roused his anger. It was the mere presentation of any note, for Russian officials take the view that the U. S., in trying to force them to re-admit all Jews, is seeking to destroy the Russian Empire."

News of the abrogation of the Treaty of 1832 caused scarcely a ripple of excitement in Russia. "The Jewish question," reported the New York *Herald* correspondent, "looms so large in Russia that the question of Russian-American relations takes a secondary place."

The Russians never budged from their stand on the Jewish problem. But they had without doubt been both surprised and shocked by the American action. The Russian diplomats had underestimated the importance of the Jews in America in their political and financial influence. The Russian Ambassador, George

Bakhmetev, wrote to Sazonov, "The American Jews adroitly deceived the Congress. This whole story proves that Americans are still at a very primitive stage of social development. Any concessions on our part are naturally out of the question, but it would be practical, in view of our future political and trade interests, to sugar the pill for the Americans."

Despite being a persecuted minority, Jews contributed a great deal to Russian cultural life, finance and business.

Abraham Zack headed a St. Petersburg Commercial Bank, which, under his leadership, became the most powerful financial institution in the Russian capital. He was offered the post of Assistant Minister of Finance, but refused it because he did not want to change his religion.

Samuel Poliakov was a pioneer railroad builder and opened the first railroad school in Russia. In recognition of his services he was raised to the nobility with the title of Privy Councillor.

Ivan Blioch, financier and railroad contractor, published a book on international peace which inspired Czar Nicholas II to issue the famous peace declaration that resulted in the creation of the Hague Court of Arbitration.

General Grulev, a Jew who remained unconverted to Christianity, became assistant Minister of War.

"Jews," wrote Rabbi Greenberg, "served as prosecuting attorneys, judges and chief secretaries in the highest judicial body of Russia, the Senate Courts."

In the world of literature, art and the theater, the Russian Jews were even more prominent. Names familiar to Americans include: Ossip Gabrilovitch, Leopold Auer, Josef Lhévinne, Mischa Elman, Efrem Zimbalist, Jascha Heifetz, Serge Koussevitzky—all men of Jewish faith who received their education in the Imperial Schools of St. Petersburg.

It would be impossible to note all the Jewish men who contributed to the building of the Russian Empire. This brief list is merely a tribute to the remarkable ability which the Jewish people, laboring under handicaps, revealed in surmounting the obstacles of Russian law and Russian prejudice, without relinquishing their religion.

the RISING SUN

On March 27, 1898, with a powerful Russian naval squadron anchored off shore, the great Dragon Banner of China was struck, and the Russian Navy's blue Cross of St. Andrew was unfurled above Port Arthur. For the first time since the cession of Alaska to the United States, Russia cut through to a vista on the ice-free waters of the Pacific.

All the major European powers had desired Port Arthur, but none had dared to take it. The Sino-Japanese War of 1894 had more than proven the fighting ability of the Japanese, who had deeply resented the return of Port Arthur to China.

Russia, under the pretext that they held a twenty-five year lease on the port, entered Port Arthur. Ever since the Crimean War Russia had been losing her military gains on the bloodless battlefields of diplomacy. The Russian government actually

329

believed that a part of the internal unrest and revolutionary activity would be stifled by enlargement of her Empire, or, if necessary, a military victory over Japan.

Almost simultaneous with the Russian occupation of Port Arthur came the news of the sinking of the American battleship *Maine* in the harbor of Havana. The Spanish-American War began with Spain the absolute loser, and in a relatively short time thereafter Russia and the United States found themselves grimly regarding each other as rivals in Eastern Asia. The United States had "arrived" in the Far East by way of Hawaii and now, as a result of the destruction of the Spanish Fleet, the Philippines. On the other hand, the Russians came by way of Siberia, Korea and Manchuria, and the two powers glowered at each other for the first time face to face.

There exists a curious parallel between the Far Eastern situation of 1902 and that of our own times. The United States is once again faced with the dangerous alternative of remaking Japan into a powerful empire in order to halt Soviet expansion, while U.S.S.R. faces the fearful requirement of making China and the yellow race, her historical enemy, dominant in Asia, if only to gain either a foothold in Japan and neutralize Formosa, or to force Japan into a neutral orbit and protect her Eastern flank.

In 1899, however, the Russians had welcomed American penetration of Hawaii and the Philippines, because it would make the United States a strong naval and commercial rival of the British Empire. When, even after the battle of Manila Bay, rumors reached Washington that certain European powers were considering intervention on the side of the Spanish, Russia was the only country among the major powers to reassure the United States by stating that she "has no interest whatever in the Philippines." The Russian Foreign Minister told the American Ambassador that Russia "would regard any attempt by the European Powers to mediate or intervene in the Philippines as wholly unwarranted."

The first Russian Ambassador to the U. S. (the United States and Russia elevated their diplomats to that rank in 1898), Count Arthur Cassini, was carefully instructed with regard to the policy he should pursue. "You will take particular heed," Foreign Minister Muraviev wrote him, "of any circumstances threatening to develop into a clash between the U. S. and England or Japan. Devote particular attention also to the tense relations that have arisen between the U.S. and Canada . . . Support the Monroe Doctrine in situations where this popular American theory opposes the ambitions of our natural enemies, particularly England." Then, turning his attention to the Pacific, Muraviev wrote, "Sooner or later the Hawaiian Islands, if independent, would fall into the possession of Great Britain, Japan or the United States. To witness the formation of a new Malta in the Pacific or to allow the Japanese to acquire such an essential link in the reinforcement of their naval power would be equally undesirable to us . . . It would be more propitious for them to form part of the territory of the United States and thus remain for us a reliable refuge and a coaling station, than that they should become a nest of hostility and danger. We fully realize that in its anxiety for the future, the American government has taken careful stock of Britain's repeated conquests in the Pacific, not to speak of the rising power of Japan. And indeed, if we consider England's conquests in recent years, we will find that with the exception of Hawaii and Samoa there is not a single piece of free base left in the Pacific."

By December, 1898, the United States had vanquished once powerful Spain. And with the American occupation of Hawaii and the Philippines, the United States and Japan, though the Americans did not yet realize it, became potential enemies in the Pacific.

In May, 1899, at the initiative of Emperor Nicholas II, the nations of the world were invited to attend a conference at the Hague for the purpose of discussing reduction of armaments, humanizing of warfare, and the settlement of international disputes by arbitration. The United States, though not among the nations burdened with armaments, responded immediately, and the American Delegation, under the leadership of Andrew White, was the only one that came to the Conference with a detailed plan for an international court of arbitration.

The major source of resistance to the formation of such a court was Germany. Andrew White worked hard with the uncompromising German delegates and even sent one of his aides to Berlin to make a special appeal to the Kaiser. "No rational man,"

Emperor Nicholas II

wrote White, "expects all wars to be ended by anything done here. The important thing is that there be a provision made for easily calling together a court of arbitration which shall be seen of all Nations to indicate a sincere desire to promote peace . . . On the other hand, if you do not do this, if you put a stumbling-block in the way of arbitration, what results?" He continued, "Whether failure or success may come, the Emperor of Russia will be hailed in all parts of the World as a deliverer and, virtually, as a saint, while there will be a wide-spread outburst of hatred against the German Emperor."

It was a great diplomatic victory for the United States when the provision for a Permanent Court of Arbitration was accepted. America was also the first power to use The Hague arbitration courts. In 1902, the long-standing dispute with Mexico over the "pious fund," a trust fund established by the Jesuits in California in the 17th century for the religious conversion of the Indians to Christianity, was settled at The Hague.

At the Disarmament Conference of 1921 President Harding opened his address with the solemn remark that the limiting of armaments was not a new idea. "It will be appropriate to recall that twenty-three years ago it was His Imperial Majesty, the

Emperor Nicholas II of Russia, who was the first in his noble declaration to propose such a conference."

The Hague Conference closed amidst renewed Russia-American cordiality, but in that same year the bonds of friendship were permanently severed. In 1900 the Boxer Rebellion broke out in China. Russia, Germany, Great Britain, Japan, France and the United States joined forces in the march on Peking. When the Russians refused firmly to withdraw their troops from Manchuria, Russian-American friendship ended.

The Boxer Rebellion was a shabby affair from beginning to end, and if Russia played no glorious role in it, the conduct of the other nations was equally questionable. England had enlarged her holdings in Hong Kong and had forced China to "lease" Wei-hai-wei. France secured a 99-year lease on Kwangchow Bay and Germany took over the permanent occupation of Shantung.

Nicholas II, when still the heir to the throne, had barely escaped assassination in Japan, and although he was pacific in his foreign policies, he was so concerned with the internal unrest in Russia that he gave little personal attention to the Far East. Other members of the government, seeing the opportunity to obtain Russian access to an ice-free port on the Pacific, were willing to risk a war. But the main body of pressure for the southern penetration of Asia came from the Siberian colonists themselves.

Prince Peter Kropotkin, the Russian anarchist, wrote:

"Only after a few years in exile in Siberia did I fully understand the attraction which southern land exercised on the Russian, the colonial effort that they made to reach the Black Sea, and the steady pressure of the Siberian Colonists southwest, further into Manchuria. It was as if the warm winds and fertile soils were an uncontrollable attraction . . ."

The United States government, alarmed by the Russian penetration of Manchuria, made repeated protests. But the Russians did not bother to answer. "The truth is," reported Ambassador Tower, "the Russian Government does not wish to answer."

Fear of Russian expansion was not dictated by American love for the territorial integrity of China, as Uncle Sam's diplomats tried to pretend. The United States was disturbed because Russian infiltration of Manchuria began to place restrictions on American

The Russian Flagship sunk in Tsushima

trade. The "Open Door in China" was still open, but it was not as wide a door as the American merchants wanted. Almost overnight, Russia became the unpopular, enormous bear "who was throwing the treaty rights of other nations in the dustbin."

Secretary Hay commented, "Russia is too big, too crafty and too cruel for us to fight, so why not give up now and be friendly?"

President Theodore Roosevelt replied, "I have not the slightest objection to the Russians knowing that I feel thoroughly aroused and irritated at their conduct in Manchuria, that I don't intend to give way and that I am year by year growing more confident that this country would back me up in going to an extreme in the matter."

On the night of February 8, 1904, without declaring war, the Japanese attacked the Russians at Port Arthur. It was no secret that Teddy Roosevelt was delighted. Almost a month before the attack, the Japanese government received assurances from President Roosevelt that the American government would go even further than the observance of strict neutrality. Two days after the treacherous attack by the Japanese, the President wrote to his son how pleased he was with the "Japanese Victory," and added, "Japan is playing our game."

The United States was to think quite differently after a similar attack thirty-seven years later—one called Pearl Harbor.

On July 24, 1905, President Roosevelt confessed to Cecil Spring Rice, the Secretary of the British Embassy in St. Petersburg, that he had notified Germany and France "in the most polite and discreet fashion, that in the event of a combination against Japan . . . I should promptly side with Japan and proceed to whatever length was necessary on her behalf."

Ironically, the first victims of the Russo-Japanese War were two Russian warships which had been purchased in the United States. Teddy Roosevelt, then Assistant Secretary of the Navy, had interested Peter Botkin, Secretary of the Russian Embassy in Washington, in their design.

The war at sea proved disastrous for Russia. The Japanese February 8th surprise engagement of a torpedo attack on the ships at Port Arthur severely damaged two Russian battleships and a cruiser. On February 11th, two Russian ships ran into their own mines. At Chemulpo, two Russian cruisers were sunk, and Japan had control of the sea. Not until August of 1904 was the battered

Russian Artillery in Russo-Japanese War

Russian fleet, in a desperation move, ordered to try to break the Japanese communication lines. Admiral Togo scattered this Russian fleet. Some of the Russian ships were captured with the fall of Port Arthur, others were sunk, and the remainder fled to neutral ports where they were interned.

During this critical period, as Russia tried to reinforce her Pacific squadrons, England did everything possible to hamper her, forbidding the purchase of cruisers in Argentina and Chile, and preventing the passage of her warships from the Black Sea. The American attitude, however, was puzzling, for while Roosevelt was pro-Japanese, the American public was only mildly aroused. In April, 1903, Secretary of State Hay wrote to Roosevelt, "It is out of the question that we should adopt any scheme of concerted action with England and Japan. Public opinion in this country would not support such a course." Thus, Russia was able to purchase six submarines, including the famous *Protector,* and with the help of an American businessman, Charles Flint, to transfer those submarines into the Baltic, despite repeated protests by England and Japan.

But while Russia managed to obtain a few submarines for her Baltic Fleet, great quantities of food, ammunition, guns, horses and mules were transported to Japan in American ships. The American banking firm of Kuhn, Loeb and Co. made important loans to the Japanese. Meetings and lectures in defence of "poor little Japan" were held throughout the United States. George Kennan, now residing in Japan, was making violent condemnations of Russia in the magazine *Outlook*. One of these articles extolled the virtues of the Japanese soldiers to the point that even President Roosevelt was forced to make a sharp criticism of Kennan. A New York *Times* editorial, bitter over American losses in Manchurian trade, proclaimed, "Whatever is gained by Russia, is lost to mankind!" Rear Admiral Francis T. Bowles announced: "It is in the interest of the United States that Japan should be victorious in this war." Regarding the Japanese surprise attack on Russia The New York *Times* wrote, "It seems hardly to become the dignity of the ruler of a great nation to complain that he has been struck before he was quite ready! To impute treachery to the Japanese . . ."

How different a shoe American newspapers wore after December 7, 1941! How many United States naval officers cursed themselves for not having studied more closely Japanese tactics in the Russo-Japanese War!

While the American newspapers bore such headlines as, "Shall Russia Dominate the World," and, "We Do Not Trust Russia," in a small corner of the *Evening Post* were the words of one W. F. Howell, "Lest we forget the arrival of the Russian fleet in 1863, I subscribe myself theirs in sympathy."

With the Russian Navy destroyed, the Japanese commenced the siege of Port Arthur. After a long, bitter series of battles, and after another Russian defeat, this time on land, in which Russian columns attempted to break the siege, Port Arthur fell. Even after the defeat of the Russians at Mukden, the Russian Army in that sector was half a million strong. Altogether the Russian forces in the Far East numbered 942,000, while the Japanese were nearer to three-quarters of a million. Thus, after the final Russian naval engagement in Tsushima Strait, in May, 1905, when their Baltic Fleet, which had made a laborious voyage around the world, was destroyed, the Russians were basically undefeated. For Russia, throughout history, has had an annoying habit of losing the battles and winning the wars.

"The Emperor," wrote Kokovtsov, a week after the Tsushima battle, "sees now no hope for a speedy victory, but he thinks one must prolong the war, in order to exhaust the Japanese and thus force them to ask for an honorable peace."

There can be no doubt that Teddy Roosevelt wanted the Japanese to win the war in Manchuria. But as the Japanese fleet began to sweep the Russian flag from the Pacific Ocean with comparative ease, he began to sense the lack of wisdom of portions of his policy. The sober thought that with the defeat of Russia a new and formidable Empire might dominate the Far East penetrated his mind. As the bloody struggle continued, Roosevelt became more and more convinced that he was fostering a dangerous power. It was not until two years after the Russo-Japanese War, however, that Roosevelt received a letter transmitted by the Chief of Staff of the United States Army, relating how a Japanese diplomat, after several glasses of champagne, had announced,

Russo-Japanese Peace Conference (Portsmouth, N. H., 1905)

"Japan will take the Philippine Islands when she desires them. She is ready now, and to take the Hawaiian Islands as well. But do you imagine *that* will satisfy us? We never forget and we never forgive a personal injury. San Francisco will see the day when she will wish that she had perished in the Great Earthquake. I tell you we will make a Japanese Colony of California and the Pacific Coast, Alaska included . . . The United States are our natural enemy, the only nation in the world that has refused to recognize us as equals!"

After the Russian naval defeat at Tsushima, President Roosevelt, through clever diplomatic negotiations, induced the Japanese to ask him to mediate for peace. He knew that this was the only way that he would be able to get the Russian Emperor to consider terminating the war. But it was no easy task, for the attitude of Russian militarists was in favor of continuing the fighting. United States Ambassador George Meyer finally gained an audience with Czar Nicholas II and pleaded for more than an hour before he was able to obtain consent to begin negotiations. "As yet," the Emperor reminded Meyer, "no Japanese foot has been placed on Russian soil." Meyer, fearing the Czar might change his mind, contrary to custom, cabled the results.

Korekiyo Takahashi, the Japanese Minister of Finance, wrote to Jacob Schiff, one of the heads of the powerful banking house, Kuhn, Loeb and Co., "I doubted that the Russian Government was sincerely intent on peace. As a matter of fact my Government had the information that there was a strong military clique in Russia who believed and insisted on continuing hostilities to the bitter end; notwithstanding the successive defeats, they seemed to stick to the view that Japan's financial strength would fall short if only they held out long enough. It was for this reason that my Government wanted further to amplify its funds before the meeting of the plenipotentiaries."

Nicholas II, in the margin of the draft of instructions to his negotiators, wrote these three comments. "I do not consider that we are defeated: our armies are intact and I have implicit faith in them! Regarding Korea, in this question I am ready for a concession—this is not Russia's land. But as to indemnity, Russia has never paid an indemnity and I will *never* consent to that."

Japan was in a peculiar position, for the Japanese had made a serious diplomatic mistake in allowing themselves to be the ones to petition for mediation; and, realizing this, they felt they had been tricked. Japan was never to forgive Teddy Roosevelt or the United States. True, the Japanese had won tremendous naval victories, but only at the cost of nearly 100,000 casualties, they had taken Port Arthur. Furthermore, it was a correct assumption on the part of Russia that the Japanese were now facing a grave financial situation. The possibility of a long indecisive war actually was more than the Japanese economy could stand. Baron Kaneko, the Japanese Ambassador to Washington, wrote to Roosevelt, "Payment of the cost of the war by Russia is absolutely necessary. Public sentiment in Japan is strongly demanding a far larger amount of indemnity . . . and acquisition of Vladivostok. Apart from this I feel that without payment of the cost of the war by Russia, we can hardly manage our national finances and economy. The war has already been a great strain upon our national economy."

Jacob Schiff, in a letter from Korekiyo Takahashi, was informed, "I meet with abundant sympathy for Japan in the

United States, but the result of my financial soundings was not encouraging." The British were also cool as far as money was concerned; and France and Germany, being friendly to Russia, could not be approached for loans.

On August 26, 1905, when the Portsmouth, New Hampshire, peace negotiations were on the brink of collapse, Schiff wrote to Baron Takahira, the special Japanese Peace Envoy, "It is true Russia will not be able to find money for a continuation of the war either in Paris or Berlin, but she will have recourse to her very considerable gold reserve and will not hesitate to abandon the gold standard. She will in the hour of her despair not flinch to secure the sinews of war. As to Japan, there will be an immediate call in the price of her foreign loans of from five to ten percent. What I apprehend, however, is that the money markets of the U.S., England and Germany will no longer be prepared to finance Japan's requirements to any great extent. It is this I deemed my duty to say to you . . . though my own firm will stand by Japan."

The Treaty ending the Russo-Japanese War was signed on September 5, 1905. There was no war indemnity or financial reparations. Russia was forced to evacuate Southern Manchuria. Japan was given the southern half of Sakhalin Island, lease of Liaotung Peninsula, and "paramount political, military and economic" rights in Korea.

There was an immediate outburst against Americans in Tokyo. The United States Minister to Japan, Lloyd Griscom, reported that on the day the Peace Treaty was made public in Tokyo "some fifty people had been killed and hundreds wounded." Teddy Roosevelt's picture was torn down from public places, and threatening letters poured into the American Legation.

The war was over. Russia salvaged a diplomatic triumph out of military and naval defeats, and the stage was set for the first great Russian revolutionary uprising. The era of the Czars was approaching its end, and the Revolution of 1905 was the dress rehearsal for the beginning of the U.S.S.R.

In that same hour the history of Asia and the Pacific began a new cycle. "Roosevelt," wrote Foster Dulles, the historian, "had in reality failed to uphold a balance of power in the East. Japan had replaced Russia as the most powerful nation in Eastern Asia.

Time was to prove that she was a far more formidable rival to American interests in the Pacific than ever Czarist Russia had been."

The commercial interests of nations do not always coincide with their political and diplomatic efforts. Thus it was that the United States fattened Japan with war materials even after it became obvious that the two nations would someday clash.

It is easy to understand, therefore, that the American repudiation of the trade treaty with Russia, a repudiation made largely at the behest of American citizens of Jewish faith, had little effect on American-Russian trade. From 1900 to 1911, Russia imported annually from the United States manufactured goods averaging close to twenty million dollars in value. Imports rose to nearly thirty million dollars by 1913 and during the First World War climbed to over forty million dollars.

For the first time in history, numerous Russian writers, musicians and composers visited the United States. In the following years Scriabin made a concert tour of the United States. He was followed by Maxim Gorky. Three years later Rachmaninov electrified American audiences with his playing. Under the leadership of Diaghilev, such outstanding dancers as Anna Pavlova, Nicholas Mordkin and Nicholas Fokine made their first American appearances. The Metropolitan Opera decided to import the entire Diaghilev Company. Gertrude Hoffman, however, outwitted the Metropolitan, and brought them to America in the summer of 1911.

It was in the June of 1911, that the American Fleet, under the command of Rear-Admiral Charles Badger, visited Russia for the last time before the First World War. For eight days the Americans were wined, dined and feted. Nicholas II, in his audience with the senior Naval officers, proposed a toast to President Taft, "The Chief of a country with whom Russia has always been at peace."

A bare three years later a shot rang out in the little town of Sarajevo and engulfed the world in a bath of human blood from which it was never to recover—at least in our time.

the curtain falls

The post of American Ambassador to Russia had been vacant for almost two years. On July 1, 1914, exactly a month before the historic afternoon when the German Ambassador was to call on the Russian Foreign Minister, President Wilson appointed George Marye of California United States Ambassador to Russia. There were, therefore, just thirty-one days left before the moment when, with "increasing signs of emotion," the German Envoy would ask Sazonov to suspend the Russian mobilization, receive the fateful negative reply, and draw from his pocket a folded piece of paper —the German Declaration of War.

Among American visitors in St. Petersburg during those portentous days were two society women—Mrs. Chauncey Depew, whose yacht was anchored in the Neva in those "last months of glamour and gaiety Russia was ever to know," Mrs. Laura Craig

342

Biddle—and Schuyler Parsons. All three attended the last peacetime parade of the Imperial Guards and the reception accorded Messrs. Poincaré and Viviani of France in Krasnoye Selo.

On the day that Germany declared war on Russia, the new American Ambassador was taking his oath at City Hall in San Francisco. Marye, upon arriving in Washington, felt that he had been given an obscure, unimportant post. Nothing noteworthy had happened in Russian-American relations since the January, 1910, dinner at the White House, when Baroness Rosen, wife of the Russian Ambassador of that day, had asked President Taft for a cigarette. The President, who was on the stuffy side, got quite flustered, but finally managed to obtain one from a musician in the dinner ensemble. Afterwards he felt bound to announce, "I hope the press will not hear of this, and I am pleased that the American women present did not indulge."

The last Imperial Russian Ambassador to the United States, George Bakhmetev, urged Marye to remain in Washington. "The Embassy [in St. Petersburg] was allowed to remain vacant for two years," said Bakhmetev. "If you go now, you will not only have all that mess to straighten out, but you will have to take care of the German interests. Wait until the war is over. It'll be over in a few months."

But Marye decided to sail.

Not being a professional diplomat, and having received his new post as a result of patronage, Marye knew nothing about Russia and less about the workings of diplomacy. On September 9, 1914, he boarded the liner *Mauretania*. These were the ominous days of the First Battle of the Marne. Upon his arrival in St. Petersburg, he found his Embassy lodged in a modest private house, and being handled by Charles Wilson, Chargé d'Affaires. Wilson was an experienced diplomat, but was hampered by his low rank in exercising his tempering influence upon the European diplomatic corps. Together, however, Marye and Wilson were to make a good team.

Less than a week after his arrival, Marye was received by Nicholas II, to whom he handed his *Lettre de Créance*. Considering wartime conditions and the chilly diplomatic relations between Russia and the United States, the audience had been granted with

Mariinsky Palace in St. Petersburg, the seat of Government

flattering promptness. Marye remarked that the Czar was an "earnest, serious man with excellent knowledge."

On December 14, 1914, Marye reported to Washington that he had discussed trade relations with Foreign Minister Sazonov. Prior to this time, most of the Russian trade had been handled by German intermediaries. The war now offered Russia an excellent opportunity to open direct trade relations with the United States. But the old passport question remained a stumbling-block to any major negotiations, even though during this period the first American Commercial Attaché was posted to St. Petersburg.

The military situation in Russia had by now grown difficult. The First Battle of the Marne had been won by the Allies largely because of the Russian sacrifice at Tannenberg. With the German drive stalled in France, the Russians now had to prepare to face a new onslaught. Warsaw fell, and the Germans advanced into eastern Poland. It was at this time that Nicholas II informed Marye, "Russia, England and France are firmly resolved to make no peace until it can be on terms which render it durable, and which will free Europe from the constant threat of German aggression."

Despite the forthright statement by the Czar, Russia was extremely hard-pressed. War enthusiasm distinctly diminished, as will happen in any country that suffers tremendous casualties. There were many false rumors in the wind indicating that Russia was seeking a separate peace with Germany. Tales linking the hypnotic evil genius, Rasputin, with the Imperial Family surpassed those of wildest imagination.

Publication of various documents by the Soviet has proven that most of the rumors, at least those concerning a separate peace, were unfounded. But toward the end of 1915 their constancy had created so many doubts in Russian hearts, that the end result was a general feeling that all information, good or bad, was necessarily unreliable. "How much of this treason is true," wrote Marye, "I do not know. Russia is a land of irresponsible *on dit* and it takes time to find out what among the things you hear is true."

On March 1, 1916, one year before the Russian Revolution put an end to the three-hundred-year dynasty of the Romanovs, Marye informed Sazonov that David R. Francis of Missouri would be the new United States Ambassador. In his last audience with Nicholas II, Marye found himself being told what many other American diplomats had heard from former Czars, "Your government makes

The Emperor Nicholas II with his family in 1914

a mistake changing its representatives abroad so often." Nicholas II, however, added, "You have now become so wealthy and important in the comity of nations that your relations with other countries will be much closer and wider than they used to be. I cannot help thinking that you will find it to your advantage to follow those methods of international intercourse which experience has shown other nations to be the best."

Marye had done surprisingly well at his post, when it is realized that his appointment was of a political nature and in a field in which he had had no previous experience. During his sixteen months in Russia, the only criticism of him was made by Negley Farson, a young Southerner, who remarked bitterly, "He has nothing to do with real Americans . . . too genteel to have anything to do with trade or business, to help us out in our various troubles with censors and obstructive Russian officials!"

On August 1, 1914, when Germany declared war, Russia had been as unprepared as France and England. The Central Powers on the other hand were fully mobilized within two weeks, but Russia found her manpower properly assembled only by the third month of the war and even then with a shortage of eleven million rifles. Her heavy artillery was less than half the minimum required, and her shell production was inadequate and unable to replace the puny amount that was then available. It was in this condition that Russia, weakened by her war with Japan and by the Revolution of 1905, had to face the combined strength of Germany, Austria-Hungary, and later, Turkey.

The Russian war plans, which had been prepared as early as 1912 in collaboration with the French General Staff, stipulated that the Russians were to withdraw their main forces slowly to the fortified zone, gradually releasing Poland to the Germans. This would not only give Russia time to strengthen her armament and her munition supplies but would also shorten her lines of communication, at the same time forcing the Germans to extend theirs. The hammer-like Schlieffen Plan and the sudden invasion of Belgium with its immediate threat to Paris induced the Allies to request Russia to cancel these original plans. In order to remove some of the pressure from France, the Russian armies were to invade East Prussia at once. The "Miracle of the Marne" was gained at the price of the disastrous battle of Tannenberg, when two Russian armies were annihilated. The massive Russian offensive, however, had forced the German High Command to withdraw two Army Corps from France and transfer them to the Eastern Front and these had come from the very hammer of the Schlieffen Plan.

"Had these four divisions been present at the Battle of the Marne," wrote British General Sir Frederic Maurice, "the history of the war might have taken a very different course."

"With the withdrawal of two Army Corps to East Prussia, the German Army was unable to reach Paris," wrote German General Ludendorff.

Regardless of the disaster of Tannenberg, Russian armies held their foothold on German soil in East Prussia until early in 1915. Germany was again compelled to concentrate more troops on the Eastern Front, increasing their strength from 114 to 153 divisions, again at the expense of their forces in the West. Despite shortages of weapons and ammunition, the Russians continued to launch offensives, capturing the Austrian fortress of Przemysl, crossing the Carpathian mountains, and invading the Hungarian Plateau.

Germany, to save her ally, threw 137 divisions against the Russians, leaving only 83 on the Anglo-French front. The Allies thus enjoyed fifteen months of relative quietness and gained precious time to increase their war production. Russia retreated, suffering terrible losses, but inflicting heavy casualties on her enemies. The grandiose plan of Hindenburg to strangle Russia in the summer of 1915 failed. Despite three million casualties and an appalling lack of ammunition, the Russian armies continued to hold the front. "These battles did not bring the desired results," wrote Hindenburg. "The Russian bear escaped the nets in which we engulfed him. He bled profusely, but he was not mortally wounded. He was saved, inflicting terrible losses on us."

At the beginning of 1916, again at the request of her Allies and again, contrary to her own strategic plans, Russia commenced a new offensive in Galicia to relieve the pressure on Verdun. Yet another offensive was launched in May to save the Italian army which had been routed at Caporetto. This offensive resulted in the greatest Russian victory of the First World War. In addition to capturing over 350,000 prisoners, 400 guns, 1300 machine guns, and sizeable amounts of ammunition, a stretch of land 200 miles wide and 60 miles deep was overrun. The war prisoners taken by Russia during this period totaled more than the combined number of prisoners taken by France and England during the entire war. Important advances were also made in Asia, where the fortified stronghold of Erzeroum and the Black Sea port of Trebizond were captured. Contact with British troops in Mesopotamia was established in May, 1916. In addition to these activities, in holding the gigantic 1000-mile Eastern Front, Russia, at the request of her Allies, dispatched troops all the way to France and Salonika. In the Black Sea the Russian Navy drove the *Goeben* and the *Breslau* back into the Bosphorus, mined the Straits, and converted the sea into a Russian lake. With the Turks no longer able to use the sea for transportation, it became necessary for the Germans to send coal to their allies overland from upper Silesia.

To retain the proper perspective of these achievements, one must remember that they were accomplished by a nation which had sustained casualties in blood amounting to almost 7,000,000 men. Allied help—munitions, planes, etc.—never reached Russia in any large proportions until after the Revolution of 1917.

Outstanding among Americans who served in the Russian Army was Dr. Eugene Hurd, who, until August, 1914, was a practicing surgeon in Seattle, Washington, and a member of the State Legislature. He spent the entire war at the Front and was decorated with three Imperial Orders for bravery. Malcolm C. Grow of Philadelphia also served out the war with the famous Siberian troops and received the St. George Cross for bravery, the highest award in the Empire. Dr. E. H. Egbert was in charge of a field hospital. And an American known only as "Death Valley Slim" was attached to the Black Sea Fleet.

American correspondents in Russia included Capt. Robert McCormick, Stanley Washburn, William Simms, and Isabel F. Hapgood. The Russian Government provided free lodging, food, and even *per diem* expenses, and the censorship was more than lax.

Although the quantities of supplies, guns and ammunition that Russia was able to obtain were pathetic, the United States, a neutral nation, contributed more to her cause (if not very much) than all the Allies combined. The Russian Army began to be familiar with such automobiles as the Ford, Hupmobile, Pierce Arrow, and the first car with four-wheel drive, the famous Jeffries.

David Francis, a former Governor of Missouri, who was to witness the Russian Revolution, arrived in Russia on April 28, 1916, alone, except for his "loyal colored valet, Philip Jordan." George Bakhmetev, the Russian Ambassador in Washington, characterized Francis as an "infinitely higher class man than Marye, a man of wide experience, 66 years of age, full of energy."

Francis was appalled with the enormous amount of work which his new post entailed. The American Embassy, since the United States was still a neutral nation, was asked to represent the German-Austrian interests. There were by now nearly a million German and Austrian war prisoners. Francis, however, who made no secret of his sympathy with the Allied cause, had come to Russia to get a new commercial treaty, and he was determined to put American affairs first and foremost, which he accomplished by simply ignoring the prisoner question.

The general situation in Russia was not very conducive to diplomatic negotiations. Although the "pale" had been broken, Jews being now allowed to live or to travel anywhere in the Empire, those Jews who would not give up their religion were still not able to become officers in the military. Nor could they rise to high political rank. The German propagandists were making use of this situation in their efforts to keep the United States neutral. But the Russians were in no mood to make changes in their internal policies merely to obtain a commercial treaty which would be of no particular consequence to them until after the war. Foreign Minister Sazonov explained to the American Ambassador, "Russia is not prepared at this time to negotiate any Commercial Treaty with any country, until all the Allies arrive at some agreement on economic problems. It was different six months ago, but now it is too late. The Allies have agreed upon a program of understanding between themselves, not only on the prosecution of the war, but on commercial relations between friendly, neutral and belligerent countries after the war."

The United States was politely reminded that it was not one of the "Allied Nations," regardless of where American sympathies might lie. Francis, disappointed, informed Washington that there was still hope for a Treaty, but not before July, 1916, when the Allied Economic Council met in Paris. Francis, a shrewd business-man, sensed that, regardless of the outcome of the war, Russia was to become an important source of trade. American goods were now pouring into Russia through Archangel and Vladivostok. Negotiations for the opening of the first American bank (the National City Bank) in Russia were in progress, with branches in Petrograd and Moscow.

In September, 1916, a few months before the Revolution, Francis brought another matter to the attention of the Russian government—a new project to link Russia and America by telegraph cable. Newcombe Carlton, the President of Western Union, had estimated the cost of the project at about six million dollars. Russian officials instantly offered to advance half of this sum. "But our Government," wrote Francis, "declined participa-tion on the grounds that it could not engage in a business enterprise."

Toward the end of 1916 the world was electrified by Presi-dent Wilson's communication to each of the belligerents requesting them to state the terms on which they would be willing to make peace. Nothing came of this proposal, and the world continued with the slaughter. Unfortunately for Russia, however, the Wilson proposal provided fodder for those unscrupulous elements within her national framework who for their own reasons wanted to withdraw from the war at any cost.

At the threshold of 1917, Russia was in a better strategic position than it had been at any time since before the battle of Tannenberg. She was the only country who had fought on German soil. For the first time her armies were properly equipped. The railroad to Murmansk was completed, and she was at last in per-manent contact with her Allies. Trained new battalions were added to her forces, and a great supply of shells, guns, planes, armored cars and helmets (which the Russians had never had and which

Breadlines in Petrograd in January 1917

had been no small factor in her casualties) were in readiness. Yet, with the coming of the Revolution, Russia, the only country that fought on German soil, was subdued without a decisive defeat being inflicted upon her by her enemies.

On February 4, 1917, a month before the Russian Revolution, the United States severed diplomatic relations with Germany. Ambassador Francis wrote to Secretary Lansing, "The Russians are very much pleased with the stand we have taken and are already beginning to treat us as allies."

It had been a severe winter in Russia, the coldest of all the three years of war. Food shortages that had been annoying city populations increased due to transportation breakdown. (The countryside as usual had an extreme oversupply.) In Petrograd (St. Petersburg before 1914) a rumor spread that the government was going to ration bread. There was a rush upon the bakeries.

On March 7, 1917, the day when the first clash took place in the streets of Petrograd, Czar Nicholas II had departed for the Front, and the symbol of order was conveniently removed from the seat of government.

That same evening, Ambassador Francis gave a dinner in honor of the new Japanese Ambassador to the Court at Petrograd, "the last function of its kind attended by members of the Russian Cabinet." The main topic of dinner conversation was the impending entry of the United States into the ranks of the Allies.

As the party came to an end, Francis bade his guests "au revoir" and expressed his hope that they would reach their homes safely. They laughingly referred to the "disturbances," and were, as the Ambassador described, inclined to accept his solicitude for their safety as "a conversational pleasantry."

As the massive doors of the Embassy opened outward, the departing guests were startled. Far away in the unfashionable sector of Petrograd could be seen a faint red glow, a glow that seemed to be increasing in intensity. The heavy doors of the American Embassy slowly closed behind them. The glow was perceptibly brighter now, and from the great *porte-cochère* the swirling snow about the first departing sleighs seemed touched with fire— fire that was soon to engulf the whole world in its flames. From this exact moment, the traditional Russian-American friendship which had begun with the birth of the young American Republic one hundred and forty-one years ago, was over. A new and terrible era was about to unfold with the imminent abdication and murder of the Czar.

Meanwhile, a Russian emigré far away in Switzerland was telling a group of comrades that he was "too old to witness the Revolution in Russia." That man was Lenin . . .

appendix

The following is the English translation
from the Russian
of the

SEALED ORDERS OF ADMIRAL LESSOVSKY

I

July 14 [26], 1863
#120

TO REAR ADMIRAL LESSOVSKY.

1. By the all-highest command of His Imperial Majesty you are appointed commander of the squadron in the Atlantic Ocean.

2. This squadron is composed of the frigates "Alexander Nevsky," "Peresvyet," and "Oslyabia"; the sloops-of-war [corvettes] "Varyag" and "Vityaz"; and the clippers "Almaz," "Zhemchug," and "Izumrud." [The last two were not sent.]

REMARK I. The frigate "Oslyabia" is at present at its station in Piraeus, and it has been proposed to dispatch her to New York in order to be there united to your squadron or to receive instructions to join it at such a place as will be designated for this by you.

REMARK II. The clipper "Izumrud" will not be ready before August and therefore will be joined to the squadron in the event that by August war will not have been already declared.

3. The aim of the undertaking of the squadron entrusted to your leadership in the event of a war at present foreseen with the western powers is to act with all the possible means available to you against our opponents, inflicting by means of separate cruises the most painful damage and loss to the commerce of the enemy, or making attacks with the entire squadron on the weak and poorly protected places of the colonies of the enemy.

4. Although the Atlantic Ocean is designated as the primary place of sojourn of the squadron, still you are not prohibited, having regard for circumstances and according to your discernment, from transferring the theatre of the activities of the entire squadron, or a part of it, to the Indian or the Pacific Oceans.

5. On leaving the Gulf of Finland, you are to direct your course with the whole squadron to the shores of the United States of North America, not putting in to any other port on the way; and upon arrival in America, you will drop anchor in New York. If it appears possible according to local conditions to remain in this port with the entire squadron, then you will there await the outcome of the negotiations on the Polish question. If our minister in Washington, with whom you will immediately establish communication upon your arrival in America, should find that the sojourn of the entire squadron in New York might give rise to difficulties with the federal government, or to other unpleasantnesses, then it is permissible for you to divide the squadron into two or three parts, and to scatter it among those ports of the North American coast which will be recognized by you as the most advantageous for this.

In advance of a declaration of war, it is left to you to determine, according to the consideration of the locality and the circumstances of the moment, whether it is possible or advisable to remain with the squadron in New York or in other North American ports until the actual outbreak of military activities or, leaving the anchorage upon the supplementing of supplies, or at a time when a declaration of war is becoming unavoidable and near, to put to sea so that at a known rendezvous, which has been previously determined, you will receive information of the declaration of war by means of a ship hired expressly for this purpose by the Councilor of State Stoeckl. It is understood that it will be necessary to preserve this arrangement with the greatest secrecy; and the place of rendezvous must not be divulged to anyone, excepting to our minister.

6. If on the way to New York you learn authentically that war is declared, then you will observe the orders which have been set out here below in this instruction as a guide for your actions in the event of the outbreak of military activities.

7. If, after your arrival in New York, you deem it necessary soon to put out to sea, then, in any event before a declaration of war, you should endeavor to hold the squadron together, carefully avoiding the places which are frequented customarily by warships and even merchantmen, in order to screen the squadron from observation, which our future opponents in all probability will try to make upon it.

If, contrary to expectation, you do not receive at the designated rendezvous the long-awaited advices from the Councilor of State Stoeckl, then, going out upon one of the commercial lanes, you are to try to obtain information about the course of political events from a merchantman, turning in preference to the ships of those powers with whom we do not expect to be at war. You must verify the information received in this manner with the parallel assertions of the skippers and with reports drawn from the newspapers which may be accessible on the ships that have been met. You must redouble your watchfulness and caution directly as the rumors and advices reaching you cause you to presume that a break and war are becoming imminent.

8. When you receive notification of a declaration of war from our minister in Washington, or when you will have received in any other kind of authentic manner the conviction that war is declared, you must then commence hostile action against the

commerce of the enemy, giving for this to the commanders of the ships of the squadron entrusted to you the detailed, pertinent instructions in proper time. You will distribute these ships with such consideration that they occupy the most frequented lanes and on which are directed the most important and the most valuable tonnage. Besides this you will designate several rendezvous for the reassembling of the entire squadron in order to examine the separate ships, to collect news concerning their activities, and to give them directions about the means of renewing the supplies of provisions and fuel, and so as to choose, according to your judgment, another scene of activity against the commerce of the enemy, or indeed to undertake enterprises against those places of the colonial power of the enemy which in your estimation and knowledge represent the probability of an easy capture, and an invasion of which promises to inflict upon the enemy a painful wound or loss.

9. For the taking of measures guaranteeing the squadron with a timely supply of provisions indispensable for its subsistence, Captain Crown, who is being ordered to America, in agreement with you, and by means of the cooperation of our minister in Washington, will arrange for the delivery of everything necessary at a designated place on a definite date. The experience and the proven capability of this staff officer is able to serve as a guarantee that this important side of the business entrusted to you will be carried out in complete satisfaction.

10. Both in your activities while examining neutral ships as well as in your actions against the enemy you should proceed in everything in accordance with the rules of international law and within the conditions of the Declaration of the Congress of Paris of 1856 relating to ocean commerce, and placed at the head of the excerpts herein enclosed, from the code of rules concerning wartime cruises, which should serve you as a guide in the matters which are confronting you.

11. If, in the course of your navigation in time of war, you should meet up with Rear-Admiral Popov, you are ordered to deliberate together with him concerning the activities which you deem the most useful and possible to undertake in the strengthened composition of both squadrons. Instructions to the same

purport have been sent to Rear-Admiral Popov according to which, it goes without saying, both squadrons must comport themselves under the direction of the elder of the commanding flag officers. [i.e. Admiral Popov]

12. The highest discretionary rights over the crew of the squadron entrusted to you are set forth in a separate instruction herein enclosed.

13. You will endeavor as soon as possible to furnish information about yourself, placing it in trustworthy hands, and reporting everything relating to your movements and surmises solely by the cypher which is entrusted to you to the number of "6" copies. You will deliver this cypher personally to the commanders, engaging them in writing to preserve it with the greatest secrecy and not to share it with anyone except the senior officer.

An identical cypher will be sent to Rear-Admiral Popov in the event that actual communication appears possible between you. On returning to Russia, you and each of the commanders must immediately hand back this cypher personally to the director of the chancellory of the Ministry of the Marine in return for his receipt.

14. While you are sailing, and whether or not war has been declared, I request you to devote especial attention to the collection of detailed and precise information of the chief routes of trade along which ocean merchandise travels, designating precisely what cargoes are dispatched from what countries. I request you also to compose, as far as may be possible, a full description of the colonial possessions of the Western nations, including therein a consideration of the possibility of an attack against them, from where and with what forces these assaults might be made, of the nature of their protection, of the importance of their military and commercial relations, etc. In addition to this you will not fail to assemble information of those places where squadrons and single ships may find refuge in times of war, and where they may be replenished with provisions and supplied with fuel.

Having been convinced that you appreciate the full importance of such knowledge, I trust that you will devote to this subject that attention which it merits.

15. In the event of a peaceful solution of the present nego-

tiations on Polish affairs, the ships of the squadron entrusted to you should be directed to a destination in a foreign station, about which you will receive the requisite notification in proper time.

It remains for me to remark in conclusion that at the present time and from this place it is impossible to guess in advance or to foresee all the occurrences which could result in a prolongation of the journey of which you are on the eve. Nevertheless, in this document there are included in their general outlines the instructions for the activities which are facing you; but it is left to you in all of these circumstances, when you perceive it to be necessary, not to be bound by the orders which have been given, and to act on your own judgment.

In giving to you such rights, His Imperial Majesty does not doubt that you will use them with that distinguished skilfulness and cleverness which, together with your other attainments, won for you an honorable renown in the fleet. Placing the honor of the Russian flag in your hands in a very important matter, His Majesty is convinced that, if the enemies of Russia shall rise up against it, our sailors, permeated with the wonderful spirit of their calling and having been animated by these sentiments which are rallying nowadays to the support of the throne from all the ends of the Russian land, then will inscribe on the waves of the ocean a glorious page in the Russian chronicle of the sea.

[signed:]   THE EXECUTIVE SECRETARY OF THE
MINISTRY OF THE MARINE
ADJUTANT-GENERAL N. KRABBE
[Minister of Marine]

[Leningrad Archives of the Army and the Fleet,
Collection of the Ministry of the Marine]

No. II

No. 250. (1 annexe)

Londres, le 5/17 Octobre 1863

ANNOTATION BY ALEXANDER II:

"Il y a beaucoup de juste dans ses raisonnements, mais ce n'est pas une raison pour renoncer au séjour de notre escadre dans ces parages."

BIBLIOGRAPhY

ADAMOV, E. A. "Russia and the United States at the Time of the Civil War," *Journal of Modern History,* II (1930).

ADAMS, JOHN. *The Works of John Adams,* ed. CHARLES FRANCIS ADAMS. 10 vols. Boston, 1852.

ADLER, CYRUS. *Jacob H. Schiff, His Life and Letters.* New York, 1928.

ALEXANDER, GRAND DUKE OF RUSSIA. *Once a Grand Duke.* New York, 1932.

ALEXANDER, W. D. "Proceedings of the Russians on Kauai, 1814-16," *Papers of the Hawaiian Historical Society,* No. 6 (1894).

ALEXIS, GRAND DUKE OF RUSSIA. *His Imperial Highness, the Grand Duke Alexis in the United States: 1871-72.* Cambridge, Massachusetts, 1872.

ANDREWS, C. L. *The Story of Alaska.* Seattle, 1931.

APPLETON, NATHAN. *Russian Life and Society as Seen in 1866-67 by Appleton and Longfellow.* Boston, 1904.

ARNAUD, C. A. DE. *The Union, and Its Ally, Russia.* Washington, 1890.

AUCAIGNE, FELIX. *L'Alliance Russo-Americaine.* Paris, 1863.

BABEY, ANNA M. *Americans in Russia, 1776-1917. A Study of the American Travelers in Russia from the American Revolution to the Russian Revolution.* New York, 1938.

BACOURT, DE. *Souvenirs d'un Diplomate. Lettres intimes sur l'Amérique.* Paris, 1882.

BAILEY, THOMAS A. "The North Pacific Sealing Convention of 1911," *Pacific Historical Review,* IV (1935).

————. *America Faces Russia: Russian-American Relations from Early Times to Our Day.* New York, 1950.

————. "Russian-American Relations: Legend and Fact," *The Pacific Spectator* (Winter, 1949).

————. "The Russian Fleet Myth Re-examined," *Mississippi Valley Historical Review* (June, 1951).

————. "Why the United States Purchased Alaska," *Pacific Historical Review,* III (1934).

BANCROFT, FREDERIC. *William H. Seward.* New York, 1900.

BARNES, THURLOW WEED. *Thurlow Weed.* Boston, 1883-84.

BARROWS, CHESTER L. *William M. Evarts: Lawyer, Diplomat, Statesman.* Chapel Hill, 1941.

BARROWS, EDWARD M. *The Great Commodore. The Exploits of Matthew Calbraith Perry.* Indianapolis, 1935.

BAXTER, JAMES PHINNEY III. *Introduction of the Ironclad Warship.* Cambridge, Massachusetts, 1933.

BELOMOR, A. "Vtoraia Tikhookeanskaya Eskadra" (Second Pacific Squadron), *Morskoi Sbornik* (Naval Records) (1914).

BEVERIDGE, A. J. *The Russian Advance.* New York, 1903.

BIRKBECK, W. J. *Birkbeck and the Russian Church. Essays and Articles by the Late W. J. Birkbeck,* ed. ATHELSTAN RILEY. London, 1917.

BISHOP, J. B. *Theodore Roosevelt and His Time.* New York, 1920.

BIZZILI, P. "Geopolitical Conditions of the Evolution of Russian Nationality," *Journal of Modern History,* Vol. II, No. 1 (March, 1930).

BLAKE, WILLIAM P. *Geographical Notes upon Russian America and the Stickeen River. A report sent to Secretary of State Seward and transmitted to President Johnson by a California scholar.* Washington, 1868.

BLINN, HAROLD E. "Seward and the Polish Rebellion," *American Historical Review,* XLV (1940).

BOSTON CITY COUNCIL. *Complimentary Banquet given by the City Council to Rear-Admiral Lessoffsky and the Officers of the Russian Fleet.* Boston, 1864.

BOTKIN, P. S. *Kartinki Diplomaticheskoy Zhizni* (Pictures from the Diplomatic Life). Paris, 1930.

BOWERS, CLAUDE G. *Beveridge and the Progressive Era.* Boston, 1932.

———. *The Tragic Era.* New York, 1929.

BRENT, JOHN CARROLL. *Biographical Sketch of the Most Reverend John Carroll, First Archbishop of Baltimore.* Baltimore, 1843.

BROWNSON, SARAH M. *Life of Demetrius Augustine Gallitzin.* With an Introduction by Orestes A. Brownson. New York, 1873.

BRUCE, W. C. *John Randolph of Roanoke 1773-1833.* New York, 1922.

BURROWS, SILAS E. *Russia and America. Correspondence, 1818-48.* Privately Printed, 1848.

BUTKOVSKY, I. Y. "Tainstvennaya Expeditzia v Ameriky v 1878" (The Mysterious Expedition to America in 1878). Istorichesky Viestnik (History Magazine), Vol. XI (1883).

BUYNITZKY, S. N. (tr.) Russian Account of the Official Mission to Russia of Hon. G. V. Fox. Washington, 1867.

CALLAHAN, JAMES MORTON. "The Alaska Purchase and Americo-Canadian Relations," *West Virginia University Studies in American History,* Series I, Nos. 2 and 3 (February-March, 1908).

———. *Cuba and International Relations.* Baltimore, 1899.

———. "Russo-American Relations During the American Civil War," *West Virginia University Studies in American History,* Series I, No. 1 (January, 1908).

CANTACUZENE, PRINCESS JULIA (COUNTESS SPERANSKY, *née* GRANT). *My Life Here and There.* New York, 1921.

CATACAZY, CONSTANTINE DE. *Un incident diplomatique.* Paris, 1872.

CHAMPLIN, J. D., JR. *Narrative of the Mission to Russia in 1866 of the Hon. Vasa Fox, Assistant Secretary of the Navy. From the Journal and Notes of J. F. Loubat.* New York, 1879.

CHAPMAN, CHARLES E. *A History of California: The Spanish Period.* New York, 1921.

CHARLES-ROUX, FRANCOIS. *Alexandre II, Gorchakov et Napoléon III.* Paris, 1913.

CHEVIGNY, HECTOR. *Lord of Alaska. The Story of Baranov and the Russian Adventure.* New York, 1943.

———. *Lost Empire. The Life and Adventures of Nikolai Petrovich Rezanov.* New York, 1937.

CHOULES, JOHN OVERTON. *The Cruise of the Steam Yacht "North Star,"* 1853. Boston, 1854.

CLARK, BENNETT CHAMP. *John Quincy Adams.* Boston, 1932.

CLARKE, BLAKE. *The Queen Who Weighed a Ton.* New York, 1941.

CLARK, HENRY W. *History of Alaska.* New York, 1920.

CLAY, C. M. *The Life of Cassius Marcellus Clay.* Cincinnati, 1886.

CLAY, HENRY. *Private Correspondence,* ed. CALVIN COLTON. New York, 1855.

CLEMENS, SAMUEL L. *Innocents Abroad.* New York, 1869.

———. *Life on the Mississippi.* New York, 1911.

CODMAN, JOHN. *An American Transport in the Crimean War.* New York, 1897.

COLEMAN, A. P. and M. M. *The Polish Insurrection of 1863 in the Light of New York Editorial Opinion.* Williamsport, Pennsylvania, 1934.

COLEMAN, MARION M. "Eugene Schuyler: Diplomat Extraordinary from the United States to Russia, 1867-76," *Russian Review,* VII (1947).

COLLINS, PERRY MCDONOUGH. *A Voyage Down the Amoor, etc.* New York, 1860.

COURANT, M. "La Sibérie, colonie russe jusqu'à la construction du Trans-sibérien," *Revue Historique* (1919).

"Correspondence of the Russian Ministers in Washington 1818-25," *American Historical Review,* XVIII (1913).

CRESSON, W. P. *Francis Dana: A Puritan Diplomat at the Court of Catherine the Great.* New York, 1930.

CROW, CARL. *He Opened the Door of Japan.* New York, 1939.

CURTIS, G. T. *Life of James Buchanan.* New York, 1883.

DALL, WILLIAM H. "Review of Bering's First Expedition," *National Geographic Magazine* (May, 1890).

DALLAS, SUSAN (ed.). *Diary of George Mifflin Dallas: While United States Minister to Russia 1837-39 and to England 1856-61.* Philadelphia, 1892.

DEKOVEN, MRS. REGINALD. *Life and Letters of John Paul Jones.* New York, 1913.

DELIVRON, A. KORVET "Kalevala" (The Sloop-of-War "Kalevala"). *Morskoi Sbornik* (Naval Records) Vol. IX, (1909).

DENNETT, TYLER. *Roosevelt and the Russo-Japanese War.* New York, 1925.

DENNIS, A. L. P. *Adventures in American Diplomacy 1896-1906.* New York, 1928.

DIX, WILLIAM GILES. *The Unholy Alliance: An American View of the War in the East.* New York, 1855.

DORR, THOMAS WILSON. "Russia and Turkey," *Providence* (R. I.) *Daily Post,,* November 25, 1853.

DOW, ROGER. "Prostor: A Geopolitical Study of Russia and the United States," *Russian Review,* Vol. I, No. 1 (1941).

———. "Seichas: A Comparison of Pre-Reform Russia and the Ante-Bellum South," *Russian Review,* VII (1947).

DuFour, Clarence John. "The Russian Withdrawal from California," *The Russians in California*. California Historical Society, San Francisco, 1933.

Dulles, Foster Rhea. *America in the Pacific*. Boston, 1932.

————. *The Road to Teheran*. New York, 1944.

Dunning, W. A. "Paying for Alaska," *Political Science Quarterly*, XXVII (1927).

Dvoichenko-Markov, Evfrosina. "The American Philosophical Society and Early Russian-American Relations," *Proceedings of the American Philosophical Society*, Vol. XCIV, No. 6 (1950).

————. "Jefferson and the Russian Decembrists," *The American Slavic and East European Review* (October, 1950).

————. "Americans in the Crimean War," *Russian Review* (April, 1954).

————. "John Ledyard and the Russians," *Russian Review* (October, 1952).

Eckel, Paul G. "A Russian Expedition to Japan in 1852," *Pacific Northwest Quarterly* (April, 1943).

Edgar, William C. *The Russian Famine of 1891 and 1892*. Minneapolis, 1893.

Egert, B. P. *The Conflict between the United States and Russia*. St. Petersburg, 1912.

Estlander, Bernhard and Ekman, Karl. *Fran Hav Och Hov. Amiral Oscar von Kraemers Levnadslopp* (From Sea to the Court. Memoirs of Admiral Oscar von Kraemer). Stockholm, 1931.

Essig, E. O. "The Russian Settlements at Ross," *The Russians in California*. California Historical Society. San Francisco, 1933.

Eyre, J. K., Jr. "Russia and the American Acquisition of the Philippines," *Mississippi Valley Historical Review* (1942).

Farrar, Victor J. *The Annexation of Russian America to the United States*. Washington, 1937.

Farrelly, Theodore S. "Aleutian Stepping-Stones," *Yale Review* (Winter, 1943).

Fricero, N. O. "Fregat *Svetlana* v Amerike v 1871-72. Iz Dnevnika Unkera Flota N. O. Fricero" (Frigate *Svetlana* in America 1871-1872. From the diary of the Ensign N. O. Fricero), *Morskie Zapiski* (Naval Records). (March, 1953).

Flandrau, Grace C. *Astor and the Oregon Country*. St. Paul, n.d.

Flint, Charles W. *Memories of an Active Life*. New York, 1923.

Foster, J. W. *Diplomatic Memoirs*. Boston, 1909.

————. *A Century of American Diplomacy (Being a Brief Review of the Foreign Relations of the United States, 1776-1876)*. Boston, 1901.

Francis, David R. *Russia from the American Embassy April 1916— November 1918*. New York, 1921.

Fremont, Jessie Benton. *Souvenirs of My Time*. Boston, 1887.

Gallatin, James Jr. A Great Peace Maker. New York, 1914.

Gerstner, Anton Ritter von. *Beschreibung einer Reise durch die Vereinigten Staaten von Nordamerika*. Leipzig, 1842.

————. "Railways in Austria," *Journal of the Franklin Institute, Philadelphia*, XXXI n.s. (1841).

————. "Railways in Russia," *Journal of the Franklin Institute, Philadelphia,* XIX n.s. (1837).

GILBERT, BENJAMIN F. "Welcome to the Czar's Fleet: An Incident of Civil War Days in San Francisco," *California Historical Society Quarterly* (March, 1947).

GILMAN, DANIEL COIT. "Letters from Russia During the Crimean War," *Yale Review* (April, 1916).

GODWIN, ROBERT R. *Russia and the Portsmouth Peace Conference.* New York, 1950.

GOLDER, FRANK A. "The American Civil War Through the Eyes of a Russian Diplomat," *American Historical Review,* XXVI (April, 1921).

————. "Catherine II and the American Revolution," *American Historical Review,* XXI (1915-16).

————. *Guide to the Materials for American History in Russian Archives.* Washington, 1917.

————. *John Paul Jones in Russia.* New York, 1927.

————. "The Purchase of Alaska," *American Historical Review,* XXV (April, 1920).

————. *Russia and Russian Alaska, The Hawaiian Islands,* ed. ALBERT P. TAYLOR and R. S. KUYKENDALL. Honolulu, 1930.

————. "Russian-American Relations During the Crimean War," *American Historical Review,* XXXI (April, 1926).

————. *Russian Expansion on the Pacific: 1641-1850.* Cleveland, 1914.

————. "Russian Fleet During the Civil War," *American Historical Review,* XX (1915).

————. "Russian Occupation of Hawaiian Islands," *American Historical Review,* XX (1914-15).

————. "The Russian Offer of Mediation in the War of 1812," *Political Science Quarterly* (1916).

GOLOVIN, IVAN GAVRILOVICH. *Stars and Stripes, or American Impressions.* London and New York, 1856.

————. "Obzor Russkikh Kolonii v Severnoy Amerike" (Survey of the Russian Colonies in America), *Morskoi Sbornik* (Naval Records), Vol. I (1862).

GOLOWNIN, VASILII MIKHAILOVICH. *Memoirs of a Captivity in Japan During the Years 1811, 1812, 1813.* London, 1824.

GONCHAROV, I. A. *Fregat "Pallada"* (The Frigate "Pallada"). St. Petersburg, 1896.

————. "Poutevia Pisma I. A. Goncharova iz Krugosvetnago Plavania" (Letters from the Journey Around the World by I. A. Goncharov), *Literaturnoy Nasledstvo* (The Literary Heritage Magazine) (1937).

GONCHAROV, V. "Expedizia Russkogo Flota v Ameriku" (An Expedition of the Russian Fleet to America), *Morskoi Sbornik* (Naval Records), VIII (1913).

GOWEN, HERBERT H. *The Napoleon of the Pacific: Kamehameha the Great.* New York, 1919.

GOWEN, JOHN S. *Personal Letters, Documents, Papers.* Unpublished.

GRAHAME, STEPHEN. *Tsar of Freedom.* New Haven, 1935.

GREENBERG, LOUIS. *The Jews in Russia.* New Haven, 1951.

GREENE, F. V. *Sketches of Army Life in Russia.* New York, 1880.

GRISCOM, LLOYD C. *Diplomatically Speaking.* New York, 1940.

HANNAN, JEROME D. "Prince Gallitzin's Experiments with Quasi-Spiritistic Phenomena," *Catholic Historical Review* (1921).

HANS, N. "Tsar Alexander I and Jefferson. Unpublished Correspondence," *Slavonic and East European Review* (December, 1953).

HANSEN-TAYLOR, MARIE and SCUDDER, H. E. *Life and Letters of Bayard Taylor.* Boston, 1885.

HAPGOOD, ISABEL F. *Russian Rambles.* Boston, 1895.

———— (ed. and tr.). *Service Book of the Holy Orthodox-Catholic Apostolic (Greco-Russian) Church.* Boston and New York, 1906.

Harper's Weekly (1863-1889).

HARRIS, TOWNSEND. *Complete Journal of Townsend Harris, First American Consul General and Minister to Japan.* New York, 1930.

HAWKINS, RUSH C. "The Coming of the Russian Ships in 1863," *North American Review,* CLXXVIII (1904).

HAWKS, FRANCIS L. *Narrative of the Expedition of an American Squadron to the China Seas and Japan, 1852, 1853, 1854; under Command of Commodore M. C. Perry, USN.* New York, 1856.

HENDRICH, BURTON JAMES. *The Jews in America.* New York, 1923.

HEYDEN, THOMAS. *A Memoir on the Life and Character of the Reverend Prince Demetrius A. de Gallitzin . . . Apostle of the Alleghanies.* Baltimore, 1869.

HILDT, JOHN C. *Early Diplomatic Negotiations of the United States and Russia.* Baltimore, 1906.

HITCHCOCK, DAVID K. *Vindication of Russia and the Emperor Nicholas.* Boston, 1844.

HOGAN, J. V. "Russian-American Commercial Relations," *Political Science Quarterly* (1912).

HOLLS, F. W. *The Peace Conference at The Hague.* New York, 1900.

IPATIEFF, VLADIMIR N. "Modern Science in Old Russia," *Russian Review,* Vol. II, No. 2 (Spring, 1943).

Istoria Russkoi Armii i Flota (History of Russian Army and Navy). Moscow, 1913.

Istoricekii Obzor Razvitiya Deyatelnosti Morskogo Ministerstva (History of Naval Ministry). St. Petersburg, 1902.

JAMES, JAMES ALTON. *The First Scientific Exploration of Russian America and the Purchase of Alaska.* Evanston, 1942.

OUR LOST EXPLORERS: *The Narrative of the Jeannette Arctic Expedition, as related by the Survivors, and in the Records and Last Journals of Lt. DeLong.* Hartford and San Francisco, 1882.

KANE, THOMAS L. "Alaska and the Polar Regions," A lecture given before the American Geographical Society. New York, 1868.

KANE, HARNETT T. with VICTOR LECLERC. *The Scandalous Mrs. Blackford.* New York, 1951.

KARPOVICH, M. M. *Imperial Russia, 1801-1917.* New York, 1932.

KASSELL, BERNARD M. "Russian Squadron in U. S. Waters in 1863," *Morskie Zapiski* (November, 1953).

KENNAN, GEORGE. *Siberia and the Exile System*. New York, 1891.
———. *Tent Life in Siberia*. New York, 1890 (?).
KHLEBNIKOV, K. T. *Zhizneopisanie A. A. Baranova* (Life of A. Baranov). St. Petersburg, 1835.
KOTZEBUE, OTTO VON. *A New Voyage Around the World 1823-26*. London, 1830.
———. *A Voyage of Discovery into the South Seas 1815-18*. London, 1821.
KRUPSKAYA, N. K. MEMOIRS OF LENIN. London, 1930.
KRUTIKOV, M. "Pervye zheleznye dorogi v Rossii" (First Railroads in Russia), *Krasny Arkhiv*, Vol. LXXVI, No. 3 (1936).
———. "Nachalo zheleznodorozhnogo stroitelstva v Rossii," *Krasny Arkhiv*, Vol. XCIX, No. 2 (1940).
KRYZANOVSKY, N. N. *Velikaya Severnaya Expeditzia* (The Great Northern Expedition). New York, 1939.
LANE, FRANKLIN K. *Letters*. Cambridge, Massachusetts, 1922.
LANGER, WILLIAM L. *European Alliances and Alignments*. New York, 1931.
LANSDELL, HENRY. *Through Siberia*. London, 1882.
LASERSON, MAX M. *The American Impact on Russia 1784-1917*. New York, 1950.
"The Last Ball in Sitka," *Century Magazine* (April, 1929).
LENSEN, GEORGE ALEXANDER. *Report from Hokhaido: The Remains of Russian Culture in Northern Japan*. Hakodate, 1954.
———. "Early Russo-Japanese Relations," *Far Eastern Quarterly* (1950).
———. *Russia's Japan Expedition of 1852-1855*. Gainesville, 1955.
LEROY-BEAULIEU, ANATOLE. *The Empire of the Tsars and the Russians*. New York, 1898.
LIFE OF ALEXANDER II. London, 1883.
LINN, WILLIAM A. *Horace Greeley*. New York, 1903.
LUTHIN, R. H. "The Sale of Alaska," *Slavonic Review* (1937).
MCCAULEY, EDWARD YORKE. *With Perry in Japan*. London, 1942.
MCCORMICK, RICHARD C., JR. *A Visit to the Camp before Sevastopol*. New York, 1855.
MCCORMICK, ROBERT R. *With the Russian Army*. New York, 1915.
MCKENZIE, RALPH M. *Jew Baiting in Russia and her Alleged Friendship for the United States. A Brief History of Russia's Relations with America*. Washington, 1903.
MAHR, AUGUST KARL. *Visit of the Rurik to San Francisco: 1816*. Stanford, n.d.
MALKIN, M. "K istorii Russko-Amerikanskikh Otnoshenii vo Vremia Grazhdanskoy Voini v S.S.A." (Russian-American Relations During the American Civil War), *Krasny Arkhiv* (1939).
MARIE, GRAND DUCHESS OF RUSSIA. *Education of a Princess*. New York, 1931.
MARKU, VALERIU. *Lenin*. New York, 1928.
MARRIOTT, J. A. R. *The Eastern Question*. Oxford, 1924.
MARYE, GEORGE T. *Nearing the End in Imperial Russia*. Philadelphia, 1929.
MASTERSON, JAMES R. *Records of Travel in North America: 1700-1776*. 3 vols. Unpublished doctoral dissertation, Harvard University, 1936.

MATTICE, HARDA A. "Perry and Japan: An Account of the Empire and an Unpublished Record of the Perry Expedition," *Bulletin of the N. Y. Public Library* (February, 1942).

MAXWELL, JOHN G. *The Czar, His Court and His People*. New York, 1848.

MAZOUR, A. G. "The Russian-American and Anglo-Russian Conventions, 1824-1925: An Interpretation," *Pacific Historical Review* (1945).

————. "The Prelude to Russia's Departure from America," *Pacific Historical Review* (1941).

MEHNERT, KLAUS. *The Russians in Hawaii*. Hawaii, 1939.

MELGUNOV, S. P. *Legenda o Separatnom Mire* (The Legend of a Separate Peace). Paris, 1957.

MEREZHKOVSKY, DIMITRI. *December 14th*. New York, 1923.

MILLER, HUNTER. "Russian Opinion on the Cession of Alaska," *American Historical Review* (April, 1943).

MIRSKY, D. S. *A History of Russian Literature*. New York, 1934.

MONTGOMERY, J. E. *Our Admiral's Flag Abroad. The Cruise of Admiral D. G. Farragut*. New York, 1869.

MORISON, SAMUEL ELIOT. "Historical Notes on the Gilbert and Marshall Islands," *American Neptune* (April, 1944).

————. *The Maritime History of Massachusetts*. Boston, 1931.

NAGENGAST, WILLIAM E. "The Visit of the Russian Fleet to the United States. Were Americans Deceived?" *Russian Review,* VIII (1949).

NORWOOD, WILLIAM. "The Russians in Honolulu," *Honolulu Star-Bulletin* (February 9, 1935).

OGDEN, ADELE. "Russian Sea-Otter and Seal Hunting on the California Coast, 1803-1841," *The Russians in California*. California Historical Society. San Francisco, 1933.

OKUN, S. B. *Rossiisko-Amerikanskaya Kompania* (The Russian-American Company). Moscow, 1939.

OTERO, MIGUEL ANTONIO. *My Life on the Frontier: 1864-1882*. New York, 1935.

PARRY, ALBERT. "A Grand Duke Comes to America," *American Mercury* (September, 1948).

————. "Cassius Clay's Glimpse into the Future," *Russian Review* (Spring, 1943).

————. "John B. Turchin: Russian General in the American Civil War," *Russian Review,* I (1942).

————. "More on General Turchin," *Russian Review* (January, 1955).

————. "Prince Golitsyn: Apostle of the Alleghanies," *Russian Review* (Spring, 1945).

————. "Washington B. Vanderlip, the 'Khan of Kamchatka,'" *Pacific Historical Review* (August, 1948).

————. *Whistler's Father*. Indianapolis, 1939.

PERKINS, DEXTER. *Hands Off: A History of the Monroe Doctrine*. Boston, 1941.

PHILARET. *Doctrine of the Russian Church*. Translated by Blackmore. London, 1845.

PHILLIPS, JAMES DUNCAN. "Salem Opens American Trade with Russia," *New England Quarterly* (1941).

PILDER, HANS. *Die Russisch-Amerikanische Handels-Kompanie bis 1825.* Berlin, 1914.

POMEROY, EARL S. "The Visit of the Russian Fleet in 1863," *New York History,* XXIV (1943).

————. "The Myth After the Russian Fleet, 1863," *New York History* (1950).

PORTER, KENNETH WIGGINS. *John Jacob Astor.* (Harvard Studies in Business History.) Cambridge, Massachusetts, 1931.

————. "John Jacob Astor and the Sandalwood Trade of the Hawaiian Islands, 1816-1828," *Journal of Economics and Business History,* Vol. II, No. 3 (May, 1930).

PRINGLE, HENRY F. *Theodore Roosevelt.* New York, 1931.

PURYEAR, VERNON J. "New Light on the Origins of the Crimean War," *Journal of Modern History,* Vol. III, No. 2 (June, 1931).

Quelques Mots, par un Chrétien orthodoxe. Paris, 1853.

RAMBAUD, ALFRED. *Russia.* Translated by Leonora B. Lang. ("Nations of the World" Series.) New York, 1900.

REED, JOHN with BOARDMAN ROBINSON. *The War in Eastern Europe.* New York, 1916.

REEVES, FRANCIS B. *Russia Then and Now. 1892-1917. My Mission to Russia During the Famine of 1891-1892 with data bearing upon Russia of Today.* New York, 1917.

REID, VIRGINIA H. "The Purchase of Alaska," *Contemporary Opinion* (1940).

"The Reverend Mr. Young's Visit to the Russian Church," *American Quarterly Church Review,* XVI (1865).

Revelations of Russia: or, The Emperor Nicholas and his Empire in 1844. By one who has seen and describes. London, 1844.

RIMSKY-KORSAKOFF, NICHOLAS. *My Musical Life.* New York, 1928.

ROBERTSON, JAMES ROOD. *A Kentuckian at the Court of the Tsars. The Ministry of Cassius M. Clay: 1861-62 and 1863-69.* Berea, 1935.

ROBINSON, GERARD TANQUERAY. *Rural Russia Under the Old Regime.* New York, 1932.

ROPES, JOHN CODMAN. *A Memoir of John Codman Ropes.* Boston, 1901.

ROSEN, ROMAN R. *Forty Years of Diplomacy.* New York, 1922.

Rousskie Otkritie v Tikhom Okeane i Severnoi Amerike v 18-19 vekhakh (Russian Discoveries in the Pacific and North America in the Eighteenth and Nineteenth Centuries). Moscow, 1944.

Russian Administration of Alaska and the Status of the Alaskan Natives. Prepared by the Chief of the Foreign Law Section, Library of Congress, Washington, 1950.

The Russian Empire. Its Resources, Government and Policy. By a "Looker on" from America. Cincinnati, 1856.

SALTER, WILLIAM M. *America's Compact with Despotism in Russia.* Philadelphia, 1893.

SAROLEA, CHARLES. *Great Russia.* New York, 1916.

SARGENT, DANIEL. *The Story of Prince Demetrius Augustine Gallitzin.* New York, 1945.

SCHAFER, JOSEPH (ed.). *Memoirs of Jeremiah Curtin.* Madison, 1940.

SEMMES, JOHN E. *John H. B. Latrobe and His Times.* Baltimore, 1917.

Sequel to the Late Visit of the Russian Fleet to the United States. St. Petersburg, 1864.

SEWARD, GEORGE F. *The Russian-Japanese War.* Newark, 1904.

SEWARD, WILLIAM H. *Autobiography and Selections from Letters,* ed. FREDERICK SEWARD. New York, 1877-91.

SINEOLOW, VLADIMIR. *La colonisation russe en Asie.* Paris, 1929.

SGIBNEV, A. "Rezanov i Kruzenstern" (Rezanov and Kruzenstern), *Drevnia i Novaya Rossia,* III (1877).

SKALKOVSKI, K. *Russkaya Torgovlia v Tikhom Okeane* (Russian Trade in the Pacific). St. Petersburg, 1883.

SOKOL, A. E. *Russian Expansion and Exploration in the Pacific.* New York, 1952.

STANYUKOVICH, K. M. *Morskie Razkazi* (Navy Stories). St. Petersburg, 1905.

STODDARD, CHARLES AUGUSTUS. *Across Russia.* New York, 1892.

STOECKL, BARONESS DE. *Not All Vanity.* London, 1950.

STOUGHTON, E. W. "Popular Fallacies About Russia," *North American Review,* CXXX (1880).

STRAUS, O. S. *Under Four Administrations.* Boston, 1922.

———. "The United States and Russia, Their Historic Relations," *North American Review* (August, 1905).

STRAKHOVSKY, L. I. "Russia's Privateering Projects of 1878," *Journal of Modern History* (March, 1935).

SUMNER, CHARLES. *The Cession of Russian America. A Speech Made by the Senator from Massachusetts in the U. S. Senate During the Debate over the Purchase of Alaska.* Washington, 1867.

TAKAHASHI, SAKUYÉ. *International Law Applied to the Russo-Japanese War, With the Decisions of the Japanese Prize Courts.* New York, 1908.

TARSÄIDZÉ, ALEXANDRE. "K 90 Letnemu Ubileu Prikhoda Russkikh Eskadr v Ameriku, 1863-1953" (Commemorating the 90th Anniversary of the Arrival of the Russian Squadron in America, 1863), *Morskie Zapiski* (Naval Records) (November, 1953 and April, 1954). Contains the list of the personnel and the specifications of the ships.

———. *Alexandrina and Alexander* (The Romance of Queen Victoria and Czar Alexander II). Unpublished.

———. "The Air-Blitz of 1812," *Russian Review* (Autumn, 1942).

———. "Berdanka," *Russian Review* (January, 1950).

———. "American Pioneers in Russian Railroad Building," *Russian Review* (October, 1950).

TAFT, MARCUS LORENZO. *Strange Siberia—Along the Trans-Siberian Railway.* New York, 1911.

TAYLOR, BAYARD. *Greece and Russia.* New York, 1880.

TCHUYKEVITCH, COLONEL. *Reflections on the War of 1812.* Translated by Eustaphieve. Boston, 1813.

THOMAS, BENJAMIN PLATT. *Russian-American Relations, 1815-1867.* Baltimore, 1930.

THOMPSON, CHARLES WILLIS. *The Fiery Epoch: 1830-1877.* Indianapolis, 1931.

THORSON, W. B. "Pacific Northwest Opinion on the Russo-Japanese War of 1904-1905," *Pacific Northwest Quarterly* (1944).

TIKHMENEV, P. *Istoricheskoye Obozrenie Obrazovania Rossiisko-Amerikanskoy Kompanii* (Historical Outline of Russian-American Company). St. Petersburg, 1863.

TOMPKINS, PAULINE. *American-Russian Relations in the Far East.* New York, 1949.

TOMPKINS, STUART R. *Alaska: Promyshlennik and Sourdough.* Norman, 1945.

VERNADSKY, GEORGE. *Lenin: Red Dictator.* New Haven, 1931.

VERNEY, EDMUND. "Old Crimean Days," *Contemporary Review* (November, 1899).

VOSE, GEORGE L. *George Whistler.* Boston, 1887.

WALWORTH, ARTHUR. *Black Ships Off Japan.* New York, 1946.

WARREN, J. G. H. *A Century of Locomotive Building by Robert Stephenson & Company: 1823-1923.* Newcastle upon Tyne, 1923.

WASHBURN, STANLEY. *Field Notes from the Russian Front.* London, 1915.

WASSON, R. GORDON. *Toward a Russian Policy.* Stamford, 1951.

WEEDEN, WILLIAM B. *Economic and Social History of New England, 1620-1789.* Boston, 1890.

WELLES, GIDEON. *Diary of Gideon Welles.* Boston, 1911.

WELLS, H. B. "The Russian Language in the United States," *American Mercury,* Vol. XXV, No. 100 (April, 1932).

WEST, RICHARD S., JR. *Gideon Welles.* Indianapolis, 1943.

WHITE, ANDREW W. *Autobiography of Andrew Dickson White.* New York, 1905.

WHITTINGHAM, BERNARD R. *Notes on the Late Expedition Against the Russian Settlements in Eastern Siberia.* London, 1856.

"William Penn and Peter the Great," *Russia* (January, 1957).

WILLIAMS, WILLIAM APPLEMAN. *American Russian Relations 1781-1947.* New York, 1952.

WITTE, SERGE. *The Memoirs of Count Witte.* Garden City, 1921.

WOLDMAN, ALBERT A. *Lincoln and the Russians.* Cleveland, 1952.

WOLF, SIMON. *The Presidents I have Known from 1860-1918.* Washington, 1918.

WOLKONSKY, SERGE. *Impressions: Sketches of American Life.* Chicago, 1893.

WRANGEL, NICHOLAS. *Memoirs.* London, 1927.

YOUNG, C. C. *Abused Russia.* New York, 1915.

YARMOLINSKY, AVRAHM. *Picturesque United States of America: A Memoir on Paul Svinin.* With an Introduction by R. T. H. Halsey. New York, 1930.

―――. "Rezanov," *Bulletin of the N. Y. Public Library,* No. 31 (1927).

―――. "Studies in Russian Americana," *Bulletin of the N. Y. Public Library* (July, 1939).

ZABRISKIE, E. H. *American-Russian Rivalry in the Far East. A Study in Diplomacy and Power Politics.* Philadelphia, 1946.

ZOLLINGER, JAMES PETER. *Sutter, The Man and His Empire.* New York, 1939.

index

ABOUT THE AUTHOR

Alexandre Tarsaïdzé was born in Tiflis, Georgia, Russia, oddly enough just a few miles from Stalin's birthplace. In fact, Stalin's first poetry was dedicated to Mr. Tarsaïdzé's great uncle, Prince Raphael Eristavi. During the First World War, he was enrolled in the Imperial Naval Academy in St. Petersburg where he remained until 1918 when Trotsky disbanded this old school founded by Peter the Great. He then returned to Georgia by a tortuous, dangerous route; in the political upheaval, the journey took a month rather than the usual three days. He served with the American Relief Administration, an organization founded by Herbert Hoover to feed the Russian people. The Soviet attack on Georgia in 1921 forced him to flee to Batum, a Black Sea port, where fortunately an American destroyer picked him up and brought him in safety to Constantinople, Turkey. He rejoined the A. R. A. and stayed on until the Turkish nationalists took power.

Mr. Tarsaïdzé is an American citizen and has lived in this country since 1923. During the Second World War, he worked for Army Intelligence as a civilian. Since then he has worked in public relations; he has been in charge of publicity and public relations at the Sherry-Netherlands and Ambassador Hotels in New York City. In 1955 he founded his own public relations firm.

It was during his time with the A. R. A. that Mr. Tarsaïdzé first became interested in Russian-American relations. He has maintained this interest through the years and explored every aspect of the history of American relations with Czarist Russia: political, social, and cultural. *Czars and Presidents* is the product of twenty years' research, much of it on little known areas of this remarkably successful relationship. Mr. Tarsaïdzé is especially qualified to write this book because of the extraordinary range of his knowledge of pre-Revolutionary Russia. On a scholarly level, he has been a frequent contributor to Russian and American periodicals and a debunker of ill-founded myths about Czarist Russia; on a somewhat different plane he is an unphased unmasker of *soi-disant* Anastasias (three).

His present activities also include the editing of a rare documentary film, "Emperor Nicholas II," which contains newsreels dating back to 1896, the time of that Emperor's coronation.

Vitiaz.

Alexander Nevski.

THE RUSSIAN FLEET, COMMANDED BY ADMIRA